# Developments in British Social Policy

edited by
Nick Ellison and Chris Pierson

**MACMILLAN**

First published 1998 by
MACMILLAN PRESS LTD
Houndmills, Basingstoke, Hampshire RG21 6XS
and London
Companies and representatives
throughout the world

ISBN 0–333–65920–1   hardcover
ISBN 0–333–65921–X   paperback

A catalogue record for this book is available from the British Library.

This book is printed on paper suitable for recycling and made from fully managed and sustained forest sources.

10   9   8   7   6   5   4   3   2   1
07   06   05   04   03   02   01   00   99   98

Copy-edited and typeset by Povey–Edmondson
Tavistock and Rochdale, England

Printed and bound in Great Britain by
Creative Print and Design Wales, Ebbw Vale

The editors and publishers are grateful to The Controller of Her Majesty's Stationery Office for permission to reproduce copyright material from Cm 3212, *The Government's Expenditure Plans, 1996/7 to 1998/9.*

# Contents

# List of Contributors

**Stephen J. Ball** is Professor of Sociology of Education in the School of Education, King's College, London, and Director of the Centre for Public Policy Research. His books include *Education Reform* (1994) and *Markets, Choice and Equity in Education* (1995, with Sharon Gewirtz and Richard Bowe). He is Managing Editor of the *Journal of Education Policy*.

**John Barry** is Lecturer in Politics at the University of Keele. His research interests lie in the broad area of green political and moral theory and in the political economy of environmental issues, as well as contemporary social and political theory. He has published numerous articles and chapters on green politics and the normative and economic dimensions of environmental problems. He has two books forthcoming: *Nature, Virtue and Progress: Rethinking Green Politics* and *The Environment and Social Theory*.

**Michael Cahill** is Principal Lecturer in Social Policy at the University of Brighton. He is the author of *The New Social Policy* (1994) and a forthcoming book on social policy and the environment.

**Laura Cram** is Jean Monnet Fellow in European Public Policy at the University of Strathclyde. She is the author of a number of journal articles and book chapters on European Union social policy and of the book, *Policy-Making in the EU: Conceptual Lenses and the Integration Process* (1997). She is currently writing a book on social policy in the European Union for the Macmillan European Union series.

**Nick Ellison** is Lecturer in Sociology and Social Policy and Deputy Dean of Social Sciences at the University of Durham. His publications include *Egalitarian Thought and Labour Politics: Retreating Visions* (1994), a number of articles on the Labour Party and social policy, and 'Towards a New Social Politics: Citizenship and Reflexivity in Late Modernity' (*Sociology*, November 1997).

**Martin Hewitt** teaches social policy at the University of Hertfordshire. He is the author of *Welfare, Ideology and Need* (1994) and several articles on social need and the future of the welfare state. He is presently writing a book on social policy and human nature.

**Paul Hirst** is Professor of Social Theory, Birkbeck College, University of London, a member of the Political Quarterly Editorial Board and Executive of Charter 88. He is the author of *Associative Democracy* (1994), *Globalisation in Question* (1996, with Grahame Thompson) and *From Statism to Pluralism* (1997).

**Mary Langan** is Senior Lecturer in Applied Social Studies at the Open University. She is General Editor of the Routledge Social Policy Series *The State of Welfare* and editor of *Welfare: Needs, Rights and Risks* (1997).

**Ruth Lister** is Professor of Social Policy in the Department of Social Sciences, Loughborough University. She is a former Director of the Child Poverty Action Group and member of the Commission on Social Justice. Publications include *The Exclusive Society: Citizenship and the Poor* (1990) and *Citizenship: Feminist Perspectives* (1997).

**Peter Malpass** is Professor of Housing Policy at the University of the West of England, Bristol, and has been involved in research and teaching on aspects of housing in Britain since the early 1970s. His publications include *Housing Policy and Practice* (with Alan Murie, 5th edition, 1998), and an edited collection, *Ownership, Control and Accountability: the new governance of housing* (1997).

**Ailsa McKay** is Lecturer in the Economics Department at Glasgow Caledonian University. She is a social economist with a background in welfare rights and housing work. Her teaching and research interests are in the areas of feminist economics and the economics of the welfare state. She is currently completing her PhD thesis on the political economy of the basic citizens' income proposal as a strategy for the harmonisation of European social protection packages.

**Sarah Nettleton** is Lecturer in Social Policy at the University of York. She is the author of *The Sociology of Health and Illness* (1995) and a co-editor of *The Sociology of Health Promotion* (1995).

**Gillian Pascall** is Senior Lecturer in Social Policy and Administration at the University of Nottingham. She is co-author with Roger Cox of *Women Returning to Higher Education* (1993) and has recently published *Social Policy: A New Feminist Analysis* (1997).

**David Piachaud** is Professor of Social Policy at the London School of Economics. He worked at the DHSS between 1968 and 1970, and subsequently in the Prime Minister's Policy Unit between 1974 and 1979. He is the author of numerous books and articles on poverty, social security and European social policy. Recent publications include *The Price of Food* (1996, with Jonathan Webb) and 'The Growth of Means-testing' in the CPAG publication, *Britain Divided* (1997).

**Chris Pierson** is Professor of Politics at the University of Nottingham. He has written extensively on the problems of social democracy and the welfare state. His most recent books are *Socialism After Communism*, *The Modern State* and *Beyond the Welfare State*.

**John Solomos** is Professor of Sociology and Social Policy at the University of Southampton. He has written widely on key aspects of race relations, including political mobilisation and the role of public policies in this field. Among his most recent books are *Race and Racism in Britain* and (with Les Back) *Racism and Society*.

**Noel Whiteside** is Reader in Public Policy at the University of Bristol. She has contributed numerous articles in various social policy and historical journals addressing these themes. Her books include *Casual Labour* (1986, with Gordon Phillips), *Bad Times: unemployment in British social and political history* (1991) and *Government, Industry and Labour Markets in Britain and France* (1997, edited with Robert Salais).

# Introduction

NICK ELLISON AND CHRIS PIERSON

In the past few years social policy has risen to the top of the political agenda in Britain. The nature of the welfare state, having once seemed uncontroversial and even dull, is now deeply contested and its institutions subject to a seemingly permanent revolution. With the total bill for social provision topping £200 billion, there is little wonder that both cost-conscious politicians and tax-weary citizens should focus so single-mindedly on the welfare state. Yet these same politicians still want to deliver the social goods, not least because voter-citizens want not only lower taxes but also improved services. All the evidence suggests that modern Britons want more and better health services, greater educational opportunities and adequate pensions, however reluctant they may be to pay the taxes to fund them. In trying to conjure up this magic combination of better services and lower taxes, social policymakers face two further problems. First, there is the rapidly changing societal context in which policies have to operate, a setting of long-term mass unemployment, new patterns of family formation (and dissolution), medical innovation and rapid ageing. Second, it is widely argued that there is a loss of governing capacity amongst nation states as their policies become increasingly subject to patterns of global social and economic transformation that lie beyond their control.

These are the circumstances of economic, social and political change under which we assess the theory and practice of social policy in Britain today. This introductory chapter sets the context for what is to follow. First, we offer a brief account of the 'Keynesian welfare state' as it evolved in the postwar period in order, second, to see how a number of key social and economic changes have challenged deep-seated assumptions about the role and nature of social provision in Britain. In the final pages we look in a little more detail at some of the most consequential of these developments, including the impact of 'deindustrialisation' and 'globalisation' as well as the likely effects of long-term demographic change, before moving to a brief consideration of the immediate future of the British welfare state under New Labour.

## Social Policy in the Postwar Era

During the decade or so that followed the end of the Second World War in 1945, the majority of Western European countries created sophisticated

1

systems of state social provision. Although these 'welfare regimes' differed in many ways (Esping-Andersen, 1990) they displayed certain basic similarities. In Britain, postwar governments (both Labour and Conservative) were committed to (1) universalising a system of *social insurance* and income maintenance to cover contingencies such as work-related disability, old age and unemployment, and (2) expanding *public services* in health (the NHS), education and housing. At the same time they endorsed the responsibility (and the capacity) of the state to run macroeconomic policies that would secure the maintenance of full (male) employment. In this they supported the ideas developed during the 1920s and 1930s by the economist John Maynard Keynes, who argued that those who exercise *political* power have a duty to intervene in the *economic* sphere to maintain and, where necessary, generate 'effective demand' and thence full employment. It was this twin commitment to more extensive and inclusive social policies plus the support of full employment that came to be described as the *Keynesian Welfare State*.

Subscribed to by all main shades of political opinion for the best part of a generation, the Keynesian welfare state appeared during the 1950s and 1960s to have solved the seemingly endemic economic and social problems of the interwar years. Although Britain's economic performance was comparatively modest throughout this period, growth was maintained and unemployment rates remained low. Real wages rose, leading to enhanced consumption amongst all sections of society whilst inflation, though rising gently, remained under control. Finally, in a context of sustained economic growth, levels of social spending increased rapidly, with the prevailing upward cycle of growth and affluence permitting the demands of social justice to be met without undermining the economic foundations of the system or unduly challenging potentially conflicting interests (Britton, 1991).

Whilst advocates of the Keynesian welfare state had seen it as a *permanent* solution to the sorts of economic and social malaise that had afflicted Britain between the world wars, by the early 1970s it was clear that the model was in real trouble. The collapse of the Bretton Woods exchange rate system and the OPEC oil crises of 1973 and 1979 (with their spectacular increases in crude oil prices) were only the most dramatic chapters in a story of sustained economic difficulty. Growth declined, while inflation raced into double figures. Unemployment, the headline measure of Keynesian success or failure, rose to over 5 per cent in the late 1970s before climbing steeply in the 1980s. 'Stagflation', the new phenomenon of low or negative growth leading to high unemployment *and* high inflation, defied Keynesian demand-side remedies, leaving British governments effectively devoid of any macro-economic strategy.

# The Causes of Keynesian Economic Decline

Nearly a quarter of a century on, the decline of the Keynesian model is still keenly debated. The earliest explanations of the dramatic events of the early and mid-1970s (OECD, 1977) tended to focus on a number of short-term and contingent causes (of which the OPEC oil price hike was the most prominent). With the persistence of economic difficulty, these explanations of a 'temporary' interruption to the pattern of postwar growth increasingly gave way to accounts that stressed much more deep-seated and structural flaws in the entire political and economic basis of the Keynesian welfare state (see Chapter 1). Initially from the left, though subsequently and more efficaciously from the new right, came the argument that the compromise of left and right or state and market that the Keynesian welfare state had consummated was unstable and, in the long run, unsustainable. For the neo-Marxist left, this expressed the inability of the state under capitalism to satisfy simultaneously two necessary but contradictory functions: securing the bases for both successful capital *accumulation* and meeting the social costs of the *legitimation* of this regime. For the right, the argument was that the nature of the state's intervention in the functioning of the economy (and the cost of supporting this) undermined the long-term viability of a market-based economy. The result was a 'fiscal crisis'. Overburdened with public spending commitments, the modern state presided over an expensive, monolithic and inefficient bureaucracy, the economic costs of which, in the opinion of the new right, could only be reduced by a return to sound supply-side policies.

These ideas or rather a vulgarised version of the new right's account has certainly had a profound and continuing impact upon the 'climate of opinion' surrounding the making of British social policy. If there is a 'new' consensus about what social policy is for and what it can do in the 1990s, it has certainly been strongly influenced by the idea that doing the things that Keynesian welfare states tried to do is undesirable or impossible or both. At the same time it is clear that insofar as both the new left and the new right held that the mixture of state and market was a societal contradiction and correspondingly unsustainable, they were both wrong. In some sense these accounts belong to a very particular historical moment. The early 1970s were marked not just by a problem of growing public indebtedness but also by levels of social and industrial mobilisation that persuaded at least a few nervous commentators (and Prime Minister Edward Heath) that Britain faced a full-blown crisis of governability. As the show somehow stumbled on, the sense of impending crisis gave way to a still rather melancholic sense of chronic long-term decline. The lasting virtues of these more alarmist accounts were twofold:

first, they emphasised that the problem of Britain's welfare state (and the social policies required to remedy it) lay in its *political economy*, that is, in the way that economic and political (and social) institutions interacted; and second, they recognised that these difficulties were not temporary and contingent but longstanding and structural.

## The Conservative Legacy

On 1 May 1997 the Labour Party secured a stunning electoral victory, gaining a majority of 169 over all other parties in the new House of Commons and reducing the mighty Conservative Party to just 156 MPs. The Conservative Party had ruled uninterrupted for the previous eighteen years and any contemporary assessment of developments in social policy in Britain must focus upon this period of unparalleled Conservative ascendancy. It is certainly possible to argue that the beginning of the end of the postwar welfare state settlement dates from the last Labour administration of Jim Callaghan which, in the wake of the IMF financial crisis of 1976, had instituted severe cash constraints in the public service and officiated over (what was then) an unprecedented rise in postwar unemployment. But the character of social policy in this period belongs more properly to the Thatcher governments and to their modest sequel under John Major's premiership.

Certainly Margaret Thatcher came to power committed to restoring the 'balance' between work and welfare. The emphasis was upon reforming the supply or 'production' side of the economy, reducing marginal tax rates, reshaping the labour market and controlling the welfare budget. At the time Ian Gough described the first Thatcher administration as 'the most far-reaching experiment in "new right" politics in the Western world' (Gough, 1983, p. 162). But whilst the private sector was lionised by Thatcher and a programme of privatisation of public corporations, income tax cuts and labour market reforms was vigorously pursued throughout the 1980s, for the best part of a decade the public provision of welfare remained curiously untransformed. Indeed social expenditure under the first Thatcher government rose by 10 per cent, increasing as a proportion of gross domestic product (GDP – the total production of goods and services in the economy in a year) from 21.7 per cent to 23.6 per cent. Of course this was not because the Thatcher government had 'gone soft' on welfare but because running a welfare state with mass unemployment was extremely expensive. Social expenditure fell in the second half of the 1980s (as the economy expanded and unemployment fell) but in the recession of the early 1990s it grew as a proportion of GDP by 5 per cent from 21.4 per cent to 26.4 per cent (Hills,

1993, p. 8). The level of social spending as a proportion of overall national production and the overall levels of taxation needed to sustain it were little different in 1995 from what they had been in 1979 (Central Statistical Office, 1995). The greatest retrenchment – and the greatest increase in disciplinary administration – tended to be focused upon those who were most dependent upon the state for income maintenance. According to one conservative estimate, 'the number of individuals in poor households rose from 5.1 million [in 1979] to 9.4 million in 1985' (Barr and Coulter, 1990, p. 333). Income inequality became more pronounced, especially after 1985, when benefits came to do rather less work in counteracting the inequalities of original (market-generated) incomes. At the same time the tax burden was shifted from direct to indirect taxes, making the overall system much less progressive and less redistributive.

## Bringing the State to Market

Ideally, new right reformers want to see the welfare state replaced by markets for welfare services. In their view the state's role should be confined to the legal regulation of these privately provided services and (perhaps) the sponsorship of those unable to fend (and pay) for themselves. This has not generally been the British experience of reform. Despite some inducements to encourage private provision throughout the 1980s, health care and education, at least, are services that are still met for most families through the state. The state is still a major provider of pensions, though it is clear that private and occupational pensions will have to carry much more of the weight of income maintenance in the future. When wholesale reform of social policy did finally get started under the third Thatcher administration, the central premise was bringing the market to the state. In this most recent period of reform, the general strategy has not been to privatise the welfare state (though significant areas of welfare provision have been 'contracted out'). Rather it has been to introduce market-like structures within the public sector in the belief that choice, competition and the power of the consumer can transform these public services without a transfer of ownership into the private sector.

At the most generic level, the strategy of reform for the public services – sometimes referred to as the 'new public management' – has sought to introduce private sector disciplines into the public sector in the expectation that the service can thus be made to deliver the sorts of service and efficiency that are identified with the private sector. Most clearly in the areas of health and education, there has been an aspiration to introduce 'internal markets' within the domain of public provision. Public funding has been retained but steps have been taken to divide the purchasers from the providers of services. Individual units are to compete for consumers of their services. The purchaser of these services should be able to move their custom between providers with relative ease and greater information should make it possible for consumers to make effective choices. With resources broadly following consumer choices, competition should encourage efficiency and reward the most successful producers.

Although the techniques of new public management have also been applied within the Department of Social Security (by far the single largest area of government administration), the idea of the 'internal market' has rather less purchase in the field of income maintenance. Here the policy changes of the last decade have been less innovative and more incremental. Although the government has sought 'value for money' its overwhelming concern has been to constrain absolute levels of spending. This is unsurprising. The social security budget constitutes the single largest item of social expenditure, at around £100 billion it represents nearly one third of all public spending. An increasingly important secondary theme has been the impact of benefit levels and entitlements upon the (changing) labour market. Conservative governments were committed to greater labour market flexibility, not least by making it more attractive to be in low-paid work than in receipt of unemployment benefit or income support (a rather ancient principle of 'less eligibility' that can be traced at least to the Poor Law Amendment Act of 1834). The carrot has been some form of income supplement for families with a low-waged breadwinner, while the sticks have been a repeated tightening of entitlement to state support and constraint upon the level of improvement of benefit rates. Most recently this tightening of terms and conditions has included the replacement of unemployment benefits and income support by a more stringently administered Job Seeker's Allowance and closer medical supervision of entitlement to Invalidity Benefit.

## Social Policy in a Changing Social World

It is clear that there have been enormous changes above all in the delivery of social provision over the past twenty years. Talk of a continuing crisis in the funding of the welfare state has scarcely relented throughout the same period. How do we reconcile these phenomena with the apparent stability (indeed in areas such as health, a very substantial increase) in the levels of funding of the welfare state? Perhaps the single most persuasive explanation lies in the profound changes that have taken place in the social world to which social policies have to be addressed. At its simplest, the scale, pattern and distribution of social need has been transformed in the past twenty-five years whilst the capacity to raise resources to meet these new needs has become ever more constrained. Here we highlight three of the most important changes: the 'demographic challenge', changing labour markets and 'globalisation'.

## The demographic challenge

Welfare states are, above all, providers for the elderly. Britain is an ageing society. The absolute numbers of those over 65 and those over 75 (the 'elderly elderly') are set to increase significantly in the next fifty years. At the same time the ratio between those in retirement and those of working age (16–64) is also set to fall. The prospect is of a growing elderly population dependent upon (taxing) the economic effort of a comparatively small working-age population. This is the trend that underlies talk of a 'demographic timebomb' – the expectation that at some time in the new century the existing welfare state will become unsustainable because of the excess of (pensioner) demands over (worker) inputs. This case is undoubtedly overstated and is repeatedly used to justify a reduction in public provision for the elderly and to induce today's pre-retirement population to invest heavily in private pensions. Nonetheless there is real pressure on a range of public services (not just pensions, but also health care and community care, for example) which arises from the ageing of the population. At the same time there are a number of other demographic pressures on the welfare state. These include the growth of single-parent families, whose heads of household have particular difficulty entering the paid workforce and which include a disproportionate number of children in poverty. The number of children in single-parent households has more than doubled in the past twenty-five years (Hills, 1997).

## Changing labour markets

The model of a postwar British welfare state anticipated in William Beveridge's celebrated 1942 report was built upon the assumption of life-long full (male) employment with a much more limited role in waged work for women, especially married women. The expectation was that a man in work would have an income sufficient to support himself and the dependent members of his family. Most social contingencies (unemployment, sickness, retirement) would be met through a system of social insurance, with only a residual role for means-tested, non-contributory benefits. The postwar welfare state never quite looked like this – but the contemporary British welfare state now looks completely unlike the Beveridge model. Clearly the most dramatic change is the move to (semi)permanent mass unemployment. Especially problematic is the incidence of high youth unemployment and persistent long-term unemployment. Unemployment rates, which seldom rose above 2 per cent in the twenty-five years following the Second World War, stayed above 10 per cent throughout much of the 1980s, dropping only in the latter years of the decade and returning to these high levels in the recession of the early 1990s. Levels of unemployment, which are now seen to contrast so favourably with our continental neighbours are at least twice what they were in the 1950s and 1960s. But patterns of employment have changed in other consequential ways. Much of the work that is available (especially for less skilled workers) is low-paid, casual and part-time. This means both that wages are *not* sufficient to support a family above the poverty line and that many employees do not earn contributory rights (to sickness leave or pension contributions for example).

According to some observers there is an increasing polarisation in the distribution of work in British society between 'work-rich', two-earner and 'work-poor', no-earner households (Oppenheim and Harker, 1996, p. 49), which has spatial, gender and ethnic, as well as traditional class dimensions (Hudson and Williams, 1995). Members of minority ethnic communities, for instance, are not only more likely to have worked in areas of manufacturing that have been hit particularly badly by industrial decline, but they are also more likely to work in the remaining (low-paid) sectors of manufacturing or in low-paid service jobs. Again, the fact that large numbers of women tend to work in the ever-expanding casual sector means that they have lower rates of unionisation and hence less employment protection. They are consequently more vulnerable to job losses than those in full-time work. Furthermore women from minority ethnic communities who work casually or part-time are more likely than white women to suffer higher rates of unemployment or earn lower rates of pay. Even those in more privileged forms of employment may find that an erosion of their terms and conditions of employment means a loss of welfare and pension rights.

An important consequence of all these changes is a shift in welfare effort and spending from contributory insurance entitlements to means-tested, non-contributory benefits. The number claiming means-tested Income Support doubled during the 1980s.

## Globalisation

'Globalisation' has become the fashionable explanation or excuse for almost every change in the contemporary world, and social policy is no exception. It is not part of the argument of this book that we now live in a fully 'globalised' economy. It is by no means clear that the international economic system has become 'autonomised and socially disembedded' (Hirst and Thompson, 1996, p. 10) to the point where transnational capital, driven by new technologies and the search for new markets, has gained such a degree of independence that national governments are effectively forced to adopt policies that accommodate rather than regulate the activities of transnational companies (TNCs). Rather, globalisation is better understood as a process, or series of processes, economic, political and cultural, by which nation-states are indeed having to come to terms with and operate within, a changing world order. Leaving the rather different issue of 'culture' aside, this order, as far as the economic and political spheres are concerned, is characterised *inter alia* by the increasing power of finance over production (Amin, 1994) and the changing nature of production itself away from goods 'designed and destined for one local or national market, to production mostly designed and destined for a world market, or at least for several national markets' (Strange, 1996, p. 44). This shift of focus has, in all probability, made it more difficult for national governments to 'manage' their domestic economies. Aided by financial deregulation, improved communication structures and so on, capital has become much more fluid – TNCs for example, are able to switch production to wherever unit costs are cheapest with the consequence that countries with high labour costs and excessive labour market rigidities have been placed at a disadvantage.

This has very real consequences for social policy. In order to remain players in and retain some control over expanding international markets, governments need to keep two elements of economic strategy in relative balance: (1) they have to ensure that the domestic economy remains open and competitive, and (2) they need to find ways of exercising sufficiently tight regulatory control over transnational capital to ensure that they are not reduced to the status of passive victims of TNC whims. The latter concerns the development of new measures of international economic governance such as international payment mechanisms and the creation of supranational bodies for the supervision of international financial institutions, and is not of direct relevance here (see Hirst and Thompson 1996, pp. 130–9). As far as the former element is concerned, what has emerged, at least in the British context, has been a dual approach which apparently accepts the logic of deindustrialisation and economic 'internationalisation'. On the one hand, it embraces the new 'flexibility' of labour (see Whiteside in this volume), in contrast to the 'job for life' assumptions of the postwar era, and offers positive encouragement to business by lowering personal and corporate taxes in order to promote 'incentives' and encourage greater activity in the marketplace. On the other hand it seeks to underpin domestic competitive performance with social policies that actively privilege market needs over social protection. This strategy stands in contrast to the Keynesian welfare state style of economic management, which sought to *reconcile* economic and social priorities even when such policies entailed the acceptance of labour market rigidities, higher taxation and so on.

Under Conservative governments during the 1980s and 1990s this approach took the form of neo-liberal marketisation policies best exemplified in financial deregulation, cuts in direct taxation, particularly for higher income groups, the attack on organised labour, and the privatisation of goods and services, including the major utilities and elements of the welfare state. These changes opened the economy to the influence of international economic forces and, partly by virtue of such exposure, fostered greater labour flexibility. The abolition of measures for employment protection and a willingness to condone lower wages and increased casualisation in the private sector were mirrored in the public sector by the contracting out of public services such as hospital catering and cleaning which led to a decline in full-time jobs in favour of low-paid, part-time and casual employment as competitors sought to reduce labour costs. In addition a growing number of jobs in both the private and public sectors became subject to short-term contracts, constituting a further step in the direction of flexibilisation (Ascher, 1987; Pinch, 1997).

Meanwhile, in welfare provision the introduction of 'quasi-markets' in education and health care, the sale of council houses and the increasing involvement of private and voluntary agencies in the delivery of care underscored the shift from Keynesian centralised state welfare institutions to the decentralised 'welfare mix' that began to characterise social policy provision in the late 1980s and 1990s. The clearest example of change, however, concerns unemployment benefits and income support. From the early 1980s individuals were increasingly held to be responsible for seeking and sustaining employment. Successive changes to the definition of 'un-employment', to the eligibility criteria for benefit and to benefit levels marked this move from the 'permissive', socially protectionist Keynesian welfare state to more 'coercive' forms of provision that stressed individual accountability and obligation. For the growing number of people not eligible for unemploy-ment benefit, social security payments became progressively more discre-tionary and means-tested, which in the view of some observers has had decidedly adverse consequences on both the individuals concerned and society as a whole (Field, 1994, pp. 14–18).

Without attempting to resolve the more general debate about the nature of globalisation, it seems reasonable to argue that we can detect in Britain a trend towards the privileging of economic competitiveness – now regarded as the *sine qua non* of national survival – which has been driven, or at least is seen to be driven, by changes in the global economy.

## Looking to the Future: New Labour's Social Policy

The tone of New Labour's election manifesto (Labour Party, 1997) suggests that, like the previous Conservative administration, enhanced national economic performance (achieved through greater economic competitiveness) is the new government's overriding objective. The party has more or less explicitly abandoned the ideal of using social policy and the welfare state to *redistribute* opportunities and, especially, incomes. This is seen as part of an exhausted tradition of 'tax and spend'. Rather social policy is to play a supportive role in creating a more competitive economy and an 'active society' with maximum 'participation', above all, in paid work. The social security system is to provide not 'a safety net' but rather 'a trampoline' propelling the displaced back into work. The overall strategy is to foster a move for individuals (and therefore for society) 'from welfare to work'. In the areas of education and social security especially, individuals are to be offered new educational, training and employment opportunities that are designed to enhance their employability. But participation in these new opportunities is not entirely discretionary. Those who fail to take up what is on offer face the threat of withdrawal of state support (Labour Party, 1997; Ellison, 1997, and Chapter 2 of this volume). In contrast to past Conservative governments, the language of social policy is framed in the new terms of 'stakeholding' which, put concisely, invites individuals and groups throughout society to participate in the twin objectives of 'social advance and individual achievement' (Blair, 1994, p. 7). Put in these user-friendly terms, Labour hopes to secure compliance for the continuing drive towards economic competitiveness by including the worst-off groups as 'partners' in the project – provided, of course, they demonstrate sufficient commitment to it.

Of course the interface between welfare state and the labour market is only one (very important) aspect of social policy. New Labour will have to respond to a number of other pressures. Amongst these are the new demands being made upon the welfare state by women, who have not only joined the workforce in ever-increasing numbers, but whose developing autonomy has begun to change the nature of marriage and family structure (Hudson and Williams, 1995). Here, Labour still has to resolve the difficult issues of child care provision, pension provision for those who do not work full-time, and the refashioning of income maintenance procedures to reflect the needs of the growing number of single parent families (Lister, 1994; Millar, 1994).

Perhaps the single greatest social policy challenge, however, is the long-term reform of old age pension provision. Although the value of pensions was reduced by Conservative governments during the 1980s little was done to alter the delivery system itself, which retains its postwar contributory character – and it is here that potential future problems lie in store. Because a fund was never built up, upon which contributors could draw when they reached retirement age, it has always been the case that those in work effectively pay their national insurance 'contributions' directly to existing pensioners. The problem is that this system clearly depends on there being (1) a sufficient number of individuals of working age to fund those in retirement, and (2) a sufficient number of people who are willing to participate in the state pension system rather than choosing private or occupational alternatives. The new government committed itself to maintaining the statutory old age pension, though this is of rapidly diminishing value. It is also committed to a full-scale review of future pensions options. Tony Blair's appointment of the radical Frank Field as minister with special responsibility for welfare state reform suggests that a very different pensions regime (with a much larger role for compulsory, state-regulated but private funds) may be envisaged. But the history of pension reform is littered with heroic failures.

## Outline of the Book

As the above discussion indicates, social policy has become a major area of academic and political interest fundamentally affecting, as well as being affected by, changes in society, economy and polity. This sense of social policy as an eclectic discipline, deeply and reflexively implicated in contemporary social change, is something that, at the most general level, this book attempts to convey. The specific themes referred to here are dealt with in greater detail in the three parts of this book (each with its own short introduction prefacing the chapters concerned), respectively devoted to (1) developments in welfare theory, (2) key policy areas and (3) a range of issues that can be expected to influence the future development of social policy.

Part I assesses the impact of changes in social policy – particularly the redefinition of the state–market relationship – on our conceptions of the role and purposes of welfare. What emerges from the discussions is necessarily ambivalent. There is, to be sure, a certain anxiety about the future of welfare in a society where ambitions of 'cradle to grave' state protection are apparently in the process of being abandoned; but there is excitement, too, about the possibility of a more democratically accountable social policy that could adapt social provision more sensitively to the needs of different social groups.

Part II elaborates at length on the nature of the changes effected in each of the main areas of social policy during the period of Conservative rule. They also speculate about the nature of future developments under New Labour. The themes of reorganisation, fragmentation and continuity – discussed in this Introduction – are clearly delineated in this central section of the book, which taken as a whole provides a sharp testament to the extent to which the British welfare state has been transformed, if by no means dismantled, over the past twenty years.

Part III is more speculative and deals with a range of issues that are likely to influence the future conduct of social policy in Britain. The thorny question of the European Union's role in this country's domestic welfare arrangements is clearly of fundamental importance, but other issues concerning the changing nature of social politics, particularly the role and scope of welfare provision in relation to the social exclusion of marginal or vulnerable groups such as women, minority ethnic groups and the poor, are of equal significance. In a rather different dimension, but one that potentially relates to poverty and social exclusion, lies the difficult issue of the relationship between social policy and the environment. How far should welfare states continue to depend on economic growth as the main source of social spending in the face of growing anxiety about the environmental effects of rising consumption? The question becomes particularly pertinent when 'consumption' is set in the general context of a rapidly expanding consumer culture, which carries specific costs for those least able to fend for themselves and who may need to rely on public services for support.

In sum, this book is about contemporary developments in the theory and practice of social policy in Britain. It is concerned with the rapid, and radical, changes imposed by successive governments (including the present one) on the welfare state and the effects of these changes, present and future, on the vast number of individuals who will require public support – because they need education, are unemployed, sick or old – at some point during their lives. It is also concerned, however, with the broader issue of what kind of society we want to fashion for the twenty-first century. The prospect of growing social exclusion, the loss of social cohesion and progressive moves towards a 'work-fare' (as opposed to welfare) state make up the nightmare scenario of those who are concerned that recent changes in British social policy have begun to make serious inroads into the previous level of social protection. But nothing is written in stone and we do have a degree of choice about our welfare future. By examining the nature and degree of change and its impact on our understanding of the welfare state, this book attempts to clarify the choices that lie before us.

# PART I

# NEW PERSPECTIVES ON WELFARE THEORY

## Introduction

It was once argued, with some justification, that British social policy lacked any real theoretical engagement with its subject matter. The business of social policy (or, as it was for long described, social administration) was to deliver an agreed agenda of social reform, not to think about it. The difficulties of the welfare state after 1970, and the critical attention of thinkers on both the new left and the new right that this attracted, gradually displaced this general (though never universal) lack of interest in the theoretical underpinnings of our social policy arrangements. We now have plenty of theories to choose from. Some of these are primarily normative (telling us what a good social order *should* be like). Others claim to have isolated general principles that show us how welfare states *actually* function (or, in many accounts, dysfunction). Most are a rather volatile mixture, identifying the general operating weaknesses of welfare states and telling us how and why these should be reformed. Chris Pierson's opening chapter is a critical guide to this wealth of new theorising, whilst Nick Ellison (Chapter 2) shows how the 'new thinking' about welfare has had its effect upon both the social policy ideas and practises of the main political parties in Britain.

The remaining three chapters in Part I make a substantive contribution to the theoretical debate. Citizenship has long been a key concept in British social policy (quintessentially in Tom Marshall's 1949 account of the new welfare settlement). In Chapter 3 Ruth Lister investigates the changing understanding of citizenship. She shows how citizenship has always meant both inclusion *and* exclusion. She considers the ways in which different axes of difference – gender, 'race', sexuality, (dis)ability and age – have been used systematically to exclude some from the benefits of citizenship. Finally, she calls for a 'rearticulation' of citizenship in which a more nuanced under-

15

standing of 'universalism' and 'difference' may generate a regime that is more authentically inclusive.

'Need' is a similarly essential, though often unarticulated, category in social policy discussions. In Chapter 4 Martin Hewitt shows how our understanding of what counts as 'need' is related to broader political beliefs and how conceptions of need have changed over time. He discusses in some detail the treatment of need by two contemporary writers: John Gray and Paul Hirst. He too attempts to overcome the seeming divide between the universal and the very particular that lies at the heart of modern discussions on need.

Finally Paul Hirst's chapter on associationalism and welfare (Chapter 5) shows how new circumstances require us to rethink the ways in which social welfare can be delivered (much of it through autonomous associations rather than through the agency of the state). It makes a radical case for the introduction of a citizens' income (a basic income guaranteed to all citizens irrespective of their wealth or employment status), a case reinforced in later chapters by Ailsa McKay and John Barry.

# CHAPTER 1

# Theory in British Social Policy

CHRIS PIERSON

There is a misconception under which both the architects of British social policy and many of its students have frequently laboured. It is that 'theory' is essentially normative (at its worst, a wish-list of the way we would like things to be), whilst what is really important are 'the facts', which once allowed to 'speak for themselves', will tell us not just what is going on, but also what needs to be done. This view is misconceived. Whilst all theories have an irreducible normative content, the purpose of developing a theory of British social policy is not to speculate about what Britain would be like if only people were nicer to each other. Rather the purpose of such a theory is to *explain* developments in British social policy. We want our theory to be *generalisable* across a number of examples/areas, *parsimonious* (explaining as much as possible as succinctly as possible) and *non-trivial* (the insights that our theory delivers should be as revealing rather than as obvious as possible). At the same time the twin belief that facts might 'speak for themselves' and, in the process, 'tell us what to do' is unsustainable. The facts always have to be divined and explained within a particular theoretical framework (however implicit and inarticulate this may be) and the view that we only have to know particular facts (about the incidence of poverty, for example) in order to be able to say what we should do about them is hopelessly naive.

## No Theory Please, We're British

Given these considerations, it is crucial that the study of social policy in Britain was for long seen to be 'untheoretical'. Building upon a Victorian tradition of incremental social reform, Britain had a distinguished record in pioneering the detailed empirical survey of social conditions (most famously in the studies of urban poverty conducted by Mayhew and Booth in London and Joseph Rowntree in York). Although there was disagreement about the responsibility of the poor for their own poverty, there was an increasingly widespread belief that such poverty was remediable and thus ought to be remedied. In the New Liberal climate of the early twentieth century, the

17

newly democratised state was seen to have a legitimate, if still secondary, role to play in relieving the destitution of at least the 'deserving' poor. Every discipline is, in significant measure, a product (and prisoner) of its own intellectual development. From its origins, social policy in Britain was self-consciously 'practical-minded' (grounded in 'the facts' about poverty, unemployment, the incidence of ill-health), aiming to feed evidence and expert advice into a governmental agenda of gradual reform. Significantly, the earliest institutional home for the study of social policy in British universities was in departments of social *administration*, fashioned after Richard Titmuss's hugely influential model at the London School of Economics. Administration suggested then, as now, the more or less routine implementation of a policy agenda whose essentials were largely agreed and non-controversial.

The high point of such agreement about the aims and purposes of social policy came in the period after the Second World War. Beginning with the implementation of the Beveridge Report, the passing of the 1944 Education Act and the inauguration of the National Health Service in 1948, this period was widely characterised as one of consensus politics within which agreement about the incremental growth of social provision was a key component. Social policy, or social administration in the more widespread and apt contemporary usage, was very largely about organising and implementing the growing provision of social services in the welfare state (income maintenance and personal social services plus public housing, health and education). The authenticity of consensus in the twenty-five years following the war is now the object of some controversy, but it is certainly the case that for most of this period social policy proceeded as if there were a near-universal agreement about the purposes of the welfare state. It is in this period more than any other that we can see social policy characterised as 'the worthy, if rather dull, province of a group of concerned specialists . . . working on a particular and practical agenda of (diminishing) poverty and (expanding) welfare provision' (Pierson, 1991, p. 2).

The extent of party political agreement in this period may have been exaggerated, but there was certainly enough of a common view within the social policy community for us to speak of a widespread professional consensus about the character (and desirability) of welfare state development. Insofar as there was a theory of social policy in this period, it was reformist, incremental, statist and premised on a belief in social progress fostered by expertise and professionalism. The perceived sources of this agreement varied. For some, social policy was above all an expression of social solidarity galvanised by the common experiences of war. For others it was part of a more general societal response to new needs generated by long-term processes of industrialisation and modernisation, sometimes brought under the rubric of a centuries-long extension of citizenship. A more political reading of the postwar welfare state saw it as a crucial element in a new social and economic settlement in which the state brokered a compact between capital and labour, a settlement that was sometimes seen to have been 'imposed' by an empowered labour movement. Whatever its origins, the purpose of social policy in this era was widely seen to be to inform and administer the growing and presumed-to-be benign social role of the interventionist state.

## 'Crisis' and the New Political Economy of Welfare

In some difficulty from the mid 1960s, by the early 1970s it was clear that the postwar pattern of sustained economic expansion in which this social policy was grounded was in serious trouble. Unemployment and inflation were both rising, whilst economic growth was faltering. Pressure on welfare state budgets rose sharply as demand increased (with unemployment) and revenue declined (with the slump in economic activity). One of the few areas of rapid growth in these years was that cottage industry which emerged to condemn the postwar welfare state and what were now seen as its complacent supporters in the discipline of social policy. In an echo of nineteenth-century arguments, the compatibility of a market economy and the welfare state (the central assumption of social policy thinking in the postwar period) was vigorously challenged. Certainly these accounts shifted the focus of theorising in social policy from problems in the implementation of a widely agreed reform agenda to disclosing conflicts built into the *political economy* of welfare states. These partially new, partially 'rediscovered' arguments, either directly or through their intellectual 'descendants', continue to exercise a profound influence upon today's thinking about social policy.

Although ideas about the incompatibility of welfare states and capitalist markets had never entirely gone away, there is some irony in the fact that this renewed challenge to the welfare establishment came initially from the (neo-Marxist) left. In Britain it is probably best represented by Ian Gough's *Political Economy of the Welfare State* (1979). Gough argued that the dominant social democratic view that social policy simply redistributed the resources and opportunities that an expanding economy could provide was unsustainable. The key characteristic of welfare states in advanced capitalist societies is that they are *contradictory*. Although they subsidise some of the costs of capital (by providing a trained and educated workforce, for example) welfare state institutions also strengthen the defensive powers of the working class. In the long run this may undermine the conditions for profitable capital investment upon which economic growth in its turn depends. A welfare state that guarantees (high levels of) income maintenance and employment will tend to strengthen the defensive powers of the organised working class and thus the capacity of labour to protect real wage levels and resist attempts to raise productivity. Under (the perhaps consequent) circumstances of sluggish economic growth, it will prove ever more difficult to finance the growing state budget without increasing inflation or further weakening growth, or both. The consequence of a stalemate between capital and labour is likely to be rising inflation, slower economic growth, escalating budget deficits and potential loss of international economic competitiveness. Broadly speaking, these were the circumstances that Gough identified in Britain in the mid 1970s. The real problem was not a temporary shortage of funds in a period of recession, but an underlying structural contradiction in the character of the postwar welfare state settlement. This had to be resolved either by socialising the investment function, that is by taking the most productive parts of the economy into public ownership (the 'socialist' solution), or else by breaking the power of the organised working class, ending full employment, restoring the disciplinary effect of labour markets and thus restoring the conditions for profitable capital investment (the 'capitalist' solution).

## The Coming of the New Right

The neo-Marxist analysis of contradictions in the welfare state has had a lasting influence upon theoretical accounts of the social policy process in Britain. Its impact has, however, been overshadowed by the politically much more efficacious account of contradictions in the welfare state that emerged in the same period under the aegis of the new right and was a key component in the legitimating ideology (though not always the political practice) of Margaret Thatcher's Conservative Party. Some of these arguments have passed into the mainstream of the governing mentality, becoming almost as ubiquitous as the earlier conventions of social democratic orthodoxy. In the new right version of this story the welfare state is unambiguously the villain of the piece. Given the almost unqualified virtues attributed to markets and to societies premised upon market principles, it is perhaps unsurprising that right-wing libertarians find a set of matching (and largely irredeemable) vices in the activities of interventionist states (Hayek, 1982). First, welfare states are seen to be *uneconomic*. They unseat the necessary disciplines and incentives of the marketplace, undermining the incentive of capital (to invest) and of labour (to work). They are *unproductive*, diverting workers and resources out of the value-generating private sector and, through the state monopoly of social services, enabling public sector workers to protect their own employment and command inflationary wage increases. The combination of state monopoly and tax funding *denies freedom of choice* and encourages *inefficiency*, with the delivery of services geared to the interests of (organised) producers rather than (disaggregated) consumers.

At the same time welfare states are *ineffective*. Despite the huge resources directed towards social policy, it fails to eliminate poverty and deprivation. Indeed new right critics argue that welfare state interventions characteristically worsen the position of the poor by trapping them in 'cycles of dependency' and setting up perverse incentives that prevent them from (re-)entering the world of work or induce them to have illegitimate children. The emergence of an 'underclass', with which critics in the United States and now Britain are increasingly concerned, is less a product of poverty than of the misconceived welfare state mechanisms that were supposed to address it. Many of the commonplace social policy initiatives of the 1980s and 1990s – various forms of 'opting out', the transfer of social administration from government departments to semi-autonomous agencies, privatisation and 'quasi-markets' – have their origins and at least part of their justification in these ideas. So, too, does much of the moralising rhetoric on dependency that has increasingly found its way into New Labour thinking on social policy reform.

## The Feminist Challenge

Although new right and, to a lesser extent, new left ideas about the welfare state have continued to be influential, theirs has not been the only challenge to the presumed complacency of orthodox accounts of the social policy process. Possibly the most influential of these alternatives has come from feminist theorising which has confronted the arguments of both orthodox and critical variants of 'malestream' social policy. This feminist critique is as old as the welfare state itself (see Pedersen, 1993). There was, for example, always a feminist critique of the differential treatment of men and women under the Beveridgean welfare state. Yet it is in the wake of 'second wave' feminism from the late 1960s onwards that we have seen the most sustained theoretical effort to underpin a distinctive feminist critique of welfare state arrangements. The trajectory of this theoretical approach is aptly characterised by Julia O'Connor (1996) as moving from a concern with 'women in the welfare state' to 'gendering welfare state regimes' (see also Sainsbury, 1994).

Much of the earliest writing in this tradition focused upon disclosing the distinctive position of women under social policies that were frequently described as gender-neutral (if gender was recognised as an issue at all). The most primitive point was that existing social policy regimes often treated men and women very differently (in terms of benefit entitlements, allowances, taxation, access to careers and so on) and generally to the disadvantage of women. Secondly, these accounts took issue with the narrow focus of social policy and its theorists upon the public sphere and the formal or monetarised economy to the neglect of production and reproduction in the domestic/ private sphere, within which most of society's welfare work was done (largely unpaid) by women. Thirdly, they registered that the welfare state is largely produced and consumed by women, though typically under the control of and in the interests of men. The state's provision of social care is disproportionately based upon the low-paid work of women (work that has historically been low-paid precisely because it is perceived to be *women's* work). Social policy reform, 'Care in the Community' for example, may involve transferring this work of care provision from low-paid women's work in the public sphere to unpaid women's work in the private sphere, with a consequent loss in women's own present and future welfare. Distinctively, socialist-feminists set out to show how existing welfare state arrangements both within and beyond the formal economy served the interests of business (and men). More generally, there was a focus upon revealing the workings of *patriarchy* (the systemic oppression of women by men) as these were mediated through social policy, both in its active interventions and, as importantly, in its areas of systematic neglect.

## Gendering Welfare State Regimes

These core areas of feminist theorising on social policy remain highly influential (though still more frequently in academic studies than in public policy making). In recent years, however, the focus of attention has shifted somewhat from disclosure of the disadvantaged position of women in welfare states to incorporating gender in the explanation of (internationally varied) welfare state regimes. Jane Lewis (1992), for example, compares a number of European welfare states in terms of their varying correspondence to a 'male-breadwinner model' in which social policy is built around the gendered division of 'breadwinning for men and caring/homemaking for women' (ibid., p. 161). Within this typification, Lewis identifies Britain as a 'strong male-breadwinner' state, which despite the removal of many explicit forms of discrimination against women, still underwrites a gendered welfare state (through, for example, its failure to make adequate child care provision): 'while no effort is now made to stop women working, the assumption is that women will be secondary wage earners and, despite the large numbers of women in paid employment, they tend to be in short part-time, low status work' (ibid., p. 165).

Similar conclusions arise from the recent feminist critique of (gendered) conceptions of welfare citizenship (Pateman, 1988; Lister, 1993). Citizenship is often presented as a universal status of the resident adult population of developed states, irrespective of gender. Yet the (social) citizenship to which women are (usually belatedly) admitted has gender-specific (and male) characteristics; for example, the presumption that the model citizen will normally be involved in life-long participation in paid employment in the formal sector of the economy. 'Treating everybody equally' in terms of criteria that vary systematically across (gender) groups will produce systematically unequal outcomes. In the case of earnings-related pensions in Britain, for example, the premium attaching to higher wages and permanent involvement in the paid workforce mean that men's incomes in retirement are systemically higher and more secure than those received by women. A disproportionate number of the elderly living in poverty are women. A further distinctive feature of this more recent feminist writing is its emphasis upon differences between individual states and a range of 'regime types'. In these characterisations Britain is often seen to compare unfavourably with its European neighbours (for example with Scandinavian countries in terms of access to paid employment or with France in terms of the generosity of financial provision for children).

## Social Policy as Exclusion: Disability and 'Race'

Feminists have undoubtedly sponsored many of the most interesting developments in recent theorising about the British welfare state. Their challenge to, and increasingly their critical engagement with, a diversity of more mainstream accounts of the social policy process has focused attention upon a series of core issues (the public–private divide, the nature of social citizenship, the bases of social 'entitlement', the interaction of equality and difference) that previously were not just neglected but often not even perceived to exist. Their focus upon the division between public and private spheres and between formal equality and substantive inequality is an insight that has been taken up and applied by, and in support of, other groups who have seen themselves to be systematically disadvantaged. Thus disability rights activists have not only mobilised to improve provision for disabled people, but have also sought to challenge society's traditional definitions of the disabled and of the bases of their entitlement to social support. Quite central to this struggle has been the claim that provision for disabled people (in terms of access to educational opportunities or adequate transport facilities, for example) is not a discretionary expression of society's sympathy but a welfare *right* grounded in the entitlement of disabled people to equality of participation (in work, education and social life) with their able-bodied fellow citizens.

Perhaps the most systematic attempt to take up the insights of feminist theory and apply them to another area of social policy has come from 'anti-racist' critics of existing welfare state provision. Here the argument is that ethnic division has operated to the disadvantage of ethnic minorities in many of the ways that gender division in social policy has operated against women's interests. The parallels are far from exact. Exclusion from formal citizenship (and exclusion of relatives from abroad) has been a more active issue and the patterns and ideologies of exclusion from the workforce for ethnic minority men and white women have often been quite different. Nonetheless there is a shared conviction that in so far as ethnic identity has ceased to be a formal reason for exclusion from full social citizenship (a process that many commentators would see as radically incomplete), it has given way to a regime in which treating quite unlike cases alike or applying a common set of rules to very different populations has reproduced the social disadvantages of minority populations. In terms of employment and its associated rights, the parallel with the position of women is quite close. Ethnic-minority populations are overrepresented in the low-paid, intermittently-employed and unemployed. They attract fewer work-related entitlements and lower pension contributions. They are more reliant upon a system of social provision that treats them less favourably than the more securely employed members of the (male) majority population.

## Contemporary Social Policy: From 'Crisis' to 'Structural Adjustment'

It was undoubtedly the prospect of a 'crisis of the welfare state' that gave such impetus to critical theories of the social policy process in the 1970s. Although the expectation of a welfare crisis is regularly dusted down and given another airing (a *Guardian* banner headline in the spring of 1997, for example, announced 'The End of the Welfare State'), after a quarter of a century a little of the original sense of urgency has been lost. Certainly the pressures upon welfare provision, especially upon its funding, have become much more severe in the last twenty-five years. Yet the spending and institutional structures of welfare provision have proven surprisingly robust in Britain and beyond (Pierson, 1994). In the face of this experience, theoretical attention has shifted from the prospect of crisis leading to an imminent systemic change towards a concern with the more gradual but still profound process of 'structural adjustment' (OECD, 1989). In essence the argument is that the international economic context has been transformed in ways that mandate change in governments' domestic economic and social policies. In the (increasing number of) areas of social policy directly exposed to international economic forces this has called for a greater focus upon competitiveness. In less exposed policy areas it has led to a growing emphasis upon cost containment and improved efficiency/productivity. (These same developments have given rise to a quite different appraisal of the need for change amongst 'green' critics of the welfare state; see Jacobs, 1996, and Chapter 14 of this volume.)

## New Public Management

One of the clearest expressions of this newer theoretical agenda is to be found in the ideas comprehended under the generic label of 'new public management' (see Hood, 1991). Though the sources of these ideas are various (including an enthusiasm for successive waves of guru-driven 'management theory'), there is a clear link with the public choice element of new right thinking in the 1970s and a pervasive concern to influence the shape of public policy. The ideas associated with the new public management have had a considerable impact upon the ideology and, to a lesser extent, practice of public administration in Britain over the past decade and a half. At the core of this approach is a critique of the traditional techniques of social administration – as bureaucratised, routinised, focused upon procedures rather than outcomes, lacking in either cost consciousness or a concern for quality, run for the (unsackable and unanswerable) producers rather than for the final consumers. The 'answer' is wherever and whenever possible to replace administration with market-like structures.

Of course the 'ideal' (new right) solution to this problem is simply to dissolve states into markets, to reduce radically those services (such as health, education and pensions) that the state now provides and to let individuals and families shop in the market (with the resources released by the collapse of the state's demand for taxation revenues) for alternatives. Whatever the merits of this position, this is not predominantly what the new public management is about. New public management is much more about introducing markets (and quasi-markets) *within* the state. Its underlying premise is that choice, competition and the power of the consumer can all be made to work their magic without a transfer of ownership. The strategy is to introduce private sector management, organisation and labour market practices into the public sector in the expectation that the public service can thus be made to deliver the sorts of service and efficiency that it is supposed the private sector (and its competitive environment) has already realised. More specifically, there has been a move to introduce 'internal markets' with competing individual units (schools, colleges or health care trusts) for consumers of their services. The purchasers of these services (parents, patients or their surrogates) should be able to move their custom between providers with relative ease. Greater information (examination results, waiting list times, proportion of successful procedures, prices) should make it possible for consumers to make effective choices. With resources following consumer choices, competition should encourage efficiency and reward the most successful producers.

As we shall see in a number of contributions to this volume, the doctrine of new public management has certainly had a significant impact upon the governing mentality across the party political divide. Whether its theoretical underpinnings have been justified by public sector experience is, as these discussions will also show, much less clear.


## Post-Fordism

In 'classical' Marxist accounts of the 1970s it frequently seemed that the 'contradictions' of the capitalist welfare state would only be resolved by getting rid of either capitalism or the welfare state. Twenty-five years on, for all the difficulties the welfare state has faced, such a view seems too stark. Perhaps the most sustained effort to understand contemporary British social policy from within a broadly neo-Marxist theoretical framework has come from those who seek to explain changes to the welfare state under the rubric of post-Fordism. Broadly speaking, Fordism refers to that form of capitalism (and its attendant social and political institutions) which predominated in the period between the end of the Second World War and the end of the 1960s. This was the epoch of full (male) employment, sustained economic growth and capitalism. It was secured around the twin commitment to broadly Keynesian policies designed to sustain full employment and economic growth, and the development of a more or less 'institutional' welfare state to deal with the dysfunctions of a market economy and deliver certain social goods to the population at large. The social and economic turbulence of the late 1960s and early 1970s was an expression of the exhaustion of this Fordist regime as a framework for sustainable capitalist economic growth. The stability that had been a feature of the postwar years had descended into rigidity. The institutions of Fordism and the Keynesian welfare state, which had once secured the grounds for capital accumulation by sustaining effective demand and managing the relations between capital and labour, had now become a barrier to further economic growth. The crisis of Fordism was thus about finding and institutionalising a new social and economic regime that could restore the conditions for successful capitalist accumulation and thus economic growth.

In the British context, the attempt to install a distinctive post-Fordist order has been characterised by Bob Jessop in terms of a transition from the Keynesian welfare state towards a *Schumpeterian workfare state*, which is consonant with a post-Fordist pattern of economic growth (Jessop, 1994). Under this new formation, the state's social policy interventions are directed towards the twin goals of sponsoring innovation and technological know-how amongst its 'own' players in an open international market economy, whilst sublimating social protection ever more explicitly to the needs of 'competi-tiveness' and a transformed labour market. In Jessop's words, 'it marks a clear break with the KWS [Keynesian welfare state] as domestic full employment is de-prioritised in favour of international competitiveness and redistributive welfare rights take second place to a productivist re-ordering of social policy' (ibid., p. 24). Similarly Phil Cerny's account (1990, p. 179) identifies a general move from 'the welfare state to the competition state' with 'a shift in the focal point of party and governmental politics from the general maximisation of welfare within a nation . . . to the promotion of enterprise, innovation and profitability in both private and public sectors'.

The attempt to inaugurate a post-Fordist regime certainly does not mean a straightforward 'withdrawal' of the state in the manner anticipated by the new right. The state certainly withdraws or at least reduces various forms of social protection. In employment-related areas the intention is generally to make labour markets more 'flexible'. Elsewhere the motivation is more straightforwardly to hold down costs. But at the same time the state may actually increase its interventions in the welfare sphere to impose a 'competitiveness' agenda. In Britain, for example, this may be seen in the reform of post-school training or the move from Unemployment Benefit to Job Seekers' Allowance (Jones, 1996). The issue is not really the 'withering away of the welfare state' but rather the further erosion of the social democratic model of welfare in favour of social policies that are more explicitly sublimated to the changing 'needs of the economy'.

## Globalisation

All of these accounts of recent change in British social policy owe something to a still broader set of conjectures about the *globalisation* of international economic activity. Indeed the recent history of British social policy might be recast as a series of 'structural adjustments' to a radically changed external environment (and its internal consequences). The idea of globalisation has been called upon to do an extraordinary amount of explanatory work in accounts of recent social and political change, and as such it has generated a vast literature and a great deal of disagreement. At one extreme are those who believe that nation states are increasingly losing their powers as we live in an ever more 'borderless world' (Ohmae, 1990). Sceptics, in contrast, doubt that there really is a new phenomenon of 'globalisation', insisting that nation states have always faced powerful transnational forces, and that in spite of these they retain significant governing capacities and policy discretion (Hirst and Thompson, 1996). Unremarkably, the truth probably lies somewhere between these two perspectives (see Perraton *et al.*, 1997). We shall confine our attention here to those aspects of globalisation that might be significant in explaining the current trajectory of British social policy.

Globalisation is clearly a multifaceted phenomenon – an 'open-ended process' rather than a given 'end state' in Perraton *et al.*'s treatment – but its most significant impact upon domestic social policy is generally seen to lie in the consequences of a seemingly exponential growth of transnational economic activity: increasing trade, rising foreign direct investment (FDI) and, perhaps above all, a rapid intensification of international financial movements. These changes in the international political economy are seen to have had at least two profound consequences. First, they have tended to strengthen the bargaining position of capital over and against labour, which cannot match capital's new-found international mobility. Second, they are seen to have undermined the authority and capacity of the interventionist state, or at least of the redistributivist state. These developments present acute difficulties for policies that are premised upon controlling investment decisions and redistributing resources and opportunities *within national boundaries*. Facing the heightened international mobility of capital, governments find themselves exposed to a 'permanent referendum' upon their financial probity in the international money markets. Competition for internationally mobile capital encourages governments to establish a favourable climate for investment – which includes flexible labour markets, low social costs and low taxation (on capital, at least). Governments that pursue expansionary economic policies are said to face the prospect of disinvestment. Newly industrialised countries, with much more rudimentary welfare states and much lower wages, are at a considerable advantage in the competition for job-creating employment. If more developed states (such as Britain) are not able to compete by offering technically more proficient workers, they face the danger of a 'race to the bottom' in terms of social protection and the creation of a permanent 'underclass' of unskilled unemployables.

There are severe reservations to be voiced against this doomsday account of the exhaustion of welfare states under the impact of economic globalisation. Mobile capital is after a good deal more than the lowest possible wages, and there is a persistent diversity in states' tax and spending profiles that defies any straightforward account of convergence at the bottom. Nonetheless accounts of this kind do indeed inform a good deal of social policy thinking in contemporary Britain and beyond. There is seemingly a new consensus amongst politicians about the necessity of improving 'competitiveness' (although professional economists are fiercely divided about this 'imperative'). New Labour has been to the fore in arguing the case for more 'flexible' labour markets and 'lifetime learning' as the essential social policy responses to a globalised economy. All parties stress the need to generate a climate in which foreign investors will be tempted to place their capital in Britain. There is also widespread agreement that the role of the state in social provision (in the costly area of retirement pensions, for example) has to be scaled back, at least in part because of the tax and revenue implications of continued state responsibility. There is a perception, substantiated by the executive autonomy given to the Bank of England, that *nobody* bucks the international financial markets and that the limits of social policy are set, above all, by what is acceptable to *this* community. Even if, as Hirst and Thompson (1996) argue, it is not a real change in the balance of global forces but rather the 'myth' of globalisation that has led political elites to conclude that 'almost nothing can be done', the consequent 'pathology of overdiminished expectations' has proved to have very real consequences.

## Conclusion

No one could argue that we lack a theoretical account of the development of social policy in Britain. This brief survey has highlighted some of the more influential approaches, but there are others. In a more explicitly philosophical/normative vein, Philippe van Parijs' *Real Freedom for All* (1995), for example, is a sustained attempt to justify an unconditional citizens' basic income as the only legitimate alternative to conventional capitalist welfare states. Paul Pierson's *Dismantling the Welfare State* (1994) (which is actually about how the welfare state was *not* dismantled) concentrates upon the policy-making processes which have so frustrated the new right advocates of retrenchment. In a quite different direction (see Cahill, 1994, and Chapter 16 of this volume), there has been a challenge to the conventional boundaries of 'social policy' itself and an attempt to bring into the domain of social policy areas of social life and, more particularly, of consumption (shopping, transport, leisure) that have been seen traditionally as lying 'outside the welfare state'. The role of the theories we have considered is complex. In part, theory has explained the social policy process but it has also sometimes informed or even shaped it. This latter impact might be quite direct (as in the activity of right-wing think tanks such as the Adam Smith Institute and The Institute for Economic Affairs during the 1980s) or quite diffuse (as in the much more general impact that neo-liberal ideas have had in shaping the governing 'climate of opinion' over the past twenty-five years) (Denham, 1996). Frequently, theories of the social policy process have sought simultaneously to describe *and* to explain *and* to pass judgement. The outcomes have not always been clear, but they undoubtedly have a central place in explaining the contemporary state of British social policy.

## Further Reading

A good short account of the postwar social democratic view of welfare can be found in D. Donnison, 'Social Policy After Titmuss', *Journal of Social Policy*, vol. 8, no. 2 (1979), pp. 145–56. On the new right, see D. King, *The New Right* (London: Macmillan, 1987) and P. Pierson, *Dismantling the Welfare State* (Cambridge: Cambridge University Press, 1994). For a discussion of the neo-Marxist account of social policy, see C. Pierson, *Beyond the Welfare State?*, 2nd edn (Cambridge: Polity, 1998). The feminist literature is extensively surveyed in J. O'Connor, 'From Women in the Welfare State to Gendering Welfare State Regimes', *Current Sociology*, vol. 44, no. 2 (1966). A useful introduction to the post-Fordism and social policy debate is R. Burrows and B. Loader (eds), *Towards a post-Fordist Welfare State?* (London: Routledge, 1994). The literature on welfare states and globalisation is growing rapidly. Amongst the best sources are: G. Esping-Andersen (ed), *Welfare States in Transition* (London: Sage, 1996) and M. Rhodes, 'Globalization and West European Welfare States', *Journal of European Social Policy*, vol. 6, no. 4 (1996), pp. 305–27. Still the most comprehensive single-volume survey of theories of social policy is C. Pierson *Beyond the Welfare State?*, 2nd edn (Cambridge: Polity, 1998).

# CHAPTER 2

# The Changing Politics of Social Policy

NICK ELLISON

This chapter is concerned with 'normative social policy' – the values and principles that shape attitudes to social welfare. It examines recent attempts by Britain's major political parties to reassess the values that underpin their ideological approaches to the welfare state in the light of the extensive social, economic and political changes of the past twenty-five years. After establishing the importance of the normative dimension for a fully-developed understanding of contemporary social policy, the chapter moves to a brief account of the Conservative Party's efforts to alter the values that informed 'Keynesian' assumptions about the role of the welfare state. It then looks at the major political parties' current approaches to social policy, as witnessed in their 1997 general election manifestoes. Striking similarities between the manifesto commitments of the two major political parties suggest that the Conservatives have been successful in forging a new 'consensus' about the principles that should imbue contemporary attitudes towards welfare, if not about the precise policy details. The bulk of the chapter focuses on the impact of these normative changes on the Labour Party's welfare ideology and asks whether 'New Labour' has effectively abandoned its egalitarian approach to the welfare state. Suggesting that the party's efforts to retain a sense of social justice in its deliberations about the future role of the welfare state are likely to be compromised by the acceptance of key elements of Conservative social policy, the chapter concludes with a brief prognosis for the welfare state under the New Labour government.

## Political Parties and Normative Social Policy

There is a tendency amongst academic observers of social policy, particularly those interested in the 'politics of welfare', to consider the values that inform ideological approaches to welfare quite separately from the actual conduct of social policy by political parties in government (see, for example, George and Wilding, 1994; Hill, 1993; Deakin, 1994). The normative dimension often seems to remain at some distance from the political process, unsullied by the inevitable compromises parties have to make when in power. This separation of principle and practice can of course be useful, not least because it allows for more detailed theoretical consideration of welfare values from which parties themselves often draw, but it ignores the fact that political parties themselves play a fundamental role in actively shaping attitudes towards social policy. In their efforts to maintain and develop distinct ideological positions, they are closely involved in developing the normative aspects of social and public policy while, as democratically accountable 'social policy makers' committed to deriving specific proposals from broad ideological principles, their deliberations provide the electorate with a degree of choice about competing conceptions of welfare.

Importantly, of course, parties rarely formulate policy in circumstances of their own choosing. Confronted by the demands of competing interests operating in a wider context over which they have little control, the policy-making process has to take account of the prevailing social, economic and political environment even as attempts are made to change it. This makes for a complex relationship between the normative components of party policy-making and the pragmatic need to produce policies capable of appealing to sufficient numbers of voters in order to secure power. The persistent need to reconcile pragmatism and principle can lead to surprising ideological contortions, particularly during periods of rapid economic and social change, which can produce seismic shifts in previously accepted ideas and practices. Such was the case in the late 1940s and early 1950s when the Conservative Party was forced, under threat of electoral extinction, to come to terms with collectivist attitudes to the state and social welfare in the emerging postwar world (Seldon, 1981). Again, as the following section demonstrates, the Labour Party's collectivist ideology itself became the subject of increasing scepticism as the egalitarian promise of the postwar welfare state fell victim to economic decline and a reinvigorated market liberal ideology in the late 1970s and 1980s.

## Changing Consensus? Conservative Social Policy in the 1980s and 1990s

Throughout the postwar period, both of the major political parties in Britain as well as 'minor' contenders such as the Liberals and others subscribed to the goal of a state-funded welfare system in which the bulk of welfare goods and services were delivered by either central or local state institutions. If 'consensus' is not an entirely happy term for what was never more than a general agreement about the economic and social case for full employment supported by a range of state welfare services (for alternative perspectives see

Lowe, 1993; Jones and Kandiah, 1996), the desire for such arrangements was sufficiently widespread to maintain the institutional apparatus of the Keynesian welfare state for the best part of a generation. As the Introduction to this book makes clear, these arrangements came under increasing strain during the 1970s as rising inflation and declining growth forced governments to curtail social spending.

The need for welfare state retrenchment, however, had to be justified by reference to principle, and with Labour unable to offer a coherent alternative to postwar Keynesianism (Ellison, 1994) the Conservative Party, replete with a revitalised 'new right' ideology (King, 1987; Pierson, 1991), proved adept at rethinking the role of welfare to reflect the new economic conditions. Importantly, as many of the chapters in this book suggest, Conservative 'rethinking' did not simply entail a straightforward acceptance of free market nostrums and the reduction of the welfare state to 'safety net' status on orthdox new right lines (Minford, 1991). Such a course would have been difficult, not least because unemployment levels, which remained obstinately high throughout the Conservatives' eighteen-year rule, necessitated correspondingly high levels of social spending. Instead Conservative governments *reorganised* methods of welfare delivery in ways that reflected their broad commitment to market solutions, significantly altering the state's role as a direct welfare provider in the process.

Viewed in retrospect, it is plain that downward pressure on social spending and the reorganisation of welfare delivery mechanisms formed part of an approach to social policy that had two principal aims. First, as part of their general scepticism about the cost-efficiency of the public sector, the Conservatives believed the welfare state would benefit from extensive institutional reform along market lines. Second, in contrast to Keynesian welfare collectivism, which they believed had created a 'dependency culture', Conservative governments wanted to use social policy as a means of revitalising what they regarded as 'traditional' ideals of individual responsibility and self-sufficiency.

On the first dimension, Glennerster (1994, pp. 322–3) has identified three changes which, taken together, transformed the organisation of British welfare and challenged assumptions about the central role of the state as a direct welfare provider:

- Budgetary devolution (though not control), for example to schools or GP fundholders in the NHS.
- The removal of local government control over many areas of social policy, notably housing and education but also residential care and the delivery of certain social services.

- The introduction of competition within specific public services in the form of purchaser–provider splits and other forms of 'quasi-marketisation'.

In each case, these changes can be read as an attempt to bring state welfare services closer to the market, either by allowing the private and voluntary sectors directly to provide particular services on a competitive basis or by mimicking the effects of market behaviour within state-run services.

As Gamble (1994) has pointed out, this sympathy for market alternatives was accompanied by a second, more 'statist' dimension, which actively used state welfare to uphold a distinct vision of individual virtue. In key areas of welfare provision, notably employment and income maintenance, governments throughout the 1980s and early 1990s insisted repeatedly that the burden of responsibility for finding employment and income security lay primarily with individuals and their families, the state being a provider of last resort. This conviction was nothing if not convenient in view of the extensive labour market changes and alarming rise in unemployment that accompanied the introduction of rigorous monetarist policies in the early 1980s. Nevertheless it informed – and continues to inform – the new welfare rhetoric that underpinned successive changes to eligibility criteria for unemployment benefit, for example, as well as the greater incidence of means testing and discretionary payments in the social security system as a whole (see Timmins, 1996, pp. 401–2; Evans, 1996). In short, the new rhetoric inverted the logic of the Keynesian Welfare State. It stressed the individual's *duty* to work and to provide for family and dependants, in contrast to the Keynesian emphasis on individual *rights* to employment and social protection (see Lister in this volume). A brief consideration of 1997 general election manifestoes will confirm how far the axis of debate about social policy has moved from its postwar position.

## Parties and Manifestoes: The 1997 General Election

Election manifestoes are of limited interest as enduring statements of a party's social and political beliefs, but they do provide a unique snapshot of how contenders for power combine principle and pragmatism at a particular point in time. Those written for the 1997 general election make interesting reading. Summing up their eighteen-year rule, the Conservatives pointed to the cost-effective nature of modern social provision while claiming that they had promoted high levels of spending in key areas such as health and education. Labour subscribed to cost-efficiency in similar vein but remained distinctly chary about committing a prospective Labour government to new spending.

The party not only ruled out increases in direct taxation as a means of funding welfare, but also promised to keep the total welfare budget within Conservative spending targets. Plans for 'extra' spending were made dependent upon the redeployment of resources garnered from the abandonment of specific Conservative programmes (the Assisted Places Scheme in education is a good example). Only the Liberal Democrats departed from the new 'consensus', retaining a vestige of their traditional centre-left approach to welfare by promising to raise income tax by 1 per cent in order to create extra resources for education and find extra year-on-year expenditure for key sectors such as the health service.

Attitudes towards social expenditure are certainly one indicator of a party's normative approach to social policy, but a fuller picture can be gained from its understanding of the *purposes* of welfare – what it believes social provision to be 'for'. Here again Labour has moved closer to the Conservative position. Throughout the 1980s, as Conservative attacks on the 'dependency-inducing' nature of contemporary social policy mounted, the Labour opposition held to its original normative stance, regarding welfare both as a means of alleviating poverty and as a vehicle for greater social equality. By the mid 1990s, however, the party's welfare ideology contained distinctly Conservative normative elements. New Labour appeared more than willing, not only to endorse the previous government's policies, which had limited the access of certain groups to specific goods and services, but also to exceed Conservative ambitions by placing a duty of 'specific performance' on those requiring state support, particularly in the areas of income maintenance, education and training (Labour Party, 1997). Again, the Liberal Democrats (1997) occupied a position somewhat reminiscent of 'old' Labour, shying away from direct attempts to limit access to welfare provision or compel particular forms of behaviour in favour of various types of pecuniary encouragement to take up training or the offer of employment.

Differences naturally continue to exist between the parties over matters of policy detail, but this brief look at the election manifestoes suggests that both major parties have accepted that the *nature* of 'welfare' has changed. The new consensus marks a shift away from the high-tax, high-spending policies of the Keynesian welfare state in favour of an approach that is designed not only to limit social spending but also to contain expectations about what governments are willing and prepared to do to help those in need. Arguably at least, British social policy is beginning to assume a 'post-welfare' character: comprehensive social protection, the normative ideal that dominated thinking about social policy throughout the postwar era, is being superseded by a new normative consensus built around the conviction that welfare provision must be conditional upon economic performance.

This change of emphasis is not simply the maverick product of Conservative political will. The emergence of the low-cost economies of Eastern
Europe and South-East Asia, with their ability to attract increasingly
footloose international capital, has meant that governments in many Western
industrial societies have felt compelled to reorganise their welfare systems to
reflect new economic priorities. In an era of 'disorganised capitalism' (Lash
and Urry, 1987), some observers have detected the emergence of a 'competitive' (Cerny, 1990) or 'workfare' (Jessop, 1994) state, one characteristic of
which is a social policy that stimulates innovation, skills and training in the
context of flexible labour markets at the expense of forms of social provision
for which there is no apparent economic return.

The point is that, irrespective of past ideological affiliations, political
parties in many advanced industrial societies have increasingly been forced
to accept the logic of the new internationalised economy and have tailored
their welfare ideologies accordingly. In ways that echo the Conservatives'
approach, this has meant refashioning rather than necessarily reducing the
state's welfare role, emphasising the part played by the state in guaranteeing
public sector efficiency and imposing a cost-effective vision of individual
responsibility. For some social democratic parties the normative change
accompanying this shift away from Keynesian welfare ideals has involved
the 'reinterpretation', and in some instances the direct abandonment, of long-
cherished egalitarian values.

## Labour's Progress: Rethinking the Normative Base of Social Policy

Labour's progress has been especially painful and protracted. During the
1980s the parlous state of the party, symbolised by the existence of huge
Conservative parliamentary majorities, meant that the search for alternative
policies was often mortgaged to the more pressing need to resolve internal
difficulties (Shaw, 1994; Heffernan and Marqusee, 1992). With deep internal
divisions continuing to exist between left wingers, committed to the party's
historic goal of public ownership, and the majority to their right, who
continued to endorse Keynesian welfarism, the party was in no position to
contemplate radical ideological adjustments. A third successive election defeat
in 1987, however, proved to be the catalyst for change as the Kinnock
leadership initiated an examination of all aspects of party policy in the shape
of a two-year policy review (Smith and Spear, 1992; Shaw, 1994).

The review marked an important stage in Labour's ideological transformation from Keynesian to post-Keynesian values, which accepted the market as

the prevailing context for the conduct of economic and social policy (Labour Party, 1989; 1990). Guided by John Smith and Gordon Brown, the party's new medium-term industrial strategy cast the state as an 'enabling' partner with the private sector, effectively ending Labour's ideological hostility to free market capitalism (Gamble, 1992). Social policy was implicated in this new vision in two ways. First, the state's enabling role was extended to a conception of welfare where citizens – frequently referred to as 'consumers' – would use the public services and opportunities offered to 'take responsibility for their own lives and to fulfil their obligations to others' (Labour Party, 1989, p. 6). Second, elements of social policy, notably education and training, began to be framed in ways that were more than simply ameliorative; that is to say, they were considered less as measures for social protection than as elements in a strategy of economic modernisation which involved the active participation of citizens themselves in making the most of the opportunities open to them. To this end, as one party document put it, Labour perceived a need for 'a massive change in attitude on the part of managers . . . and on the part of potential trainees, who often do not see training as relevant or leading to greater opportunities' (Labour Party, 1990, p. 11).

Endorsed by the great majority of the party, the momentum of renewal instigated by the policy review survived the disappointment of losing a fourth general election in 1992, but thereafter it took on a different and more urgent quality. In the immediate aftermath of the election, Neil Kinnock's successor, John Smith, took the unusual step of 'contracting out' responsibility for developing new social policy proposals to the independent Commission on Social Justice (CSJ) – an initiative imitated by Liberal Democrat leader Paddy Ashdown, who sponsored a commission (the Dahrendorf Commission) to enquire into 'Wealth Creation and Social Cohesion in a Free Society' a year or so later.

The CSJ was created for the express purpose of developing new normative foundations for Labour's social policy, but both commissions effectively acted as *ad hoc* think tanks for new ideas about the role of welfare in a way that traditional political parties could not. Notionally independent of party control, they proved to be convenient devices for presenting new thinking in a format that rendered their creators less vulnerable to criticism either from internal party factions or external opponents. Because the party leaderships were not obliged to accept their recommendations, the commissions were useful vehicles for generating ideas that effectively moved the normative core of centre-left welfare ideology further from the traditional association with Keynesian principles towards a set of priorities that endorsed certain elements of Conservative social policy.

## Commissioning social justice

The normative assumptions of both commissions were broadly similar (McCormick and Oppenheim, 1996), and displayed a more individualistic interpretation of social justice than is usually associated with centre-left thinking. Recognition of the 'equal worth' of all citizens in a context of equal access to resources and opportunities for education, training and employment were the key elements of an approach to social justice that emphasised a rough 'equity' of input rather than equality of outcome. To be sure, the commissions acknowledged the importance of 'social inclusion' and 'social cohesion', but as part of a refashioned conception of 'citizenship' perceived as a mix of rights owed to, and duties owed by, individual members of society. This new approach to social justice chimed with the acceptance of the free market as the dominant method of economic organisation, the belief being that economic and social policy could be combined in ways that would sustain both social equity and economic efficiency. In the CSJ's view (1994, p. 97) the two were interdependent, the 'economic high road of growth and productivity . . . also [being] a social high road of opportunity and security'.

This conviction was reflected in ideas for the reform of the benefits system, and particularly in the interest displayed in 'welfare-to-work' programmes designed to ease individuals' passage into employment (ibid., pp. 239–65; Dahrendorf Commission, 1995, pp. 85–91). Both reports considered unemployment to be 'the greatest threat to wealth creation and social cohesion', in the words of the Dahrendorf Commission (1995, p. 85), and discussed possible methods of raising employment levels in conditions of greater labour flexibility – one of which was to impress upon individuals that they had a 'duty' to find work. Again, both the CSJ and the Dahrendorf Commission discussed the possibility of funding education and training through the provision of a National Learning Bank (CSJ) or individual learning accounts financed by contributions from employers and employees (Dahrendorf), on the basis that 'investment in people simultaneously contributes . . . to social justice and to national economic strength' (CSJ, 1994, p. 97). Finally, both commissions outlined proposals for a new approach to old age pensions that would require individuals to make their own arrangements for a 'second pension'. Each report underlined the fact that, if the current arrangements were to continue, they would not only fail to guarantee older people's living standards but would continually confront the state with the most expensive of all options: having to pay for successive pension increases out of general taxation, with potentially adverse economic consequences (ibid., pp. 268–9; Dahrendorf, 1995, pp. 66–7).

The twin themes of a more individualised conception of social justice and the belief that social policy could be used as a vehicle to pursue social justice *and* greater economic efficiency carries more than a hint of the Conservative approach to social policy. Although the preoccupation with social justice obviously continues a long tradition of left-wing theorising, the individualist turn, particularly when accompanied by acceptance of the centrality of markets, belies Conservative influence. Moreover the conviction that the welfare state can work proactively to shape individual behaviour owes something to Conservative beliefs. In this regard it is important to note that the CSJ accepted Conservative 'availability for work' tests and, pushing further, proposed the payment of a 'participation income' to those individuals who met prescribed criteria for 'active citizenship' (CSJ, 1994, p. 264).

## New Labour, New Values?

New Labour enlarged upon these more directive aspects of the commissions' reports after Tony Blair became leader, following John Smith's death in 1994. In the two years before the 1997 general election, party leaders became increasingly convinced that individual opportunity and social responsibility should comprise the twin goals of social policy in a society that accords economic competitiveness the highest priority. Blair's vision of 'a new settlement on welfare for a new age, where opportunity and responsibility go together' (Blair, 1996, p. 19), informed a raft of proposals for education, income maintenance and employment that not only took the reciprocal nature of the relationship between the individual and the wider community – the symbiotic quality of rights and obligations – as a common starting point, but linked it with the *economic* rationale for fairness and social justice. To quote Blair once again, 'social cohesion – a society in which there is not gross inequality nor the absence of opportunity for a significant number of citizens – is an indisputable part of an efficient economy' (ibid., p. 116).

But, quotations apart, is it plausible to suggest that social policies can somehow reconcile individual interests with the collective interest of the wider community, or the ideal of social cohesion with the needs of the free market? Current debates within the Labour Party suggest that not everyone is convinced, the remaining representatives of 'old' Labour continuing to press the case for Keynesian welfare solutions, which they believe will protect the most vulnerable sections of society, and fostering collective interests and social cohesion against the excesses of self-interest encouraged by the new competition state (Hattersley, 1997a). This debate – principally between ex-Shadow

Chancellor Hattersley and Chancellor Gordon Brown – indicates the degree to which Labour in power is continuing to distance itself from the party's traditional ameliorative concerns.

While this is not to imply that the new government is unmoved by the existence of poverty and inequality, it is distinctly possible that New Labour no longer sees itself as *primarily* responsible for the well-being of the worst-off. Instead it considers the state's welfare role to be that of a facilitator. Brown's (1997) comment that 'our modernisation of the welfare state will create work, make sure that work always pays, and provide recurring opportunities for lifelong learning' suggests that the Labour government will offer 'life chances' rather than increase direct social provision – although he is careful to say that 'the sick and the elderly' will be protected and defended. A similar view is offered by Peter Mandelson (1997), who argues that 'it is the job of the government to *play its part* in guaranteeing "flexibility plus" – plus higher skills and higher standards in our schools and colleges, plus partnership with business to raise investment . . . plus an imaginative welfare-to-work programme to put the long-term unemployed back to work' (emphasis added). These views contrast with Roy Hattersley's (1997b) more forthright concern to alleviate poverty in the short term, even if this involves breaking election promises and raising direct taxation to pay for immediate benefit increases.

Hattersley's fears may be well-placed, but it is possible that a more insidious danger could accompany Labour's new approach to welfare; one born not out of an intentional lack of generosity but out of failure to achieve the desired harmonisation of economic and social policy. The potential threat, examined at some length below, is this: in periods of economic adversity the government could be tempted to adopt a more 'regimented' – even coercive – attitude towards welfare than anything envisaged by the CSJ or Dahrendorf in an effort to ensure that the welfare system really does contribute to economic efficiency. In fairness, Labour would almost certainly wish to 'encourage' rather than coerce, but as discussed above, its conception of social policy is sufficiently influenced by the 'competition mentality' to undermine other potential values from which alternative ideas of social justice could be derived.

Such a prospect is not of course inevitable, but much depends on how successful Labour is in convincing key sections of society of the viability of its new normative position. Here a good deal of weight is placed on currently fashionable ideas of 'stakeholding' and 'partnership', for it is by operationalising the values implicit in these ideas that the government hopes to bridge potential contradictions between its economic and social goals. Stakeholding is applied to different areas of economy and society in different ways, but its abiding principle lies in the conviction that individuals will better sustain their commitment to an enterprise, community or society if they feel that they have a genuine interest or 'stake' in it. Where welfare is concerned, stakeholding conveys a sense of 'ownership' of or rights to particular resources, but also a corresponding obligation to make use of the resources on offer. In this way the idea is used to describe a relationship between state and individual based upon a 'partnership', where the state provides opportunities for employment, education and so on that individuals are effectively obliged to take up. Both sides derive benefits from the duties performed for the ultimate economic benefit of society as a whole.

It is worth devoting a little space to an examination of the policy details behind these ideas because they are so central to Labour's social policy. In education, for instance, Labour makes much of the need to promote a 'culture of responsibility' for learning within the family to support the work done in schools(Labour Party, 1997, p. 8). Parents, pupils and teachers are expected to work in partnership to make the most of the opportunities and resources provided by the state, with penalties being imposed where one or other party fails to carry out its obligations satisfactorily. At the time of writing, new proposals to speed up procedures for dismissing incompetent teachers are under discussion and formal contracts for the amount of time to be spent on homework are being actively considered, together with penalties for pupils who fail to complete the work they have 'contracted' to do.

Stakeholding is also currently being applied to income in old age, where Labour MP Frank Field has advocated a system of compulsory saving towards second, 'stakeholder pensions'. His reasoning epitomises the new approach to social policy. Instead of continuing to rely exclusively on the expensive state system, an explicit appeal should be made to *self-interest*, individuals being encouraged to transfer more of their current income (which they must do if immediate costs are to be covered) in such a way that 'each individual gains ownership over any new assets which are built into the scheme' (Field, 1996, p. 21). Field's point is that gains accrue not just to individuals as direct beneficiaries, but also to society as a whole, for state and economy will benefit from being able to devote fewer resources to combating poverty and inequality in old age.

Finally, the clearest example of stakeholding as it applies to social policy unquestionably lies in Labour's 'welfare to work' policy. In Blair's (1996, p. 302) view, 'the most meaningful stake anyone can have in society is the ability to earn a living and support a family', and to this end he argues that the state has a duty to attack unemployment, providing jobs and therefore opportunities for individuals to benefit from this most basic of all forms of belonging. However, although the supposition is that those out of work actually want employment, the state 'guarantees' job and training opportunities only on the condition that offers are taken up. If an individual refuses to comply, he or she is likely to incur loss of benefit, just as those who do not make the most of educational provisions can be penalised, or those who fail to make appropriate pension arrangements may face a poorer old age.

On one reading this 'carrot and stick' approach to social welfare does not automatically imply a lack of concern for those who turn to the state for support; after all there is nothing necessarily reprehensible about requiring individuals to make the most of available opportunities. And yet it may be the case that, as the dominant 'partner', the state could offer less 'carrot' and more 'stick' in circumstances where resources are constrained, not only providing a lower quality of services and opportunities but becoming increasingly demanding about the kind of behaviour deemed acceptable for individuals to remain eligible for welfare provision. Whether or not the British welfare state will adopt this 'post-welfare' character greatly depends on how other key sections of the community understand their roles as stakeholders and partners.

## New Social Policy, Old Problems?

Stakeholding, as those who advocate it make clear (Hutton, 1995), does not only apply to social policy. If Labour is to achieve the twin goals of equity and efficiency, then wealth producers as well as welfare consumers have certain obligations. The question is whether they will feel the need to carry them out.

The sharpest example concerns the business sector. Whereas in the past the relations between Labour and private enterprise were often far from friendly, New Labour has gone out of its way to reassure business that it sees 'healthy profits as an essential motor of a dynamic market economy', and that it will 'build a new partnership with business to improve the competitiveness of British industry for the 21st century' (Labour Party, 1997, p. 15). To ensure optimum conditions for the free market, particularly labour market flexibility, Labour has promised to retain the bulk of Conservative industrial relations legislation and has also ruled out any reversal of Conservative privatisation policy. In return, business will not only have to accept minimum wage legislation and Britain's acceptance of the Social Chapter of the Maastricht Treaty – both of which were major manifesto commitments – but will be encouraged to act 'responsibly' by putting long-term investment in social as well as economic infrastructure before the self-interested 'short-termism' that typified the British economy in the 1980s. Participation in activities designed to support the government's social policy goals will be a significant sign of a willingness to accept this responsibility. Private sector involvement in educational and training initiatives, and especially in the welfare-to-work programme, is considered a *sine qua non* of the new approach to welfare.

There are, however, difficulties with this cooperative vision. The key issue, and one that has never been successfully resolved by social democratic governments in the past, is whether or not the private sector can really be persuaded to sacrifice short-term gain in the interests of long-term stability. As Hutton (1997, pp. 64–5) has recently commented, the task is to design 'institutions, systems, a wider architecture which creates a better economic and social balance, and with it a culture in which common humanity and the instinct to collaborate are allowed to flower'. But the problem is the perennial one of how the corporate sector can be encouraged 'voluntarily to operate in ways that reflect the costs that individualist action motivated by self-interest necessarily imposes upon the rest of us' (ibid., p. 65) – how, in other words, powerful institutions can be persuaded to accept a wider social responsibility that in many cases will impinge on their ability to maximise immediate economic potential.

And *persuasion* will be the main weapon available to a Labour government that is entirely dependent upon the private sector for the success of key aspects of its welfare strategy. In contrast to the CSJ, Labour did not include a commitment to full employment in its election manifesto, but the party did promise that 'our goal will be educational and employment opportunities for all' (Labour Party, 1997, p. 11). The much-vaunted windfall tax on the privatised utilities apart, if this ambition is to be realised private sector cooperation will be necessary over the long term – but why should this be forthcoming during periods of recession, for example, when it is needed most? In rather different vein, it is hard to see how the commitment to labour market flexibility – considered vital to Britain's international economic competitiveness by government and business alike – can be made compatible with Labour's social goals. Ideals of fairness and social justice would surely demand, for instance, that an individual's citizenship rights be placed above the immediate requirements of economic efficiency, but the logic of the 'competition state' would, equally surely, assume the opposite.

The thrust of the new government's social policy is premised on the assumption that it will never have to choose between its economic and social objectives, yet Labour may well be confronted by just such a choice if growth proves elusive. Whereas past Labour administrations attempted to 'reconcile' or balance these competing elements, preserving certain levels of social protection (Piachaud, 1980; Ellison, 1997), even when this entailed tax rises for the better-off, this course is not one that New Labour appears willing to take. Lacking any formal control over the corporate sector and with a wary eye to the international economy, social policy may be used progressively more 'coercively' to ensure compliance with designated economic goals. Individuals could incur increased penalties for specific performance failures, for example, even as the opportunities on offer become less appealing. With the potentially contradictory commitments to flexible labour markets *and* low unemployment levels it is difficult to see how any government could continue to offer high-quality employment opportunities during periods of negative growth. Indeed those most dependent upon increasingly meagre state services would stand to lose most, being forced to take the lowest-paid job or training opportunities which by implication will yield low benefit entitlements, adding to their vulnerability in sickness and old age.

## Conclusion

By accepting the logic of the 'competition state', New Labour has effectively abandoned the egalitarian collectivism that underpinned the party's approach to social policy during the postwar period. This is not to suggest, however, that the party has entirely jettisoned its concern for 'social justice'. As this chapter and others in this volume make clear, New Labour has adjusted previous normative assumptions to endorse a conception of social justice as 'equity' rather than 'equality'. To this end, Conservative notions of state welfare as expensive and dependency-inducing have not so much been discarded as given a positive twist. The state will actively 'invest' in those who are prepared to help themselves, the 'return' coming partly in the form of enhanced life-chances and 'inclusion' for the individuals concerned, but partly, too, in the shape of greater economic competitiveness and social cohesion across society as a whole.

This vision is seductive. The difficulty is that it is a vision for fair economic weather and the equation of 'individual self-interest plus-communal benefit' upon which it is based could disintegrate in the face of recession. At that point Labour would be forced to choose between its economic and social ambitions – and the indications are that the present government, preoccupied as it is with Britain's place in the global economy, would choose the former, effectively consigning social policy – and those dependent on social provision – to much the same position it occupied during the long period of Conservative rule.

This contradiction, which strikes at the heart of New Labour's approach to social policy, has the effect of making the current Conservative and Liberal Democrat positions appear more ideologically straightforward. Despite their current lack of direction, the Conservatives remain sceptical about state welfare and the champions of market solutions – certainly the new Hague leadership has said nothing so far to suggest that the party will reject this essentially 'Thatcherite' perspective. Conversely, as suggested above, the Liberal Democrats have become progressively more concerned about the inadequacy of existing levels of social provision. If their 1997 party conference is anything to go by, they appear to be adopting the role of Labour's social conscience. The Liberal Democrats are not serious contenders for government, however, and as the Conservative Party is likely to remain in the political wilderness in the immediate future, the fortunes of the British welfare state undeniably lie with New Labour.

## Further Reading

The best single treatment of the politics of social policy in the 1980s and early 1990s is Nicholas Deakin's, *The Politics of Welfare: continuities and change* (Hemel Hempstead: Harvester Wheatsheaf, 1994). Vic George and Stewart Miller (eds), *Social Policy Towards 2000: squaring the welfare circle* (London: Routledge, 1993) has a good first chapter by the editors that takes account of some of the issues discussed in this chapter, while Martin Jones, 'Full Steam Ahead to a Workfare State?', *Policy and Politics,* vol. 21, no. 1, pp. 3–16, discusses the nature of the emerging 'workfare' or 'competition' state. Frank Field's *Stakeholder Welfare* (London: Institute of Economic Affairs, 1996) provides a clear insight into a possible welfare future. Finally Nick Ellison, 'From Welfare State to post-Welfare Society? Labour's social policy in historical and contemporary perspective', in B. Brivati and T. Bale (eds), *Labour in Power: Precedents and Prospects* (London: Routledge, 1997) takes a more detailed look at Labour's changing value base than space has allowed here.

# CHAPTER 3

# New Conceptions of Citizenship

RUTH LISTER

Citizenship has been described as 'a strategically important idea in late twentieth century Western society' (Roche, 1992, p. 1). This chapter begins by examining how and why citizenship has assumed this strategic importance. A central issue is citizenship's contested nature. This is explored in relation to (1) a shift in emphasis in British political discourse from a rights- to an obligations-based construction of citizenship, and (2) the ways in which citizenship operates as a force for exclusion as well as inclusion. In conclusion, a possible re-articulation of citizenship will be suggested on the grounds that the exclusionary tensions inherent in citizenship do not invalidate its use as an important theoretical and political concept for social policy.

## The Revival of Citizenship

The last two decades of the twentieth century have seen the re-emergence of citizenship as a focal concept both politically and academically. In Britain, we have had a Commission on Citizenship, a Citizen's Charter, proposals for a 'citizens' service' and 'citizenship education', and the Charter 88 campaign for civil and political citizenship rights. At the European level, the Maastricht Treaty of 1992 created the new category of 'Citizens of the Union', which grants European Union (EU) citizens the right to vote in local and European elections in their country of residence, regardless of nationality. The placement of citizens' rights 'at the heart of the Union' was a key objective of the 1997 Treaty of Amsterdam. In the United Nations (UN) European region, the promotion of citizenship and social rights has been identified as a priority in applying the global UN Guiding Principles for Social Developmental Welfare policies. Academically, the international literature on citizenship has burgeoned across a number of disciplines.

Citizenship's new-found currency has been attributed to a number of developments. One is the repositioning of the nation state, which provides the context for the European Commission's promotion of European citizenship through its 'Citizens first' campaign, as a means of winning loyalty to a developing political union. In the words of the Comité des Sages, established by the European Commision, Europe cannot be built on 'an inadequate sense of citizenship . . . If it wishes to become an original political entity, it must have a clear statement of the citizenship it is offering its members. Inclusion of civic and social rights in the Treaties would help to nurture that citizenship' (Comité des Sages, 1996, p. 13). The reshaping of national boundaries and growing pressure for regional autonomy in some nation states, concern about the impact on national autonomy of 'globalisation' and the implications for citizenship of the growing movement across national borders of migrants and asylum-seekers have, in different ways, problematised the relationship between citizenship, the nation and the state. The achievement of citizenship rights in Central and Eastern Europe and South Africa has reverberated beyond their own frontiers, contributing to a re-evaluation of civil and political citizenship rights in other societies. At the same time, in many Western societies the values of social citizenship embedded in their welfare states have been challenged in the face of economic crises and political backlash.

As the 'chief European testing ground for New Right theory' (Marquand, 1991, p. 329), Britain has witnessed a particularly vibrant debate on citizenship. The centralisation of state power (in the name of a minimal state), the erosion of local democracy and of a range of civil rights have all helped to highlight the fragility of democratic institutions in a country that lacks a constitution or bill of rights and whose members are technically not citizens but subjects of the crown. The rhetoric and philosophy of social citizenship have been deployed by academics and campaigners in defence of welfare rights. At the same time more radical writings on the welfare state have emphasised the values of citizenship and democracy in an attempt to fashion a new approach to welfare, grounded in user involvement, which addresses the paternalism and lack of accountability that characterised the postwar model.

For a while in the late 1980s, citizenship was promoted by some as the new 'big idea' for the British centre-left. It was seen as providing a means of reconciling the collectivist tradition of the left with notions of individual rights, in recognition that the alternative to the political credo of the new right cannot discard the individual, to whom the latter directed its appeal. Tony Blair, in his first exposition of the meaning of socialism (or social-ism as he chose to recast it) after taking up the Labour leadership, set out his interpretation of the 'left view of citizenship' and included 'the equal worth of each citizen' as one of the values of democratic socialism (Blair, 1994). In the event, citizenship was not adopted as New Labour's big idea; nevertheless its language is deployed extensively (including in Blair's first social policy speech as prime minister) and permeates important texts on the centre-left, most notably Will Hutton's best-selling *The State We're In* (1995).

Citizenship has also been invoked by Conservative politicians. The Thatcherite John Moore, when social security secretary, set out to correct 'the balance of the citizenship equation' by emphasising the work obligations of social security claimants. In contrast the promotion of active citizenship can be interpreted as an attempt to soften the harsher edges of Thatcherism. John Major's Citizen's Charter appropriated the language of the citizen to re-commit the Conservatives to public services, but in a manner that emphasised consumerism.

## A Contested Concept

The appropriation of citizenship for very different political ends reflects not only the flux of contemporary political debate but also citizenship's roots in divergent political traditions: civic republicanism and liberalism. Adrian Oldfield (1990) has conceptualised these two different approaches as citizenship as a status versus citizenship as a practice. The one prioritises the rights of the individual citizen, the other the interests of the wider community. Civic republicanism reaches back to classical Greece, where political participation as civic duty represented the essence of citizenship. Whilst this political construction of civic duty lives on and has undergone something of a revival in recent years, especially in the United States, citizenship obligation is, as we shall see, today being construed by politicians in primarily non-political terms.

The liberal tradition, born in the seventeenth century, emphasises the rights of the individual. The most famous twentieth-century exposition of those rights is that provided by T. H. Marshall, who divided them into three main categories: civil, political and social. Civil and political rights originate in the classical liberal tradition in which the role of government is confined to the protection of the 'negative' freedoms they embody. Social rights imply a more proactive role on the part of the state in the promotion of a 'positive' notion of freedom as the ability to participate in society as full citizens. In Marshall's words, they 'range from the right to a modicum of economic welfare and security to the right to share to the full in the social heritage and to live the life of a civilised being according to the standards prevailing in the society' (Marshall 1950, pp. 10–11). The Beveridge Report and those who implemented it appealed to the values of social citizenship, as did one of the key postwar figures in social policy, Richard Titmuss.

## From rights to obligations

The late twentieth century has seen a challenge to the legitimacy of social rights from classical liberals in the form of the new right , but also a greater willingness on the more radical left to engage in a rights discourse. New categories of rights have emerged, for example reproductive rights. What has been most significant, though, in relation to the contested nature of citizenship, has been the shift in the dominant paradigm from a rights to an obligations discourse (Roche, 1992).

This shift started in the 1980s on the political right, heavily influenced by US new right thinkers. Conservative social policy reforms that bear its imprint include the Job Seeker's Allowance (of which more below) and the Child Support Act, with its emphasis on parental responsibility. In many ways the shift has been even more marked in the thinking of the centre-left, as the discourse of responsibility became the hallmark of New Labour during the 1990s. When Tony Blair talks the language of citizenship, it is to emphasise obligations and responsibilities. This is reflected in the statement of values that replaced Clause 4 of the party's constitution. This offers the ideal of a 'community . . . where the rights we enjoy reflect the duties we owe', a formulation that implies that duties exist morally and logically prior to rights. Gordon Brown, announcing his 'new deal' on youth unemployment as shadow chancellor, promised that 'opportunities and responsibilities' would dominate Labour's modernisation of the welfare state. Jack Straw, when shadow home secretary promoting ideas of community responsibility, attacked the Tories for presiding over the growth of a culture of 'dutiless rights'. The latter phrase echoes the work of David Selbourne, one of the populist communitarians who has influenced New Labour thinking. The other is an American, Amitai Etzioni (1993, p. 4) who has called for 'a moratorium on the minting of most, if not all, new rights', together with reestablishment of the link between rights and responsibilities and recognition that the latter do not necessarily entail the former. Such ideas have been popularised further by influential journalists such as Melanie Phillips, who has regularly attacked 'rights-based individualism [for] destroying fundamental civilised values' (*Observer,* 15 September 1996).

## Work obligations

It is often forgotten that Marshall himself addressed the question of the balance between citizenship rights and obligations, even though the question was not central to his renowned exposition. Moreover, under the general obligations of citizenship he included 'the duty to work'. However (a voice from a different age), he suggested that 'the essential duty is not to have a job and hold it, since that is relatively simple in conditions of full employment, but to put one's heart into one's job and work hard' (Marshall, 1950, pp. 79–80). Today, when conditions of full (male) employment are long gone, the duty 'to have a job and hold it' has been a primary target of the shift from a rights to a duties discourse. Unlike Marshall, neoconservatives such as Lawrence Mead and Michael Novak argue that social citizenship rights should be contingent upon the duty to engage in paid work, which they maintain represents 'as much a badge of citizenship as rights' (Mead, 1986, p. 229). It is a duty that is prescribed for welfare recipients, particularly those with families to support, while those with independent means can afford to ignore it, if they so wish. Thus although notions of the 'common good' are invoked in justification, it is a common good in which the interests of the poor and powerless are subordinated to those of the rich and powerful.

Such thinking has been influential in a number of countries, especially, though not exclusively, in the Anglo-Saxon world, where it has led to 'work-welfare' programmes, including most radically, work-fare in the United States. In Britain, the widely accepted, long-standing principle that unemployed claimants should be available for work and should accept a reasonable offer of work or training has been subject to increasingly punitive interpretation and application. By the end of the Major government, pilot work-fare-type schemes had been introduced and unemployment benefit had been replaced with the Job Seeker's Allowance (JSA), designed to 'make clear to unemployed people the link between their receipt of benefit and the obligations that places upon them' through a mandatory 'job-seeker's agreement' (Employment Dept Group/DSS, 1994, p. 10). Although Labour opposed the introduction of the JSA it has refused to commit itself to its abolition. Labour has made clear that its commitment to tackle youth and long-term unemployment must be matched by the exercise of responsibility among unemployed people themselves; otherwise they will suffer a benefit penalty that will be even harsher than under the Tories. The difference is that at least there is recognition of the state's responsibility to ensure that employment or training opportunities are available, unlike in the one-sided contract imposed by the Tories.

In the United States, it has been (primarily black) lone mothers, including those of very young children, rather than the unemployed who have been the main targets of work-fare policies. It has thus been both a gendered and a racialised construction of citizenship obligations. It has, however, also exposed some of the tensions within new right thinking about citizenship. For some, such as Novak, the presence of children to be supported intensifies the work obligation; for others, such as George Gilder, this position is regarded as undermining family responsibilities.

Britain is unusual in exempting lone parents on benefit from the paid work obligation until their youngest child is aged 16. Surprisingly perhaps, Conservative governments have not challenged this, despite their obsession with welfare 'dependency'. In the conflict between different strands of neoconservatism, unlike in the United States, the 'pro-family' construction of mothers' primary obligations won out. Instead the Child Support Act, coupled with benefit incentives, was used to encourage a shift from reliance on income support to an income package combining child support, wages and in-work benefits. Labour's policy is to place more emphasis on encouraging lone parents to take paid work, without actually requiring them to do so.

In a number of EU countries, alongside the growing emphasis on work obligations in social security policy, an alternative understanding of citizenship is being promoted under the rubric of basic or citizen's income (see Chapter 7 of this volume). Here, decoupled from work obligations, social citizenship rights are totally unconditional. One of the arguments deployed in its favour is that it would provide recognition of (primarily women's) unpaid work in the home. However it would do so in an indiscriminate way, providing equal recognition for care work and basic house work. It is care work that a number of feminists, both in the early twentieth century and today, have argued should be acknowledged as an expression of citizenship responsibility.

## Active citizenship

In the same way that the contemporary mainstream discussion on work obligations tends to discount the importance of unpaid care work, so has that on 'active citizenship'. The term was first coined by Conservative ministers in the late 1980s in the name of social cohesion, as an exhortation to discharge the responsibilities of neighbourliness, voluntary action and charity. Given the context of the rundown of public services and growing inequalities, it was largely discredited. More recently, all the main political parties have given their backing to some kind of citizens' service to provide volunteering opportunities for young people, thereby, in David Blunkett's words, helping to 'develop a sense of citizenship which our country needs to replace the alienation, disaffection and individualism that young people have experienced' (*Guardian*, 2 October, 1996). Blunkett links citizens' service to complementary plans for education for citizenship, which has been the subject of some debate in education circles in recent years.

In a critique of citizenship education as currently conceived, Wilfred Carr and Anthony Hartnett (1996, p. 82) argue that 'the only kind of civic education which can prepare citizens for life in a fully democratic society is one which acknowledges *both* that the meaning of citizenship is perennially the subject of contestation, *and* that it is through this process of contestation that the relationship between the citizen and the state is being continuously redefined' (emphasis in original). This implies that more radical notions of active citizenship can be identified in the shadow of the conservative model. Ray Pahl, for instance, offers as an alternative definition: 'local people working together to improve their own quality of life and to provide conditions for others to enjoy the fruits of a more affluent society' (Pahl, 1990, p. 8). This is a form of active citizenship that disadvantaged people, often women, do for themselves rather than have done for them by the more privileged; one that creates them as subjects rather than objects.

Examples of such active citizenship are proliferating in the form of both a myriad of local community groups and the increasingly visible direct action movement. A primary focus of the latter is the environment, as exemplified in a series of roads protests in the late 1990s. More broadly, the green movement has developed the idea of ecological citizenship duties that stretch beyond the geographical and temporal boundaries of the individual citizen's community. Green citizenship action unites the local with the global. Similarly radical forms of active citizenship can be witnessed at the supranational level both in the EU (an example being the Permanent Forum of Civil Society, which has proposed a European Citizens' Charter) and in the developing networks of global civil society, such as those that helped shape the agenda and outcome of major UN conferences in the 1990s. Again, women have been at the forefront of such networks.

## Inclusion/Exclusion

These different notions of active citizenship bear the imprint of opposite templates: one identifies citizenship as a force for inclusion, the other as a force for exclusion. Until recently it has been primarily as a force for inclusion, within the confines of national boundaries, that the idea of citizenship has been promoted in the British social policy literature. Critical social policy theory has, however, attempted to shift the focus both to citizenship as a force for exclusion and to how this force operates at the boundaries of the nation state. These different perspectives reflect the Janus-faced nature of citizenship, simultaneously drawing the boundaries of inclusion and exclusion. As Nira Yuval-Davis (1991, p. 61) observes, 'constructing boundaries according to various inclusionary and exclusionary criteria, which relate to ethnic and racial divisions as well as class and gender divisions, is one of the main arenas of struggle concerning citizenship that remain completely outside the agenda of Marshallian theories of citizenship'.

The boundaries of inclusion and exclusion operate at both a legal and a sociological level through formal and substantive modes of citizenship. The former denotes the legal status of membership of a state, as symbolised by the possession of a passport; the latter, as observed above, refers to the possession of rights and obligations within a state. In practice, at both the legal and the sociological level exclusion and inclusion represent more of a continuum than a simple dichotomy. Thus, for example, certain rights and duties can apply to those who are not formal citizens, and the rights associated with residence in and membership of a state can be seen as more of a hierarchy than a sharp division between citizens and non-citizens. Conversely, formal citizenship does not necessarily guarantee full and effective substantive citizenship, as the experience of New Commonwealth immigrants to Britain exemplifies.

## Exclusion of nation state 'outsiders'

Nevertheless, for those physically excluded from a particular citizenship community, exclusion can operate as an absolute. The right to enter, or remain, in that community is a critical issue for citizenship. It is an issue that is taking on greater salience in the face of the growing number of migrants and asylum-seekers (many of whom are women) attempting to cross national boundaries in an increasingly economically polarised world. Paradoxically, nation states in the North and the West are exercising their boundary-staking powers more aggressively, with the aid of modern technology, at a time when the autonomy of the nation state is under pressure from both globalising and localising forces. This serves as a reminder of the role the nation state is continuing to play in delineating and enforcing the frontiers of citizenship at a time when it is fashionable to portray its demise.

In Europe this role is exercised at the level of both individual states and the EU, as symbolised by the image of 'Fortress Europe'. Strict external border controls, measures to restrict immigration and the rights and number of asylum-seekers admitted, and provision for the swift expulsion of unwanted aliens, all backed up by a comprehensive computer network, constitute Fortress Europe's barricades. Their construction has made possible the abolition of most internal border controls in the name of free movement within the EU, which, with concomitant employment, social and political rights, comprises a key ingredient of European citizenship. It is a right confined to citizens of the EU and their families; a citizenship for Europeans rather than for all those living in Europe. As such it serves to reinforce symbolic as well as actual racialised borders between Europeans and non-Europeans and to feed racism within Europe's borders.

In Britain, the boundaries of exclusion have been tightened steadily in relation both to rights of entry and residence and to social citizenship rights. A succession of immigration and nationality laws have undermined the rights of black Commonwealth citizens and virtually closed off their lawful entry to Britain. Under the Conservatives, asylum-seekers faced not only tougher procedures but also drastic curtailment of the right to claim social security benefits. This is but the most recent example of how more restrictive immigration policies have been underpinned by more restrictive welfare policies, a trend by no means confined to Britain and taken to the extreme in the United States, where federal legislation has removed the right to welfare benefits and services from legal immigrants who have not yet become citizens. Most immigrants are now allowed to enter Britain only on condition that they do not take 'recourse to public funds'; in addition certain groups are admitted only under the 'sponsorship' of a relative, who is then responsible for their maintenance. New regulations in the mid 1990s, including the introduction of a 'habitual residence test', have served to tie benefit entitlement ever more closely to residence or immigration status. Access to housing and free hospital services has also been affected. This armoury of rules designed to limit access to welfare also serves as a system of internal immigration control to detect people in breach of immigration laws. The impact is felt not only by citizen 'outsiders' but also black 'insiders', for '*all* black people are made accountable for their presence in the UK because the inevitable political practice is that it is black people who are most likely to be interrogated as to immigration status' (Cohen, 1995, p. 137, emphasis in original).

## Exclusion of nation state 'insiders'

This is one example of how internal and external boundaries of exclusion can overlap and reinforce each other. Gendered processes of exclusion similarly impact on both outsiders and insiders, for example through the construction of women as dependants in immigration and nationality laws on the one hand and in social security laws on the other. Indeed citizenship was originally predicated on the exclusion of all women and their inclusion has been on different terms to those enjoyed by men, so that women can still be said to enjoy second-class citizenship status. Feminists have underlined how this exclusion has been far from accidental. In both the liberal and civic republican traditions, the citizen stands as the abstract, disembodied individual demonstrating the (male) qualities of impartiality, rationality and independence in the public sphere. In a classic double bind, women have been banished to the private realm of the family, either physically or figuratively, because they are deemed not to display such qualities, and because of their association with the private realm they have been considered incapable of developing them. It is thus the 'patriarchal separation' (Pateman, 1989, p. 183) between the public and private that underpins the very meaning of citizenship, as traditionally understood, and also women's exclusion from it.

Although women have now achieved full *formal* citizenship status in most societies, in practice their position as public citizens continues to be constrained by their responsibilities for care in the private sphere. Conversely, men's citizenship continues to be privileged by a gendered domestic division of labour, which frees them to participate in the public sphere. At the same time the public sphere itself places obstacles in the way of women achieving their full potential as citizens. The upshot is that women continue to be grossly underrepresented in positions of political and economic power, and despite equal treatment legislation they tend to have inferior social citizenship rights than those enjoyed by men, reflecting their labour market position.

Thanks to feminist scholarship, the limits to the universalist cloak in which citizenship has been wrapped have been revealed, together with the decidedly male citizen hidden beneath it. More recently, feminism's challenge to political and social theory's false universalism has been matched by a similar challenge to the false universalism of the category 'woman' and hence also 'man', so that the identikit male citizen turns out to be a white, non-disabled heterosexual male of working age.

The citizenship status of members of minority ethnic communities, as we have seen, is compromised by their association with nation state 'outsiders', regardless of their place of birth. The substantive citizenship of black citizens and residents is further undermined by racial discrimination, harassment and violence. Homophobic violence and harassment likewise serve to curtail the citizenship of lesbians and gays. In most countries, including Britain, their legal status is still inferior in certain spheres, including the armed forces, the former locus of citizenship. Homophobic attitudes and practices make it difficult for lesbians and gays to 'come out' as homosexual citizens in the formal political sphere, in the context of implicitly heterosexist constructions of citizenship, although the failure of a homophobic campaign against a publicly gay candidate in the 1997 general election suggests that this is beginning to change. As members of 'sexual minorities', gay and lesbian activists have been fighting for a citizenship status that does not require them to deny their sexuality.

The paradigm of citizenship has been adopted by the disabled people's movement in their fight for equality and inclusion. Thus, for example, Mike Oliver (1996, p. 160) has argued that, in Britain, disability spells the denial of social, political and civil citizenship rights and that the achievement of anti-discrimination legislation 'must be seen as a platform for the continuing battle for citizenship, not as a sign that citizenship has been achieved'. More fundamentally, Helen Meekosha and Leanne Dowse (1997) warn that 'the very language and imagery of citizenship is imbued with hegemonic normalcy', so that disabled people's capacity for citizenship is thrown into doubt. The same could be said to apply to elderly people, despite the patronising 'senior citizen' label that is commonly applied to them. At the other end of the life span, youth represents a time of transition to the rights and responsibilities of adult citizenship; a transition that has been made harder for many young people in Britain in the face of a changing labour market and cutbacks in social security entitlements.

In practice, the implications for citizenship of the different axes of difference – of gender, 'race', sexuality, (dis)ability and age – depends in part on how they interact with each other. For any individual, they can either be mutually reinforcing of privilege or oppression or they can cut across each other. Thus, for example, the quality of citizenship in old age will depend in part on the gender and 'race' relations experienced earlier in the life course. Critical too is class position, a dimension that is often missing from theoretical discussions on difference. In contrast social class is the one dimension of inequality that traditionally citizenship theorists such as Marshall (1950) have addressed. Indeed the relationship between citizenship and social class is a central theme of Marshall's essay, which more or less ignores other dimensions of inequality. The continued power of social class, in interaction with other sources of exclusion, to shape the contours of citizenship should not be underestimated. At one extreme, poverty under-mines citizenship rights; at the other, wealth can buy dispensation from its obligations (Scott, 1994).

## Re-articulating Citizenship

The contradiction between citizenship's universalist claims and the exclusions in which it is implicated has led some to question its value for a progressive social policy and politics. Nevertheless, as Denise Riley (1992, p. 187) argues, despite the dangers in a claim to universal citizenship that masks real differences, 'importantly, it also possesses the strength of its own idealism. Because of its claim to universality, such an ideal can form the basis for arguments for participation by everyone, as well as for entitlements and responsibilities for all . . . Citizenship as a theory sets out a claim and an egalitarian promise.' The challenge is to rearticulate citizenship so as to address its exclusionary tensions and reconcile its universalistic claims with the demands of difference. In this final section I will briefly sketch out the form such a re-articulation might take in relation to nation-state 'outsiders' and 'insiders' before speculating on how citizenship is likely to inform social policy developments in the next few years.

## An internationalist agenda

Large-scale migration, ecological concerns that cross geographical borders and the economic and political pressures on the nation state all raise a question mark over our traditional nation-state-bound understanding of citizenship. One response has been to sketch an alternative, multilayered model of citizenship, operating on several frontiers from the local to the global. This embraces the idea of global citizenship, which reflects at the international level the rights and responsibilities associated with national citizenship. In so doing, it contains the potential to challenge, or at least temper, citizenship's exclusionary force in two main ways, both involving a link between citizenship and human rights.

First, a framework of global citizenship encourages a focus on the responsibilities of the more affluent nation states towards those that lack the resources to translate human rights (as defined by the United Nations to embrace economic, social and cultural rights) into effective citizenship rights. It is accepted by a number of citizenship theorists that principles of distributive justice, together with ecological imperatives, demand an internationalist interpretation of citizenship obligations in the context of global economic and physical interdependence. Such a perspective is beginning to be reflected in social policy analysis, where it is being argued that issues of human need, poverty and social cohesion have to be addressed at the global as well as the national level through more effective institutions of global governance and redistribution than exist at present (Doyal and Gough, 1991; Deacon B., 1995; Townsend, 1996).

Such institutions could also provide the key to circumscribing nation states' exclusionary powers. As enforcers of international human rights law they could subject these powers more effectively to an internationally agreed set of principles governing rights of entry, residence and citizenship. Such principles might include, for instance, those of non-discrimination and observance of basic human rights. This would furnish 'outsiders', in particular refugees and asylum-seekers, with a potentially powerful legal and discursive resource in the name of a more inclusive internationalist citizenship framework.

## A differentiated universalism

Within the nation-state context, the dilemma at the theoretical level is how to combine universalism's promise with a recognition of difference. At first sight the two might appear to be incompatible. Yet arguably a genuine universalism has to acknowledge difference; otherwise it represents a particular standpoint masquerading as the universal. An important strand of radical political theory is attempting to 'particularise' the universal in the search for 'a new kind of articulation between the universal and the particular' (Mouffe, 1993, p. 13). Such a synthesis also forms the heart of an attempt by Simon Thompson and Paul Hoggett (1996, p. 21) to sketch a postmodern social policy on the basis of 'a sophisticated universalism that, while committed to equality, is able to be sensitive to diversity'. Their argument is that 'any justifiable universalism, or egalitarianism must take particularity and difference into account; and any legitimate particularism or politics of difference must employ some universal or egalitarian standard' (ibid., p. 23).

This points to what we might call a 'differentiated universalism'. Such a principle opens up the possibility of a re-articulation of citizenship at both the theoretical and the policy level, thereby addressing, in relation to nation-state 'insiders', the exclusionary tensions discussed earlier. This can be illustrated in relation to citizenship both as a practice and a status, and also the interaction between the two. Specifically from a gender perspective, the 'universalist' yardstick against which citizenship is measured needs to be stripped of its male bias. Thus, for example, unpaid caring work would enter the equation of citizenship obligation alongside paid work. This would involve social policy questioning the privileges enjoyed by citizen-the-earner over citizen-the-carer in the distribution of social rights and creating the conditions in which citizen-the-carer/earner can flourish. It would mean recognition of the ways in which the interaction between the public and private spheres differentially shapes the access of women and men to citizenship.

More generally, rights can be particularised without sacrificing principles of equality and universality. They can take account of the situation of specific groups both in the reactive sense of counteracting past and present disadvantages that may undermine their position as citizens and in the proactive sense of affirming diversity, particularly with regard to cultural and linguistic rights. Examples of the former are affirmative action programmes and the kind of wide-ranging disability discrimination legislation enacted in the United States. Examples of the latter are the specific rights enjoyed by indigenous American Indians alongside their rights as US citizens and language policies that give official recognition to the languages of significant minority ethnic groups. The backlash against such policies in a number of countries does, however, underline their politically sensitive nature. Moreover the 'multicultural' model of citizenship, which implicitly or explicitly underpins some of them, is not without its problems. In particular it runs the risk of homogenising cultural groups and both minority and majority communities in denial of differences such as gender, age, sexuality and class.

This points to the parallel need for a more pluralistic understanding of community as the locus for a citizenship politics that likewise accommodates difference. Anna Yeatman (1993, p. 231) calls this a 'politics of difference', involving 'a commitment to a universalistic orientation to the positive value of difference within a democratic political process' and to 'an inclusive politics of voice and representation'. On the one hand, it would mean recognising, as an expression of citizenship, the kind of informal community politics in which women are more likely to be involved, and on the other, opening up the channels of the formal political system to this informal politics of difference.

## Looking to the future

There is little sign at present that the formal political system will respond to a radical pluralist agenda of this kind, although the presence of significantly more women in parliament is symbolically (and potentially practically) important for women's citizenship. The disengagement from formal politics of a number of groups, including many young people, during the 1997 general election campaign highlights the continued flowering of informal forms of politics in which alternative constructions of active citizenship can be forged. The challenge will be to reconnect the two.

The most significant implications for citizenship of the election of a New Labour government are likely to be political and constitutional, with the devolution of Scotland and, to a lesser extent, Wales, reform of central and local government, and the incorporation of the European Convention on Human Rights into British law in the context of a greater emphasis on European citizenship. Rights will thus be strengthened and extended in the civil and political spheres. On the social front, apart from a stronger emphasis on anti-discrimination, it is, as indicated already, a communitarian construction of citizenship that will inform policy in a wide range of areas, in particular social security and 'law and order'. The two come together in the drive against benefit fraud, which is being promoted as 'our expression of responsible citizenship' (DSS press release, 25 June 1997).

Blair's (1997) vision of 'a decent society' is infused with the language of strong families and communities, duties and responsibilities, independence, opportunity and 'one nation'. He promises a society in which 'each of us has a stake, a share', but – marking the break with 'Old Labour' – not one of *equal* stakes or shares. Significantly, the payment of taxes is not stressed as a citizenship obligation by New Labour, giving rise to a possible structural imbalance in the allocation of responsibilities and rights that could reinforce rather than challenge existing inequalities.

## Further Reading

The ideas explored here are developed further in Lister, *Citizenship Feminist Perspectives* (London: Macmillan, 1997), which provides an extensive bibliography on the subject. A good introductory text is Dawn Oliver and Derek Heater's *The Foundations of Citizenship* (Hemel Hempstead: Harvester Wheatsheaf, 1994). For an overview of contemporary debates, see Roche (1992) and Bulmer and Rees (1996). More detailed discussions of social citizenship can be found in Hartley Dean, *Welfare, Law & Citizenship* (London: Prentice-Hall/Harvester Wheatsheaf, 1996), Fred Twine's *Citizenship and Social Rights* (London: Sage, 1994), John Scott's *Poverty and Wealth: Citizenship, deprivation and privilege* (London: Longman, 1994) and Lister's *The Exclusive Society. Citizenship and the Poor* (London: CPAG, 1990). For a series of radical accounts of citizenship see David Taylor (ed.), *Critical Social Policy: A Reader* (London: Sage, 1996) and *Feminist Review*, no. 57 (1997).

# CHAPTER 4

# Social Policy and Human Need

MARTIN HEWITT

Until recently the topic of human need was a largely neglected area of social policy. However in the 1980s and 1990s social policy discovered the central importance of need in defining the scope of its subject matter. This importance is soon grasped if one considers some of the reasons why social policies are made and implemented in the form of social provisions. The main reason is that social policies are meant to meet the needs of people in various ways: providing cash benefits to offset poverty; health services to maintain physical and mental well-being; housing services to provide shelter; education and training to enable people to live independently and participate fully in economic, scientific and cultural life; and so forth. Each service represents an important area of human need without which individual existence would be seriously deficient, if not impossible.

The logic of social policy is not, however, quite so straightforward. The needs of other sections of society, apart from welfare recipients, must also be met, such as the needs of business for a healthy, educated and flexible workforce and of government for a regulated and content population. Unfortunately the human needs reflected in social policy and the needs of business and government do not always coincide, as in the 1980s when the Thatcher government criticised the 'nanny' welfare state and tried to engineer the creation of an enterprise culture.

In this chapter our approach is threefold. First, we examine the different ways political ideologies have conceptualised need. This will enable us to identify the role played by particular conceptions of need in the development of social policy and to consider the role they might play in new developments. However, whilst it is helpful to understand need from the perspective of political ideology, there is at present a debate about whether the major political ideologies that have shaped modern society over the last two centuries are relevant to the profound changes of the last quarter century. One form this debate has taken in social policy is concerned with the nature of change in 'postmodern' society. This notion assumes an important break has occurred that distinguishes postmodern from modern societies, and that demarcates new social, political and cultural forms of life from the forms that have emerged during the last two hundred years or more. At the core of these new forms of life are new needs that new social policies must address.

Our second concern is to discuss the impact on thinking about need of the new politics associated with social and political diversity and the new social movements of feminism, ecology, disability and so on. Two writers in particular, coming from different political perspectives, are providing influential accounts of political change and its impact on social policy, namely Paul Hirst and John Gray. We will compare their notions of need and the responsibilities they accord individuals and government in meeting need.

One implication of the new politics of welfare is to revisit the relationship between universal and particular needs. This is the third concern of the chapter, to examine some of the ways in which the different needs distinguishing one individual or group from another are configured in relation to the basic needs we all share.

## Conceptions of Need

This section introduces five conceptions of need that have shaped social policy this century, each reflecting a particular perspective on human nature and motivation and supporting particular ideologies of welfare. The first three – basic, residual and mutual needs – represent views that have influenced mainstream social policy. The last two – Marx's concept of 'radical' needs and feminist concepts of gendered needs – offer important critiques of mainstream thinking.

Until recently the dominant idea in twentieth-century social policy has been that individuals share *basic needs* that are universal to humankind. This idea informed the notions of the national minimum, introduced by the 1906–14 Liberal government and implemented more fully in the 1940s Beveridge reforms. It influenced the thinking of Fabians such as Sydney and Beatrice Webb, of Beveridge, the architect of the postwar welfare state, and postwar Fabians such as Crosland, Titmuss and Townsend, who have supported the idea of universal welfare for all. Similarly, the history of poverty research – from Charles Booth and Seebohm Rowntree to Peter Townsend today – represents a tradition that sees basic needs as shared by all and believes that poverty and want represent a denial of basic human needs. For these researchers, basic needs have an objective basis – the material objects of food, warmth, shelter and clothing, as well as social participation – that is shaped by culture and can be identified empirically. Rowntree, for example, provided an empirical definition of physical deprivation based on the need for food, housing, clothing, light and fuel (Rowntree, n.d., p. 119), which influenced subsequent poverty studies. This definition depicted a core of the poorer classes as 'those whose total earnings are insufficient to obtain the minimum necessaries for the maintenance of merely physical efficiency' (ibid., p. 117). This notion of basic need was later incorporated into the different types and rates of benefit Beveridge devised in his 1942 report, as part of his 'diagnosis of want' (Beveridge, 1942, p. 7), which formed the basis of postwar social policy.

The idea of basic needs is used to argue for the universal rights of individuals to basic welfare provision and the obligation of government to undertake such provision. By virtue of the existence of common needs, all individuals have a universal right to sufficient resources and opportunities to fulfil these needs. In this vein, the Webbs asserted that 'the maintenance of a definite standard of civilised life is certainly a universal obligation' and the mark of civilised society where no one's needs go unmet (Webb and Webb, 1911, p. 297). Government endeavours should ensure that basic needs are met either by state welfare or by enabling individuals, through education, training and labour market policy, to acquire the means to meet their own needs. Providing for basic needs has been an important part of the twentieth-century political agenda of ensuring that welfare provisions are universally available to all citizens. The social rights of the welfare state have been a central component of citizenship, augmenting civil and political rights in the modern constitutional state (Marshall, 1963).

A second *residual* conception of need is found in rightist social policy, such as in key documents of the postwar Conservative Party (for example Powell and Macleod, 1952) and especially in Conservative government policy between 1979 and 1997. This view, like the preceding one, holds that individuals share basic needs as well as having individually different needs, but that the market rather than the government is the first order of provision, enabling individuals to satisfy their personal needs in diverse ways and develop their talents. Government is left to supplement the market by extending minimum provisions to those unable to access markets because of poverty or incapacity. It is responsible for meeting the residual needs of those who cannot meet them themselves. Such a view appeals to an atomistic model of society in which separate individuals are motivated by self-interest. The market is the best means of enabling individuals to pursue their different self-interests freely and to combine with other individuals in voluntary associations when their self-interests stand to benefit. According to Hayek (1960), markets are preferable because they operate with minimum external interference in an ordered and predictable way.

In social policy, this atomistic and individualistic view of society has supported a residual conception of need that recognises some individuals are unable to participate in the labour market and require their minimum needs to be met. Nineteenth-century poor law and twentieth-century means-tested provisions have appealed to this view of need in the belief that these measures would keep the non-active separate from the economically active, and minimise the disturbance of the free circulation of labour in the market. State welfare should be pitched at an absolute minimum level to avoid giving out false signals or 'perverse incentives' that discourage individuals from making their livelihood through gainful employment. For this reason needs are defined in subsistence rather than basic terms, and welfare provisions are kept at a level that is residual to the market place. Furthermore, 'residual needs' implies a narrower band of needs than common basic needs. Unlike the universalism of basic needs, this conception supports a residual and selective approach to welfare that directs resources to the poorest alone.

A third *mutualist* conception holds that there are some needs that can best be met through mutual and supportive relationships between different individuals at work, in the family and in the community. Needs such as respect, recognition and 'fellowship' or comradeship are also basic needs, alongside physical needs such as food, shelter and clothing. However they are unlikely to be met by bureaucratic state provision or competitive markets, but must rely on mutual forms of relationship and cooperation. Furthermore, through mutual help even basic physical needs that are normally met by the state are met in a way that might be considered more humane. Alternatively, however, personal acts of giving can be taken as intrusive and patronising by recipients who prefer the impersonal relationship of bureaucratic state welfare. Perhaps mutual welfare works best in institutions that encourage relations of reciprocity and equality between giver and receiver – what Terrill, Richard Tawney's biographer, calls 'right relationships among free and equal individuals' (Terrill, 1974, p. 217). In theory, through cooperative ventures of labour, individuals come to recognise in each other their common and their different human needs. Reciprocity creates the conditions for realising universality and solidarity in humankind within a framework that includes a large element of voluntary obligation.

This conception animated the nineteenth-century movement for working-class self-help, as represented by friendly societies, cooperatives and trade unions. It pervaded the thinking of the British idealists, who in the late nineteenth century influenced the new Liberals and the Charity Organisation Society. The idea is less evident in the Webbs' writings but resurfaces later in the writings of Tawney and Titmuss, in Beveridge's ideas on voluntary action (1948) and in recent proposals for mutual welfare and stakeholding (Field, 1996 a or b; Hutton, 1996, ch.12). Today it is making a comeback in the speeches of Tony Blair (for example Blair, 1995) and among Christian socialist social policy writers such as Bob Holman (1993). Traditionally this conception referred to the qualities of 'fellowship', 'comradeship' and 'fraternity' to designate the third part of the socialist trinity of 'equality, liberty and fraternity'. However in the writings of recent thinkers and politicians associated with New Labour, such as Frank Field, mutualism is not synonymous with altruism, but is seen as a new philosophy that puts self-interest before other-interested motivation, so that 'satisfying self-interest in ways which promote the common good should be the major objective of welfare policy' (Field, 1996a, pp. 2–3). The organic view of the relationship between self-interest and altruism in New Labour's thinking is a revival of the ideas of the nineteenth-century British idealists (Vincent and Plant, 1984).

The fourth and fifth conceptions of need – *Marxist* and *feminist* – offer powerful critiques of mainstream thinking in social policy. Marx's conception of need influenced socialist thinkers earlier this century and received renewed interest in the 1970s and 1980s (Gough, 1979; Soper, 1981). In his early writings Marx appealed to a notion of need that he described as 'radical' and 'human', which he used to criticise the notion of basic need found in the work of the classical political economists of the early nineteenth century. According to Norman Geras (1983, pp. 84–5 *et passim*) there is a continuity in the notion of need that Marx developed in his early and late works, and this provides a consistent standard for critically assessing arrangements for meeting need in capitalist societies, including their welfare policies.

Marx began his critique of basic needs with an attack on Adam Smith and the classical political economists' notion of basic need. For Marx, this notion represented 'the absolute minimum necessary; just enough for [an individual] to exist not as a human being but as a worker and for him to propagate not humanity but the slave class of the workers' (Marx 1975, p. 287). It is this idea of basic need that influenced the concept of poverty and national minimum discussed in the first conception of need above. Marx described in derisory terms this conception of human satisfaction, which embodies the idea of humankind as 'a stomach', with 'minimum bodily needs', reduced to the 'paltriest minimum necessary to maintain his physical existence' and relegated to become no more than a 'servant of the flesh' or a 'prisoner of crude practical needs' (ibid., pp. 285, 290, 353).

Marx saw human needs as shaped by the structure of society and specifically by the dominant mode of production. In his later works on historical materialism he examined the processes of producing for need embodied in the development of the technological means and social relations of production under capitalism. His earlier focus on human nature and needs broadened to take into account the material structures that shape production and consumption and determine the modes of life and consciousness that govern individual existence. In this respect Marx's account is significantly different from social democracy's account of the formation of needs and their means of satisfaction. In essence Marx argued that humankind must struggle to overcome the dominant mode of capitalist production – and not merely reform it – in order to inaugurate socialist production for need rather than for the accumulation of further capital and profit. With the demise of capitalism and the rise of socialism would come 'a fresh confirmation of human powers and fresh enrichment of human nature' (ibid., p. 358).

In contrast to the notion of basic needs, Marx suggested that meeting 'truly human' needs involves meeting more than physical needs alone. For the satisfaction of human needs involves an enrichment of existence that gives form to the diverse content of human experience. For Marx and Engels the mode of production must not be considered simply as the reproduction of the physical existence of the individual. Rather it is 'a definite form of activity of these individuals, a definite form of expressing their life, a definite mode of life on their part. As individuals express their life, so they are' (Marx and Engels, 1976, p. 31).

Ted Benton (1993, p. 49) argues that Marx was affirming that 'in a fully human, or "true" practice of production, physical needs would be met in a way that was aesthetically and cognitively satisfying', and that there are many different ways in which human society meets its needs in this enriched way. The expectation in modern democratic societies that government policies provide for basic needs has been understood in a minimal sense that pays little attention to the full needs that constitute the human mode of existence. This has been partly a matter of financial constraints on government. But it has also been a matter of modes of welfare delivery that have been constrained by a government assumption that recipients are passive and possess minimum or limited needs.

The fifth and final conception of need represents not a single notion but several different notions unified by their *feminist* perspective. These notions address the different conceptions of need that arise from the politics of difference, waged in part in social policy. They share a concern to address the needs of women specifically, though in a way that also has implications for social relations between men and women, and provides important challenges to the political traditions discussed here. For example the social democratic notion of basic needs asserts that needs are universal and by implication common to one single human nature. However if the different needs claimed by feminists are taken seriously, then notions of common human needs and universal rights to welfare become highly problematic.

Feminist theory provides four different responses to universalist theories of need. First, liberal feminists have responded by affirming the existence of a core of human needs shared by all, but, nonetheless argue that there are some significant gender differences in connection with need. For instance women share with men the same health needs, but suffer health problems in different ways (depressive illness is one example). Furthermore, they experience specific conditions that do not affect men at all (such as gynaecological and obstetric conditions) and require specific gendered forms of care. The failure of social democratic social policy to extend to women the same egalitarian considerations it gives to most men is seen as a failure that could be remedied by a stronger affirmation of universal values in social legislation by extending to women the rights enjoyed by men.

Second, some radical feminists respond to the failure to acknowledge the identity of women by asserting the existence of fundamental differences in the gendered needs of men and women, in their biology, physiology, psychology, sexual and genetic make-up, and even suggest that men and women need fundamentally different modes of life (Firestone, 1971).

Third, other radical feminists respond to the patriarchal attitudes that violate their identity, not by asserting a differently human nature, but by arguing that human needs are a social construction that men impose on women and which does not have its own objective existence (Butler, 1990). In this vein, feminist politics and policy is about constructing a female power base that resists and subverts male definitions of women's needs.

Finally, Marxist and socialist feminists have recently advanced the idea of a struggle for recognition that sees the politics of difference as the struggle between subaltern groups of women whose universal needs are not recognised and dominant groups of men whose needs are recognised. For socialist feminists, the struggle around the politics of difference leads to a deeper recognition of identity and difference in the needs of women and men – a conception similar to the mutual conception of need discussed earlier.

## Understanding Need in a Changing Society

Welfare ideologies are a useful approach to understanding different conceptions of need. However there is now a strong intellectual movement arguing that these ideologies have exhausted their relevance in an age of fundamental social change, when national economies have succumbed to world capitalism, traditional industries to new world competition, and labour markets have become increasingly insecure. This new intellectual movement believes that modern political thought, which began with the intellectual Enlightenment of the late eighteenth century, is being supplanted by a more pragmatic, 'post-Enlightenment' politics that has serious implications for social policy. The implication is that the notion of common basic needs embodied in uniform state provision and supported in the post-1945 welfare state by most of the ideologies discussed above (except feminism), is now no longer relevant to the social needs of today. In particular, social provisions have proved insensitive to the new diversity of needs and life styles that characterise a 'postmodern' age (Williams, 1992; Penna and O'Brien, 1996).

Among those writers who have addressed the passing of traditional politics and ideologies, Paul Hirst and John Gray have advanced influential new ideas about welfare and politics, what they term respectively 'voluntary associationalism' (Hirst, 1994) and 'communitarian liberalism' (Gray, 1997). These ideas also suggest new ways of thinking about need. We will compare their accounts of the organisation and scope of welfare, and extract from these accounts their thinking about need and the responsibilities individuals and government have in meeting need.

From a socialist perspective, Hirst has responded to the exhaustion of politics by advocating the renewal of the associationalist tradition bequeathed by an earlier generation of socialist thinkers such as G. D. H. Cole and H. Laski (Hirst 1994, ch. 2). Associationalism turns the traditional relationship between state and voluntary organisations 'on its head': 'It treats self-governing voluntary bodies not as secondary associations, but as the primary means of both democratic governance and organising social life' (ibid., p. 26). Nonetheless, Hirst recognises the role government must play in raising public funds to finance voluntary initiatives, in policing these finances and maintaining standards in the voluntary sector (ibid., p. 24). In so doing he advances an approach that meets individual, mutual and common needs. According to Hirst, the provision of basic needs can be met better by voluntary associations than by the state. This opens up the possibility of addressing basic and mutual conceptions of needs in new ways. For if it is possible to meet basic needs through voluntary provision, then it is also possible that they could be met in ways that satisfy mutual needs for human recognition and comradeship (with the safeguard of government provision for the needs voluntary organisations fail to meet). This would enlarge the scope of need satisfaction beyond mere physical satisfaction to permit the meeting of needs normally not met by the state or the market. In this respect there is scope for realising human needs in a way that accords with Marx's 'truly human' needs.

We can capture the sense in which basic, mutual and individual needs can be met by outlining Hirst's account of an associational system of welfare (Hirst, 1994 and Chapter 5 in this volume). First, universal cash benefits tied to a national minimum would be given to cover basic needs. This is the classic social democratic principle that universal needs require universal benefits, such as a guaranteed minimum income or a 'citizens' income'. Individuals would use these benefits to acquire goods or services in the market place or from voluntary organisations that belong to local circles of mutual aid involving local exchange trading schemes, credit unions and voluntary agencies. In mutual organisations the exchange would be multi-layered and not solely economic. Exchange could be geared towards meeting basic needs of the kind that social democrats have traditionally relied on the state for, as well as the complex of individually different needs that motivate mutual or market exchange. Second, individuals with particular needs – what Hirst calls 'status' needs (ibid., p. 178) – would be assessed by relevant experts (for example diagnosing specific forms of illness and disability) or acquire a demographically defined status (as schoolchildren, the elderly and lone parents). Individuals with status needs would have right of access to formula-funded voluntary organisations such as schools, hospitals, residential or assisted accommodation and would take their funding with them (for example as vouchers) when they join the organisation and exercise their right to membership. Such rights would not interfere with their right to purchase provisions from commercial providers. Third, discretionary payments would be available for individuals facing certain contingencies whose needs could not be adequately legislated for. Environmental catastrophes such as floods, fires or earthquakes would be covered by this.

We can compare Hirst's account of new welfare with that of Gray, a former advocate of the radical right. Gray now sees Thatcherism as a 'self-undermining project', which, having successfully laid social democracy to rest, has itself finally succumbed to economic and social processes beyond its control (Gray, 1997, p. 11). The major outcome of the collapse of the left and right is that the dramatic policy choices that were once proclaimed by the old ideologies – such as between universal and selective welfare – are no longer available. In their place, Gray argues for more diverse options to suit different needs framed by a more practical and realistic approach to policymaking. Policies would be arrived at via more conditional and fluid agreements struck at the local level. In this vein, Gray argues that

> there is no one set of policies, no one structure of institutions, in which an enabling welfare state is best embodied. There is instead a diversity of local settlements, never final and always provisional, in which conflicting claims are given a temporary reconciliation, and the values of autonomy and community are accorded a more or less complete embodiment and expression (1992, p. 63).

For Gray, the question of social need is no longer one that can be settled only in the market place, but arises in the diverse ways in which different individuals go about meeting their needs in families, communities and markets and exercising their autonomy. By autonomy, Gray means 'the capacity for rational deliberation and choice', and acquiring the resources needed for a life that is at least partly self-directed (ibid., p. 26). For Gray autonomy is the most important of human needs whose fulfilment rests on the satisfaction of other needs. It is central to Gray's argument about welfare in a plural society, where markets exist alongside informal, mutual and governmental provision, that needs are understood as *satiable needs*; that is, as basic needs that can be satisfied not fully but to an agreed level of satisfaction by fixed amounts of provision. Once this level is reached, Gray argues, 'the content of the welfare claim which guarantees their satisfaction is exhausted' (ibid., p. 66). State provision is not obliged to meet basic needs beyond this level. Whereas social democrats have argued that the key distinction shaping need is the division between basic and non-basic needs, Gray argues that a more relevant line dividing basic needs is that portion of basic need that must be satisfied in order for an individual to choose whether and how to meet him- or herself what remains unsatisfied. If this content of satiable need defines what public welfare should provide, and if its satisfaction is achieved through provisions sufficient for this level and no more, then it follows that 'reasoned public discourse can occur as to the content of basic needs, which invokes the shared norms and common life of the society' (ibid., p. 67). The notion of satiable need represents a level of basic need satisfaction that is universal to a particular society. Once satisfied, individuals are free to meet these needs by their own means at the higher levels of satisfaction they choose as part of their own projects of autonomous self-development.

Both Hirst and Gray arrive at conceptions of basic needs that have the following in common. They both address the basic needs for which government is ultimately responsible even though some members of society will opt to meet these needs through voluntary or commercial agencies. Furthermore, basic needs are universal in the limited sense of reflecting the shared values that different members of a particular society embrace. However they differ on the construction and satisfaction of human needs. For Hirst, there is a sense that each basic need is a definable entity, with physical and mutual components that should be financially underwritten by government and in most cases met by voluntary associations. Gray, who advocates the satisfaction of basic needs to the point of satiability, as distinct from fulfilment, retains the liberal assumption of a sovereign individual who is ultimately responsible for his or her own fulfilment. In departing from liberal individualism, Gray introduces the concept of common satiable needs that are arrived at by consensus and met collectively. Of course, British welfare, whether social democratic or rightist, has historically satisfied need at a sub-optimum level and rarely offered optimum fulfilment.

## Universal and Particular Needs

One response to the criticisms that Hirst and Gray make of 'old' welfare is to revisit the problems of reconciling particular and universal needs, posed in the way social policy seeks to satisfy the needs of different individuals as well as the common human needs of all. In the practical world of social policy, social democratic and rightist ideologies draw on different and sometimes conflicting conceptions of need. For social democrats this has meant a strategy of meeting basic needs through collective provision and individual needs through market, mutual or voluntary provision; while those on the right have advanced a strategy of residual state provision for the poorest and market provision for the majority. Nonetheless the traditional ways of configuring universal and particular needs remain inadequate. Whether collective or market welfare, these approaches are insufficient to meet the diversity of needs that constitute a profoundly transformed postmodern society.

In confronting these new circumstances, several recent discussions of need have sought to clarify the relationship between universal and particular needs and to describe its implications for social policy. However there are significant voices in social policy (for example Taylor-Gooby, 1997) who question whether the transition from modern to postmodern society involves the far-reaching social changes postmodernists suggest. What can be said is that postmodernists who stress the need to reexamine the nature of particular needs still have to consider the need for universalist perspectives if different need claims are to be dealt with justly.

Thompson and Hoggett's move towards a 'postmodern' social policy is a case in point. They define particularism as a set of social policy arguments that stress 'social diversity rather than commonality and thereby give emphasis to the particular needs, moral frameworks and social expectations of different groups' (Thompson and Hoggett 1996, p. 31). Such arguments demand that social policy address the specific identities of the groups in question, namely 'the things they want, value and need' (p. 32), arguments that appear to reject universalist claims about basic needs, values and aspirations. On the other hand, Thompson and Hoggett recognise the need for a universal perspective and suggest that there are different approaches to reconciling particular and universal needs. We shall examine three such approaches: Doyal and Gough's (1991) thoroughgoing universalist view of human needs, Thompson and Hoggett's (1996) approach, to postmodern reconciliation and Seyla Benhabib's (1992) approach, which retains a universalist perspective whilst responding to the postmodern nature of social change. Though they each adopt different positions on postmodern politics –

the first two dismiss it and the latter three accommodate it critically – they all share a belief in the significance of communication as a means of coming to recognise others' needs.

Doyal and Gough present a thoroughgoing case for welfare universalism by arguing that, whilst different communities have their own interpretations of need, they nonetheless all share the same core problems of meeting need. Needs are universal not only because there is one common human nature, but also because there is one relatively finite material world that all peoples share, even though they approach the tasks of resource utilisation and need satisfaction in ways that are shaped by their own cultures. An important implication of the existence of universal need is the moral obligation it imposes on society – local, national and international – to provide individuals with the means to meet their needs.

For Doyal and Gough, needs are universal in two ways. First, needs are essentially material nature, in consisting of basic needs for food, warmth, shelter and higher needs such as nurturing relationships, learning, fulfilment and so forth. Second, the technical, moral and political choices made in connection with meeting needs are essentially rational, and thus open to public scrutiny. These two factors mean that needs have an objective and empirical existence independent of the subjective judgements of different individuals, and that their identity is open to public and rational discussion (Doyal and Gough, 1991, p. 41). It follows that decisions about the identity and satisfaction of need should be democratic and as far as possible impartial.

In contrast the particularities of need become increasingly apparent the closer one gets to the everyday practical tasks of meeting need in a community. Indeed Doyal and Gough acknowledge that 'there is no escape from the rules and discourses of one's form of life, there is no neutral reality to which one can turn to assess which approach to need-satisfaction is "best"' (ibid., p. 7). However, although they acknowledge the cultural specificity of needs, they nonetheless stress the importance of the core activities that make up social life in different cultures, for these core activities are 'at the heart of our ability to understand the similarities between alien cultures and our own' (ibid, p. 81). It is, they argue, the ability of individuals to enter into other cultures' need-satisfying practices – practices that are similar to their own – that enables them to translate other cultures' languages, rules and norms into terms that are similar to their own. Because of this, practices constitutive of universal forms of human achievement – for example production, reproduction, cultural transmission and political authority – form a 'translation-bridgehead' in cross-cultural understanding. They contend that what is special about need-satisfying activities is that they are intelligible in all forms of cultural life and hence provide the basis for practical understanding 'which is equally immune to cultural variation' and is constant between different cultures (ibid., p. 82). For example, building a roof requires a system of physical supports, and agriculture a regular supply of water, whatever the culture.

In contrast to Doyal and Gough's universalism, Thompson and Hoggett seek a postmodern social policy that is more attuned to social difference. However they recognise that a balance must be maintained between the claims for universal and particular needs, in that 'any form of universality not able to be sensitive to the differences between different cases is indefensible, and any form of particularism unable or unwilling to compare different cases will collapse into an untenable relativism' (Thompson and Hoggett, 1996, p. 35).

Thompson and Hoggett's approach to reconciling particular and universal needs is to suggest that, at the level of logic, any argument that professes to treat the claims of local or different groups justly must itself derive from a general principle that differences should be respected (ibid., p. 34). The implication is that 'to conceptualise difference that is not sheer "otherness" is already to bring the things distinguished under a common signifying order' (ibid.) In other words this 'signifying order' stands as a framework of universal principles under which the conflicting political claims arising from social differences are subsumed and arbitrated. For example the assertion that women have particular needs that are different from those of men would mean that recognition of these needs and their fair treatment should draw on a universal principle about treating different needs justly. Women who are excluded from the labour market because of the demands of motherhood (in a way that fathers generally are not) have a right to pre-school and out-of-school provision that will enable them to enter the labour market and pursue a career. The provision of these facilities for women who choose to work is a means of responding to their particular needs in order to extend to them a universal right to seek work without unreasonable impediment. Recognition of the particular needs of difference in this case is ultimately justified by reference to a universal principle.

However, some feminists claim that women have needs that are radically different from those of men (as we saw in the above survey of different feminist conceptions of need), and therefore cannot be subsumed under a universal principle applying to women and men alike. Indeed the feminist argument might be that some women's needs stem from a radically different human nature – a woman's nature – which gives rise to principles defining need that apply to women alone. If we take the example of women's need for childbirth, abortion and contraception provision, which men do not have in the same way, we are dealing with particularistic claims where there is no clear universal principle to appeal to. There is only an appeal to the specific needs of womankind, qualities that are specific to their otherness. We can discern two contrary interpretations of this need. One might be that women and men do indeed share a universal duty to exercise responsibility in sexual relationships and parenting, which they fulfil differently because of their biologically different roles at conception and birth. Gender differences in no way allow men to avoid their responsibilities in these respects. The argument for shared parental responsibility is a strong one, but could be used – as it is by the Roman Church – to condemn abortion and contraception and deny women 'the right to choose'.

However a second argument suggests that women have fundamental biological and psychological differences that afford them the right to control contraception and childbirth, while men do not have that right. This argument is different from the former in appealing to some fundamental difference that cannot be justified by appealing to universal principles that respect differences; that there are – to use Thompson and Hoggett's telling phrase – differences that stem from 'sheer otherness'. Where advocates of particular needs do insist on subsuming particular claims under a universal framework, these claims are ultimately reduced to the same level as men's claims to fair treatment, so that women's differences become at best secondary to the universal needs shared with men (see, for example, Spicker, 1996, p. 231).

Thompson and Hoggett suggest that one way out of the problem of particularism as sheer otherness lies in acts of communication between different others, that 'relatedness provides the necessary condition for communication across the boundaries that differentiate us' (Thompson and Hoggett, 1996, pp. 34–5). This implies that there is no essential order of difference between human beings (such as between the insane and sane, black and white, women and men) that cannot be transcended through acts of recognition and communication. In recent years some philosophers have revived the idea of a politics of recognition, of whom Charles Taylor (1992) is a leading example. In fact the possibility of communication across boundaries of social difference has become an important theme in social politics, one shared by all the writers discussed in this section.

For Benhabib (1992), the politics of recognition involves addressing a different type of universalism from the abstract notion of a 'signifying order' subsuming differences, referred to above. The problem with universalist theories of justice and ethics is their construction of moral persons as disembodied subjects governed by impartial and abstract faculties of reasoning and capable of discerning the common good over more particular concrete interests. Benhabib insists that a universal reasoning must be developed that addresses concrete moral subjects who are capable of engaging in moral conversations aimed at understanding each other's particular needs. What she terms 'interactive universalism' in welfare and politics arises from mutual recognition between concrete individuals who each have their own needs, histories and aspirations. Despite fundamental differences of identity between individuals, the assumption is that an ethical understanding can prevail, which leads to 'universal respect and reciprocity' (that is, taking the other person's viewpoint) and which

> does not deny our embodied and embedded identity, but aims at developing moral attitudes and encouraging political transformations that can yield a point of view *acceptable to all*. Universality is not the ideal consensus of fictitiously defined selves, but the concrete process in politics and morals of the struggle of concrete selves, striving for autonomy (Benhabib, 1992, p. 153, emphasis added).

In this account of the relationship between universal and particular needs a 'dialectic of recognition' unfolds whereby real differences are encountered by real individuals who are capable of reaching agreement over their differences. In this agreement some means of need satisfaction are sought collectively, and other means are sought that by agreement, are exclusive to each party. In human recognition, different individuals and even conflicting parties learn to agree and to disagree whilst maintaining a way of existing together.

One could accuse Benhabib and the other writers of betraying a degree of idealism that is out of kilter with social policy retrenchment throughout the West. However it is worth recognising that the politics of recognition represents a movement in social politics that in its mutualist guise had a significant practical impact on early social policy, and is being revived when discussing new social movements. Despite wide-ranging changes, a case for continuity can be made by acknowledging the continued presence of earlier ideas in New Labour's thinking today. Ideas about basic, residual and mutual needs remain active. What remains to be seen is the form these conceptions of need will take, and the balance accorded to common and particular needs, as Labour's social policy takes shape as we move into the twenty-first century.

## Conclusion

The chapter has described five different conceptions of need in twentieth-century social policy. The role played by each conception has changed with the shifting fortunes of welfare politics. Ideas about basic, residual and mutual need, in particular, still inform welfare debates at the close of the century. What has changed is the configuration between them.

At its height, social democracy configured three notions of need: a notion of basic needs that are shared by all and underwritten by government national minima; individual human needs that individuals are free to meet in the market once common needs are secure; and mutual needs where groups of individuals act cooperatively to meet their common and different needs. In addition the continuation of means-tested provision for the poorest kept alive the Poor Law idea of residual needs. In contrast, the right, at least in principle, saw the market as the primary order for satisfying need and state welfare as supplementary provision for those unable to buy in the market. Individualist and residual conceptions of need were combined. In this configuration, the state minimum did not act as the first line of defence for all, as did the national minimum, but rather provided a residuum available only to the poorest. In this way the right reversed the social democratic order between basic needs met by the national minimum and individual needs met in the market or by voluntary welfare. For the right, the first line of welfare was the market and the second the residual minimum. In practice Tory governments between 1979 and 1997 retained some of the remnants of basic need provision, whilst increasingly operating welfare services like business concerns exposed to a volatile mix of market forces and public interest. In this climate the national minimum gave way to a residual minimum concerned with residual rather than basic needs.

The previous two sections argued that the mutualist conception of need has received growing attention in welfare thought recently, especially as expressed in the significance given to communication and recognition in the politics of welfare. Whilst representing different positions on how to reconcile universalism and particularism, new pluralists such as Hirst and Gray, postmodernists such as Thompson and Hoggett and universalists such as Benhabib, Doyal and Gough all acknowledge the significance of mutual recognition in the way different individuals and groups come to understand their needs in an increasingly diverse society. The mutual recognition of need is an important motivation for different individuals to pool their energies and resources in the event of hardship. However, though an important strand in welfare thought, mutualism cannot survive without support from broader and stronger structures. The experience of Victorian mutualism was one of solidarity among members combined with the exclusion of vulnerable individuals who posed bad risks. Mutual needs may be universal, but mutual welfare alone cannot count as universal welfare. Today the experience of mutualism is mixed. On the one hand, former mutual organisations such as building societies have succumbed to the pressures and allures of the market by converting themselves into public limited companies. On the other hand, new forms of mutualism have emerged, for example local exchange trading systems, credit unions, job clubs and self-help organisations. The survival of mutualism depends on national and international governmental support.

The traditional social-democratic structures configuring basic, mutual and individual needs have been replaced by new structures based on independent but government-aided agencies in the voluntary and market sectors, with the government concentrating residual support on the poorest. The structures that once placed voluntary, commercial and mutual provisions on the foundations of the state minimum – so defining the contours of basic, individual and mutual needs – no longer exist. However, despite wide ranging changes, ideas about basic, mutual and residual needs remain active in welfare politics today. How these conceptions of need will develop as we move into the next century remains to be seen.

## Further Reading

A recent discussion of the concept of need is L. Doyal and I. Gough's *A Concept of Human Need* (London: Macmillan 1991). J. Bradshaw's typology in 'The Concept of Social Need', *New Society*, 30. March 1971, has been influential in categorising the administrative definitions that practitioners deploy in policy making. For different views on the implications of postmodernity for social policy, see F. Williams, 'Somewhere over the rainbow: universality and diversity in social policy', in N. Manning and R. Page (eds), *Social Policy Review 4* (Canterbury: Social Policy Association, 1992) M. Hewitt, 'Social Movements and Social Need', *Critical Social Policy*, vol. 37, pp. 52–74 (1993); S. Penna and M. O'Brien, 'Postmodernism and Social Policy', *Journal of Social Policy*, vol. 25, no. 1 (1997); and P. Taylor-Gooby 'In defence of second-best theory: state, class and capital in social policy', *Journal of Social Policy*, vol. 26, no. 2 (1997).

# CHAPTER 5

# Social Welfare and Associative Democracy

PAUL HIRST

As must already be clear from the preceding chapters, state-provided welfare is in crisis throughout the advanced industrial world. Even labour and social democratic parties, for whom universal benefits and collectivised state services were a defining political doctrine, are now contemplating a radical reduction of the scale and scope of the welfare state (see Chapter 2 of this volume). There are many reasons why welfare funding and services are now under pressure in the advanced countries: low growth, widespread unemployment, an ageing population, tax aversion and a growing disinclination to subsidise the 'feckless'.

Despite all the heartsearching and the rhetoric of 'thinking the unthinkable' the solutions proposed are predictable and unlikely to promote welfare: restriction and rationing of services, privatisation of provision, and targeting state services on those too poor to provide for themselves. The results are all too predictable: a large proportion of the population inadequately covered by private insurance, and pauper welfare services that everyone pays for but only the desperate use. Roughly the position at the end of the Victorian era.

The question that is seldom asked when the crisis of funding of the welfare 'state' is discussed, is which part of the phrase is the problem? Is it welfare or the state? I shall suggest that for many purposes conventional state welfare has run its course, but that there is an option that combines public funding, collective consumption and personal choice. That option is associationalism, - in which welfare services would be provided by self-governing voluntary associations in receipt of public funds proportional to their subscribing members. Thus health, education and social protection would combine public entitlements with consumer choice; everyone would have access to a minimum level of service and those with the resources could top up their provision. All would thus benefit from public but non-state provision, and the well-to-do would have a rationale for staying with common services and contributing to collective consumption. In a pauper welfare state, such services are seen as a pure tax and their level needs to be kept as low as possible. In an associationalist system the successful would have incentives to invest in advanced services for themselves, but also contribute to the common pool.

Assocationalism would be possible without a citizens' income scheme, which would provide a guaranteed minimum income to all. But it can be argued that a citizens' income – a guaranteed minimum income to all adults either in the form of a transfer payment or a tax credit - would help to mitigate the tendency towards inherent inequality in an associationalist system, and also that some such form of basic income would be inevitable given major changes in the economy, employment patterns and demographics (for a fuller discussion of the idea of a citizens' income see Chapter 7 of this volume).

In order to see why a radical change in the way services are provided is necessary, but also why commonly available, publicly funded health, education and social protection will become more not less necessary, I shall consider three processes: automation, globalisation, and the ageing of the population. Each will increase the need for protection against risk, and each will undermine the conventional economic institutions and patterns of funding that underlie the existing welfare state.

## Automation

Most contemporary discussions of welfare still envisage working life paid employment as the economic basis for social citizenship. However technological changes may well undermine this assumption (Rifkin, 1995). In the 1960s the great automation debate got the future completely wrong. Predictions of a society of mass leisure and the complete automation of manufacturing processes proved hopelessly optimistic about both technology and the social effects. The electro-mechanical systems of the time could not effectively control most manufacturing processes. In fact new technologies let people work 'smarter' and harder – the hours worked per employee in Britain have actually increased since the 1960s.

Now, however, the old predictions may be coming true but in a less comforting form. The combination of computing power, informatics and robotics is beginning to transform both manufacturing and services. We may be on the edge of an economic revolution in which wholesale job displacement will be the norm. It is already beginning to happen, especially in the hitherto secure sectors of banking and financial services. Employment is differentiating into a highly skilled minority and a low-wage, low-skill mass with an intermittent history of employment. The public sector can no longer function as the employer of last resort, since it is under intense fiscal pressure.

Economists generally challenge this scenario. They argue that dramatic increases in productivity actually tend to *increase* overall employment: reducing the costs of products, thereby increasing demand and freeing resources for consumption elsewhere. Our history, they argue, is one of a steady transfer of employment from agriculture to manufacturing to services, driven by improvements in productivity. Moreover displaced labour will be a cheap resource that stimulates demand for it in new industries; provided mobility is not blocked by restrictive labour market policies.

These arguments are a mixture of economic theory and analogies from economic history, and they may prove to be wrong. In fact no major new sector is emerging to take up displaced labour – other than the personal services component of the service sector. But such jobs are frequently extremely ill-paid, and it is difficult to see demand rising significantly unless wages are very low. The current combination of steady productivity growth and restrictive macroeconomic policies that constrain growth will inevitably lead to high levels of unemployment. Employment at poverty wages is hardly a substitute, and already large numbers of working poor in the United States are unable to meet many of their basic needs (Gordon, 1996). Such people will certainly not be able to build up credible levels of private social protection insurance.

The key problem with the automation revolution in a system that depends on wage labour and that cannot grow at more than 2–3 per cent on average, is that it is not clear how the economy can sustain itself in the long run (Leontieff and Duchin, 1986). A 'Bladerunner' society is a familiar dystopian vision, in which a wealthy and privileged corporate elite lords it over an impoverished and excluded mass. Modern mass consumption capitalism is not like this, it requires a large affluent middle class to buy its products. One cannot act out a feudal logic in a market society. Elitist societies have been extractive, they have taken the agrarian wealth produced by the masses in the form of rents and taxes. Under modern conditions if people do not work or are paid very badly then they cannot consume – our corporate elites have to sell in order to be rich.

There are no easy solutions to this problem of structural unemployment. Labour market "reforms" can only significantly increase employment if wages are allowed to rise and fall like any other commodity. But wages are a social institution, they are supposed to support the worker (Solow, 1990). Work sharing is a palliative to job losses driven by technology, but only if wages are reduced *pro rata* and the indirect social costs to employers are reduced. Yet the welfare system cannot currently accommodate either of these developments. The answer is a citizens' income based on redistributive taxation (Jordan, 1987; Van Parijs, 1992). This would provide a sufficient

basis for people to supplement their social stipend with paid employment –
unlike in present welfare systems, participation in the labour market would
always be positive, and people could cushion themselves against low-paid,
part-time and intermittent employment. Such a system would make it
possible to meet the demand for personal services such as nurseries, care
for the aged and so on, whether through low-cost paid employment or
voluntary work.

The standard tax experts' answer to any citizens' income scheme is that it
implies that unacceptably high levels of taxation will be inflicted on the
employed to pay for it (see Commission on Social Justice, 1994, pp. 261–5).
However if the alternative is 30 per cent unemployment, social unrest and
economic stagnation, then radical redistribution may be necessary not only in
the interests of social justice but also to sustain effective demand. The fiscal
experts assume the wage labour system is the norm, but if labour is displaced
on the scale that the new technologies make possible, a new form of
distribution of social wealth will become necessary. The prediction of the
end of work may prove alarmist, but in case it comes true it would be well to
have experimented with guaranteed minimum income schemes so that their
scale could be increased in the next two decades if necessary. As it happens a
modest citizens' income scheme is affordable, would have a marked effect on
inequality (Parker and Sutherland, 1994) and can be justified on grounds
both of its administrative economy compared with targeted benefits and of
social justice. A citizens' income is an essential element in any viable
associationalist welfare system.

## Globalisation

Politicians, journalists and academics insist that the forces of globalisation are
unstoppable and that national societies are now subject to intense
international competitive pressures. The result is that no social welfare
provisions, labour market policies and tax levels that depart significantly from
the international norm will face sanctions from the multinationals and
financial markets. Such societies will suffer capital flight and a dramatic loss
of inward investment.

One could argue endlessly about the nature and extent of globalisation. Let
us assume the real issues at stake are a high degree of integration into world
financial markets and a high ratio of external trade to GDP (gross domestic
product) (Hirst, 1997a; Hirst and Thompson, 1996). A highly internationalised economy depends for its performance on its internationally traded
sector. But it is a simple truism that it is not *societies* that are competitive

but *companies*. Japan and Germany are not in competition. Toyota and Volkswagen are. Provided the key companies that make up the internationally traded sector of the economy are competitive, then what happens in the rest of society is a matter of relative indifference. There is little evidence that wage costs or social overhead costs are the most significant factors in company competitiveness: if that were so employment would have shifted far more dramatically to low-wage countries in internationally-tradable products (Krugman, 1994). Productivity, product quality and sales and service standards appear to be the key determinants of competitive performance for most major companies.

Thus France is often presented by British commentators as a country whose extensive welfare state and regulated labour markets are making it internationally uncompetitive. It does have higher unemployment than Britain and its managements are finding it hard to adapt to new commercial practices. But in the 1990s it has run a substantial balance of trade surplus compared with Britain's persistent deficits, and it attracted an average annual inward investment of $19 billion between 1991 and 1995, as against Britain's $17.2 billion (IMF data in the *Observer*, 27 April 1997). Thus the strategy of promoting 'national competitiveness' by driving down wages and social overhead costs to attract inward investment on the part of Britain does not seem a good bargain.

The effects of a high degree of internationalisation on the national economy and society are more complex. The economy is exposed to external shocks and must develop means to cushion itself against them. Major events such as the 1973 OPEC (Organisation of Petroleum Exporting Countries) oil crisis, which increased oil prices by 400 per cent, are difficult to make provision for; nevertheless those societies with effective corporatist institutions and strong traditions of social solidarity weathered the crisis best. In normal times sectors, firms and individuals need institutions that provide protection against the effects on them of internationally-induced changes. Peter Katzenstein (1985) has shown that small, highly internationalised countries, such as the Netherlands have combined traditions of solidarism and consensus in economic policy making to coordinate organised economic actors, with high levels of welfare and training to protect individuals against the effects of uncertainty. Thus a high level of internationalisation, far from requiring cut-throat competition between firms and the slashing of welfare provision, has actually tended to promote cooperation and social protection in the smaller advanced economies of Europe.

The issue now is whether such national responses are still possible. Dani Rodrik (1997) has argued that the very factors that increase the need for insurance against external shocks may actually work to undermine it.

Companies and markets may refuse to accept such protective regimes. Sweden seems to be a case in point. Since the 1980s its elites and major companies have been insistent that domestic tax and welfare policies are damaging their competitiveness and have regularly threatened to defect abroad. Yet the people of Sweden still support the welfare state, even if the political class is in retreat. Moreover Sweden's experience is unusual and hardly a model for small states in world markets. Thus Denmark too has high levels of taxation (51.6 per cent of GDP) and welfare provision, but it has not suffered the same economic difficulties nor, despite rumblings in the press, is the welfare state seriously under threat. Denmark has a diverse and very successful internationally traded sector with a large number of small and medium-sized enterprises.

The main sanctions that internationisation does impose is the ability of individual companies to use the threat of relocation when bargaining over wages and conditions, and of the corporate sector as a whole to restrain taxes on capital. Thus welfare states will have to be financed domestically from incomes and sales taxes. That throws the main burden of sustaining welfare on the employed workforce and the level of welfare provision will depend on the willingness to pay for social solidarity (Rodrik, 1997).

In the highly internationalised British economy before 1914, welfare provision and labour regulation were both weak (Hirst and Thompson, 1996, table 2.5). However the main cushion against economic shocks was migration, adjusting the labour force by flows to the rapidly growing economies of North America and Australasia. Between 1945 and the 1980s countries such as the United States and Japan had low trade to GDP ratios and could thus insulate their domestic economies and pursue their own full-employment strategies. Migration is no longer an option in the advanced world and the vast majority of OCED countries now have a high degree of international openness.

Thus the arguments for extensive welfare provision are reinforced by international openness, not undermined by it. Too many politicians are quite unaware of this, advocating that we should emulate countries such as Singapore, with its very low ratio of public expenditure to GDP (20 per cent). It might appear that this point favours conventional state welfare. On the contrary, it gives priority to systems where the taxpayer feels he or she is a stakeholder. Internationalisation puts some degree of pressure on welfare systems to offer workers value for money. If welfare has to be funded from domestic personal taxation then, for it to be sustained, workers will require services they can identify with and that offer proportionate benefits. Associationalism could act to increase such identification by empowering the welfare consumer.

## An Ageing Population

There is an extensive international debate on whether the advanced countries can support their ageing populations at the current standards of welfare. On existing demographic projections many countries will have very low support ratios of adults of working age to those over 65 (3:1). Britain may be better off than countries like Italy, with a higher than average projected ratio (Hills, 1994). In some countries, for example Australia, these demographic projections have been used to question the viability of existing pensions and health insurance standards, arguing that 'intergenerational equity' should not burden future workers with the obligation to service today's lucky working-age adults. Equally there are fears in Britain about the impact of the current level of the elderly on health service provision.

These arguments seem beside the point. Just as there is considerable uncertainty about the future of work, so we have very little idea of what the aged in, say, 2025 will be like and the demands they will make on welfare. For example it is possible that they may place less burden on health care than now because of a switch to healthier lifestyles, improvements in therapy and acceptance of euthanasia for the terminally ill and grossly incapacitated. But a large number of healthy and active old people will pose a very real problem – at 60–65 people are unlikely to accept 20 years of inactivity, especially if they do not have the resources for affluent retirement. An associationalist welfare system would tackle this issue of compulsory withdrawal from economic activity at its root. It would avoid a rigid divide between employment and unemployment, and in the same way it could reduce the divide between work and retirement. Individuals could continue to take paid employment to supplement their citizens' income, which would replace public retirement pensions. Moreover associative welfare would create a vast third sector between the state and the market in which the active aged could offer voluntary service, helping to keep down welfare costs whilst providing fulfilling activity. Given the increasing trend towards single person households, voluntary associations could provide elderly people with substitutes for services formerly provided by families and at least partially on the basis of mutual aid and voluntary service. A state-organised service based on wage labour could not do this, or only at a greatly increased cost.

## Why is There a Crisis of the Welfare State?

We shall now return to the question of whether the problem of the welfare state refers to welfare or the state. In the 1980s social democrats believed that the main problem with welfare was how to pay for it; that the existing services were desirable and that the constraints were entirely fiscal. For the new right, in contrast, the problem with welfare lay with the state: public services were inherently inefficient, encouraged dependency and crowded out wealth-generating markets. New right remedies clearly failed wherever they were tried – markets could not guarantee the kind of basic security for all that public welfare was intended to do. Yet the negative part of the economic liberal critique was successful, primarily because increasing costs coincided with a wide range of consumer dissatisfactions with welfare. There were problems with *how* services were provided that made people resistant to their cost. Modern centre-left pragmatists have absorbed the cruder lessons of the new right, thus they embrace marketisation and imagine they are offering an alternative with communitarianism and self-help. Yet they have no distinctive and coherent theory of reform: no response to the problem of how to provide services in new ways while ensuring widespread access.

In the first phase of modern state welfare, citizens were mostly grateful to receive national, bureaucratically administered basic services such as un-employment insurance, basic workers' housing and elementary education. These services were uniform and standardised in content, easy to replicate locally and to administer by well-tried bureaucratic methods. In the 1960s, as welfare states expanded they not only consumed a growing proportion of GDP and imposed a new direct tax burden on workers, but they also diversified, offering a wider and more varied range of services. Such services became more difficult to deliver uniformly as they became more complex, and they also became more expensive as they came to rely on increasingly professionalised workforces. At the same time, and in substantial measure as an effect of the achievements of the health, education and welfare sector, the public became more sophisticated, more diverse in its values and expectations, and much less deferential.

Several problems came together in the 1970s and early 1980s to challenge the new composite welfare states. Inflation and recession imposed severe fiscal constraints. Expanding services such as higher education, sophisticated medical procedures and care for the aged fought for limited budgets with an enhanced demand for basic services such as unemployment benefit. Public attitudes were changing. Intense dissatisfaction with ill-administered basic services such as council housing went hand in hand with widespread aspiration to and attainment of hitherto 'middle class' benefits such as occupational pensions, owner-occupation, life insurance and so on. Services that were acceptable when the bulk of the employed population were struggling and insecure manual workers were now less satisfactory to the majority. Compulsory, collective, state-administered services no longer met with mass expectations. People were increasingly less willing to submit to administrative discretion, to wait, and to be treated as supplicants. People were extending the consumer mentality to public services, and they often found them wanting. Welfare providers failed to respond to these changes in conditions and attitudes in the way that manufacturing firms responded to a similar crisis in the 1970s, switching from standardised mass production to more customised products and more flexible production systems (Sabel, 1995).

In a sense welfare personnel had few opportunities. In Britain they were trapped between the hostility of conservative governments and the conservatism of their own universalist and social democratic ethos. Increasing numbers of successful citizens began to see 'going private' as the better option. Intellectual debates about welfare were obsessed with the public–private divide – as if a service wholly changed its nature with its constitutional position. Even intelligent critics of extended public service states such as Robert Skidelsky (1996) have argued the need to get back to the public spending to GDP ratios of the early 1960s (30 per cent). Yet the rationale for this is unclear in economic terms. At one level it is an obsession with national accounting conventions, treating transfer payments as public expenditure rather than as exchanges between citizens with the state as intermediary; at another level it assumes that state provision is inherently less efficient than private. In fact advanced societies spend broadly similar total amounts on health, education and social protection; the division between public and private spending, and how fair the outcomes are, being secondary matters to the crude fact that resources consumed in this way are unavailable for other purposes. A pound spent in a public hospital is not that different from one spent in a private clinic. A social choice to consume collectively through state provision poses no obvious macroeconomic problem, unless it is assumed that state employees or welfare recipients are paid too much or that the services are grossly inefficient. As neither is generally the case, the argument that high levels of public expenditure are a threat to economic performance has little foundation (Slemrod, 1995; Atkinson, 1995).

Thus the case for associationalism is not based on an assumption of the superiority of private over public choice. Far from wishing to privatise welfare, the associationalist argument for radical reform starts from the increasing irrelevance of the divide between state and civil society in modern societies. In fact associationalism is as concerned to democratise civil society as it is to devolve the powers of state to voluntary organisations. The public–private divide is increasingly as irrelevant politically as it is economically. Our obsessions with it stem from the fact that we continue to imagine society very differently from how it actually is. We believe we live in a liberal capitalist society in which state and market, and public and private choice are separate spheres. In fact this old liberal architecture no longer fits what is a post-liberal organisational society (Hirst, 1997b). The public–private divide is increasingly confused, and on both sides of it are large hierarchically-administered organisations with essentially similar characteristics – corporate bureaucracies and public institutions. Both exercise governance powers and public governance is increasingly modelled on that of the private sector. Public institutions increasingly adopt the form and methods of private corporations, and private corporations increasingly compete to perform public functions. In neither sector, however, is there much genuine accountability. The interests affected by such institutions – customers, ordinary shareholders, employees, service recipients and local communities – have little effective voice.

Associationalism is not a form of privatisation. It prioritises voluntarism and self-governance, emphasising the role that the combination of voice and the potential of exit have in ensuring accountability and consumer satisfaction. In fact many private welfare institutions offer poor, extremely variable or unnecessarily expensive services. The pensions, life insurance and health insurance sectors offer ample evidence of this. After scandals such as the widespread mis-selling of pensions in the wake of the government's privatisation of SERPS, consumers ought to be more critical of the private sector than they are. As public services are transformed by the new public management and run as if they were commercial corporations, and as public bureaucracies became semi-autonomous agencies, the difference in style and content between the public and private sectors becomes difficult to determine.

## An Assocationalist Welfare State

Thus the key issue for radical reform is treating the whole societal welfare system – public and private – as an integrated package, and not just seeing the welfare state as the problem. The priority is to find effective governance mechanisms that confront the reality of an organisational society and fit the complex of provision that now spans the public–private divide. For a start that means enhancing the protection of consumers in the private sector and extending consumer choice in the public sector. Indeed the ideal would be to fuse the two systems – allowing people to top up a publicly funded minimum level of service if they could afford it, whilst still receiving their basic public entitlement. Only if this can be achieved will citizens be willing to spend more on welfare, receiving benefits proportional to their spending, and being willing to use the same institutions as poorer citizens.

What would an associationalist welfare system look like? Obviously space prohibits more than the barest sketch here, but I have tried to develop a model in *Associative Democracy* (Hirst, 1994, Introduction, ch. 7), and this is illustrated in Figure 5.1. Firstly, a citizen's income would replace most existing state benefits. Unemployment insurance and state pensions would be abolished, and citizens would be able to supplement their basic income without losing benefits. The system would be administratively simple, and it would encourage people to do paid or voluntary work. Far from being a disincentive to employment, it may be a bulwark against chaos in a society where conventional, well-paid, full-time jobs are less readily available than they were in the heyday of mass public welfare.

Secondly, services would be provided in the main by self-governing voluntary associations (police, prisons and compulsory mental health services apart). Such associations would ideally be partnerships between the recipients and the providers of a service in areas such as health and welfare – seeking to give consumers and producers a proportionate voice in how the service is run and delivered. Such associations would be formally democratic, each affected interest electing an appropriate proportion of the governing body, and recipients would have an annual right of exit.

Citizens would thus choose from a range of competing service providers that which is most appropriate to their values and needs. Consumers would be able to 'craft' their own welfare state, choosing the pension plans, hospital schemes and schools they deem best. Competing providers would be under constraint to be efficient and to offer distinctive products. Existing organisations such as churches and trade unions would be able to offer their members distinctive welfare services and use public money to do it. In an increasingly pluralistic society people could create a welfare system that is appropriate to their own values and in common with others in their chosen community.

Such organisations would be formally funded according to the number of members who had elected to join them. They would be obliged to provide a minimum level of service for such funds, but allowed to offer enhanced services to those who could pay extra. Organisations would be constrained by the possibility of exit – members would have the powerful sanction of voting with their feet and thus would have considerable power both of choice and control without excessive participatory involvement.

Any voluntary organisation – church, charitable trust, a cooperative of former state employees – would be able to establish as wide or narrow a range of services as it and its members deem appropriate. For example a Muslim charitable foundation might establish schools, hospitals, old people's homes and so on. Therefore in most urban areas there would be several competing providers of a service. To receive public funds, associations would have to guarantee certain standards: minimum service levels, members' rights to exit

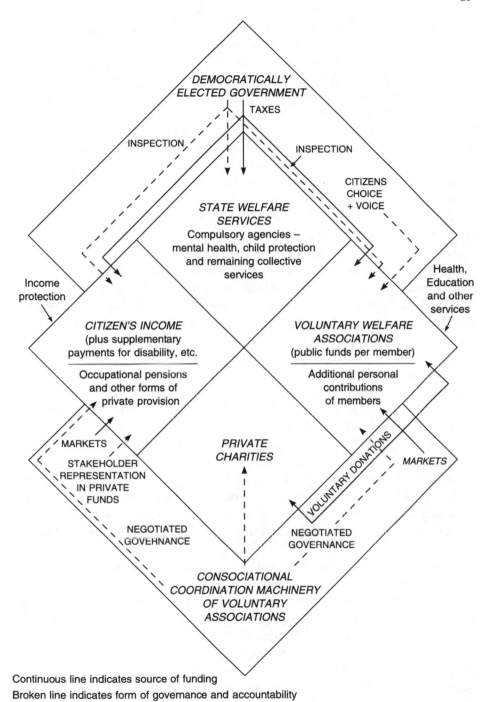

Continuous line indicates source of funding

Broken line indicates form of governance and accountability

**Figure 5.1   Funding and governance in an associated welfare state**

and voice and the obligation to spend funds committed by formula to education on that purpose and none other.

Such a system would provide the possibility of choice; in effect everyone would enjoy the twin benefits of public funding and private choice. As the poor would receive their basic allocations, the system would not be equal in what it offered. But, then nor is the current system. What it would offer the poor is empowerment. They could quit unsatisfactory services and if they want, they could, build their own forms of provision, using public money to obtain the services they would subsequently control, and removing the prospect of having to submit to the patronising treatment of state service providers in the process (Hirst, 1994, ch. 7).

The system could limit duplication of complex services by collaborating, networking and subscribing to common collective services for training, shared use of expensive equipment and so on. In *Associative Democracy* (Hirst, 1994) I have outlined an associational structure for a federal welfare state, one that would combine decentralised provision with the possibility of cooperation.

Clearly, not all services could be provided by basic formula funding. The citizens' income would provide the security of minimum subsistence; more specific entitlements would depend on needs and status. Thus disabled people would receive additional funds. Funds would follow the citizen, and thus the system would be quite different from, for example, the purchaser–provider split in the NHS, where funds are distributed bureaucratically and patients are dependent on their doctor or health authority. It is assumed, although there would be an annual right of exit, that most citizens would stay with the same service provider. The advantage of this system is that as associations would depend on citizens' choice, they would have real power. Inevitably, certain public services would have to remain outside the system – people could hardly choose their own police force, or butcher's shops, their own health inspector – nor would the central state be dissolved, it would remain as a standard setler, inspector and determiner of overall funding levels.

Associationalism would not just be another way of providing welfare services, it would also renew modern society through democratisation. It is the one doctrine of governance that could come to terms with the fact of an organisational society and make a virtue of it. It would convert the particular governments that exist on both sides of the public-private divide into political societies, voluntary organisations chosen by their members and whose policies they give consent to (Kelly *et al.*, 1997). At the same time the decentralisation of power from state institutions and agencies to voluntary organisations would help to restore representative democracy to its role as a source of accountability and a standard setter. Currently, big government is enmeshed in the contradictory roles of service provider and source of accountability for the service.

The aim is thus not to convert big government into small government, to do less, but to change the loci and methods of governance from state to associations. The aim is to offer extended welfare, supported by public funding but without state bureaucracy. Public funding combined with decentralised provision and citizen choice is the essence of associative democracy. This is the one doctrine that can continue the aim of social democracy (to offer citizens security in a market society) in a new social setting, in which the old institutions of the welfare state become less and less effective. Such a system could offer greater accountability and a greater willingness to spend on collective consumption, since citizens would choose what to receive. It may be the only route to social solidarity in a pluralistic and individualistic society.

Associationalism has the great advantage that it can be implemented experimentally and by iterative stages. It is not a big bang reform. Moreover it would supplement rather than supplant the institutions of representative democracy and the market, allowing the one to be a more effective protector of the common interest, and enabling the risks inherent in the other to be contained.

## Further Reading

Modern statements of associationalist principles of governance are Erik Olin Wright (ed.), *Associations and Democracy* (London: Verso, 1995), especially the major essay by Joel Rogers and Joshua Cohen; and John Matthews, *The Age of Democracy* (Melbourne: Oxford University Press, 1989), Boris Frankel, *The Post Industrial Utopians* (Cambridge: Polity Press, 1987), discusses a number of Green and post-industrial thinkers, notably André Gorz, who share elements of the associationalist agenda. On the history of associationalist ideas see David Nicholls, *The Pluralist State,* 2nd edn (London: Macmillan, 1995); Paul Hirst (ed.), *The Pluralist Theory of the State* (London: Routledge, 1989); and Darrow Schecter, *Radical Theories* (Manchester: Manchester University Press, 1995). On the history of voluntary welfare in Britain and its demise see Frank Prochaska, *The Voluntary Impulse* (London: Faber and Faber, 1998), and David C. Green, *Reinventing Civil Society – The Rediscovery of Welfare Without Politics* (London: IEA Health and Welfare Unit, 1993). Accounts of the basic income principle by economists of very different opinions are David Purdy, *Social Power and the Labour Market* (London: Macmillan, 1998, chs 9–11), and Milton Friedman 'The Case for the Negative Income Tax: a view from the right', in J. H. Bunzel (ed.), *Issues in American Public Policy* (Englewood Cliffs, NJ: Prentice-Hall, 1968). In *Life After Work: the arrival of an ageless society* (London: HarperCollins, 1991) Michael Young and Tom Schuller indicate the radical social transformations that are necessary in a society of mass longevity.

# PART II

# BRITISH SOCIAL POLICY IN THE 1990s

## Introduction

The chapters in this section examine recent developments in each of the major areas of the welfare state. While it is not the case that all areas of provision have been affected in identical fashion, clear 'common denominators' of change can be observed in the majority of cases. In particular the contributors to this section dwell on the marked trend towards the *fragmentation* of welfare state services – a trend that has taken a variety of forms.

In Chapter 6 Noel Whiteside discusses the implications of the abandonment of full employment as an overriding social, political and economic objective. In her view the shift towards labour market flexibility and the emergence of Hutton's 30–30–40 society has contributed to widespread insecurity, the implication being that the strains caused by this 'employment policy' lie at the root of a range of other social problems. Ailsa McKay continues in similar vein in Chapter 7, where she examines the shift away from the contribution-based income maintenance system in the wake of high unemployment progressively eroding the foundations of the Beveridge model. The increased incidence of means-tested benefits, as Conservative governments sought to tighten eligibility rules in the face of mounting costs, has, McKay believes, led to social fragmentation in the form of rising poverty as growing numbers of claimants fall into the 'poverty traps' that this approach to income maintenance inevitably creates. She suggests that a citizens' basic income could prove a fairer, more socially cohesive method of ensuring that individuals have access to sufficient income in conditions of 'jobless growth'.

High unemployment and increasingly tight income maintenance arrangements (which have increased the cost of housing) have all contributed to *social* fragmentation because they have accentuated the divisions amongst different social groups, highlighting in particular differences of class, race and gender. Other areas of the welfare state have clearly been affected by these processes as they have had to deal with the increasing demands being placed upon them. But these areas have also fallen victim to a rather different kind of fragmentation, being 'broken up' as service delivery systems are decentralised. The impact of these changes on education, health and personal social services are discussed in turn.

In Chapter 9 Stephen Ball examines the impact of educational reform following the 1988 and 1992 Education Acts, concentrating on the consequences of greater financial autonomy in schools and the effects of grant-maintained status as well as changes in further and higher education. Importantly, he notes the central paradox of welfare state reform: while the decentralisation of delivery systems has involved various forms of privatisation and 'marketisation', the central state has increased its powers of prescription and surveillance as well as retaining ultimate control of budgets. The chapters by Sarah Nettleton and Mary Langan (Chapters 8 and 10) which look at health and personal social services, bear testimony to this fact. Nettleton charts the extensive changes made to the NHS since 1987 in the wake of the 'new managerialism' and the creation of the internal market. She examines the impact of these changes by analysing a number of key themes that have come to dominate health debates. If aspects of the NHS reforms clearly have merits, one of the most contentious issues that Nettleton identifies concerns rationing and priority setting – questions that have also dominated the reorganisation of the personal social services. Langan discusses a wide variety of changes, ranging from child protection to community care, as the old centralised social service departments of the 1970s have been fractured and decentralised along quasi-market lines. She is in little doubt that considerations of cost-efficiency dominate those of meeting stated needs in the brave new world of the 'mixed economy of welfare'.

Finally in this section, Peter Malpass considers the extensive changes experienced by the housing sector during the 1980s and 1990s. Chapter 11 takes account of the effective elimination of local authority housing programmes and the Conservatives' privatisation of public housing – initiatives reflected in similar policies in the rented sector. Malpass also examines the impact of these significant changes, not least their social and economic costs, as the housing boom of the mid 1980s turned into the slump of the early 1990s – a time of rising rents and soaring repossessions.

Much has been said about fragmentation and change, but can we detect any continuities with the type of social provision delivered in the past? The answer is unquestionably 'yes'. Even far-reaching change builds on preceding ideas and assumptions, and even areas such as health and personal social services, which have plainly experienced radical reorganisation, contain elements of past practices. Medical treatment in the NHS remains free at the point of need, for example. The income maintenance system retains elements of its original Beveridgean principles, at least insofar as contributory benefits have a continued, if increasingly precarious, presence. State schooling, meanwhile, remains broadly 'comprehensive' despite the dilution of this collectivist ideal by the creation of a grant-maintained sector, city technology colleges and so on. Where housing is concerned, Malpass makes the point that policies to increase owner-occupation and residualise public housing were in place well before 1979, although he is careful to point out that the irreversible onslaught on public housing during the 1980s has placed housing policy firmly on Tory ground.

To end this short introduction where it began, there is one area in which there has been a total break with the past: employment policy. Successive governments, including the present Labour government, jettisoned the goal of full employment, thus abandoning the clearest *social and political* as well as economic objective to emerge from the Second World War.

# CHAPTER 6

# Employment Policy

NOEL WHITESIDE

For Britain, as for other European countries, the chief labour market problem in the 1990s has been unemployment, and most employment policies have focused on how this might be contained. In academic and political terms, labour markets and employment are commonly viewed as the remit of economic policy. Recent and current unemployment crises appear as a residual of a poorly functioning economy – where the production of goods and services is insufficiently competitive, high taxation discourages entrepreneurship, labour costs are too high and other market 'rigidities' prevent the production and sale of commodities at a commercially viable price. From this perspective, labour is a commodity much like any other, whose attractions for employers depend on its skills, mobility and the wage it commands.

This neglects aspects of labour that make its market different from, say, that for capital equipment or raw materials. Unemployed workers cannot be abandoned. The country 'pays' for high unemployment through higher social security expenditure and lower income tax receipts. Furthermore, when jobs are scarce, older workers (whose skills are assumed to be outdated) and those in less than perfect health tend to be more likely to be made redundant and to experience greater difficulty in finding new employment. This means that the labour market tends to bifurcate, marginalising older, sicker and less skilled workers. The poverty following persistent unemployment means that standards of living fall, mortgage repayments become forfeit – sometimes resulting in homelessness – placing a strain on marriages and on the children of such marriages, who tend to be underweight at birth, to suffer poorer health, to underperform at school. Areas of high unemployment, notably inner cities, suffer from higher crime rates (Hakim, 1982). While it is impossible to 'prove' that unemployment is the sole cause of all these ills, communities with high unemployment also suffer a variety of other social ills, which translate into higher social expenditure on the police, health and social services.

The real costs of unemployment are less obvious than they initially appear. Not all those who lose their jobs in a recession join the official count of 'the unemployed'. Since 1979 the economic activity rate of men over the age of fifty has dropped dramatically; those losing work are more likely to be seen as in early retirement or as suffering from long-term sickness (whose incidence has risen by a factor of five) (Lazco *et al.*, 1988). The classification 'social dependency' does not reflect some hard and fast social reality; all categories of claimant tend to expand during economic recession (Whiteside, 1988). Furthermore, labour-market restructuring has led to a rise in the number employed part-time or who have become self-employed. These categories can lose work through reduced hours without this being reflected in the unemployment count; together with those employed on short-term contracts, those in 'irregular' employment now comprise about one third of the workforce (Casey and Creigh, 1989).

It has thus become hard to determine a 'real' level of unemployment. Over thirty changes in the official counting method have been introduced since 1979, all but one of which reduced the official figure, but the spread of less formal employment makes it difficult to translate job loss into a specific head count of unemployed individuals. New systems of 'outsourcing' and sub-contracting – the advent of the flexible labour market – have encouraged the growth of less regular and less secure jobs, spreading job loss among a larger number of people during an economic downturn than is commonly supposed, without necessarily creating 'unemployment' as such. In all cases, however, both present claimants (however classified) and the less regularly employed are unable to provide for themselves or their dependants. Labour market problems over the last two decades have left a legacy of low or no savings, of inadequate contributions towards a retirement pension, and a persistently high social security budget that shows no sign of diminishing (Hills, 1997). Thanks to persistent unemployment, at the time of the 1997 general election around 4.5 million people of working age lived in households without work, over one million had not worked since they left school, and all were permanently reliant on state benefits (*The Independent*, 2 June 1997).

New Labour made employment policy a priority in its 1997 election campaign. In his first budget, Chancellor Gordon Brown introduced a 'windfall' tax on the privatised public utilities to fund a 'welfare to work' initiative, designed to secure jobs or training for all those unemployed for more than six months. Return to work is also central to projected social security reforms (as outlined by Frank Field, 1995; see also DSS, 1998), which seek to restore contributory insurance as the central pillar of a new, individualised system of benefit rights. If social dependency is to diminish, then participation in the world of waged work is essential – even for those categories (such as single parents) whose responsibilities, some argue, should exempt them from such obligations.

To help us evaluate the feasibility of this objective, this chapter examines recent employment policies and their impact. The first section sets the context by outlining recent labour market restructuring and its promotion. The analysis then focuses on manpower and training initiatives. Finally, labour market outcomes will be assessed and British policy will be viewed through European eyes. For it is the European context, where employment policy is central to social protection, that will prove the most significant forum for policy debate on these issues in the future.

## From Full Employment to Flexibility: The Changing Policy Context

During the 1980s, forms of employment underwent fundamental restructuring and the policy objective of full employment disappeared. Until the 1970s, economic and social policies reflected the assumption that the government should play a central role in managing both the economy and levels of employment. In reaction to the mass unemployment of the interwar period, postwar governments adjusted tax levels, interest rates, public expenditure and investment in order to regulate consumption, thereby sustaining the full deployment of national economic resources, including labour. State intervention in Britain, however, remained confined to the realm of macroeconomic policy. Unlike their counterparts in Germany and France, for example, British governments never introduced industrial and manpower policies or planning mechanisms to regulate the nature or direction of economic development. All political parties respected the voluntarist tradition of industrial relations, which allowed manning levels, working conditions and wage rates to be determined by free collective bargaining. Social policy issues were considered politically separate from these areas, even though private systems of welfare supplemented negotiated working agreements. This helps explain why a legal minimum wage, central to social protection in most continental countries, has yet to be introduced in Britain. Even so, state intervention in the labour market expanded by the 1970s, providing a legal right to redundancy pay, legal protection against unfair dismissal and outlawing discriminatory employment practices based on race or gender.

By the mid 1970s, however, the labour market was no longer as buoyant as it had been in earlier years. Inflation rates in excess of 20 per cent were corroding domestic savings and devaluing long-term investment, thus stimulating swingeing pay demands and rising industrial unrest, which in turn generated a series of generally unsuccessful attempts at voluntary and statutory systems of pay restraint. Attempts were made to correct widely perceived fundamental economic problems. Since the 1950s Britain's eco-

nomic growth had been slower than that of most other European countries –
a result variously attributed to low investment, unprofessional management,
appalling industrial relations, essential skill shortages, low productivity,
general uncompetitiveness and too much (or too little, depending on your
viewpoint) state intervention. Both Labour and Conservative administrations
tried to contain shopfloor militancy and to improve training and manpower
policies. Arguably, such initiatives delivered too little too late, as Britain's
performance continued to compare badly with the more regulated economies
of France, Germany and Sweden as well as the less regulated one of the
United States. The Conservative governments of the 1980s and 1990s were
convinced that Britain's problems stemmed from too much state regulation,
not too little – and proceeded to 'deregulate' the labour market to secure
improved performance.

Before turning our attention to this, we need to note major changes in the
international economic climate that helped justify and promote changing
attitudes towards firm structure, management and employment, and the
state's role in economic regulation. The postwar buoyancy of international
markets – and the stability of the US dollar – faltered during the 1970s;
growth rates for all developed countries proved less stable, and with the
development of competition from Far Eastern economies (initially Japan and
Singapore, later Korea and Taiwan) European and American dominance in
manufacturing production vanished. The floating of exchange rates and the
subsequent removal of exchange controls left international capital free to
roam the globe in search of the most profitable investment, generating a vast
market of financial transactions whose size dwarfed the national budgets of
even medium-sized nations. The stability of any currency is no longer judged
directly by the relevant countries' balance of payments situation or similar
criteria, but on a more amorphously defined market confidence, which is
easily damaged by the possibility of higher taxation and the rumours of higher
social expenditure.

Faced with greater market uncertainty, international conglomerates abandoned mass production of standardised goods, diversified their holdings and
decentralised managerial control. This restructuring involved 'outsourcing':
component supply, company services, marketing and sales were subcon-
tracted to independent agencies, a strategy that fostered competition and
shifted some risk away from the parent company, permitting it to switch the
location of product design and marketing, at will (Amin, 1994; Introduction).
In more uncertain world markets, firms and retailers preferred to delegate
authority to individual branch managers, whose performance was judged
against predetermined criteria and whose future in the company depended on
how well his or her profits compared with those of others in the same group.

Similar strategies have permeated service industries in Britain. Milk delivery firms now lease out the float and sell the milk to a self-employed driver, whose own income thus directly depends on the sales she or he makes – not on a negotiated salary. Many driving schools similarly lease both car and booking services to self-employed driving instructors, whose incomes now directly depend on the number of pupils taught, unsupported by a basic salary. Loss of custom forces the driver to quit, not the firm to go broke. Such restructuring is justified in terms of providing incentives, rewarding enterprise and hard work, but it offers no protection against recession or sickness, and no retirement pension in old age.

In this way the 'flexible' firm gave birth to the 'flexible' labour market. By the late 1970s, academic analysis focused on the emergence of 'secondary' labour markets, composed of the less skilled, women and ethnic minority workers, whose employment was intermittent and insecure in comparison with a firm's full-time employees, its 'core' workers. Segmentation theories explained the core–periphery division in various ways, attributing it to new forms of labour exploitation by firms whose profit margins were being squeezed in an increasingly uncertain economic climate, or to the rise of post-Fordist production methods, based not on mass production, but on coalitions of smaller firms that were less capable of maintaining full-time, permanent jobs (Rubery and Wilkinson, 1994; Introduction). Changing firm strategies and structures became central to the analysis of diversifying forms of employment: such changes were viewed as essential to competitive advantage and growth. Flexibility, both within firms and between firms, became the watchword for economic success. Firm strategy and human resource management, studied by university business schools, stressed the importance of individualising the relationship between employer and employed, of abolishing old systems of collective bargaining, of establishing work incentives through the creation of strategic performance indicators, of using short-term contracts to permit the evaluation of each employee's performance – in short, of professionalising employment relations and promoting responsiveness to business opportunity. Such developments were not universally welcomed. In the context of high unemployment and falling union or state protection, many analysts suggested they simply signified the return of old, exploitative types of labour management, not the development of new systems (Jessop *et al.*, 1991; Pollert, 1991; McLaughlin, 1994).

Certainly the Conservative governments of 1979–97 endorsed the free play of market forces and reinforced managerial authority, seeking to free business from the perceived constraints of state regulation. The commitment to secure full employment ceded precedence to the control of inflation and the restoration of business confidence as cornerstones of economic policy. State aid to industry (in the form of regional policies and public investment) ended; taxation was cut to reinforce work incentives. Workers were encouraged to 'price themselves into jobs', the ratio of benefits to wages fell and constraints that prevented wages from falling in line with market demand were removed. Corporatist institutions – which had involved representatives from both sides of industry in the policy making process, for example the National Economic Development Council – were scrapped. The early 1980s witnessed a series of measures designed to restore the rule of 'the market' in employment. Access to unemployment benefit became increasingly difficult; rates of benefit became attached to the cost of living, not average wages. In 1995 unemployment benefit was replaced by the Jobseekers' Allowance, which was only available for six months and conditional on the applicant 'actively seeking work'. In 1980 employment protection was confined to those who had held the same full-time job for more than two years. The right of trade unions to secure a closed shop (making union membership compulsory), to strike and to picket was progressively reduced. Trade unionism became identified as the 'enemy within', working against the restoration of market forces and Britain's economic prosperity; unions' struggle to protect workers' standards of living was held up as a major cause of high unemployment. The government systematically sought to eradicate national collective bargaining, notably in the public sector. Nationally negotiated wage rates were to be replaced by performance-related pay. In similar vein, there was an attack on wages councils, whose origins predated the First World War and which set minimum pay rates in low-wage industries. In the mid 1980s their coverage of the under-25 age group was removed, and they were finally abolished in 1993.

These changes were justified by the rationale of free market economics. Only by eliminating inflation, the Conservatives argued, could investment in British enterprise be encouraged and 'real' (as opposed to publicly funded) jobs sustained. Competition and free enterprise would secure efficient production and distribution of goods and services. State intervention was distorting market mechanisms and diverting the finance available for investment to fund state benefits, which were undermining incentives to seek work. The state should not foster social dependency in this way, but should remove impediments to wage flexibility and encourage labour mobility. Deprived of the cushion of state support, the unemployed would compete for work by offering their services at lower wages, thus reducing production costs and making the economy generally more competitive. Lower wages would create more jobs in the long run; high levels of youth unemployment in particular were attributable to the comparatively high marginal costs (and lower productivity) of new labour market entrants (policies to lower the cost of employing this group gained a high priority). Attempts to create jobs through higher public expenditure would require higher taxation and stimulate inflation. The non-accelerating inflation rate of unemployment (NAIRU) – the irreducible minimum level of joblessness – is determined by changing levels of market activity and is adversely affected by state intervention. Any attempt by government to reduce unemployment below NAIRU would drive up inflation, discourage investment and threaten to raise levels of unemployment to new heights in the longer run.

However logically attractive, the removal of state intervention in the labour market was not a feasible option. By the mid 1980s, average wages were not falling as neo liberal theory suggested they should. Instead, as noted above, the labour market was bifurcating. Average wage rates were stable – even rising – for those in full-time work; but some workers were being marginalised in poorly paid, insecure jobs, while the unemployed were becoming residualised, with the result that the rate of long-term unemployment (those out of work for twelve months or more) reached unprecedented heights in 1985–6. The government created several schemes to persuade employers to hire the unemployed, particularly the long-term unemployed, not only to remove a political embarrassment but also to drive down wages by making claimants compete for jobs. Many of these initiatives came under the euphemism of training (described in the following section). Others took the form of tax incentives and grants to employers and the unemployed, to foster their return to work. Job subsidies – for example the New Works scheme, introduced in 1986 for 18–20 year olds on less than £65 per week, and the Workstart pilot scheme, introduced in 1993 for the long-term unemployed – were offered to private employers to persuade them to hire the victims of recession.

On the employee's side, the Enterprise Allowance scheme offered financial assistance to the registered unemployed seeking to set up their own business. In 1993, subsidies became available to those long-term unemployed who accepted part-time work. Since 1995 the Job Finder grant has given £200 to every long-term unemployed worker who finds a job. Work Trials offer employers free unemployed labour for a three-week trial period, during which the new recruit continues to receive state benefit. Other initiatives include National Insurance Contribution (NIC) 'holidays' for employers taking on long-term claimants, and a plethora of schemes – Job Plan Seminars, Restart, Workwise, Job Review Workshops, Job Search Assistance, which regularly call in the unemployed for an interview, offer advice about job applications and generally seek to prevent the apathy, depression and torpor that are commonly associated with joblessness from undermining the claimant's search for work (Tonge, 1997).

The Blair government's welfare to work programme will largely build on these existing initiatives (Toynbee, *The Independent*, 30 June, 1997). Labour's 'New Deal' will give four options to those aged 18–24 who have been out of work for more than six months: a subsidised job with a private firm, voluntary work, work with an environmental task force or full-time education. Higher subsidies will be available to employers taking on those of any age who have been unemployed for two years. Refusal of a placement will result in loss of state benefits. The cooperation of private employers will be central to the success of Labour's strategy, but here the omens are not good. First, a similar programme launched in Australia in 1995, the Job Compact, was abandoned because employers found the public subsidies insufficient compensation for the problem of coping with unskilled, unmotivated people forced on them by the public service, and many left the scheme as a result (*The Economist*, 28 June, 1997). Second, Labour's programme is being introduced during an economic upturn. With unemployment falling and demand relatively buoyant, employers will be willing to take on extra hands – especially subsidised ones. But when economic conditions change, as they inevitably will, the scheme may find itself with rising numbers of participants but falling employer interest and dwindling revenues. The windfall tax is a one-off exercise to fund the welfare-to-work programme. Thereafter the scheme is expected to pay for itself, as rising numbers of claimants are transformed into tax-paying workers. However when economic recovery falters, larger numbers will be pushed back onto environmental projects – necessarily involving more public expenditure. Such an outcome will test New Labour's resolve.

However the Blair government has no intention of restoring the old, regulated labour market: more flexible employment is interpreted as one of Margaret Thatcher's more positive achievements, and in this at least the Labour prime minister is her torchbearer. Blair has been an outspoken advocate of labour market flexibility as the means to cure the employment sclerosis afflicting the European Union: a policy received with sceptical interest by some European politicians, but regarded with hostility by European workers and electorates, who are liable to be affected by the privatisation and deregulation required to further such a strategy. In many European countries, social protection is directly attached to the employment contract and is safeguarded by law. Unemployment, particularly among school leavers, translates into social exclusion – no right to a pension, health care or unemployment benefits. Preferred strategies to combat social exclusion have varied widely, involving employer subsidies, publicly funded works projects, collective programmes for early retirement or reduced working hours (without loss of pay) – all of which seek to solve the problem through collective solutions without undermining existing structures of social protection. Violent strikes greeted the French government's attempt to restructure public sector employment in 1995–6; its programme of public expenditure cuts resulted in the defeat of the Gaullist administration in the election of June 1997 and the return of a socialist government committed to conventional systems of job protection and publicly funded programmes of job creation.

The close relationship between work, wages and welfare rights in the European Union is reflected in the Maastricht Treaty's Social Chapter, which John Major's government refused to sign (on the ground that any official regulation threatened jobs) but which the Labour government supports. By introducing a minimum wage, which forms a common theme in European labour law outside Britain, the Blair government will move Britain more towards the heart of European practice. Possibly this will make Blair's message about flexibility and its advantages more palatable, but only if those in irregular employment are endowed with more social rights than they possess at present.

## Training and Manpower Policies

Employment policy is not solely a matter of job subsidies, labour mobility and the restructuring of work. It also involves workers being trained in the skills and aptitudes required for economic growth. Here British manpower policies have long been very weak. In Germany, Scandinavia and France the state (local and national) has worked closely with both sides of industry in the process of skill formation – or 'investment in human capital' as education and training is sometimes called. In Britain the greater part of public investment in training has traditionally gone to the university sector, to professional training, while training in technical and manual skills has been neglected. Traditionally, British training has taken place 'on the job', through systems of apprenticeship and direct work experience. This instils the skills that are required immediately, but does not promote an understanding of state-of-the-art technologies, nor does it help firms to develop new production systems. Moreover, when profits are squeezed and workers are laid off, apprenticeship schemes are commonly suspended, impeding the inflow of skilled young workers needed for recovery. When business picks up, firms either import skilled labour from overseas or poach trained manpower from other employers with the promise of better pay and conditions – driving up wages in the process. Hence unemployment can be viewed as a problem of mismatch: vacancies exist for specialisms and skills that the unemployed do not possess, but could acquire with more state investment in training.

Sporadic attempts have been made by central government over the last century or more to correct the deficiencies in British industrial training.

These efforts were renewed in the 1960s through the Industrial Training Boards (ITBs) and in the 1970s, following the creation of the Manpower Services Commission in 1973; however the impact of government policy on real skill shortages remained minimal. The Manpower Services Commission swiftly found its manpower strategy swamped by the surge in unemployment in the mid 1970s. From that point, political objectives switched from promoting economic performance by raising general levels of skill to trying to get the unemployed – particularly school leavers – any foothold on the labour market at all. The purpose of job training became inextricably entangled with the instillation of work discipline, and with alleviating public irritation at the prospect of the unemployed claiming benefits indefinitely and not having to do any work at all. Hence the terms 'training' and 'work experience' have become indistinguishable as a variety of programmes with a myriad of titles have been introduced for the unemployed, particularly the young unemployed, over the last twenty years.

Throughout the last decade the idea of compulsory 'work-fare' (as the Americans call the system of working for welfare benefits) has come up for regular discussion. Arguably, Labour's welfare to work initiative contains elements of work-fare; claiming benefit while remaining idle will no longer be an option for its target groups. The main arguments against such a strategy stem less from compassion for the unemployed than from the expense – and the complications – consequent on such a policy. First, there is the problem of substitution: if one private employer hires a number of state-subsidised young workers, his or her wage costs will be lower than that of the competitor who employs none. There is a consequent risk that the firm using 'scheme' labour will drive others out of business, thereby creating more unemployment. Second, if governments try to avoid this by placing workers in commercially unviable projects (with voluntary agencies, or on environmental projects), then it will fail to train workers for 'real' jobs in the 'real' economy, thereby prolonging their dependence on the state. Finally, there is the question of cost, for it is cheaper (and easier) to keep unemployed school leavers on benefit than to place them in training or jobs. To date, compulsory work experience and training have been more or less confined to the under-25s. New Labour promises to extend this to all long-term claimants, which may well revive the arguments against the viability of such strategies with the launch of welfare to work in April 1998.

Even so, from 1987 16–18 year olds were excluded from claiming state benefits (unless under emergency regulations) and required to undertake training, whose content and value were dubious as the then Conservative government remained unwilling to invest in training programmes. When unemployment began to fall in 1988, the Manpower Services Commission was abolished and the Employment Department briefly took over responsibility for the main training schemes then in operation (Youth Training and Employment Training being the largest), setting up 82 local training and enterprise councils (TECs), voluntary bodies run by local employers that still implement training packages and supervise work placements (Farnham and Lupton, 1994). Central funding of training was cut the following year (and never restored, even during the recession of the early 1990s), effectively placing the privatisation of training in the hands of local employers and restoring a neoliberal, voluntary policy to replace state direction in this field (King, 1993; 1997). Devoid of resources and reliant on voluntary goodwill, the content of TEC-based training schemes varied widely from place to place. During the recession of the early 1990s, official claims that training places were available for all unemployed 16–18 year olds were no longer true; a large number of school leavers remained reliant on their families or, when their families refused to take responsibility, wandered the streets, begging for a living. In 1995 the Department of Employment was merged into the current Department for Education and Employment and all pretence of centrally directed training and manpower policies disappeared, at least until the election of New Labour in 1997.

In the 1990s, there have been sporadic attempts to countermand the academic bias in Britain's education system and to raise the status of vocational qualifications. Under the Technical and Vocational Education Initiative (TVEI) in the mid 1980s, technical training was introduced into the secondary school curriculum. This initiative was supplemented by the promise of 20 city technology colleges; however these were to be funded by industry – not the Treasury – and so deprived of resources, they never flourished. Perhaps more significantly, the spread of work skills under the OND and Higher National Diploma programmes, run by further education colleges and some of the new universities, has fostered education qualifications that are more directly related to employment. However, this search for equity has had partial results. While OND and HND have spread successfully in service sectors such as health and social care, art and design, entertainment and leisure, they have had far less impact on manufacturing, where Britain's economic performance has been particularly weak. Britain possesses no equivalent to the German or French systems of vocational qualifications, which offer access to specific trades and skills. Furthermore, although the bias is changing, larger employers still look at GCSE, A-level and graduation results when seeking new recruits. The value and status of new and different qualifications permeate the consciousness of personnel departments at a snail's pace. This means that alternative qualifications such as certificated completion of a training scheme or NVQs hold little status or meaning in recruitment terms.

At the lowest rung on the training ladder, the Training and Enterprise Councils rely on fees from the Treasury (and the cooperation of the local business community) for each client placed; however with few resources and not many qualified instructors, they have no means of monitoring the training they offer. In 1994 less than 50 per cent of young people completing Work Based Training (which replaced the Youth Training programme) had found work six months after finishing their course (*Hansard*, PQ, 7 July 1995). The Restart programme for long-term claimants, introduced in 1987, did facilitate entry to work or training (White and Lakey, 1992), but mostly to temporary jobs, which meant that clients were eventually liable to find themselves back on benefit. Commentators are divided in their views on the impact of state training on unemployment. Some argue that, by reinforcing time discipline, self-belief and competitiveness among the un-employed, government programmes have had a salutary effect in raising aggregate demand for labour. They see feasible demand for labour as limited by feasible supply: by stimulating the supply of employable individuals the government increases the demand for their services (Layard *et al.*, 1991). In such a perspective, Restart and similar programmes had a positive effect on reducing the unemployment level during the expansion of the late 1980s. It is, however, difficult to determine how much credit should go to the economic upturn of those years in producing that effect. Some government schemes have had less than impressive results: in 1989, in a period of expansion, 42 per cent of employment training participants returned to unemployment on completion of their course. The exclusive focus on labour supply, which has dominated state policy in recent years, cannot be the only solution: some attention has to be paid to the nature of demand. Government trainees rarely enter full-time, secure employment; those gaining a foothold in temporary work seldom find a permanent job. Government training to date appears to be more associated with work-fare systems (King, 1995) than with endowing the unemployed with any real, marketable skills.

Labour's welfare to work package promises to change all that. The £3 billion raised by the windfall tax offers the resources to provide proper training for the young and the long-term unemployed. Government funding, however, will only cover six months and we might question the amount of training that could be achieved in so short a time. The project appears to be better suited to returners to the labour market – single mothers, for example, whose return to work the Blair government wants to encourage – than to the 250 000 young unemployed who have never worked and whose joblessness is attributable to more deep-seated problems – illiteracy, innumeracy, mental difficulties, drug addiction, criminal records. Nonetheless, when placed in the wider context of tightening standards in schools and broadening access to higher education, Blair's promise to end the culture of dependency rests fundamentally on improvements in training and employability. Whether this continuing stress on the supply side alone will generate the employment opportunities necessary to achieve this goal, however, remains an open question.

## Conclusions: Evaluating the Flexible Labour Market

Thanks to the relative absence of institutional or other constraints on the British executive, Conservative governments were able to proceed further and faster with deregulating the labour market than in any other European nation. In other EU countries, legal and constitutional obligations limit policy options. Labour representation at all levels of policy making and its implementation is strongly defended – not least by trade unions and left-wing parties – and is reinforced under the Maastricht Social Chapter. In Britain, where consultative processes have rested on voluntarist foundations, the opposition of organised labour could be undermined without threatening the whole basis of constitutional government. Most European labour markets remain subject to greater regulation; employment policies form a central component of social protection and welfare. Any extension of less conventional forms of employment would necessarily entail the extension of social rights to those at present excluded – part-time and contract workers, of whom there are generally far fewer than in Britain – as well as provision of work to the unemployed. A new marriage of an efficient labour market and universal protection has yet to be established; the British experiment, for many Europeans, offers the prospect of insecurity and instability for very little return.

Has deregulation cured the problems of the British labour market – and do past policies and present proposals point the way forward for the future? Within the European context, as advocates of deregulation point out, Britain has secured competitive advantage, partly because English is the international language of business, but also because manufacturing overheads are low – the product of lower corporation and payroll taxes, of tight controls over public expenditure and minimal levels of welfare. Unlike in other European countries, where an employment contract stipulating working hours, wage rates, welfare protection and so on is underwritten by the state, Britain has increasingly reinforced employers' control over employment. The advantages are seen in rising productivity, stable inflation and higher rates of inward investment than anywhere else in Europe. Flexible labour markets permit firms to respond to opportunities in today's competitive markets. Part-time jobs have allowed women, particularly women with child-care obligations, to return to work; few such workers want a full-time job, and in this respect the spread of part-time employment has promoted new opportunities.

Recent developments have, however, been heavily criticised. Rising productivity is less the consequence of investment in new capital equipment than extensive 'downsizing' – particularly in the newly privatised utilities – where lay-offs have spelt an increased workload for some and redundancy for others. In his book *The State We're In* (1996), Will Hutton describes the consequences of deregulation for rising social inequality and job insecurity. In his 30–30–40 society, one third remain stuck on state benefits, and the second third struggle in casualised, insecure and low-paid jobs. Neither of these groups can contribute to the future of themselves or their dependants; those in part-time or temporary work and most of the growing numbers of self-employed do not have any form of social protection and less than 10 per cent of those employed in this sector of the casualised labour market manages to move into secure employment. The top 40 per cent of employees – those in full-time work, the self-employed who have survived for more than two years, part-time workers in the same job for five years – form a privileged elite. These are the winners of the Conservative tax cuts, who retain full social protection in both private and public forms. Hutton estimates that 50 per cent of the population live in poverty and/or insecurity, and that the resulting stress produces broken marriages, poor parenting and thus (indirectly) the delinquency, vandalism and problem children whose numbers have risen in recent years. This explains the proliferation of unmarriageable men and the rocketing social security budget - both of which are consequences of labour market deregulation and the employment policies that helped secure it.

From this perspective the labour market reemerges as the source of most other social problems, which makes the need for an effective employment policy all the more urgent. As the economies of the EU countries become increasingly enmeshed, and as the remit of social policy within the EU is rooted in labour market regulation under the Social Chapter, so the solution to Britain's difficulties must be found within a broader European context. Economic and social goals cannot be divorced; any solutions to our employment problems have to be rooted in a common European consensus. Future historians may view the Thatcher – Major years as a political aberration in the renewed struggle by governments to bring labour market efficiency into line with social welfare for all.

## Further Reading

H. Compston (ed.), *The New Politics of Unemployment* (London: Routledge, 1997), provides a country by country guide to the dimensions of the unemployment crisis in the European Union and the policy initiatives to counteract it. F. Field, L. Halligan and M. Owen, *Europe Isn't Working* (London: ICS, 1994), offers a more general – and more politically slanted – critique. Both books advocate more extensive state action. D. J. Snower and G. de la Dehesa, *Unemployment Policy: Government Options for the Labour Market* (London: CEPR, 1997), offers the opposite conclusion (for the economically literate only!)

For Britain, M. White (ed.), *Unemployment, Public Policy and Changing Labour Markets* (London: PSI, 1994), offers an excellent overview. (See also M. White, *Against Unemployment* (London: PSI, 1991), the flexibility debate is discussed in B. Jessop *et al.* (eds), *The Politics of Flexibility* (Aldershot: Edward Elgar, 1991) and A. Pollert, *Farewell to Flexibility* (Oxford: Oxford University Press, 1991) J. Rubery and F. Wilkinson (eds), *Employer Strategy and Labour Markets* (Oxford: Oxford University Press, 1994), provide a carefully researched assessment of the impact of labour market restructuring. For the late 1980s, before the most recent recession, D. King, 'The Conservatives and Training Policy, 1979–92', *Political Studies*, vol. 51, no. 2 (1993), analyses ideological changes underpinning the last government's policy initiatives. The PSI has published a number of useful policy evaluations (for example M. White and J. Lakey, *The Restart Effect* (London: PSI, 1992), Frank Field, *Making Welfare Work: Reconstructing Welfare for the Millennium* (London: Institute of Community Studies, 1995), gives a broad rationale for New Labour's new employment policy. See also DSS, *A New Contract for Welfare* (London: HMSO, 1998), and D. King, 'Employers, Training Policy and the Tenacity of Voluntarism in Britain', *Twentieth Century British History*, vol. 8, no. 3 (1997), 383–411.

# CHAPTER 7

# Social Security Policy

AILSA McKAY

Income transfer programmes are a fundamental component of the welfare state in most, if not all, advanced Western societies. We know this from the proportion of government budgets devoted to such programmes; from their primary role in the establishment and subsequent development of the welfare state; and from the universal impact that social security and taxation have on the economic well-being of families and individuals (Mitchell, 1991, p. 1).

Why are income transfer programmes deemed necessary? What is the function of state supported income maintenance programmes and how do these programmes interact with other areas of state welfare provision? What types of programme can modern welfare states continue to sustain financially, given the changing nature of the economy and in particular the structure of contemporary labour markets? Is there continued political will to support the public provision of income maintenance, and if so should programmes be universal or selective? Have the problems that programmes are designed to address been adequately identified? These are the main issues faced by policy makers with regard to income maintenance.

When assessing the effectiveness of policy, questions of economic efficiency, administrative feasibility and political acceptability must be addressed, alongside issues centring on citizenship rights, gender equality and social justice. Income maintenance policy must therefore be analysed within a framework that takes account of its function in the overall performance of modern welfare states. The main aims of this chapter are to provide an overview of contemporary income maintenance policy in Britain, focusing on the tension between the principles of 'universality' and 'selectivity', which has plagued debates on future policy direction; and to introduce the basic citizens' income model, a reform proposal that requires a radical rethinking of the purpose, nature and structure of income transfers in modern welfare states.

## Defining Income Maintenance Policy

Income maintenance policy in Britain encompasses a whole range of measures. Cash benefits and tax allowances are direct income transfer mechanisms. Government activity in the housing market, the public provision of free or highly subsidised health care and education, and government policy in the field of employment all indirectly impact on individual incomes. In addition various forms of private insurance exist alongside public provision, and the importance of these schemes in supporting the state system has been emphasised in recent years. The subject matter of this chapter is the operation of cash transfer mechanisms that are financed and delivered directly by the state, therefore the focus will be on cash benefits and tax allowances. The term income maintenance policy will be used for the remainder of the chapter to refer to this narrower area.

Within Britain the terms 'income maintenance' and 'social security' are often used synonomously to refer to the area of state welfare provision that involves direct cash transfer payments. The rationale for state-supported income transfer payments covers a range of objectives that can be categorised under four main headings, as follows.

## Poor relief

State-supported income maintenance provides people with financial assistance in times of need and therefore is often directly associated with the social problem of poverty (see for example Alcock, 1987; Brown and Payne, 1994, ch. 2; Atkinson, 1989; A. Deacon, 1995; Spicker, 1993). However cash transfer mechanisms can also be employed to enable individuals to spread their income over the lifecycle and to insure against financially risky situations such as unemployment or ill-health. The actual design of policy will determine whether the intention is to relieve poverty, defined in its narrowest sense as being without an income, or to prevent poverty by influencing consumption behaviour.

## Reductions in inequality

Both cash benefits and tax reliefs or allowances have redistributive effects and therefore it is possible to associate such policy with the goal of equality, or rather with the goal of reducing income *inequality* (Barr and Coulter, 1990, pp. 274–5; Mitchell, 1991, p. 11).

## Promoting social solidarity

Beneficiaries of cash benefits may not be poor, and likewise all of those who contribute to the funding of those benefits may not be rich. State provision of benefits to the elderly and those with young families acknowledge the fact that various stages in the lifecycle are more financially demanding than others. This example of policies aimed at preventing poverty and promoting economic security also reflects the 'way in which social security systems enforce solidarity between generations' (Spicker, 1993, p. 106). Child Benefit in Britain, which is tax-funded, exemplifies this notion of solidarity in that working people without children contribute to a scheme that provides guaranteed financial support, regardless of other means, to families.

## Supporting the market economy

The design and delivery of income maintenance measures can play a crucial role in supporting and thus preserving the political and economic structures associated with advanced capitalism (see for example Hill, 1990 p. 3; Piven and Cloward, 1993; Dean, 1991). Linking income maintenance policy with particular patterns of behaviour assumes a set of social relations compatible with market-based economies and industrial progress. Policies that emphasise labour market participation and encourage or even reinforce particular family structures typify the function of social security in producing behaviour that conforms to 'dominant norms' (Spicker, 1993, p. 106).

A final point to note when discussing the objectives of income maintenance policy is that income transfers do not operate in isolation but rather interrelate with other areas of government policy. For example methods of financing will influence the government's fiscal stance, levels of benefit will influence patterns of consumer spending, and both the type and the level of support may influence the incentive to work and save. The transfer of incomes within groups is the main source of finance for modern state welfare provision and has come to play an increasingly important role in economic and social policy. The social security budget, the government's largest expenditure programme, will represent around 30 per cent of planned public expenditure for 1997/98. For 1996/97 spending was estimated to total £96.7 billion; a real increase of eight times the original amount in 1949–50 (the first full year of operation of the postwar Beveridge scheme) and twice the rate of growth in the economy as a whole (Department of Social Security, 1997, pp. 9, 11). This growth, particularly from 1978/79, has been attributed to demographic and social factors, economic performance and political policy commitments (Department of Social Security, 1993a, p. 9). Income maintenance policy should be therefore be analysed in terms of its impact on the structure of the economy as a whole.

## Approaches to Income Maintenance

In order to make sense of the British income maintenance programme it is essential that each type of benefit is understood in terms of its justification and claiming principle, which in turn will determine the method of delivery and financing arrangements. Four approaches have been identified that form the basis of direct income transfers within modern welfare states:

- Contributory benefits.
- Means-tested benefits.
- Universal or non-contributory contingency-based benefits.
- Tax relief or allowances.

The first three approaches are associated with the award of cash benefits. Tax advantages such as specific tax relief or personal tax allowances are implicit transfers in that they do not involve an actual cash payment but rather a reduction in tax liability (Barr, 1993 p. 170). In Britain the proportion of public money allocated to these implicit transfers does not appear in the government's official figures on public spending unlike cash benefits. As with all tax expenditure, they are viewed as negative revenue due to the reduction they make in income tax receipts and are therefore an 'invisible item in government accounts' (ibid., p. 182). However this is not an indication that tax relief is an 'invisible' element of income maintenance policy.

Tax relief and allowances play a crucial role in the operation of income maintenance policy in Britain in two particular ways. The tax system is used to promote various forms of saving with the intention of reducing overall government spending in the future. Tax relief is applied to interest payments on mortgages and contributions to 'tax approved' pension plans. Income tax allowances, on the other hand, effectively complement cash benefits designed to provide financial assistance to those on low incomes. The late 1980s and early 1990s witnessed major changes to the structure of income tax in Britain. The basic rate was reduced to 23 per cent, with a lower rate of 20 per cent applicable to the first £4100 of taxable income (announced in the November 1996 budget), and the rate for high-income groups was substantially reduced from 60 per cent to 40 per cent in 1988. These reductions were accompanied by an overall shift in the tax burden from direct income tax to other taxes, both direct and indirect. The most notable, with regard to their effect on those living on low or fixed incomes, were as follows:

- Value Added Tax (VAT) – the main rate increased from 15 per cent to 17.5 percent in 1991 and the VAT base was extended to include domestic fuel from 1994.

● National Insurance contributions increased from 9 per cent to 10 per cent from 1994.

Considering these changes in relation to the adequacy and generosity of benefits involves examining how the tax and benefit system interact in such a way as to impact on individual decisions about entering the labour force.

Incomes in and out of work are primarily determined by the structure of taxes and benefits. Individuals on the margins of social security and income tax will experience high marginal tax rates, that is, the proportion of increased gross income that is lost through a combination of benefit withdrawal, increased income tax liability and National Insurance Contribution deductions. In 1994/95 over 700 000 individuals in Britain were faced with marginal tax rates in excess of 70 per cent (Department of Social Security, 1997, fig. 34, p. 57). High rates of benefit withdrawal combined with low wages and low tax thresholds effectively trap people in a situation of welfare dependency. The poverty and associated unemployment traps are inevitable consequences of a system that is heavily reliant on means-tested benefits and a tax structure that is skewed in favour of higher earners.

All three approaches to explicit transfers, that is, cash benefits funded and provided by the state, are employed in the British social security programme. Table 7.1 provides a framework of the principles, entitlement basis and purpose of benefit for the three approaches, identifying current British examples.

**Table 7.1 A typology of approaches to income maintenance policy**

| Principle | Benefit basis | Purpose of benefit |
| --- | --- | --- |
| Contributory | Social insurance | To compensate for lost earnings, e.g. Job Seekers Allowance (JSA) – contributory |
| Individual need | Means-testing or social assistance | Specifically to relieve poverty and provide a safety net of provision through which no individual should fall, e.g. Income Support (IS) |
| Universal citizenship rights | Categorical, conditional or unconditional benefits | To promote common citizenship by helping to meet additional costs faced by specific categories of people, e.g. universal Child Benefit (CB) |

## Social insurance: contributory

Social insurance is based on the principle that benefits are a form of return on contributions made whilst in paid work. Individuals insure themselves against loss of income by contributing to a state-supported insurance fund. The basis of entitlement is past contribution records, that is, evidence of paid social security contributions by both employee and employer. The purpose of social insurance is to provide social protection and economic stability to individuals whose capacity to earn is temporarily or permanently removed. The main contributory benefits in Britain include the Job Seeker's Allowance (*contribution-based*), the state retirement pension and various sickness-related benefits. These benefits are categorised as 'earnings replacement benefits' and are financed through the National Insurance Fund.

The main advantages of social insurance schemes are that they incorporate the notion of a right to benefits and that in theory they can be designed to ensure they are largely self-financing. However social insurance is limited in its ability to provide social protection for all citizens. The eligibility criteria include a past contribution record and thus previous work experience. This effectively excludes a large number of individuals who may require social protection but fail to meet the qualifying conditions, for example young single mothers with limited work histories or earnings below the contribution threshold (Spicker, 1993, p. 137). Consequently this approach to income maintenance policy demonstrates the principle of universality only when the contribution condition is satisfied, and does not aid those individuals who have never had an income to lose or never will have an income from which to make sufficient contributions. National insurance is 'essentially an approach geared to the average needs of the working population as society interprets these at any given time' (Brown and Payne, 1994, p. 23). The decision to adopt and implement a social insurance policy may therefore be influenced by policy makers' opinions on the structure of society and their interpretation of 'need'.

## Means testing: social assistance

Means-tested benefits often exist alongside social insurance programmes and serve to fill the gaps in coverage. Benefits are conditional in that they are awarded on the basis of a test of existing income or capital. Entitlement criteria require individuals to be categorised as poor or in need of assistance, and therefore means-tested benefits are associated with the principle of targeting resources. Means-tested and non-contributory benefits in Britain are financed from the Consolidated Fund (general taxation), which currently covers over 50 per cent of the total expenditure on social security (Department of Social Security, 1997, p. 6). The principle means-tested benefits are the Job Seeker's Allowance (*income-based*), Housing Benefit, Council Tax Benefit and Family Credit.

Social assistance or means-tested benefits represent a 'safety-net' of income through which, theoretically, no one should fall. However 'in 1992, there were a total of 4,740,000 people (including children) living below the income support level. . . One of the principle reasons that people are living below the income support level is that they are not taking up means-tested benefits to which they are entitled' (Oppenheim and Harker, 1996, pp. 30–2). Low take-up rates are an inherent feature of means testing. Targeting benefits involves categorising and therefore stigmatising people as poor. Furthermore any system of aid that is subject to a test of existing economic resources requires investigation into individual circumstances in order to determine eligibility. Such intrusion serves to weaken the notion of the right to benefits and necessitates complex administrative procedures. In turn this can serve to deter people from claiming.

Additionally, depending upon the nature of the system and the specific rules governing receipt, the distinction between actual resources and access to resources can become blurred. Problems arise regarding the classification of diverse individual circumstances and the dynamics of social living. Government departments assigned the task of carrying out the means test can interpret the rules at their discretion, which inevitably results in unequal treatment. Means testing can therefore be criticised in terms of its ability to relieve poverty, reduce inequality and promote social cohesion. The minimum income guarantee is not a right within such a system in that it 'is not based on either past contribution or universal entitlement, but on political discretion' (Rainwater *et al.*, 1986, p. 131).

## Universal: categorical, conditional or unconditional

The third principle behind state-supported cash benefits is the notion of universal citizenship rights. A programme of universal benefits would involve the granting of benefit to every resident of the country, financed from general taxation. The link between contribution and receipt would be indirect in that although citizens would contribute to the programme through their individual tax payments, the payment of taxes would not be a condition of entitlement and there would be no barrier to entitlement for non-taxpayers.

Certain benefits within the British system illustrate a degree of universality in that they are paid to all members of a particular demographic category or to those meeting predefined disability criteria. Examples include Child Benefit, Attendance Allowance for people over the age of 65 and the mobility component of the Disability Living Allowance. Benefits available to severely disabled people are a form of selective universalism. The qualifying criteria are determined by perceptions of the needs associated with varying degrees of disability, and entitlement is not automatic but must be supported by medical evidence of the disability. Conseqently, as with means-tested benefits, there is scope for discretion and benefits may not actually reach all those in the targeted group. Where ill-health is concerned, individual circumstances are diverse and fluid therefore delivery becomes complex and this affects take-up rates.

The closest approximation to a universal system of social security is Child Benefit, introduced in 1976 to replace the Family Allowance and income tax allowances for children. As a universal benefit it enjoys widespread public support, high take-up rates, ease of administration in that the target group is readily identifiable and remains stable over a long period of time, and there are no disincentive effects. However universal cash benefits financed from general taxation are costly and as the primary redistributive effects are horizontal – that is, they redistribute income from those without children to those who have – rather than vertical, which would involve redistribution to families with lower incomes, they do not directly address the problem of income inequality. It was for these reasons that Child Benefit came under scrutiny in the 1980s. Attempts to introduce means testing were thwarted, mainly due to the 'strong support for Child Benefit from the powerful Conservative Women's lobby and many MPs on both sides of the Party' (Lister, 1989, p. 207). Instead the real value of the benefit was eroded when it was frozen at the 1988 rate and the emphasis on child support was switched to the new means-tested benefit for working families: Family Credit. The operation of this benefit alongside Housing Benefit compounded the problem of the poverty trap. Child Benefit was, however, uprated in the first post-Thatcher administration and it remains intact, increased on an annual basis in line with inflation.

Although the British social security system draws upon all three methods of direct cash transfer together with tax allowances and relief, in recent decades means testing has become more central to the system in an attempt to target benefits more efficiently and ultimately reduce costs. However expenditure on social security is largely demand-led, which makes overall control of the spending level difficult. A summary of the main changes to the design of the British system will illustrate that measures to constrain expenditure have continually taken precedence over reforming the system in line with current circumstances.

## The Design of the British System

The British social security programme currently comprises over thirty separate cash benefits, covering a wide range of circumstances. Overall responsibility for the development and monitoring of the system rests with the Department of Social Security (DSS). Responsibility for the implementation, delivery and administration of benefits is devolved to the DSS's five executive agencies, launched in the late 1980s and early 1990s as part of an overall strategy to improve service delivery by establishing clearly defined areas of responsibility and accountability. A number of other organisations are involved with the administration and payment of certain benefits, for example employers are responsible for the delivery of statutory sick pay and local authorities or district councils deal with Housing Benefit and Council Tax Benefit. Administration procedures can vary enormously, the rules for assessing entitlement are complicated and, in the case of discretionary benefits, are open to misinterpretation.

From at least the mid-1980s attempts to cut costs and make greater use of selective targeting have served to undermine the contributory principle within the British system. Recent changes to the main contributory benefits include the following:

- On 7 October 1996 the Job Seeker's Allowance replaced Unemployment Benefit and Income Support for those required to look for work.
- In April 1995 the state Sickness and Invalidity Benefits were relaced by Incapacity Benefit.

For both new benefits the eligibility criteria are more stringent than those for the previous systems. The Job Seeker's Allowance requires claimants to draw up a 'jobseeker's agreement', in cooperation with the benefit office, which clearly defines the steps they are willing to take to secure employment. Furthermore the contributory element of this benefit is only valid for six months – thereafter claimants are subject to a means test. The main intention of the new system is to reinforce the pre-condition for entitlement, that is, an active search for work on the part of the claimant, and to target the available resources at those identified as being most in need by introducing a means test after six months, rather than the 12 months that prevailed before. Even if a claimant is officially entitled to the Job Seeker's Allowance it may not be paid due to the imposition of a 'sanction': benefit can be suspended if a claimant fails to carry out the tasks detailed in the jobseeker's agreement or is deemed to be voluntarily unemployed, either because of dismissal due to misconduct or for leaving a job without good cause. The practice of 'sanctioning' is harsher than the previous voluntary unemployment deduction rules in that no benefit at all is paid for periods of up to 26 weeks.

The new Incapacity Benefit requires claimants to submit to a medical test to prove their incapacity for work. Individuals unfit for work continue to receive statutory sick pay from their employer for the first 28 weeks, thereafter those who have a sufficient contribution record are eligible to claim Incapacity Benefit. Those not entitled to statutory sick pay are eligible to claim Incapacity Benefit at a lower rate from the beginning of their period of incapacity. Two medical tests are involved:

- The 'own occupation' test assesses a claimant's ability to carry out the duties associated with the occupation in which she/he is, or was, engaged and must be undergone by those claiming sick pay, or those deemed to have a 'regular occupation, for the first 28 weeks of claim'.
- The 'all work' test assesses a claimant's ability to perform certain physical and mental functions without any reference to her or his most recent or previous occupation(s) and must be undergone by those who are not entitled to sick pay and have no 'regular' occupation, as well as all claimants after 28 weeks.

These recent reforms clearly indicate that a more punitive system is being favoured over the rights-based element of contributory benefits. Other developments contributing to the weakening of the insurance principle include more limited coverage and reduction of the level of benefits. From April 1988 benefits for 16 and 17 year olds and most full-time students were abolished. Only those demonstrating exceptional hardship were eligible for limited assistance. Their limited access to the labour market effectively rendered young people ineligible for insurance-based benefits, but the new legislation meant that even full-time students with sufficient contribution records witnessed the removal of their right to benefits altogether. From 1980 benefits were uprated in line with inflation, rather than earnings, and in 1982 the earnings-related additions to short-term contributory benefits were abolished. In the case of long-term incapacity benefit, earnings-related supplements have been abolished for all new claims and frozen at the 1994/95 rate for existing claims. In combination, these developments have effectively eroded the real value of benefits.

Expenditure concerns have also affected pension provision. Measures were taken in the late 1980s to encourage the growth of private pensions, which primarily involved giving rebates on National Insurance contributions to those opting out of the State Earnings Related Pension Scheme (SERPS) and the granting of tax relief on approved private schemes. This has had the effect of gradually shifting the overall burden for pensions from the public to the private sector. As a result many pensioners have surrendered their right to a guaranteed income and as a consequence their living standards are now determined by the performance of the highly volatile private financial market (A. Deacon, 1995, p. 90).

Changes in benefits designed to meet child support costs have further demonstrated the emphasis on reducing the demand on the public purse and the drive to replace public responsibility with private provision. The Child Support Act, introduced in April 1993, was designed to ensure that both parents accepted and maintained financial responsibility for their children. This piece of legislation was primarily aimed at forcing absent fathers to pay child support, thereby reducing the public dependency of lone mothers. The Act serves as an example of how income maintenance policy can be employed to encourage and promote a particular set of familial norms in that it has the power 'to regulate and enforce breadwinner obligations in a way which is impossible within households' (Hooper, 1996, p. 158). However the Child Support Act has been highly criticised for failing to meet its objectives. In fact in 1997 one of the first tasks of the newly appointed secretary of state for social security, Harriet Harman, was to initiate a wide-ranging review of the operation of the Child Support Agency, the department responsible for administering the Act.

The current structure of the principle means-tested benefits was largely determined by the Social Security Act 1986, implemented in April 1988. This piece of legislation was an attempt to simplify the system and introduce a uniform structure of entitlements common to the three main income-related benefits (Dilnot and Webb, 1989, pp. 244–5; Hill, 1990, p. 60). A necessary step in this process was the abolition of discretionary awards, previously available to claimants of Supplementary Benefit. Additional payments were replaced by weekly 'premiums' added to standard Income Support allowances, available only to certain groups, and the practice of making lump sum payments to individuals in exceptional circumstances was abolished altogether. In its place the Social Fund was introduced – a radical development in British social security policy:

> [The Social Fund] was quite different from any previous type of British social security provision in that it was cash-limited not demand-led; it could make grants, but most payments were in the form of loans; claimants became applicants to the social fund, as they had no rights to a social fund payment and all decisions were discretionary; finally there was no independent right of appeal (Walker, 1993, p. 14).

The operation of the social fund has proved highly controversial and has been heavily criticised for contributing to the poverty experienced by many claimants rather than alleviating it (A. Deacon, 1995, p. 90). As the majority of financial aid provided by the fund is in the form of loans (only 25 per cent of the decisions made on Community Care Grant claims resulted in awards in 1995/96: Department of Social Security, 1996a, table A5.04, p. 87), individuals already living at the 'safety net' income level are experiencing greater hardship in that repayments are deducted from their benefit at source.

The 1986 Act firmly placed 'means-tested benefits at the heart of future benefit provision' (Walker, 1993, p. 14). The number of individuals claiming and receiving only contributory-based unemployment benefit fell from 555 000 in May 1991 to 314 000 in May 1995, a reduction of 43 per cent. At the same time the number of individuals claiming unemployment benefit and receiving either a combination of contributory and means-tested benefits, or IS only, rose from 1 314 000 in May 1991 to 1 708 000 in May 1995, an increase of 30 per cent (Dept of Social Security, 1996a, derived from table C1.01, p. 122). This trend among unemployed claimants is set to continue as a result of the six-month rule in the Job Seeker's Allowance. The proportion of the overall population receiving means-tested benefits rose from 17 per cent in 1979 to 25 per cent in 1992/93 (Oppenheim and Harker, 1996, p. 25). Means testing is therefore performing a fundamental and ever increasing function within the British social security system and this switch in emphasis has formed the basis of much of the political and economic debate on the future direction of social security policy.

## Income Maintenance: The Reform Agenda

Reforms of our welfare state are essential. They are essential above all in the interests of those who most depend upon the welfare state. Beveridge largely destroyed the 'evil giant of want'. The only thing which would bring it back to life would be a system which both outstripped and undermined the nation's ability to pay (Lilley, 1993, p. 22).

The British experience of escalating costs is not unique. Funding pressures are common to all EU member states. The combined effects of competing demands on public expenditure, low rates of economic activity and the imposition of political and economic restraints on deficit financing have restricted the capacity of modern welfare states to meet the needs of contemporary society. The perceived 'crisis of social protection' has led to the emergence of a widespread political debate at the EU level on the future of state welfare provision, a core focus being containment of the explosive growth of public spending (see for example Department of Social Security, 1993b). According to the political right, generous social security benefits promote welfare dependency and the large resources devoted to programmes negatively impact on overall economic performance. Those on the political left tend to argue from a user's point of view, claiming that means testing traps people in poverty and exacerbates the problem of social exclusion. The Commission on Social Justice, set up by the Labour Party in 1992, examined the social security measures employed in Britain at the time in an attempt to develop a reform package aimed at modernising the system. The Commission reported the following objectives for any system of benefits, tax allowances and private provision (Commission on Social Justice, 1994, p. 224):

- To prevent poverty where possible and relieve it where necessary.
- To protect people against risks, especially those that arise in the labour market and from family change.
- To redistribute resources from richer to poorer members of society.
- To redistribute resources of time and money over people's lifecycles.
- To encourage personal independence.
- To promote social cohesion.

As indicated above, recent policy developments in the area of income maintenance have served to stigmatise the poor further and curtail the coverage and level of benefits, and rather than promote independence, they have substituted public dependence with various forms of private dependence. The focus of social security policy in Britain has altered from a rights-based insurance scheme to a residual system of safety-net provision that has had a negative impact on individual welfare; 'poverty has grown significantly over recent years and by 1992/3, between 13 and 14 million people in the United Kingdom – around a quarter of our society – were living in poverty (Oppenheim and Harker, 1996, p. 24).

Given this evidence it is clear that social security provision in Britain is failing to relieve the poverty of many individuals. The Job Seeker's Allowance, currently paid at a weekly rate of £49.15, represents 14.84 per cent of average full-time earnings (according to the *Labour Force Quarterly Bulletin*, no. 19, March 1997, the average full-time wage in autumn 1996 was £331 per week). The objective of maintaining living standards is clearly not being met, and when considering the issue of insuring against risks, or even promoting economic security current benefits provide only minimum levels of protection.

Likewise gender inequalities are exacerbated within the current British social security framework. The direct relationship between insurance-based benefits and paid work directly disadvantages women due to their historically limited access to the labour market and their lower earnings relative to their male counterparts. Means-tested benefits in Britain are calculated on family income, therefore women married to employed men (16 hours or more of paid work per week is now considered full-time employment) are denied access to Income Support regardless of their own income level. Evidence suggests that those most affected by the poverty trap are women married to unemployed men, as the amount they would receive from paid employment would not equal the benefits they would lose by going out to work (see for example Dilnot and Kell, 1989).

The child-care cost 'disregard' has been increased from £40 to £60 per week for the purposes of Family Credit and the Parent Plus Initiative, a pilot programme offering lone parents help with accessing jobs, was introduced in April 1997. The focus is clearly on improving work incentives. Social security programmes that are linked to the formal labour market and continue to assume the traditional male-breadwinner family model implicitly promote the citizenship rights of workers whilst denying the full inclusion of many individuals, particularly women and children, by assuming their dependency on men.

Future reform of the British tax and social security system must take all of the above factors into account. The landslide victory of New Labour in the May 1997 general election indicated the possibility of a fresh approach to social security policy. Labour's election promises contained few specifics about social security policy, specifically, but it was clear that there was a firm pledge to enact measures that would improve access to the formal labour market, thereby tackling poverty and reducing future demands on the social security budget. Gordon Brown, now chancellor of the exchequer, reaffirmed this commitment in an election address:

> The unemployed men and women I meet in my constituency don't want to settle for an extra pound and a life on benefit . . . They don't demand the right to benefit they demand the right to work . . . Therefore our first priority – the purpose of our windfall tax – will be to cut unemployment, modernise the Welfare State, reduce social security bills and get our people back to work . . . A tax system for work, and the reform of the Welfare State to encourage work, that will be our first priority (Gordon Brown, speaking at the Scottish Labour Party Annual Conference, 8 March, 1997).

It would appear that the current political and economic climate dictates continued emphasis on reducing expenditure and a renewed commitment to enacting social security reforms that support contemporary labour market processes. It can only be assumed that this narrow approach to the reform agenda will bring with it more of the same rather than embracing a radical rethinking of overall income maintenance policy. One particular proposal, which represents a radical reform of both the tax and the benefit system, is the citizens' basic income model. Support for this proposal has been gaining ground throughout Western Europe within a wide variety of intellectual and political arenas.

## Basic Income Maintenance versus Basic Income

A basic income is an income unconditionally paid to all on an individual basis, without means test or work requirement. In other words, it is a form of minimum income guarantee that differs from those that now exist in various European countries by virtue of the fact that it is paid:

- to individuals rather than households;
- irrespective of any income from other sources;
- without referring to any present or past work performance, or the willingness to accept a job if offered (Van Parijs, 1992, pp. 3–4).

In practical terms a citizens' basic income policy would involve the granting of a regular equal income to each adult member of society. Children would receive an age-related grant, paid to parents or guardians. This income would be tax free and calculated in accordance with relevant cost of living indicators. All existing income maintenance benefits would be replaced by the citizens' basic income and the scheme would be financed via general taxation. This would therefore involve the abolition of all personal relief against income tax as this would be classified as a benefit and would entail full-scale integration of the tax and benefit mechanisms.

The current tax and benefit measures are criticised for their complex delivery structures and their failure to reach the targeted client groups. A citizens' basic income model would benefit from simplicity in administration. The information required to establish entitlement would be clearly defined, simple to collect and monitor, and is not readily open to misinterpretation. The advantages with regard to take-up rates are obvious with such explicit and uncontroversial eligibility criteria. Likewise the contributors would be easily identified as all those in paid employment. Mechanisms for the collection of pay-as-you-earn taxes are well established in modern capitalist systems, with technological advances resulting in improved information flows and a consequent reduction in administrative costs. One of the main attractions of this simplified tax-transfer system is the favourable framework it provides for promoting European-wide implementation, given the current emphasis on integration and harmonisation in economic and social policy.

Integration of the tax and benefit systems would remove the worst aspects of the poverty trap. The gains to be had from paid employment would always be positive. Unlike the existing tax and benefit structures, which create a disincentive to work, the citizens' basic income model would promote labour market participation within a system that clearly delineates the functions of receipt and provision.

A citizens' basic income should be welcomed as a proposal that meets the needs of a labour market adapting to technological change, the phenomenon of 'jobless growth' and intensifying international competition. Throughout the late 1970s and 1980s modern labour markets were characterised by accelerated growth in precarious and more flexible forms of employment. Corresponding increases in income inequalities were accentuated by the implementation of government policies informed by supply-side economics. Policies aimed at alleviating the plight of the poor must therefore take account of the dual aspects of marginalisation and exclusion. Individuals may find themselves excluded from employment for extended periods which would force them into a situation of welfare dependency, or they may find that inclusion into the labour market depends upon taking jobs that are insecure and low paid. This process of labour-force fragmentation between 'core' and 'periphery' employment is associated with microflexibility in labour markets and the consequence is effectively to marginalise those who are unable to secure full-time, regular jobs. Marginalisation within the labour force has become one of the main sources of the 'new' poverty that is evident across Europe (Cross, 1993; Standing, 1992, p. 52). Furthermore Cross (1993, p. 7) identifies marginalisation as 'typically affecting identifiable groups, with few chances for advancement or wealth accumulation'. Social security systems institutionalised at a time of high and stable levels of employment, with full-time male jobs as the norm, are no longer effective in meeting the needs of the ever-expanding number of individuals joining the ranks of the new poor.

The provision of a basic income would enhance individuals' opportunity to make real choices with reference to economic and non-economic activities throughout the course of their lifecycle. The need to predefine specific life situations that render individuals or groups of individuals vulnerable to poverty, an essential ingredient of effective targeted programmes, would no longer be necessary. Given the volatile nature of modern labour markets and uncertainty about the future, an antipoverty strategy that would not involve the categorising and continual re-categorisation of eligible beneficiaries appears promising. A citizens' basic income would serve to meet the two-pronged objective of preventing poverty and enhancing labour flexibility.

Despite the existence of convincing theoretical and practical arguments that justify a basic income (see for example Van Parijs, 1992), to date no single model of a universal, unconditional, minimum income guarantee exists within any modern apparatus of state welfare provision. A policy that advocates paying people in exchange for nothing would be difficult to achieve given the value modern society attaches to paid work, and the costs associated with extending a universal benefit scheme to the whole population are believed to be unaffordable given the present economic climate. Various proposals, such as a 'participation income' or a 'partial basic income', have emerged with the intention of addressing these criticisms and making a citizens' basic income more politically palatable and economically feasible (see for example Atkinson, 1996; Parker, 1989). However, such modifications to the model would limit the role a citizens' basic income could play in addressing the problems of unemployment, poverty, inequality and economic insecurity within a modern socioeconomic context. Furthermore in Britain the accounting practice of showing tax expenditure as negative revenue, means that the introduction of a new cash benefit, to replace all tax relief and allowances would distort the government's accounts by showing an exorbitant increase in spending. This leads Monkton (1993, p. 6) to the conclusion that, 'unless the Treasury is forced to mend its ways, it will always block the consideration of any universal benefit scheme, erroneously believing it to be in all circumstances unaffordable'.

## Conclusion

It would appear that, for New Labour, the role to be played by social security policy in eliminating poverty and ending the culture of dependency will be subservient to the role played by the formal labour market. The prospect of a radical change in policy direction seems unlikely. Cost considerations continue to dominate the reform agenda. However escalating costs are mainly due to increased demand. Policy makers should therefore consider the dynamics of modern socioeconomic conditions when designing possible reform options. The continued preference for means-testing as a method of targeting resources more efficiently, together with minimal levels of benefits to encourage labour market participation and policies designed with the formal work and pay relationship in mind, effectively render the British social security programme a system of basic income maintenance with little prospect of a move towards a citizens' basic income model in the immediate future.

# Further Reading

A useful starting point for students of social security policy in Britain is Hill (1990), which gives an account of policy developments form the days of the early Poor Law up to the late 1980s. More up-to-date information can be found in the Child Poverty Action Group's (CPAG) journal, *Poverty*, and in their *Welfare Rights Bulletin*, published bi-monthly. Specific details of all available benefits are given in the CPAG's annual guides to welfare benefits and a range of statistical information can be located in the Department of Social Security's annual report, which also provides details of planned policy developments. Students interested in the economics of social security should consult N. Barr, *The Economics of the Welfare State*, 2nd edn (London: Weidenfeld and Nicolson, 1993); A. B. Atkinson, *Poverty and Social Security* (Hemel Hempstead: Harvester Wheatsheaf, 1989). and A. Dilnot and I. Walker (eds), *The Economics of Social Security*, 1989, Oxford, Oxford University Press. An analysis of methods of financing can be found in H. Glennerster, *Paying for Welfare* (Hemel Hempstead: Harvester Wheatsheaf, 1992).

The various publications of the Commission on Social Justice provide an informative summary of the reform debate. C. Glendinning and J. Millar (eds), *Women and Poverty in Britain the 1990s* (1992), and S. Baldwin and J. Falkingham (eds), *Social Security and Social Change* (1994), both published by Harvester Wheatsheaf (Hemel Hempstead), discuss the limits of current measures in light of changing socioeconomic conditions. The theoretical case for a citizens' basic income model is best covered in P. Van Parijs, *Arguing for Basic Income: Ethical Foundations for a Radical Reform*, (London: and New York: Verso 1992). The Citizens Income Trust (Citizens Income Study Centre, St Philips Building, Sheffield Street, London WC2A 2EX) publishes a twice yearly bulletin, *Citizens Income*, which contains a range of articles covering developments in the reform debate, both in the British and the European context.

# CHAPTER 8

# Health Policy

SARAH NETTLETON

In common with many other countries, the transformation of health policies in Britain in the 1980s and 1990s has been profound (Ham, 1997). There have been policy changes with regard to both health care services and health itself. In relation to health care there have been two interrelated developments: a new system of management, and the introduction of the 'internal market'. In relation to health, a strategy has been designed to improve the nation's health by way of a commitment to prevent disease and illness and promote better health (Department of Health, 1992). These developments represent a significant departure from the health policies of the post-war years through to the late 1970s. They also mirror changes in other areas of welfare such as education, housing and social services, which have all seen the introduction of new forms of managerialism, the development of quasi-market relationships and attempts to encourage prevention and personal responsibility for welfare. Nevertheless, as a system of health care the National Health Service (NHS) remains unique in that it is funded principally out of taxation and, according to official policy documentation, there is continuing commitment to its founding principles of universality, comprehensiveness and equity.

After briefly summarising some of the problems that contemporary policy makers face in relation to health and health care, this chapter will go on to identify the key developments in health policy during the last decade. First the reforms in the delivery of health care will be examined and then the development of policies designed to improve health will be discussed. From a review of policy developments it is possible to decipher a number of themes that have come to dominate the current debate on health policy: the affordability of health care; rationing and priority setting; patient choice and the involvement of users; and inequalities in health and health care.

## Health Policy: Problems and Dilemmas

The NHS was established in 1948 and is widely considered to have been a success. It was then, and remains today, an immensely popular institution

(Klein, 1995, p. 135), and compared with similar institutions in other nations it provides health care at a relatively low cost (Holliday, 1995). Predominantly funded out of central taxation it remains for the most part (with the exception of charges for prescriptions, dental services and so on) free at the point of use. Despite its success, over the last five decades the NHS has been beset with a number of enduring problems. The NHS is characterised by escalating costs. More and more resources have been channelled into the service year on year, and yet it always appears to be starved of resources. Health professionals and the media constantly proclaim that the NHS is on the verge of a financial 'crisis'. Simply putting more money into the service does not however seem appropriate as demand for health care is seemingly insatiable. This fact is compounded by the development of new and often expensive drugs and technologies, designed to treat previously intractable conditions. This raises a number of questions that are by no means easy to answer. For example, how should the health service be financed? Can we afford the NHS?

A further problem is the power wielded by health professionals, and in particular the medical profession. To a significant extent the costs incurred by the NHS are a result of the millions of decisions made by clinicians each year. These decisions are made in the 'best interests' of given patients on a given day, which forms the basis of the doctors' so-called 'clinical autonomy'. This means that those providing care have significantly shaped the ways in which resources are used, even though this may not be in the best interests of the population as a whole. The central problem, therefore, is a tension between regulation and autonomy. Should providers of care have constraints placed on their clinical decision making or should decisions invariably depend on the clinical needs of individual patients. Should some services be rationed and/or prioritised?

A third problem has been that the views of individual patients, and 'consumers' of health care more generally, have not been taken into account, with the consequence that those who the health service seeks to care for have actually had little influence on the nature and content of health care services. According to some critics the NHS has become a professionally dominated, unwieldy bureaucracy that is not sensitive to the needs or wishes of patients and users (Seale, 1993) .

A fourth problem since the inception of the NHS has been the allocation of resources between different types of health care, with the more powerful groups amongst the medical profession winning the bulk of the resources. Hospital medicine and acute services have taken the lion's share of the health budget (Ham, 1992, p. 65), with the consequence that other community based services, primary health care and preventative services have lost out. Inequalities between various sectors of the NHS have also been compounded by geographical inequalities, with some parts of the country being over-or underprovided (Mohan and Woods, 1985). This is sometimes referred to as the 'inverse care law': those areas in greatest need of health care receive disproportionately fewer resources (Tudor-Hart, 1971). These geographical inequalities reflect broader socioeconomic inequalities in health. Essentially, those people who are materially worse off are more likely to experience worse health.

These are the kinds of problem that health policy analysts and politicians have been grappling with since the 1950s (for more details see Klein, 1995). A wide range of solutions and policy initiatives have been developed, and in particular the NHS has undergone a whole series of reorganisations. For example in 1974 new tiers of management were introduced, as was a new style of 'consensus' management. This structure was subsequently changed and modified: some tiers of management were removed, and other tiers were added. But in essence the nature of the NHS remained the same: a highly bureaucratic organisation with a hierarchical structure and functioning as a 'command and control economy' (Allsop, 1995, p. 172). As such it epitomised what Butcher (1995) refers to as the 'public administrative model of welfare delivery'. During the 1980s however, the new right Tory governments attempted to confront these problems by radically altering the way in which the health service was organised and managed. The 'old administrative model' gave way to a new-style 'managerialism' and the control and command economy was replaced by a managed internal market: these two developments now form the core of the 'new' health service.

## New Managerialism and the NHS

The so-called 'new managerialism' within the health service refers to the displacement of diplomatic consensus management and administration with a more dynamic style of 'strong' management, derived from models of private sector management that emphasise 'accountability, results, competition and efficiency' (Gray and Jenkins, 1993, p. 12). Within the 'old' model of the NHS, health service administrators served and supported the work of health care professionals (Harrison et al., 1990). Within the new NHS health service managers are encouraged to manage these same professionals – to make sure that these providers of care work efficiently and do not waste resources. The change is not just about semantics: health service administrators were reactive in that they responded to problems, but health service managers are expected to be innovative, dynamic, responsible and accountable. What was lacking within many health service settings was a 'boss'. This was the conclusion reached by a team of four businessmen, headed by Roy Griffiths (managing director of Sainsbury's supermarket), following their review of the NHS. Their report contained the now famous sentence: 'If Florence Nightingale were carrying her lamp through the corridors of the NHS today she would almost certainly be searching for the people in charge' (Department of Health and Social Security, 1983, p. 12).

Their solution was a system of general management. All the health authorities (regional health authorities, RHAs; district health authorities, DHAs; and family health service authorities, FHSAs), hospitals and other services were to appoint a general manger who would be responsible for the strategic direction of the NHS. In other words general managers were to be responsible for semi-autonomous units. Griffiths maintained that strong management and a private sector ethos would 'stimulate initiative, urgency and vitality' and ensure a 'constant search for change and cost improvement' (ibid., p. 12). The driving force behind this was to be two new bodies at the top of the NHS hierarchy: the NHS Supervisory Board (later the NHS Policy Board) and the NHS Management Board (later renamed the NHS Executive). Alongside the move towards centralised strategic direction was an attempt to involve health care providers at all levels. An example of this was the resource management initiative, which devolved budgetary responsibilities to clinical directorates within hospitals. Doctors and nurses were given greater responsibility for the management of resources, the idea being that doctors would become more cost conscious and aware of the broader consequences of their individual decisions.

Change was not easy. The problems outlined above became increasingly apparent. Furthermore applying business practices to the NHS proved more difficult than Griffiths had anticipated (Strong and Robinson, 1990). Unlike much of the private sector the NHS is highly charged politically. Managers may try to act strategically and rationally, but ultimately they will be constrained by political factors. The consequences of a child not receiving treatment or a hospital being closed make for good media copy and may scupper attempts to implement policies and programmes designed to make the service more effective and more efficient. Not surprisingly perhaps, managers and health professionals have not found it easy to work together. Part of the underlying rationale for the new managerialism was to curb the power of the medical profession: studies had found that the balance of power was predominantly in the hands of the medical profession (Hunter, 1991) and there was no 'disciplining agent' (Holliday, 1995). The latter, the politicians hoped, might come in the form of the internal market.

# The Internal Market and the NHS

The government white paper *Working for Patients* (Department of Health, 1989) formed the basis of the NHS and Community Care Act 1990. The main aims of the policy and legislation were to extend patient choice, secure better value for money and, wherever possible, devolve responsibility. It was envisaged that these aims could be achieved by creating an internal market. The government had been introduced to the idea of an internal market by a visiting American policy analyst, Alain Enthoven, who, in an influential paper, had diagnosed the main problems within the NHS and offered suggestions for change (Enthoven, 1985). A striking feature of the white paper and the subsequent legislation was their lack of detail. The proposals were not a blue-print for change, instead they outlined a new set of market structures, and it still remains to be seen just how the nature of the organisation will develop. As Allsop (1995, p. 174) has observed: 'As the reforms were implemented, a variety of patterns of service developed, based on local circumstance. This meant that there was no standard pattern – indeed the intention had been to encourage local enterprise and innovation.'

Far from becoming a seamless service, as the original architects of the NHS had hoped, it was looking more like a 'patchwork quilt' (Webster, 1991). Furthermore, as Holliday (1995, p. 2) has argued, whilst the introduction of new managerialism introduced regulatory dynamic within the health service, the introduction of the internal market has contributed to a dynamic of fragmentation, which has done much to 'undermine the strategic control of the service'. It was also hoped that the internal market would increase efficiency, cost effectiveness and consumer responsiveness, and that it would 'discipline medical behaviour' (ibid., p. 58).

In practice the formation of the internal market involved splitting the former district health authorities (DHAs), which had previously provided health care services, into purchaser and provider units. When provider units were separated from the health authorities they established themselves as Trusts and were free to operate as independent non-profit organisations. The state, however, retained ownership of the provider agencies and they are financed by the Treasury. The former health authorities, initially at least, became the main purchasers and were able to 'buy' or 'commission' services (many purchasers are now called 'health commissions') from the trusts or any other provider of health care in both the public and the private sector, thus opening up the potential for an expansion of private health care provision.

The idea was that trusts would compete for contracts from the purchasers, who would be funded on a weighted capitation basis. Trusts could also negotiate contracts with the other key players within the internal market, that is, the general practitioners. Commissioning authorities would be encouraged to 'buy' services on the basis of local health needs assessments and local health strategies which, in turn would be designed to optimise 'health gain' (see below).

Purchasers would also be charged with the responsibility of ensuring that the services delivered by providers were effective, efficient and appropriate. Thus contracts with provider services would be monitored to ensure that they delivered what they said they would deliver.

All this has proved more difficult than was initially envisaged. A particularly tricky problem is translating the findings of needs assessments into contracts (Robinson 1996). In theory, priorities should be based on health needs assessments, all interventions should be based on evidence of their effectiveness, and they should also be evaluated. These evaluations should measure outcomes as well as processes. However problems often arise because there is insufficient information about the relative cost effectiveness of various treatments and interventions. Another problem is that priority setting is invariably affected by the wider political context and short termism.

The contract is pivotal to the internal market. The idea is that through its formation and negotiation purchasers will rationally decide, on the basis of needs assessments, what to buy on behalf of their patient population and they will be able to agree costs, outcomes, indicators of quality and measures of performance. This new 'contract culture' is compatible with the other key change in the health service, the development of a new style of management. In particular they both emphasise performance measurement, the defining of goals, the setting of targets, the evaluation of outputs rather than inputs and ensuring greater 'value for money'. However, one of the major criticisms of the contracting process is that it requires a substantial bureaucracy to administer it (Robinson, 1996). The Labour government has indicated that it will replace contracts with 'comprehensive health care agreements', which will be on a longer-term basis and involve the commissioning of the full range of services, which should be supplied to agreed standards by the providers (Labour Party, 1995). This does not mean that the market will disappear altogether, but rather that 'periodic competition for markets replaces competition in the markets' (p. 34).

## Purchasing Primary Health Care

Perhaps one of the most controversial features of the reforms was the establishment of GP fundholders. A fundholding practice is one that controls its own budget, within the confines of which it must buy and provide a range of services. Since April 1996 there have been three types of fundholders:

standard fundholders – practices that can shop around for secondary care; community fundholders who are able to purchase a more limited range of services; and total purchasing fundholders, who can buy all the services they require on behalf of their patients. The main criticism of fundholding is that it has caused a two-tier system in that fundholding practices are able to secure hospital care services more quickly on behalf of their patients than non-fundholding practices, and there is evidence to support this view (Audit Commission, 1995). The new Labour government has been quick to defer applications for fundholding for 1998/9 while it reviews alternative models of commissioning health care (Department of Health, 1997).

A non-fundholding practice is one where secondary care is bought on its behalf by a health purchaser. Such practices are therefore not able to choose their own service providers, although developments such as area commissioning, locality commissioning and partnership schemes have meant that health authorities and GPs have developed ways of working together. Although no single model of locality commissioning exists, it seems likely that certain features of it are likely to endure. For example, practices that cover the same geographical location have agreed to work collaboratively both to influence the health authorities' purchasing work and to encourage local providers to agree to changes that can then be incorporated into local authority contracts (Mays, 1997, p. 1212). Such experimentation and the development of new initiatives is currently underway, and has been facilitated by the Primary Care Act 1997, which followed the Conservative White Paper *Opportunity and Choice: primary care the future*. The core of this Act is flexibility, as the government then wanted to encourage 'local flexibility so that services can be delivered in a way which is better attended to local needs and circumstances' (Department of Health, 1996a). The Labour government will pursue this but will shift the emphasis from GP fundholding to new and varied types of GP commissioning groups (Department of Health, 1997); Labour has argued for a 'diversity of practice which respects the diversity of local need' (Labour Party, 1995).

These policy developments are congruent with a more profound aim of health policy in recent years: to develop a primary health-care-led NHS. This goal is not confined to British politicians, it is also seen by health analysts as crucial to the development of efficient and effective health care. The World Health Organisation's global health strategy, Health for All by the Year 2000 (HFA 2000), is based on the premise that 'primary care is the key to obtaining health for all' (WHO, 1985). Investing in primary health care arguably has many benefits over sinking resources into secondary, 'high tech' acute care (Coote and Hunter, 1996). It has the potential for improving the quality of health care, after all 98 per cent of the population are registered with a general practitioner. It is likely to be more patient centered and holistic in that primary health care workers such as health visitors, community psychiatric nurses, GPs and practice nurses are closer to patients and tend to care for the 'whole' individual and their entire patient base. Finally, it is less costly than secondary care and therefore has the potential to increase cost effectiveness.

## Health Care in the Community

Perhaps one of the most dramatic differences in health care provision in the twenty-first century will be the demise of large-scale, high-tech hospitals and the growth of primary and community-based services. For a range of user groups the policy of deinstitutionalisation can be traced back to the 1950s, when the idea that elderly people, people with learning disabilities, those experiencing mental health problems and others would be much more appropriately located and supported in community settings rather than large-scale institutions (Walker, 1993). Today large-scale hospitals that provide acute care are also beginning to look outmoded. Health care needs are different and the needs of patients with chronic conditions might be better served at home. Also technological developments are such that many of the treatments that hitherto required inpatient care can now be treated on an outpatient basis. Those patients who are admitted to hospital are now being discharged earlier. For example between 1979 and 1990 the average length of stay in the acute sector for patients aged 45–64 fell from 10.2 to 6.7 days (Marks, 1992). The transition to home care will however take time, and as we can see from Figure 8.1 the acute sector still consumes the bulk of the resources.

Tomlinson (1992) chaired a review of hospital services in London and concluded that there was over provision of hospital-based services and resources should be diverted to community-based care. Such findings have been replicated in other major cities throughout Britain. Hospital closure however, is an emotive business and not one that politicians feel comfortable with. However the rationalisation of large, high-tech hospitals forms but part of the more general reorientation of health care, which aims to be more holistic and patient-centred. A social model of health would encompass not just the control of disease but also the social consequences of experiencing illness, and it would also involve attempts to promote health and well-being.

## Policies to Improve Health

In concert with the reforms of the health care services have been the formation of policies to improve the general health of the population: to

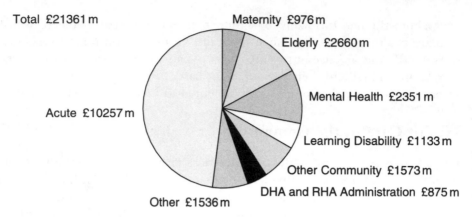

Total £21361 m    Maternity £976 m

Elderly £2660 m

Mental Health £2351 m

Acute £10257 m

Learning Disability £1133 m

Other Community £1573 m

DHA and RHA Administration £875 m

Other £1536 m

*Source*: Department of Health (1996b).

**Figure 8.1    Hospital and community health services gross current expenditure, by sector, 1993–94**

prevent disease and illness and to maximise health gain. The term 'health gain' is in vogue in the 1990s, it refers to the improvement of the health status of groups and populations as opposed to the benefit that specific health interventions may have for given individuals. The emphasis is very much on improving 'health' and wellbeing, rather than just treating disease. It forms the core of what Klein (1995, p. 210) refers to as 'a new health policy paradigm', which has come to dominate the health policy agenda in the 1990s. 'In short', Klein writes, 'the Government acknowledged that it had responsibilities for the health of the population that went beyond the provision of a health care system' (ibid., p. 210). For example, when purchasers make decisions about which services to buy they are required both to assess health needs and to try to ensure that their purchasing decisions will maximise the health status of the populations they serve. Interestingly this constitutes a radical departure in health policy, in that since the establishment of the health service there have been few policies that have actually been designed to improve health. Indeed the health service has often been dubbed the 'sickness' or the 'disease' service! The White Paper *The Health of the Nation* (Department of Health, 1992) formed the basis of a new strategy to improve health and constituted a genuine attempt to buck this trend.

Like the attempts to shift the balance in favour of primary care, the attempt to redress the imbalance between prevention and intervention draws upon frameworks developed internationally by the World Health Organisation's HFA 2000 initiative (WHO, 1985). A number of further factors in concert with these global initiatives have intensified the impetus for a commitment to prevention and health promotion. First, the limitations of the biomedical approach to health care have been recognised, and policy makers have come to recognise that increasing investment in technological medicine has resulted in diminishing returns. Second, the nature of the disease burden has changed: a decline in infectious diseases has been matched by a relative increase in chronic conditions such as heart disease and cancer which are often precipitated by social and behavioural factors. Third, demographic changes mean that the growing proportion of elderly people in the population are placing a great strain on an already overburdened health service. Fourth, the financing of a health service that has to deal with an infinite demand for health in a period of retrenchment is becoming untenable. Finally, the pursuit of a policy that shifts the responsibility for health from governments to individuals is congruent with the ideologies which underpinned health and welfare policies in the 1980s and early 1990s. Although the *Health of the Nation* emphasises the need for governments, the NHS, local authorities, employers and other organisations to work together to create 'healthy alliances', ultimately the aim is to encourage individuals to change their behaviour and lead more 'healthy' lifestyles.

The *Health of the Nation* identified five key areas where substantial improvements in health could be achieved, and within these set national targets to be met by the year 2000. The five areas are coronary heart disease and stroke, cancer, mental illness, HIV/AIDS and sexual health, and accidents. Whilst good progress is being made towards some targets, other trends have turned in the opposite direction, for example smoking amongst young people and especially young women, obesity in men and over-consumption of alcohol by women (Coote and Hunter, 1996, p. 11). The *Health of the Nation* policies have been much criticised for their emphasis on the behaviour and lifestyle of individuals and the relative neglect of factors such as poverty and social inequality (Benzeval *et al.*, 1995). Indeed the Conservative government subsequently published another document, *Variations in Health* (Department of Health, 1995a), which conceded that unless such factors as social inequality were addressed it could not hope to achieve its targets. However as yet the promotion of health has been dominated by attempts to modify behaviour, in particular what have come to be known as the 'holy trinity of risks' – smoking, lack of exercise and poor diet.

It is now accepted that any attempt to improve health must extend beyond the provision of health care services, and in particular must move beyond the interventionist, hospital-based medicine that has dominated health care systems for the major part of this century. In 1997 the participants of a World Health Organisation conference endorsed this view (Ress, 1997, p. 1407). Whilst technical health care intervention may reduce the impact of disease it cannot ensure that people are actually living 'healthier' lives. Life expectancy in Britain has increased significantly during the twentieth century: in 1994 it was over 74 years for males and over 79 years for females, an increase of just over 60 per cent compared with the beginning of the century (Central Statistical Office, 1997). However surveys of morbidity suggest that this has not been accompained a by general improvement in health (Dunnell, 1995). For example the percentage of people reporting a chronic sickness (that is a long-standing illness, disability or infirmity) has actually risen over the last twenty years. Whilst the likelihood of suffering from chronic sickness increases with age, a higher proportion of people in all age groups in Britain reported chronic sickness in 1995–6 than in 1974. This would seem to indicate that the need and demand for health care are unlikely diminish, so troublesome issues are likely to dominate health policy debates well into the next century.

## Contemporary Debates in Health Policy

### Is the NHS underfunded?

The NHS has always been plagued with funding problems and heated debates about the extent to which it is underfunded have raged ever since its inception. The under-funding problem is highly complex, not least because there are a number of ways of calculating what needs to be spent and no consensus as to which is the most appropriate measure (Klein, 1995, p. 179–181). As can be seen from Figure 8.2 expenditure on the NHS increased by over 40 per cent between 1985–86 and 1995–96.

Large amounts of increased funding are rapidly consumed by the health service for at least four reasons (Holliday, 1995): (1) NHS inflation is higher than the standard retail measure of inflation; (2) wages and salaries amount to over 70 per cent of the NHS resources; (3) technological developments are rapid and extremely costly; and (4) an ageing population is making greater demands on certain types of service. Although spending on the NHS has increased in real terms in recent decades, the NHS is relatively cheap: for example in Britain in 1995 health care expenditure formed 6.8 per cent of GDP, whilst the United States spent 15.7 per cent; Austria 8.2 per cent and France 9.2 per cent. That Britain spends proportionately less of its resources on health care is taken by some commentators as proof that the NHS is indeed underfunded. For others it is evidence that a system funded out of central taxation is more cost effective than insurance-based health care systems.

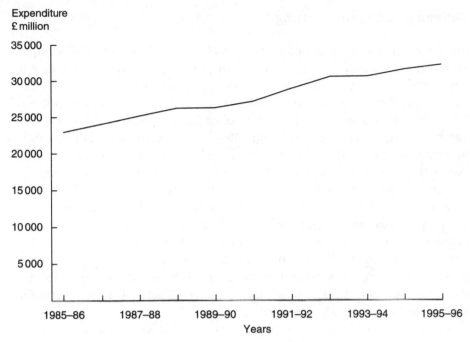

*Source*: Department of Health (1996b).

**Figure 8.2  Growth in NHS gross expenditure (1994–95 prices)**

There is no objective answer to the question: is the NHS underfunded? This is because 'the answer requires value judgements that will inevitably give rise to disagreements' (Dixon *et al.*, 1997, p. 314). Dixon *et al.* reviewed the debate on this issue and identified seven different approaches that have been used to support the case that the NHS is underfunded, all of which, they concluded, have flaws. The problem revolves around the fact that whilst most people would agree that the NHS could do with more money, it is not clear what the 'right' level of funding should be. The funding question also needs to be placed in the wider context of welfare spending. Despite the much talked about 'cuts' in public spending on welfare, the actual level of spending has not decreased. This is largely due to increased spending on social security due to high levels of unemployment, and demographic factors such as the ageing population. For the current Labour government, resourcing the financially hungry health service will involve a highly complex economic and political conundrum. Alongside the question about the amount of funding the NHS should receive are questions relating to how the existing funds should be awarded or allocated and who should be eligible to receive them. In other words, how do we go about rationing health care resources?

## Rationing and priority setting

One of the founding principles of the NHS was that health care would be provided on the basis of clinical need. In practice, however, health care has always been rationed. During their everyday practice clinicians routinely make clinical decisions about whether or not to administer treatments. Such 'rationing' decisions are said to be implicit in that there is no reference to agreed systems or criteria (Lenaghan, 1997). The health care reforms, and in particular the fact that services are purchased, means that rationing (decisions about the allocation and eligibility of resources, treatments or services) is becoming more explicit, rather than remaining implicit. The health authorities are having to make tough decisions about which services they are prepared to pay for and for whom. For example one survey found that couples in Scotland were seven times more likely to obtain in vitro fertilisation on the NHS than those in the South-West region (cited in ibid., p. 967). However, as yet there are no universally agreed principles to guide these decision and there remains considerable variation between authorities (House of Commons Health Committee, 1995).

The case for and against explicit rationing is hotly debated within health policy circles (Klein *et al.*, 1996). The case of Child B, a ten-year-old girl who was suffering from leukaemia and was refused treatment by Cambridge Health Authority, stimulated intense debate on the issue. The child's father took the case to the High Court of Appeal, which ruled that the health authority had acted rationally in refusing to spend the £75 000 on her treatment (for more details of this particular case see ibid., pp. 77–82). After describing this case in some detail, Klein and his colleagues usefully identify a number of points that this case serves to highlight. First, the case received a massive amount of media attention and this is characteristic of such issues – decisions about whether or not a person should receive care makes for good copy. Second, the decision not to treat was informed by the perceived likelihood that the intervention would not be effective. But what is the cut-off point when it comes to assessing the probability of success? Two per cent, 10 per cent, 20 per cent – who can say? Third, could the £75 000 be more effectively spent on other treatments for other illnesses with a better chance of success. This relates to the basic logic that presumes a need for rationing in the first place; that is, there is so much demand that we cannot meet it all and therefore we have to ration. Fourth, who should make the decision in cases such as this? Should it be the patient, the parents or other relatives and carers, the health authority, the medical profession, the taxpayers, the general public, or perhaps of all of these? Fifth, Klein *et al.* point out that despite the rhetoric such decisions are not purely financial. The medical advice to the health authority had been that the treatment required by Jaymee Bowan was such that it would have a detrimental effect on her quality of life. A sixth observation is that the High Court's decision in this particular case has had the effect of strengthening the position of health authorities in their capacity to take rationing decisions. Finally, and not unrelatedly, the decision made in this case was overt. It was not implicit, we all knew about it. This is an effect of the purchaser–provider split.

Arguments against implicit rationing include the fact that it is wasteful as clinicians cannot take cost effectiveness into account if, in incremental fashion, they base decisions on individual cases. Those who argue for explicit rationing are keen to see the development of clear criteria to inform those who are charged with the responsibility of making such decisions. A tall order. The extent to which explicit rationing is achievable is still being debated (ibid.). A further argument for such an approach is that it encourages policy analysts to listen to the views of patients and the general public. However others have cautioned that debates on the best ways of going about rationing may gloss over more fundamental questions and fail to ask whether or not rationing is inevitable or desirable.

## Patient choice and the involvement of users

According to the gurus of the new managerialism, the key to an organisation's success is responsiveness to its consumers. As Roy Griffiths, author of the Griffith's Report, has noted: 'the hallmarks of the truly great organisations in the private sector is that they place quality and customer satisfaction first, and profit for a long time simply emerged as the by-product of effective services' (Griffiths, 1991). The principle of 'extending patient choice' was one of the key themes in the reforms and was made quite explicit in *Working for Patients* (Department of Health, 1989). The idea that the introduction of the market would force services to respond to patients' demands is however misleading. In practice, as we have seen, services are bought not by patients themselves, but by a third party, be that a health commission or GP fundholders. This said, health authorities have been encouraged to set up mechanisms by which they can consult the views of the people they serve and they have to demonstrate that they are listening to 'local voices' (NHSME, 1992). It is not always obvious, however, that what they hear is actually used to inform their subsequent decisions.

In the context of the health care reforms, greater 'consumer awareness' has come to involve a focus on the provision of adequate information; improving the standards of health care, ensuring the quality of services by consulting consumers, reducing waiting times for treatment and encouraging patients to complain if they are not satisfied with the services they receive. The procedures for making complaints have been much improved since the early 1990s. In many respects this represents a significant achievement because the complaints machinery within the NHS has been subject to substantial criticism for many decades (Nettleton and Harding, 1994). Problems with the system, however, still abound. The nature of the current concerns reflect a particular model of consumer awareness which is congruent with private sector practices. This is evidenced by the fact that despite the consumer–oriented rhetoric, the functions of the NHS statutory bodies set up to represent consumers – the Community Health Councils (CHCs) – have not been extended; in fact with the health care reforms their functions have been curtailed.

Whilst patients and other consumers of the health service have been provided with more information about such matters as waiting times, and mechanisms are being devised to elicit their views, there is little evidence that consumers have any power to actually participate in decision making. This may be because consumer awareness within the NHS context has to some extent been imposed on patients and users. Klein (1995, p. 238) captures this point when he notes that 'Inherent in the NHS's linguistic transformation of the patient into the consumer is a curious paradox. This is that the new rhetoric of consumerism is a response to top-down policies rather than bottom-up demands.'

## Inequalities in health and health care

We have discussed above how current health policies aim not only to ensure that people are treated then they fall sick, but also to prevent people from becoming sick in the first place. Clearly there are good social, economic and moral reasons for this. There is a common assumption that economic growth leads to improved health. It is certainly the case that the growing prosperity of countries since the industrial revolution has been accompanied by an improvement in people's health and well-being. However there is growing evidence to support the view that economic prosperity *per se* does not improve health, but rather what is critical is the socio-economic distribution of that material wealth. For example one study in the United States found that, in Harlem in New York, at most ages the death rates where higher than in rural Bangladesh (cited in Wilkinson, 1996, p. 53). According to Wilkinson this is supported by three pieces of evidence. First, mortality is more closely related to relative income within countries than between them. Second, national mortality rates are lower in countries with lower levels of relative deprivation. Third, increased life expectancy is not invariably associated with long-term economic growth rates. The explanation for these findings is that more equitable societies have greater social cohesion, and it is the quality of this social fabric that impacts upon people's physical and mental health.

Reducing inequality is one of the most important challenges confronting health policy and it is one that the new Labour government has recognised. A Minister for Public Health has been appointed, and tackling the question of health inequality forms part of her brief. Health services need to be developed in such a way as to tackle the problem effectively. Simply improving the existing services in ways that are not sensitive to the existence of inequality can actually exacerbate it, so it is important that resources are directed to where the need is greatest. But more importantly perhaps, health policies that are concerned only with treating illness cannot tackle the issue of health. Health status is shaped by broader socioeconomic and environmental factors, and policy domains such as social security, education and housing, which are dealt with in other chapters of this volume, are absolutely fundamental to health. Even the most effective, efficient and streamlined health service cannot overcome the social and enviromental factors that predispose people to poor health in the first place. A major challenge for health policy is to aspire to a 'healthy society' and to ensure that health issues are placed on all social policy agendas.

## Further Reading

There are many excellent texts on health policy. A useful place to start for a straightforward account of the health service reforms is Ian Holliday, *The NHS Transformed: a guide to the health care reforms* (Manchester: Baseline Books, 1995). A thorough and readable account of health policy is Rudolf Klein, *The New Politics of the NHS*, 3rd edn (London: Longman, 1995). Much detail can also be gleaned from Chris Ham, *Health Policy in Britain: the politics and organisation of the NHS* (London: Macmillan, 1992) Health policy changes rapidly and a good source of current developments is the *Health Service Journal*, which is published weekly.

# CHAPTER 9

# Education Policy

STEPHEN J. BALL

Since Margaret Thatcher's first government came to power in 1979 the administration, funding, control, content and form of educational provision in England and Wales have all been subject to major reform. At the same time the provision of education has become a major political issue, with Tony Blair famously declaring that his first government's three leading priorities would be 'education, education and education'. In this chapter I consider the principal policy changes that have been introduced since 1979, measure their outcomes and assess their likely consequences.

## The Architecture of Reform

The centrepiece of reform over the last decade has been the 1988 Education Reform Act. The only significant prior piece of Conservative education policy under Thatcher's leadership was the Assisted Places Scheme (1981 Education Act), which provided state funding for 'high ability' children from 'low income' families to attend private secondary schools (see Edwards *et al.*, 1989). The new Labour administration elected in 1997 pledged to abolish the scheme and use the funds released to reduce to 30 the maximum class size for all 5–7 year olds.

The passage of the Education Reform Act of 1988 heralded a decade of unprecedented change in which educational provision has been transformed from a locally administered system loosely based on the principles of social welfare to a centrally regulated quasi-market. The key organising features of this transformation have been competition between providers, choice for parents and students, per capita formula funding and the local management of schools – that is, budgetary devolution and institutional autonomy. These changes have been underpinned by a national curriculum, a regime of national testing for schools and a national system of vocational qualifications for further education and training. The role of local government in the planning and control of education has either been much reduced or, in the case of further education institutions, polytechnics and grant maintained (GM) schools, eradicated entirely. In effect there has been a dual process of

146

change, with moves towards both decentralisation and centralisation. Along-side budgetary devolution, institutional autonomy and incorporation, the secretary of State for education (and employment) acquired a raft of new powers under the provisions of the 1988 Act (Seddon, 1994). This dual process has 'altered the basic power structure of the education system' (Maclure, 1988, p. ix).

The major aspect of decentralisation came with the transfer of decision-making powers from local education authorities (LEAs) to schools them-selves. Local management of schools (LMS) introduced a system of delegated budgets for schools covering teachers' salaries and other staffing costs, equipment and books, heating and lighting, rates, examination fees and all internal maintenance. LEAs remain responsible for capital expenditure but no longer have the power to direct how much a school can allocate for items in its own budget. The actual budget figure for any school is calculated annually from an LEA formula, approved by the Department for Education and Employment, determined mainly by student numbers and weighted by age, but with small adjustments for social need, special educational needs and the maintenance of the curriculum in small schools.

Under the 1988 legislation, schools were offered the possibility of being funded and regulated in one of two ways: they could either stay within LEA 'control', with their budgets 'top-sliced' for central service costs (approxi-mately 15 per cent of annual income for each school); or they could adopt grant maintained (GM) status, and thus receive a budget, without 'top-slicing', directly from the Funding Agency for Schools, so ending their formal relationship with the LEA. GM status provided schools with the possibility of access to other sources of funding (for example capital grants, technology grants) and offered additional 'autonomies' such as the freedom to introduce partial selection. Schools moved to GM status via a vote by the governors and then by the parents. A simple majority of those who vote was needed for acceptance. The original intentions of GM status were to 'break' the LEA's 'control' of schools and to create a group of schools that would be more innovative, risk-taking and entrepreneurial than their LEA counterparts. In fact research suggests that GM schools are if anything more traditionalist and conservative than their LEA counterparts (Halpin *et al.*, 1997). As of autumn 1996 there were 1115 grant maintained schools in England and Wales. About 2 per cent of primary schools and 16 per cent of secondaries (accounting for about 10 per cent of the school-age population) are now grant-maintained.

Perhaps the most important aspect of centralisation was the introduction of the national curriculum. The national curriculum mark 1 consisted of three core subjects (English, mathematics and science), eight other foundation subjects (all set within a common structure expressed in 10 levels of attainment with programmes of study for each subject and four key stages, at the end of which every child is assessed) and non-compulsory, cross-curricular themes and dimensions. The cross-curricular themes quickly disappeared from view. In 1993 the then Secretary of State for Education, John Patten, admitting that the government's reforms had gone 'badly wrong', announced a review, to be headed by Sir Ron Dearing. The national curriculum mark 2, based on this review, came into operation in August 1995. The prescription of content for non-core subjects was 'slimmed down', freeing up to one day a week for discretionary use by schools; the number of attainment targets was reduced; the amount of monitoring and testing required of teachers were also reduced; and greater flexibility of options for 14–16 year olds was introduced, which was intended to allow for the development of a vocational pathway that would 'enhance motivation for many students who are not getting adequate benefit from school' (Dearing, 1994, para. 5.52).

Britain is not alone in pursuing this sort of an educational reform agenda. Whilst the reforms have been pursued with particular rigour and zeal in Britain, the same processes can be seen at work in many other countries around the world, and not just in the sphere of education. As in Britain, other areas of social welfare and state service provision are involved and subject to the same transformational policies.

> Throughout much of the industrialised world the 1980s saw governments divesting themselves of responsibility for designing, organising and providing services for their citizens. In country after country, the ideology of the market swept away ideas of rational planning, and massive privatisation programmes of state-owned manufacturing and service organisations have resulted (Walford 1997a, p. 7).

I shall argue later that the quasi-market system in education has provided the government with new possibilities for the design and organisation of services – 'steering at a distance'. However it is also important to make the point that these generic elements of reform are embedded in and inflected by the specificity of national cultural and historical trends. Thus in England and Wales, school reform has to be viewed historically and politically in relation to what went before – that is, the trends towards comprehensivism and progressivism, in the 1960s and 1970s as against the postwar 'grammar school tradition' of selective education. Educational reforms in, say, France and Germany, which bear a strong resemblance to those in Britain, are grafted on to very different national histories (see Van Zanten, 1996; Weiss and Steinert, 1997) and policy cultures (see Cerny, 1990), although the social effects of the changes may be similar. Hence in France 'it is clear that the ideal of the common school and of equality of opportunity for all citizens is being replaced by the ideal of the "patterned" school geared towards the satisfaction of specific customers' (Van Zanten, 1996, pp. 72–3).

## Policy Developments in Compulsory (4–16) Education

Schools in England and Wales are now funded primarily on the basis of the number of students they recruit. Need is no longer a significant factor in the distribution of educational resources. On average only 1.5 per cent of the general schools budget (GSB) is distributed on the basis of social need. In areas where there are surplus places, per capita funding is encouraging schools to compete. Glossy brochures, advertising, promotional events and carefully choreographed 'open evenings' are now commonplace. In areas of population growth or social isolation, formula funding is not generating the same competitive effects, although more general changes in the discourses and practices of school management are having an effect all the same. In practice, education markets are local and diverse (see Gewirtz *et al.*, 1995). Parental choice also works to facilitate and drive competition. Theoretically, every parent has the possibility of choosing the primary and secondary school and post-16 education or training that is best suited to their child (as they see their child's needs). In practice, geography, transport and other costs, and increasingly selection by schools, are inhibiting freedom of choice for certain groups of parents. There is an important difference between 'making' and 'getting' a choice. Appeals against allocation decisions by parents have been steadily increasing since 1988.

An education market requires not just parental choice but also a diversity of provision (see Tooley, 1996). The GM initiative was seen by Conservative governments as one way of introducing greater supply-side diversity into the school system. Other attempts to extend diversity have been (1) the city technology colleges initiative (Whitty *et al.*, 1993) and, more recently, technology and sports colleges (schools that were to deliver a distinctive and more specialised curriculum); (2) the various regulations that have made it easier for schools to introduce overt selection on various bases; and (3) the possibility offered by the 1993 Education Act for the governors of existing private schools or groups of independent sponsors to apply to the secretary of state to establish 'sponsored GM schools'. Labour are introducing legislation to encourage further specialization and selection – the 1998 School Standards Bill. Altogether in the secondary sector there are 162 grammar schools (approximately half of which are GM), 600 GM schools, 500 voluntary or grant-aided, mainly church, schools, and about 200 other LEA-maintained schools specialising in either technology or languages. Taken together, these schools account for about 40 per cent of the sector but they are very unevenly distributed geographically.

Another essential requirement of a quasi-market for education is information. Since 1991 all secondary schools have been required to publish annually a range of performance indicators, as specified by the secretary of state for education. The most important of these are student achievements in GCSE and A-level examinations, which are reproduced in local and national newspapers in the form of 'local league tables'. National curriculum test scores in 'core' subjects are also now being published for primary and secondary schools. This introduces another dimension to the competition between schools and is a powerful but indirect mechanism for government control of schooling. The stated policy intentions of the control and publication of performance indicators, as part of the paraphernalia of the quasi-market in education, are to drive up academic standards, thereby improving Britain's position in the global economy, to expose 'weak' or 'failing' schools and to provide market information for parent-choosers. However in this way the Department for Education and Employment is able to impose various limits upon the autonomy of schools as schools clearly have to operate within the parameters set by local league tables and enrolment competition.

Furthermore, there is an apparent contradiction between the ideas of diversity and competitive, responsive, entrepreneurial schooling on the one hand and the introduction of a centrally determined national curriculum on the other. We can think about this in different ways: on the one hand it represents the ideological concerns and political aspirations of two different trends within Conservative thinking, the former being a clear expression of neoliberal market ideology applied to the public sector, the latter reflecting neoconservative concerns about national identity and solidarity and the maintenance of political authority. On the other hand there may be no real contradiction here. This is a perfectly sensible form of the 'strong state/free market' coupling that exists in commercial market arenas (Whitty, 1989). Indeed it is possible to see the reform of education in Britain, as elsewhere, as a logical extension of the workings of the 'competition state' in an increasingly open world marketplace (Cerny, 1990). Insofar as the performance and production of the education system is seen to be crucial to the competition of the nation in world markets, then we must expect to see 'the total amount of state intervention . . . increase, for the state will be enmeshed in the promotion, support and maintenance of an ever-widening range of social and economic activities' (ibid., p. 230). Thus we might expect to see the state maintaining or even increasing its interventions in the education process. But these interventions may increasingly be oriented around the needs of an internationally competitive economy rather than the particular needs of individual students.

A further crucial feature of the reform process has been a concern with 'testing' and the agenda of 'standards' and 'performance'. This agenda has been pursued through a privatised and increasingly prescriptive system of school inspections (under the auspices of the Office for Standards in Education, OFSTED), which is also used to identify 'failing schools' and 'incompetent teachers', the take-up of models and schemes of school effectiveness and school improvement, and, at various times, the sponsorship of particular pedagogies and classroom arrangements, such as setting and whole-class teaching, and the criticism of others, such as mixed-ability and group work. These elements were embraced and pursued with vigour by the Labour opposition, and one of the first moves of the new Labour secretary of state for education was the establishment of a Standards and Effectiveness Unit headed by school improvement guru Michael Barber. Labour has gone further: local league table information is to be extended to include performance trends; LEAs will be inspected; the identification and sacking of 'incompetent teachers' is to be speeded up; lists of 'failing schools' have been published; and firmer targets are to be set for school and national educational performance. The 1997 education white paper laid out a programme of legislation which includes limiting class sizes to 30 for 5–7 year olds; establishing School Action Zones; a General Teaching Council and a new advanced skills teacher grade, the setting of students by ability, and at least an hour a day devoted to both numeracy and literacy in all primary schools. In addition the July 1997 budget allocated £1.3 billion from 'windfall tax' for school repairs and equipment and £1 billion from reserves to help raise school standards. While not intending to remove the paraphernalia of the education market, the emphasis of the Labour government is more directly on a planned and directive approach to education provision. This is may be seen as one manifestation of what Blackburn (1997, p. 15) calls 'New Labour authoritarianism and conformism' based upon 'populist appeals for punitive measures'.

## Policy Developments in Post-Compulsory Education

In the post-compulsory education and training sector a set of parallel reforms were introduced by the Conservatives. The 1992 Further and Higher Education Act removed colleges of further education, sixth form and tertiary colleges (and polytechnics) from LEA control and 'incorporated' them. In effect they were transformed into freestanding, competitive business enterprises. Emphasis has switched from LEA-planned provision of courses within each locality to a system of individual student/customer choice between competing providers (colleges, training and enterprise councils and private companies all compete for some sorts of courses and training). This is animated by a complex funding system based on recruitment, retention and student achievement of qualifications. Funds are transferred on the basis of five audit points (one for recruitment, three for retention and one for achievement of the qualification). Courses are funded by a standard unit cost formula, set at a relatively low level, which for most colleges has meant the need to bring about a 25 per cent growth in enrolment to maintain their existing levels of income – a target that a large number are unable to achieve. Concomitantly, 'savings' are being pursued by colleges by reductions in permanent staff, increases in class sizes and the imposition of new contracts on remaining staff that require longer working hours and increased contact time.

Alongside these changes the local planning and funding of vocational and employment training passed to 82 employer-led TECs. In addition national targets for education and training (NTETs) have been introduced to structure a system of job-related national vocational qualifications (NVQs) and vocationally relevant GNVQs – the former being work-based while the latter are college or school-based. The NTETs are expressed in terms of the acquisition of competencies and the measurement of outcomes and originated from the Confederation of British Industry: 'They are a commitment by the government and others to raise the level of qualifications held by the British population, as part of the drive to upskill the workforce' (Hodkinson *et al.*, 1996, p. 14).

In higher education, formula funding was introduced in 1986. More recently there has been an increased separation of the funding of teaching from the funding of research, the latter now being driven by the 'research selectivity exercise' (which rates and differentially funds all departments on a 1–5 scale) and competitive grant-getting from research councils. The change in funding mechanisms has also encouraged a shift in the style and culture of university management, with a very marked take-up of business and market methods (Mace, 1995). In 1991 the Committee of Vice-Chancellors and Principals set up an academic 'audit' unit, based upon the concepts of quality control and quality assurance used in the business sector. The Conservative government's stated intention with regard to these changes was to increase the efficiency and accountability of universities. Despite the abolition of the 'binary divide' (which had formerly divided universities from polytechnics) in 1994, one of the clear effects of the changes in funding has been the development of a new hierarchy among universities, with most research income now being attracted by approximately 15 of the 100 universities.

These internal changes have been accompanied by a massive increase in the age participation rate (APR) of those going on from school to higher education from around 13 per cent in 1980 to around 30 per cent in 1995:

> These developments have many similarities to the restructuring being effected within the school, health and personal social service systems. In all these, the thrust is to make providers operate as far as possible as entrepreneurs in quasi-markets, subject to new forms of regulation intended to make competition more effective (Rustin, 1994, p. 178)

Clarke and Newman (1992) argue that the insertion of what is called 'new management' into public sector institutions serves a dual purpose. On the one hand it is a vehicle for the introduction and naturalisation of the norms of efficiency and effectiveness. The use of various technologies of surveillance and monitoring relates performance more directly to cost and ties individual effort to organisational goals. On the other hand it works by attrition to weaken and transform the 'bureau-professional regimes' of public sector organisations. The values and culture of professionalism are replaced by those of business and management. Research suggests that both purposes are having their impact on school and college cultures and practices. However critics of the Conservative reform package have argued that the new emphasis on efficiency and cost do not automatically translate into more effective education, at least not for all students.

> At the level of the individual school, LMS seems to be encouraging resource decision-making which is consciously efficiency enhancing. However, the conception of efficiency used here is extremely input oriented, and it is not clear how choices made by schools about their patterns of resource acquisition and deployment relate to intended or actual teaching outcomes (Simkins, 1995, p. 30).

## The Outcomes and Effects of Change

After a decade of reform, how 'successful' has the process of institutional change been? Have educational outcomes improved, and if so, for whom? How have the roles of both teacher and those taught been changed? And what have been the unanticipated side effects of the reform process?

### Performance measured

In the simplest sense, the evidence for the success of these policies is contradictory. It is possible to point to an improvement in GCSE and A-level examination pass rates, but these improvements were called into question by the Conservative government's own concern about 'slippage' in the standard of examination marking. Political panic about national test results, reading age scores and Britain's performance in international assessment comparisons, fuelled by media coverage, have recurred throughout the period of reform. The 'politicisation of performance' can be seen both as indicating the importance attributed to education in contributing to national economic competitiveness, and as a political tactic for destabilising the education system for the purposes of reform.

Nonetheless it is clear from a range of evidence that schools have responded with great seriousness to the publication of local league tables and the general issue of competition for student recruitment (for example Abbott *et al.*, 1994; West and Sammons, 1996). And HMI (Her Majesty's Inspectors of Schools) and Ofsted reports have continued to identify supposedly significant percentages of 'incompetent' teachers and 'unsatisfactory' lessons. Among the responses to the latter has been a series of measures changing the ways in which teachers are trained: the inspection and grading of teacher training courses; a shift of emphasis away from college-and-university based courses to 'school-based' preparation; and a national curriculum for teacher training, which emphasises to classroom skills and competencies and eschews the use of educational 'theory'.

However this kind of evidence of 'outcomes' really tells us very little about the effects of policies on teachers' work, on schools and colleges as organisations, and on service users. Research evidence can be marshalled to suggest that across both the compulsory and post-compulsory sector these effects have been profound, although some commentators warn us that research on change in education may lead to a systematic neglect of powerful continuities (Power, 1992).

## Institutional change: the impact on cultures, values and practices

It is impossible for most schools and colleges to escape from the rigours of the market mechanism. Recruitment cannot be ignored – institutional survival depends upon it. LMS means that senior managers in schools are now responsible for financial management, student recruitment, marketing, employment relations and management of their plant and facilities. As a consequence the nature of school management and the role of the headteacher have changed significantly (Grace, 1995). These and other changes have also effected the nature of and created new tensions in the relationship between teachers and their managers (Bowe *et al.*, 1992). The former are now more than ever focused upon classroom and curricular concerns, while the latter are increasingly embedded in the languages and perspectives of their new generic tasks.

The market mechanism is also changing relationships within institutions, between institutions and their communities and between institutions and their clients. In many localities the possibility of cooperation and coordination between providers has been replaced by suspicion and overt rivalry, although there are some exceptions to this (Bridges and Husbands, 1996). Thus while the market mechanism is clearly a structural device it also brings about cultural and value changes. It significantly alters the moral environment within which teachers and managers work and make decisions. The market incentives give primacy to self-interest, and to shrewdness rather than principle (Heelas and Morris, 1992). Financial rather than 'professional' decision making lies at the core of the market form. Two groups have been profoundly affected by the changes: teachers and education's 'service-users'.

## Teachers' Work

The reforms of the past decade have changed not just the teacher's task but the very nature of what it is to be a teacher. LIBRARIES NI
WITHDRAWN FROM S C

### Employment

Teachers are now employed directly by schools and colleges. The security of their employment is based upon the continuity of their institutions' budget, and furthermore their pay is being increasingly deregulated. Since 1987, when teachers' negotiating rights were removed, general pay scales have been set by the secretary of state, based on advice from the School Teachers' Review Body, but governors and headteachers have considerable flexibility in the sorts of contract and levels of pay they offer. One outcome of this, related in particular to year-on-year budgetary uncertainties, has been a rise in the number of short-and fixed-term contracts. Incentive payments are now also used and experiments with performance related pay have been undertaken. The use of average staffing costs rather than actual costs in the calculation of budgets has put financial pressure on institutions with a more stable and experienced staff. In some cases this practice has led to the replacement of older, more expensive staff members with younger and cheaper ones. All of this is contributing to, and is an indicator of, the changed and weakened role of the teacher unions – although overall membership of the main teacher unions has increased since 1988. The emphasis on institutional survival and competition undermine both intra- and inter-institutional solidarities (Sinclair *et al.*, 1995).

## Classroom practice

It is more difficult to gauge the impact of reform on classroom practice. The national curriculum and national testing in schools, and the structure and assessment regime of GNVQs in colleges means that there is much greater external control or determination of the substance, pace and progression of classroom topics – the implication being that the scope of teachers' professional judgement has been narrowed (Pollard *et al.*, 1994). Nonetheless some evidence suggests that at least some teachers feel that their professional expertise has been enhanced by these changes. The filtration into the classroom of new management practices and the pressures emanating from student recruitment and public performance indicators is much less obvious. However the introduction of management techniques from business to achieve closer monitoring of teachers' work; the backwash effects of league table performance and intra- and interschool comparisons; the attempts to relate rewards more closely to performance; the more regular testing of children; and the sponsorship by government, inspectors and some academics of more 'traditional' teaching techniques, including the regrouping of students by ability – all these factors appear to be combining, at least in the secondary sector, to standardise teachers' practices and alter the balance between spontaneity and routine.

Almost all of the above also apply to the post-compulsory sector, although with some differences in emphasis. For example the further education funding regime, with its five audit points, acts directly on the teachers' classroom work, and colleges are responding to the financial demands of retention by paying more attention to pastoral care and guidance, student monitoring and student counselling (Ball *et al.*, 1997).

## Service users

Here there are two basic points to be made. The first is the ways in which the indicators and funding systems that drive the system lead to the overvaluing of some sorts of clients and the undervaluing of others. The second is the ways in which the market form trades upon skills and resources, inclinations and capacities, which are unevenly distributed across the population.

At school level, the use of academic indicators and a non-discriminatory funding system means that schools that are able to select (and deselect) their 'clients' have a strong incentive to do so. Disruptive students or those with special learning needs or difficulties are (1) unlikely to contribute to the improvement of a school's league table position; (2) more costly to provide for than other students; (3) may draw resources away from or inhibit the performance of other students; and (4) in some cases may damage the reputation of or give a particular emphasis to the image of the school. A number of consequences flow from this. First, all schools tend to compete hardest for the same types of student – girls, students with 'supportive and motivated parents' (often a euphemism for middle class), and certain Asian students, generally those with a prior record of high achievement or potential. This orients the schools towards certain programmes and activities and leads to certain common emphases in public presentations and publicity. Second, established expertise in the support of students with special educational needs is played down (Bowe *et al.*, 1992) for fear of discouraging the parents of more highly valued prospective students. Third, there has been a massive increase (since the introduction of local league tables in particular), of expulsions from school. In 1991–92, 2910 students were permanently excluded from schools in England and Wales; by 1994–95 the figure had risen to 12 500, 84 per cent of them from secondary schools (*Guardian*, 14 September 1996, p. 4). In a MORI poll published in 1993 nearly half of the chief education officers questioned identified competition between schools as the major factor in the dramatic rise in expulsions (*Time Out*, 10 July 1996, p. 13). Certain groups, African-Caribbean boys in particular, are overrepresented among these expulsions. Finally, there are indications that the social pattern of selection and expulsion, together with the uneven distribution of skills, are increasing the social segregation between schools, with working-class students and those with certain special needs and difficulties being grouped in particular schools. Typically such schools are undersubscribed and therefore have smaller budgets and fewer resources than their oversubscribed counterparts (Echols and Willms, 1995).

As for the second major trend, evidence suggests that middle-class parents are the main beneficiaries of choice and open enrolment policies inasmuch that they display the strongest inclination to choose, and they also possess the appropriate skills and resources to exploit to the full the opportunity to choose. They are also best placed to respond to the increased use of overt and covert selection procedures by schools, which are intended in any case to attract parents like them. Research by Echols and Willms (1995) into parental choice in Scotland indicates a thoroughgoing set of relationships between choice and social class. Our own research (Gewirtz *et al.*, 1995) and research from elsewhere (for example Waslander and Thrupp, 1995) confirms this finding.

During John Major's second term of office the reintroduction and extension of selection was a recurring theme. For example the promise of 'a grammar school in every town', together with changes in regulations by the Department for Education and Employment (1993 and 1996), provided the possibility for grant maintained and local authority schools to introduce partial selection on the basis of ability in music, art, sport or technology, without the necessity of further approval. Furthermore schemes were established for grant maintained schools to specialise as technology and sports colleges. For the former, schools are required to obtain £100 000 of sponsorship from industry in order to receive matching funding from the government. Walford (1996, pp. 55–6) notes that, 'such extra resources to a limited number of schools can lead to substantial differences between the learning environments of neighbouring schools'. Clearly, however, there is a basic tension between choice and the disciplines of the market on the one hand, and selection on the other. Choice is intended to reduce the power of providers, but selection enhances their power.

In post-compulsory education the most significant change in participation patterns is an increase in the number of 16 year olds staying on in some form of education and training. As a press release from the Department for Education and Employment (27 June 1996) stated, 'the proportion of 16-year-olds in education or training at the end of 1995 is estimated at 86.4 percent, an increase from 83.1 percent 5 years ago' (the equivalent figures for 18 year olds were 59.6 per cent and 45.7 per cent respectively). These figures still compare unfavourably with other developed countries, however, and are a direct reflection, and result, of the collapse in the youth labour market. In 1974, 61 per cent of Britain's 16-year-olds were employed, by 1993 this had fallen to 24 per cent, and many of the jobs were part-time or temporary (Coles, 1995). Furthermore, within these staying-on rates there are some stark social differences. Students from ethnic minorities are significantly overrepresented in the further education sector and underrepresented in the school sixth form sector. It would appear that for many of these students, further education provides an alternative or a fresh start after unsatisfactory experiences at school. As in the school sector, certain students carry higher 'value' than others. A-level students are the most sought after and not surprisingly the social backgrounds of such students are different from those choosing the vocational (GNVQ) and employment-based (NVQ) routes, and the rates of retention within the routes differ markedly. Ainley and Green (1996) describe this separation of routes as a 'new tripartitism'.

## Conclusion: Towards a New Polity?

In the ten years from 1988 to 1998 we have seen a fundamental and multifaceted reform of British education system. New logics, technologies and discourses have been inserted into and established in the institutions of education, right through from the primary school to the university. These reforms have contributed to fundamental changes in the nature of the relationship between civil society, the economy and the polity. Specifically they have shifted many aspects of public provision out of the sphere of local government and into a quasi-commercial environment. School governance, at least on paper, now rests in the hands of the governing bodies of individual schools (made up of elected parents and appointed members – there are now over 300 000 school governors in England and Wales). Deem *et al.* (1995, p. 162) describe governors as 'state volunteers', and drawing on their research argue that 'governors are either unaccountable to, or only very loosely accountable to, the local community that they and their schools are supposed to serve'.

The market, together with the cognate technologies of enterprise and entrepreneurship is a transformational force that carries and disseminates its own values. Choice and market systems reinterpolate key actors such as families, children and teachers, reposition schools and rework and revalue the meaning of education. The education market encourages competitive individualism and instrumentality. Thus, writing in more general terms, Ranson (1995, p. 442) argues that 'the economic, social and political transformations of our time are altering fundamentally the structure of experience: the capacities each person needs to flourish, what it is to live in society, the nature of work and the form taken by the polity'. Within all this, children themselves are positioned differently and evaluated differently in the education market, they are 'commodified'. In systems where recruitment is more or less directly related to funding, then the educational and reputational 'costs' of the child become part of the producers' response to choosers. The changes taking place in the ethico-political terrain of education may be seen as part of a broader set of shifts in 'the categories and explanatory schemes according to which we think ourselves, the criteria and norms we use to judge ourselves, the practices through which we act upon ourselves and one another' (Rose, 1992, p. 161). Social welfare is on the way towards thoroughgoing incorporation into the ontology of the market.

## Further Reading

Journals are probably the best general source of further material on education policy, in particular the *Journal of Education Policy* and the *British Educational Research Journal*. The chapters in J. Docking (ed.), *National School Policy* (London: Fulton, 1996) provide a good summary of educational reform, with suggestions for further reading. S. Ball, *Politics and Policy Making in Education: Explorations in Policy Sociology* (London: Routledge, 1990), examines the background to the 1988 Act based upon interviews with the major protagonists. I. Lawrence, *Power and Politics at the Department of Education and Science* (London: Cassell, 1992), offers a recent policy history of the DES.

# CHAPTER 10

# The Personal Social Services

MARY LANGAN

This chapter is about the transformation of personal social services in the 1980s and 1990s. After expanding and flourishing in the decade following the 1968 Seebohm Report, which advocated the integration of separate mental health, child care and welfare services, local authority social services departments were thrown on the defensive in the 1980s. At a time of rising demand for services, social services suffered from the general squeeze on public spending and local government. The seemingly endless stream of child abuse scandals had a damaging effect on social workers' morale and confidence. The Children Act (1989) and the NHS and Community Care Act (1990) initiated a process of reorganisation around child protection and care in the community, characterised by some as a 'revolution' in social services. Continuing controversies about the balance between family support and intervening to protect children, and about the harsh realities of 'needs-led' assessment and allocation of resources in the community, suggest that the difficulties facing social services are far from being resolved.

> The Government will rapidly find that the whole range of personal social services are as important and as potentially volatile as the health service (Feature on 'the new agenda' in the social services after the Labour Party's election victory, *Guardian*, 7 May, 1997).

There was little that was new in the agenda facing the new Labour government in the social services after its landslide victory in May 1997. In the early months of 1997 the media reported the latest in what appeared to have become an endless succession of scandals in the spheres of child protection and community care.

- A man who had been allowed by six different social services departments to foster 19 children over 18 years – despite an earlier conviction for sexually assaulting a boy – was sentenced to six and a half years in prison after admitting ten charges of indecent assault.

- An independent inquiry into the handling of the case of Rikki Neave, who was killed in 1994 at the age of six while on the 'at risk' register of Cambridgeshire social services, confirmed earlier reports of 'demoralisation, internal wrangles, unbearable case loads and poor management'.
- The director of two private homes for people with learning disabilities in Buckinghamshire was convicted of wilful neglect and ill-treatment of residents. The homes had been inspected every six months over 'a ten-year regime of terror'.

For the *Guardian* there was no difficulty in setting out the 'millennium tasks' facing the new government in the social services: 'to define clearer standards of service, to raise and fund overall training requirements, to blend health and social care into more locally-accountable arrangements, and to make more explicit the interface between public and personal funding responsibility for social care' (*Guardian*, 7 May, 1997). Furthermore, given the firmness of New Labour's pre-election commitment to keep a tight grip on public expenditure, the government was now expected to fulfil these tasks without providing additional resources to local authority social services departments.

Neither Labour's manifesto nor its first Queen's Speech proposed any specific measures to tackle the widely publicised problems of child protection and community care. Indeed the Conservative manifesto included a commitment to a £50 million respite programme for carers, which was more specific than Labour's bland endorsement of the mix of public and private provision introduced by the Conservatives and a proposed charter for standards in community care. Recognising the difficulty – if not the impossibility – of reconciling the conflict between demands and resources, the new government promptly proposed a Royal Commission to investigate the provision and financing of long-term care for the elderly.

Net expenditure on local authority social services increased approximately tenfold in real terms between the mid 1970s and the mid 1990s, to reach £7.8 billion in 1996. Spending expanded particularly rapidly in the early 1990s as responsiblity for long-term institutional care for older people was transferred from the social security budget. Though the Conservative governments of the 1980s and 1990s might not have been well-disposed towards local authority social services departments and social workers, both expanded in the Tory years. The total social services staffing level grew from 213 000 in 1984 to 238 000 in 1994, and the number of social workers from 24 000 to 35 000 (though only 15 per cent of the total, they certainly attracted the lion's share of the publicity, although unfortunately this was mostly adverse). Long dissatisfied with the performance of social services, the departing government had commissioned detailed reviews of particular departments: these would now report to a new secretary of state, but no doubt one equally concerned to tackle waste, inefficiency and low standards.

To gauge the scale of the problems facing the new government in social services and its prospects of success, it is necessary to trace the evolution of the current crises in child protection and community care.

## Social Work on the Defensive

The 1980s was a grim decade for social services departments and the social work profession, both of which had expanded rapidly in the previous decade in the wake of the 1968 Seebohm Report (Langan, 1993a). There were problems of resources, fierce controversies over cases of child abuse and allegations that the services were inefficient and unresponsive to users' needs. Let's take these issues in turn.

### The community care crunch

There were a number of reasons for the rising demand for social services. Fluctuating mass unemployment in the 1970s became a permanent feature of British society following the recession of the early 1980s and the collapse of substantial sections of the manufacturing industry. Increasing poverty, homelessness and family breakdown inevitably imposed greater demands on social services. Another problem was a growing mismatch between the rising numbers of elderly and disabled people wanting to live at home and the declining availability of carers (Henwood, 1992, p. 23). This was a result of demographic factors (the declining number of young adults following a long-term fall in the birth rate), economic factors (the increasing number of women going out to work) and social changes (increasing family breakdown, smaller family units).

Finances were increasingly constrained (Bebbington and Kelly, 1995, p. 409). There was a steady reduction in the grant from central government: in 1977 this accounted for 60 per cent of local authority income; by 1988 it had been reduced to 44 per cent. Councils that attempted to raise revenues above the levels approved by government were subjected to 'rate-capping', and the consequences of this were particularly severe in a number of inner London boroughs. The squeeze was further intensified, especially in the north, by the low growth in the local tax base of councils. Thus according to Oldman (1991, p. 5), resources were 'grossly inadequate' at a time when local authorities faced 'new responsibilities'.

## The child abuse double bind

In the course of the 1980s there were 18 official inquiries into cases of child abuse, most of which had led to fatality and often involved children under some form of social services supervision (Department of Health, 1991b). Several of these cases – perhaps most notably that of Jasmine Beckford, who died at the age of four of cruelty and neglect in Brent, North London, in July 1984 – provoked extensive media coverage. Social workers were condemned as lacking in commonsense and for taking a liberal attitude towards child abuse. Social services departments were targeted as callous, indifferent and unrepentant (Franklin and Parton, 1991, pp. 16–19). Strident editorials echoed judges and politicians in demanding a more authoritarian approach to families in which children were deemed to be at risk.

However the revelation of alleged child sexual abuse on a large scale in Cleveland in 1987, and the removal over a three-month period of around 120 children from their homes, provoked a different response and another conflicting set of demands on social workers. The social worker was no longer a fool or a wimp, but a bully or a zealot, motivated by feminist prejudice or academic theory (ibid., pp. 19–24). Subsequent allegations of 'satanic' or 'ritual' abuse in Nottingham, Rochdale, the Orkneys and else-where provoked similar responses. Now newspaper editors and politicians demanded more protection for families against interventionist professionals.

The official response to Cleveland, contained in the Butler-Sloss report and subsequent guidelines to concerned professionals, tried to balance the concern about protecting children with the rights of parents (Butler-Sloss, 1988). Many social workers, however, felt they were in a 'no-win' situation, 'damned if they did, damned if they didn't' interfere. The inevitable result was widespread demoralisation and a tendency to adopt a defensive style of practice.

## The bureau-professionals under attack

Social services departments also found themselves under attack as a conservative bureaucracy committed to an obsolete pattern of service provision. There was a convergence here of pressure 'from above' (from the government, the Audit Commission and various 'new right' think tanks) and a critique 'from below' (from individuals and organisations concerned about the lack of responsiveness of local services to particular needs).

An Audit Commission survey judged local authority social services to be expensive and in some areas wasteful (Audit Commision, 1986, p. 2). A recurrent criticism was that social services departments were inefficient at providing an optimal level of services for a given input of resources. One indication of this problem was the wide variation in the provision of services and the level of expenditure among different authorities. A survey in the child care field, for example, revealed 'huge differences in the quantity, quality and style of the services provided, in spite of a shared legal framework and broadly similar aims and policies' (Department of Health, 1991c, pp. 59–60).

The government complained that social services lacked the kind of rigorous data on local need that was necessary to deploy resources efficiently. Furthermore managers lagged behind other public services in identifying performance indicators. The Audit Commission criticised the reluctance of social services staff to accept hierarchy and formal managerial styles, with the result that performance-related pay remained 'conspicuous by its absence' long after it had become commonplace in the private sector (Kelly, 1991, p. 181).

The Audit Commission further commented on the 'low level of strategic rationality' in the management of social services. This led to a reluctance to advance clear and specific policies and instead allowed 'happenstance' to dictate the persistence of anachronistic patterns of service provision and staff allocation. According to one authoritative account, social services departments became less efficient in the 1980s as rising unit costs swallowed up increased expenditure: the result was a 10 per cent reduction in the volume of services (Bebbington and Kelly, 1995, p. 385).

Much social services capital and current expenditure was tied up in homes for children or older people and could not be readily redeployed in the community. As well as being expensive, institution-bound services tended to be centralised, standardised and inflexible: provision was service-led rather than needs-led. However in many authorities the interests of the institutions and those who worked in them still tended to take priority over the needs of the individual applicant.

Organisations representing people with physical disabilities, mental illness, learning difficulties and older people were all critical of local authority services. Groups representing women and minority ethnic communities complained about the discriminatory assumptions often made by service providers, the lack of culturally appropriate services and the inadequacy of information.

Towards the end of the 1980s some authoritative commentators considered that social work as a profession was destined for 'perpetual marginality' and that local authority social services departments might soon cease to exist (Baldock, 1989, p. 23; Bamford, 1990, p. ix). In fact both survived a major process of legislative and institutional reform, though their functions and style of working changed substantially.

# The Transformation of Social Services

Despite the controversies surrounding social services in the 1980s, it was not until the third term of Conservative rule after 1987 that the government set about restructuring them through two key pieces of legislation. The Children Act, introduced in 1989 and implemented by October 1991, created a new framework for the care and protection of children. The NHS and Community Care Act was introduced in 1990 and implemented in April 1993. It sought to change the role of the local authority social services department from that of a provider of services to that of 'enabler' or 'purchaser' of services from a mix of public, voluntary and private sources.

Instead of removing the responsibility for child protection from local authorities and handing it over to an independent agency, as some hostile commentators advised and many social workers feared, the Children Act in fact ratified the place of the social services department and the role of social workers. It sought, however, to establish clearer spheres of professional responsibility and lines of accountability.

An important feature of the Children Act was the extension of the juridical sphere into social work with families, removing from social workers some of the discretionary powers they had exercised in the past. Under the new framework, social workers retained statutory powers but were much more accountable to the courts. The legislation signalled a shift from a paternalistic and bureaucratic ethos to one of liberal individualism and juridically sanctioned rights. Nigel Parton identified a redefinition of the problem from a socio-medical one of child abuse to a socio-legal conception of child protection (Parton, 1991).

The two key features of the community care reforms were the 'purchaser–provider split' and a shift in the balance of provision from the state to voluntary, private and informal agencies. The objective, in social services as in other areas of welfare, was to extend the influence of market forces within social services (see Flynn, 1997). In practice the purchaser–provider split meant that, instead of directly providing services, 'care managers' used their devolved budgets to commission or purchase services from a variety of sources. The idea was that the market would encourage a shift from service/supply-led provision to needs/demand-led provision.

Competition among independent agencies was expected to expose (and reduce) the cost of services and offer a wider choice to users. Cutting costs was a particular concern to social services because of the perverse move towards private institutional care for the elderly that had resulted in the dramatic expansion in the number of old people in nursing and retirement homes during the 1980s – and an even more dramatic increase in costs. One of the central aims of the community care programme was to push this expenditure back on to the social services budget, where it could be more readily brought under control.

The community care reforms envisaged key roles for senior 'strategic' managers and for care managers, squeezing out superfluous intermediaries. It was up to senior managers to take the lead in deciding strategy, planning change, taking stock of resources, defining and measuring local needs and establishing priorities and targets. To achieve the goals of what the Audit Commission called the 'community revolution', managers would have to take the lead in 'challenging power structures and vested interests' (Audit Commission, 1992). They would also need to harness the latest information technology and financial systems to ensure the efficient devolution of administrative and budgetary responsibility to the care managers. It was considered essential that resources should flow to the point in the system where user needs were assessed.

The distinctive role of care managers was to assess the needs of particular individuals and devise appropriate packages of care services. The authorities emphasised that the care manager was not merely the familiar social worker with a new hat. Whereas the social work function involved both assessment and provision of services, the care manager combined the task of assessment with that of contracting for services from others – who might include social workers. For the Audit Commission, such a combination of needs-led assessment and targeting of resources offered great scope for flexible and innovative home-based services. It was also promoted as a device for putting power in the hands of the user of social services – now less of a troublesome client and more a valued customer.

One consequence of the reform of social services was the diminution of the power and independence of social work as a profession (Langan and Clarke, 1994). Though social workers retained a role in relation to child protection, this was circumscribed by the courts and by the requirement to collaborate with other agencies. In community care they were largely reduced to the task of needs assessment and subordinated to managerial discipline and market forces; there no longer seemed to be much place for their wider professional skills in counselling and therapeutic work with individuals and families. The transformation of social work education, downgrading sociological theory and elevating technical 'competencies', appeared to ratify the deskilling and degradation of the social work profession (Cannan, 1994/95).

Despite all the media brouhaha around social services and social work, the Children Act and the Community Care reforms were among the least controversial legislative reforms of the Tory years. But did they deliver what they promised?

# Family Support or Child Protection?

Though the Children Act was welcomed by social services departments, it failed to resolve the contradictory pressures on social workers. On the one hand the main emphasis of professional and academic authorities was on the importance of working in partnership with families. The aims were to provide support for those in difficulties, to safeguard the welfare of children and to prevent cases of neglect and ill-treatment. On the other hand the message coming from the inquiries into particular cases of abuse, amplified by politicians and the media, was that social workers should not hesitate to carry out their statutory policing responsibilities and intervene in families considered to be at risk.

Developments in the 1990s did not make it any easier to reconcile the conflicting perspectives of family support and child protection. The tendency, encouraged by the high public profile of voluntary organisations such as the NSPCC and ChildLine, towards a wider definition of abuse (including emotional neglect as well as physical and sexual abuse), together with a general heightening of public awareness of these issues, contributed to a dramatic increase in referrals of cases of suspected or alleged child abuse. It was also apparent that the vast majority of familes subjected to any form of child protection intervention were poor. Yet the Children Act was vague about what level of deprivation constituted a need for child welfare services.

It soon became apparent that the coercive aspects of the child protection system were taking priority over the supportive approach to child welfare. An Audit Commission report in 1994 concluded that the wider aims of the Children Act were not being achieved (Audit Commission, 1994). It reasserted the importance of preventive work, against the trend for social services to reduce their role to 'reactive' intervention and the provision of 'residual' services. In 1995 the government published an even more comprehensive indictment of the drift into coercive child protection: the result of a series of research projects commissioned in the wake of the events in Cleveland in the late 1980s (Department of Health, 1995b). The central message of the research was that social services departments had over-emphasised the 'forensic' aspects of child protection, wasting resources on largely fruitless investigations, while neglecting long-term treatment and preventive work in families considered in need of help.

However, while these reports called for a 'rebalancing' of social services activity in child protection in favour of support and away from coercion, there was no let up in the stream of gruesome court reports – and their familiar aftermath. For example the 1995 report of the inquiry into the case of 'Paul', who died of neglect at the age of 16 months while under the jurisdiction of

Islington Council in North London, criticised social workers for regarding the family as one in need of support, rather than one that was highly dangerous to its youngest member. The grisly case of Fred and Rosemary West, which revealed the systematic physical and sexual abuse and murder of up to a dozen young women, including family members, in Gloucester over a 20-year period, led to questions about the role of social services, the NSPCC and the police – all of whom had had contact with the family.

As Parton (1998) noted, the abuse inquiries had the effect of encouraging a legalistic outlook. For example a report by the Social Services Inspectorate in 1993 appeared to place greater importance on social workers following the correct child protection procedures than on providing appropriate support to families in need. For social workers, their anxiety about making a decision that was *defensible* came to outweigh their responsiblity to make one that was, in their professional judgement, in the best interests of a particular child.

## Needs-led or Resource-limited?

Though the principle of care in the community was popular, implementing this policy in such a way as to satisfy the diversity of needs – at a time when such needs appeared to be multiplying at a much faster rate than the resources available to meet them – proved difficult in practice. Let's look more closely at some of the problems of community care in the 1990s.

For Jane Lewis and her colleagues, who undertook a major study of the impact of the community care reforms in five local authorities, 'the most fundamental dilemma' facing social services departments was the 'tension between needs and resources' (Lewis *et al.*, 1995). From the moment the community care legislation came into effect, there were concerns about 'a care gap' between the level of need and the available services, because of the alleged underfunding of the transfer of elderly people in residential care from social security to social services responsiblity (*Guardian*, 3 October 1992).

In 1996 the Social Services Inspectorate reported that 'during the year a number of authorities announced that they had to raise their criteria for service provision in order to manage within their budgets' (SSI, 1996, p. 9). One example illustrates the consequences of such measures. Gloucestershire county council, facing a £2.5 million shortfall in its social services budget, removed home care services from more than 1000 people. When some of them – including 81-year-old Michael Barry, who had had a stroke, several heart attacks, a hip replacement and impaired vision – took the council to court, the case was ultimately decided (in the House of Lords) in favour of the council (*Guardian*, 21 March, 1997).

Some authorities transferred funds from their community care budgets to cover the mounting costs of maintaining an increasing number of children in care (*Guardian*, 1 January, 1997). Thus, for example, Oxfordshire moved £1.1 million from services for the elderly to those for children and people with learning disabilities; Essex moved £1.3 million from community care to children's services.

The process of 'needs assessment' rapidly became an exercise in reducing consumer expectations, as the government's own circulars candidly conceded: 'Practitioners will, therefore, have to be sensitive to the need not to raise unrealistic expectations on the part of users and carers' (quoted in Lewis *et al.*, 1995, p. 92). Care management became a process of rationing resources rather than one of extending choice. The process of 'raising the criteria' of need meant in practice reducing eligibility for services to those considered to be at risk of 'significant harm' if the service was not provided. In her survey, Lewis identified a trend for fewer people – those targeted as being at high risk – to get better services. The other side of the coin was that those at lower levels of need – considered merely to be at risk of loss of independence or of being unable to maintain a satisfactory quality of life – could no longer expect much care in the community.

What about empowerment and choice? In a comprehensive survey of the structural and informational imperfections of the new social care markets, Julien Forder and his colleagues concluded that they 'cannot be guaranteed to deliver the range of services required to meet community care objectives' (Forder *et al.*, 1996, p. 201). Following a study of four user groups, Stevenson and Parsloe (1993, p. 6) pointed to 'inconsistencies and conflicts' arising from the new policy, that 'raise doubts as to the sincerity of the intentions'.

Quasi-markets in welfare present a number of problems. On the purchaser side, the care manager controls the budget on behalf of the service user, but she or he has no direct control over the services themselves, and depends on contract specification and monitoring to guarantee the quality of service. Indeed in many instances she or he 'purchases' only nominally, within the framework of block contracts already negotiated. Block contracting serves to minimise uncertainty for purchasers as well as contractors, particularly for first-time buyers, who have no experience of this market and little information upon which to engage in bargaining. The same conditions are likely to promote contracting relationships with familiar providers, rather than producing 'market stimulation' (Wistow *et al.*, 1992). At the same time the user may receive the services she or he is assessed as needing, but has no control over the assessment or the allocation of resources. The position of users is that of quasi-customer, exercising sovereignty at second hand through the care manager.

Despite the rhetoric of 'user-led, customer-oriented services' accompanying the community care reforms, user demands for diversity has clashed with managerial concerns about cost-effectiveness. Though the discourse of empowerment has encouraged a challenge to bureau-professional paternalism, it is difficult to identify any enhancement of the power of the service user. Marion Barnes has identified a series of 'barriers to effective user involvement' in community care plans, including the exclusion of those considered incapable (people with learning disabilities), and those with different languages (including those reliant on sign language), the neglect of the old and the elevation of carers over users, the fact that consultation is with client groups defined by the authorities (which may not be accepted by users) and is based on an agenda set by the authorities (Barnes, 1996).

Organisations representing people with disabilities and minority ethnic groups have vociferously challenged the assumptions of the community care programme. For Michael Oliver, the very language of community care has served 'to deny disabled people the right to be treated as fully competent, autonomous individuals, as active citizens' (Oliver, 1992, p. 31). He argues for a 'rights-based welfare' that emphasises entitlement, independent living, social support, personal assistance, activity, organisation and empowerment. From a black perspective, Adele Jones rejects needs-based assessments as promoting 'pathology, inadequacy and inability as the basis of who has what services' (Jones, 1992, p. 38). For her, the focus on needs rather than human rights is 'in direct conflict with the concept of empowerment'.

Another promise of the community care programme was to deal with the problems at the interface between social services and other welfare agencies and thus to move towards the goal of 'seamless' care services. From the outset some experts were sceptical. For Tessa Harding the seamless blanket looked more like a net full of holes: 'as each area of public service narrows its focus, the gaps between them become larger' (Harding, 1992, p. 7). The problem for social services has been that people who have fallen through other nets have all tended to end up on their doorstep

One of the most publicised failures of the community care programme has been in the sphere of mental health services. In the early 1990s a series of fatal attacks on members of the public and care workers by recently discharged psychiatric patients led to a public clamour for a more coercive policy towards potentially dangerous individuals with mental illness. This led to the allocation of specific funds for improving services and, in 1995, to the policy of 'supervised discharge' under which mentally ill individuals considered at risk of violence remained under surveillance in the community.

# Conclusion

In the long run-up to the 1997 general election, the Conservative government threatened drastic measures to deal with the chronic problems in the social services. In response to a series of scandals in residential child care in 1996, health secretary Stephen Dorrell once again raised the question of whether responsibility for child protection should be removed from local government (*Guardian*, 16 October, 1996). In a white paper published only weeks before the general election, the government proposed further measures to push local authorities into selling off their remaining care institutions and purchasing services from private and voluntary providers.

In the event, of course, the Conservatives were defeated, leaving the Labour Party with the ambivalent legacy of the reforms of the early 1990s – but without much in the way of clear policy commitments. What were the options facing the new government as it set about planning social services into the new century?

With regard to child protection, some experts suggested that the institutional separation of the tasks of child protection and family support might help to resolve conflicts (Parton, 1996, p. 20). Recognising that social services had become primarily a child protection agency, Parton argued that the wider responsibilities for child and family welfare might be better discharged by some other department of local government or voluntary organisations.

A parallel argument in community care proposed a clearer separation between the processes of needs assessment and those involved in the commissioning and purchasing of services (Lewis *et al.*, 1995). Lewis was, however, concerned about the pressure to reduce expectations in community care, emphasising the continuing importance of recording need, even if it could not be met. The importance of defining 'unmet need' was that it at least raised aspirations for a new pattern of provision that was genuinely responsive to individual needs.

Other alternatives were advanced by those on the receiving end of community care. In an attempt to develop the 'independent living' model, disability organisations demanded that people with disabilities be enabled to act as their own care managers. The notion of 'service brokerage', in which, for example, the parents of a person with learning disabilities have the power to act as intermediaries between that person and the social services department, originated in Canada. Others emphasised the role of advocacy, particularly in relation to people with mental health problems or learning disabilities.

For social services departments and social workers the future remained uncertain. Back in 1991, former social worker Tessa Jowell told a conference on community care that 'our professional world is spinning so fast it is hard to maintain one's bearings and the uncertainties, real or speculative, are in danger of sabotaging competence, creativity and confidence' (Jowell, 1991). Six years later Jowell was appointed junior minister in the Department of Health (though not with personal responsibility for social services). While the world of social services was still spinning, perhaps at an even dizzier rate, expectations were high that a government whose members had more experience and expertise in the fields of social care might at last begin to realise some of the higher aspirations of those who had stood up for children's rights and for care in the community.

## Further Reading

The fragmentation of social services in the 1990s is reflected in the literature: general overviews of the field of social work seem to have disappeared with the generic social worker. However A. Webb and G. Wistow's *Social Work, Social Care and Social Planning* (London: Longman, 1987) remains a useful assessment of the two decades following Seebohm, as does T. Bamford, *The Future of Social Work* (London: Macmillan, 1990) For subsequent developments in the sphere of child protection there is no better guide than Nigel Parton's *Governing the Family: Child Care, Child Protection and the State* (London: Macmillan, 1991) and *Child Protection and Family Support: Tensions, Contradictions and Possibilities* (London: Routledge, 1996). The Department of Health's report, *Child Abuse* (1991b), provides a comprehensive – and deeply depressing – survey of the child abuse inquiries of the 1980s. Marion Barnes' *Care, Communities and Citizens* (London: Longman, 1996) provides a valuable survey of the development of community care and a well-informed discussion of the issues and controversies that are likely to remain at the centre of the policy debate over the next few years. For the perspective of those trying to push through the 'community care revolution' from above, the publications of the Audit Commission and the Social Services Inspectorate are invaluable. A consistent voice from below, from the perspective of the disability movement, is that of Michael Oliver, Britain's first professor of disability studies. His *Understanding Disability: From Theory to Practice* (London: Macmillan, 1996) contains a powerful critique of the record of social services.

# CHAPTER 11

# Housing Policy

PETER MALPASS

For twenty five years after the Second World War governments in Europe developed housing policies against a background of, on the one hand, serious housing shortages and problems of unfitness, and on the other hand, a prolonged period of economic expansion and virtually full employment. In Britain there was agreement about the need to build as many houses as possible (using both the private and the local authority sector), and to demolish unfit houses as part of an ambitious urban renewal plan. Of course there were arguments about some aspects of policy, such as whether there was too little or too much building by local authorities, too little or too much slum clearance, and there was debate about the level and distribution of subsidies. But successive governments, both Labour and Conservative, accepted that new building by local authorities had a significant part to play in meeting housing needs. From the early 1950s onwards there was also a gathering consensus of support for the expansion of home ownership, underpinned by the generally favourable economic climate. In the case of private renting the continuing long-term decline led to a policy that was effectively one of managed decline, with little realistic expectation of significant amounts of new investment.

In recent times housing has lost much of its political salience: in 1945 it was seen as one of the key electoral issues (Hennessey, 1992, p. 85) and for many years after the war politicians in both main parties sought to garner votes by pledging to build large numbers of new houses. In 1979, promising council tenants' the 'right to buy' was seen as a vote winner for the Conservatives, and in 1987 a raft of new policies on housing were rolled out during the election campaign (Malpass, 1990, 1993). By the general election of 1992, however, housing seemed to be an issue that no one wanted to talk about, and the same was true in 1997. Nevertheless, throughout their eighteen years in office the Conservatives never lost sight of the importance of housing and they retained an active legislative programme right up to the end, with two major Acts in 1996. Such a long period in power gave the Conservatives the opportunity to stamp their ideological imprint on housing policy and the housing system, with the result that in 1997 the incoming Labour government inherited a situation that was very different from the one that the Callaghan administration had left behind in 1979.

In constructing a review of developments since 1979 it is tempting to concentrate exclusively on change, but this would be a mistake, for there are significant elements of continuity, or at least consistencies in the direction of change. The emphasis on the growth of home ownership, the parallel residualisation of council housing, and the policy of shifting from general housing subsidies to income-related assistance were all in place well before 1979, but they were accentuated under the Conservatives. A distinctive feature of the Thatcher governments, maintained under John Major, was a deep hostility to local authority housing. From 1979 new building by local authorities was reduced, the sale of existing houses was promoted and ministers took the view that local authority housing was actually part of the problem to be solved. This has to be seen in the context of their ideological belief in the superiority of private-sector, market-driven solutions, and their hostility to all things municipal, epitomised in the abolition of the metropolitan counties and the Greater London Council in 1986. It is important to recognise that although the Thatcher administrations will be remembered as the most ideologically driven of British governments, they retained a degree of pragmatism, as illustrated by their resistance to demands for reform of mortgage interest tax relief for home owners throughout the 1980s, their willingness to abandon or modify failed initiatives (such as tenants' choice and housing action trusts) and their espousal of successful ideas emerging from outside government (especially the large-scale, voluntary transfer of council housing to new landlords).

Housing was a success story for the Conservative Party from the late 1970s through to the late 1980s. The party had something positive to offer to significant groups of electors: six million council tenants were given the right to buy their houses at heavily discounted prices and home owners in general enjoyed the benefits of substantial capital gains from increasingly rapidly rising house prices in the period 1983–89. By the mid 1990s, however, the situation was very different, with the housing market continuing in recession, house prices generally significantly below their 1989 levels, at least a million households in negative equity, and nearly 1000 households each week facing repossession. In contrast to the positive policy stance of the 1980s the situation was dominated by cuts across the board: in local authority housing subsidies, in housing association grant (HAG) rates, in individual housing benefit entitlement, in mortgage interest tax relief, in income support to unemployed mortgaged home owners and in the capital programmes of providers of social housing.

# Public Expenditure on Housing

The main components of public expenditure on housing are capital investment by local authorities (including renovation grants to private owners) and the Housing Corporation (together with Scottish Homes and Tai Cymru) and, on the revenue side, local authority revenue subsidies, housing benefit and mortgage interest tax relief. A complete measure of assistance to consumers would need to include the value of discounts given to purchasers of homes owned by councils and housing associations. The DOE white paper of 1995 (Department of the Environment, 1995, p. 8) put housing expenditure (not including discounts) in 1994/5 at £18.2 billion, which it claimed was in real terms very close to the 1979/80 level. There were some very important differences in the pattern of expenditure, however, with income-related benefits to tenants having increased from 10 per cent to 49 per cent, and investment expenditure having fallen from 68 per cent to 27 per cent.

Whereas in 1979 local authorities built some 75 000 new houses, by the mid 1990s their building programmes had been effectively eliminated and their capital expenditure was devoted either to renovation of the existing stock, or to loans to housing associations to build new dwellings. Central government provision for local authority capital expenditure has been on a downward trend since 1992/93, and the 23 per cent cut for English councils announced in the budget of November 1996 was even greater than implied in earlier plans. Housing associations have suffered a similar fate. In the early 1990s they enjoyed a major expansion of their capital programme, supported by grants from the Housing Corporation, but since the peak year of 1992/3 they have experienced deep cuts each year, and the cut in 1997/8 was 40 per cent. This left the programme standing at little more than a quarter of the 1992/3 level.

There are two further points to make about the capital side. First, only about 50 per cent of housing association capital spending counts as public expenditure, the remainder being generated as loans from private financial institutions. Second, both local authorities and housing associations are now subject to competitive allocation systems, the introduction of which has had a big impact on their behaviour. In the case of housing associations it means that they have come under competitive pressure to bid for schemes at lower and lower levels of subsidy (social housing grant). In order to do so they have had to raise more in private loans (with implications for rents) and/or cut the standards of new houses.

On the revenue side of housing expenditure, general housing subsidies to local authorities have been cut back considerably in recent years, but the

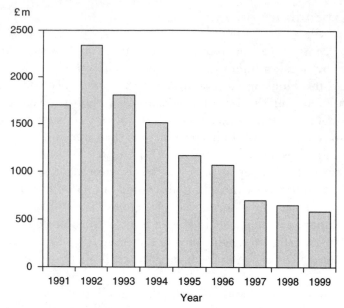

*Source*: Wilcox (1997).

**Figure 11.1   Housing Corporation Expenditure, 1991–2000**

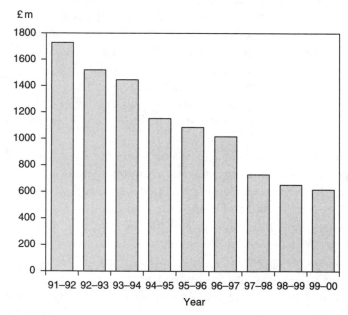

*Source*: Wilcox (1997).

**Figure 11.2   LA capital expenditure, England, 1990–2000**

consequence has been a huge increase in spending on housing benefit, fuelled also by the deregulation of rents in the private sector since 1989. Total housing benefit expenditure in 1995/6 was estimated to be £11 billion, or 22 per cent above the level of 1992/3. The growth of housing benefit expenditure was a planned outcome of changes in rents policy, but the scale of the increase was not foreseen, and tackling the problem has become a priority for government.

The other large component of housing expenditure is mortgage interest tax relief, which stood at £7.7 billion per annum in 1990/1, but has now fallen to around £2.5 billion. The decline is due to two main factors: the fall in interest rates and cuts in the level of assistance given.

## The Organisation and Delivery of Housing Services

A distinctive feature of British housing policy since 1979 has been the form and scale of privatisation of social rented housing. The most important privatisation measure, in terms of the numbers of dwellings involved, has been the sale of local authority houses to individual owner occupiers. This has been complemented by a series of other measures designed to reduce the stock of dwellings retained by local authorities. Tenure diversification has been a key element in initiatives such as Estate Action, City Challenge and Housing Action Trusts, while proposals emerging from outside central government, specifically large-scale voluntary transfers and local housing companies, have sought to retain and enhance the supply of social rented housing by transferring it to new not-for-profit owners.

Privatisation has underpinned commitment to the growth of home ownership, which has remained the primary objective of housing policy, as confirmed by the White Paper on housing in 1995. In the period 1979 to 1995 the stock of social rented housing in Britain declined by more than a quarter and contributed nearly half of the growth in home ownership (Forrest *et al.*, 1995). Further growth in the coming decade will require the continued sales of local authority houses on a significant scale. However sale to individual owners have been running at substantially lower levels in the 1990s, at around a third of the rate achieved in 1989. The declining level of sales can be attributed to a number of factors. First, the deep and prolonged recession in the first half of the decade led to reduced earnings, high unemployment and greater job insecurity. It is difficult to quantify the impact, but this must have reduced the number of 'right to buy' sales. Second, it is reasonable to infer that the collapse of the private housing market must have acted as a deterrent to at least some potential right to buy purchasers. Third, there has been a decline in the number of desirable dwellings in the right locations, and the experience of tenants who bought flats during the property boom in the late 1980s has had a deterrent effect on the sale of this type of accommodation in the present period. Accounts of heavy service charges and difficulties with reselling have dealt a severe blow to the market for local authority flats.

A fourth factor is that social rented housing has been affected by the longer-term increase in the proportion of households with no income from employment. Between the early 1960s and the late 1980s the proportion of all households with no income from employment doubled to 34 per cent, but the proportion of local authority tenants with no earned income showed a more than fivefold increase to 60 per cent (Holmans, 1991). More recent statistics suggest that only 28 per cent of local authority tenants have an earned income (Wilcox, 1995). This very high rate of dependency on pensions and state benefits means that the majority of current local authority tenants are financially unable to exercise their right to buy.

In the early 1980s the main policy theme in relation to rented housing was privatisation, and it was not until the latter part of the decade that a review of policy gave a new emphasis to the need to enhance the provision of rented housing, in terms of stimulating the private sector and housing associations, and tackling some of the problems in the council sector. What emerged in the late 1980s, then, was a rented housing strategy consisting of four main elements:

- Provisions for council tenants to have new landlords.
- A strategy to revive investment in private renting.
- A new financial regime for housing associations.
- A new financial regime for local authority housing.

Space does not permit a detailed discussion of each of these elements (Malpass, 1993), but briefly the proposals for landlord change involved Housing Action Trusts (HATs) and tenants' choice (a scheme allowing approved landlords to bid to take over parts of the local authority stock). HATs were bitterly opposed by tenants in the first areas to be designated and although six were eventually set up they were on very different terms from those initially envisaged. Tenants' choice made very little impact, and fewer than 1 000 dwellings were transferred out of local authority ownership by the time the scheme was abandoned in 1995. There has been a substantial stock transfer programme since 1989, however, but it has resulted from an initiative by local authorities themselves. By the start of 1997, 50 local authorities had transferred 230 000 dwellings into the ownership of other landlords, in nearly every case a housing association set up for the purpose. The DOE white paper of 1995 said that the government 'would like to see all authorities consider transfer as one of the options for dealing with housing problems'

(Dept of the Environment, 1995, p. 29), and in February 1997, shortly before the end of the Conservative government, the minister of housing issued a consultation paper on proposals to require all housing authorities to include stock transfer plans in their housing strategies.

The revival of private renting involved two elements: legislation in the Housing Act 1988 to deregulate rents and alter security of tenure, and the introduction of a financial inducement to investors in the form of tax breaks for investors in companies set up specifically to invest in new rented housing (this was an extension of the Business Expansion Scheme, BES). Deregulation of the private rented sector took the form of phasing out fair rents and regulated tenancies and replacing them with market rents and assured tenancies, giving landlords greater access to vacant possession of their properties. Implicit in the deregulation of rents was acceptance that additional housing benefit costs would be borne by the Treasury.

The new financial regimes for housing associations and local authorities were distinct in their form and detail, but they were united by the objective of shifting from 'bricks and mortar' subsidies to means-tested housing benefit assistance. In the case of housing associations the new system that operated from 1989 was that capital subsidies in the form of housing association grants should be gradually replaced by private finance, borrowed directly by the housing associations from the private capital markets. In order to attract private finance it was necessary to introduce legislation to change the nature of housing association tenancies, and since 1989 new housing association tenants have been given assured tenancies, with no right to buy. However the Housing Act 1996 introduced a right for housing association tenants to acquire their homes, but the right applies only to tenants of properties built since the Act came into effect.

In the local authority sector the Local Government and Housing Act 1989 established a new subsidy system designed to give the centre renewed leverage on rents (Malpass *et al.*, 1993). Each year the DoE sets guideline rent increases related to property values in each local authority area, and if these increases exceed the notional increases in permitted expenditure the subsidies are withdrawn.

## Impacts on Tenants and Home Owners

Looking at the outcomes of the government's rented housing strategy, there are two main aspects to consider: the supply of new rented housing and the shift to income-related assistance with housing costs. The increase in private renting in Britain as a whole amounted to some 0.2 per cent of the total stock, or 214 000 units in the period 1989–93. However Crook and Kemp (1996) conclude that, 'whilst there has been a significant increase in the number of dwellings, much of this can be attributed to the short-run impact of the BES and to the property slump (as frustrated owner occupiers unable to sell temporarily let out their houses), rather than to rent deregulation'. Housing associations in Britain as a whole built 143 000 new units in the same period, while the local authority building programmes were virtually eliminated (in 1994 only 1 664 new council houses were built). In terms of the supply of rented dwellings the strategy seems to have had a short-term effect, but the market failed to produce convincing evidence of long-term growth in private renting, and the government itself cut back the resources for the development of the social rented sector.

Turning to the question of the redirection of subsidies away from bricks and mortar into income-related assistance, there was mounting evidence of a change of policy in the face of escalating costs as rents rose in real terms. In the local authority sector the government pursued a policy of guideline rent increases above inflation each year from 1990/1 to 1995/6, with the result that council rents rose by an average of 40 per cent in real terms (ADC/AMA, 1995, p. 3). Housing association rents at the end of 1994 were 80 per cent higher than at the start of 1989, in a period when prices generally rose by only 30 per cent (NFHA, 1995).

The housing benefit budget was always intended to 'take the strain', but what happened was that the cost rose faster than had been anticipated. Rent allowances (covering private and housing association tenants) grew at an annual rate of 22 per cent between 1988/9 and 1993/4; this compares with only 7.6 per cent for local authority rent rebate expenditure (Department of Social Security, 1994, p. 11). Private sector tenants constituted just over a third of all housing benefit claimants but their rent levels meant that they accounted for nearly half of all housing benefit expenditure (DSS press release, 30 November 1994).

The rising cost of housing benefit produced two policy responses. First, the government rediscovered the virtues of bricks and mortar subsidies and signalled a change of approach to rents in the social rented sectors. The DOE white paper of 1995 admitted that 'The most cost-effective way of ensuring that people with permanently low incomes have a decent home is to give a direct subsidy to landlords to provide social housing at rents below market levels' (Dept of the Environment, 1995, p. 26). The white paper also referred to an intention to reduce the rate of increase in local authority guideline rents, implying that by the end of the decade rents would increase broadly in line with inflation. However the process was speeded up in November 1995 and the government announced that the guideline increase in April 1996 would be pegged to inflation. In addition it was revealed that any local authority that decided to increase rents by more than the guideline amount would not be entitled to an additional subsidy to cover the cost of extra housing benefit.

Thus the long march towards a policy based on means-tested assistance in the local authority sector slowed to a halt, and the system that was used for six years to force rents to rise was turned into a mechanism to restrain local authorities from making further increases.

The second response to the rising cost of housing benefit was that in the housing association and private rented sectors the Conservative government introduced restrictions on housing benefit entitlement in cases where the rent was deemed to exceed the average for the locality. The assumption under-pinning this move was that tenants would be given an incentive to negotiate rents downwards, or that they would seek cheaper accommodation, although this was highly questionable in a market where shortages continued.

Turning to events in the housing market since 1980, there have been cycles of boom and slump, which have had important implications for consumers. The economic recession of 1981 resulted in a serious downturn in housing market activity, with new private sector output reaching a 25 year low point. Although the recession in the early 1980s had an impact on real house prices, the effect of inflation was to protect home owners from the psychologically damaging experience of seeing the value of their homes falling in cash terms. It was in 1983 that real house prices began to recover, launching the third and most damaging boom–slump cycle since 1972. Prices went on rising ever more steeply until 1989. Thus for established home owners and those able to get a foot on the ladder, in this period home ownership was a highly attractive investment, with prices rising by an average of nearly 24 per cent in 1988 alone, the third year running that average increases had been in double figures (CML, 1991).

It all began to go wrong for the government in the summer of 1988, following the chancellor's budget announcement of the impending end of multiple tax relief (this was the anomaly under which unmarried couples had each been able to claim interest relief on up to £30 000 of mortgage debt). Advance notice of the withdrawal of this arrangement encouraged more purchasers into the market, and activity became frenzied as buyers competed to beat the deadline for double tax relief. Mortgage interest rates had dipped below 10 per cent during the spring of 1988, the first time for a decade that they had been so low, and this naturally added to the activity in the housing market. The more frenzied the market became the higher the prices were driven, dragging the price to income ratio to its highest level since 1973, thereby taking house purchase beyond the reach of growing numbers of would-be home owners.

In July 1988 interest rates began to rise again, reaching record levels (in excess of 15 per cent) by early 1990. House prices fell in nominal as well as real terms, and activity in the housing market fell by nearly 50 per cent in five years. Whereas in the boom there had been concern about whether home ownership was becoming unaffordable in the sense of it being difficult to gain access (Bramley, 1994), in the early 1990s the emerging problem was that a growing numbers of people who had gained access could no longer afford to remain home owners, but as prices fell they could not afford to sell either. Their problem was compounded as the economy sank into deep recession, in which unemployment nearly doubled between the start of 1990 and the start of 1993; the rate of increase in unemployment was above the average in precisely those regions that had experienced the most active housing markets during the boom (Wilcox, 1994, p. 99).

The collapse of the housing market produced an explosion of mortgage arrears and repossessions on a scale never before experienced in Britain. In 1980, for instance, the building societies recorded 15 530 cases of mortgages that were in arrears by 6–12 months, and by 1992 the figure had grown to 205 000. In the early 1980s repossessions were running at less than 10 000 per year, but in 1990 there was a sudden leap to 43 890 from 15 810 in 1989. The peak year was 1991, when 75 540 houses were taken into the possession of mortgage lenders. Although things have improved somewhat since then, repossessions are still running at more than twice the highest ever annual rate before the 1990s.

The term negative equity, referring to situations where the amount of loan secured against a property exceeds its current market value, entered the language of housing debate after the housing market collapse. There is some disagreement about the scale of negative equity and what to do about it, but estimates suggest that over a quarter (26.4 per cent) of 1988–91 buyers had negative equity in 1993 (Dorling and Cornford, 1995, p. 161), and that the number was 1.7 million at the end of 1995 (Nationwide, 1996).

In addition to the cuts in mortgage interest tax relief there has been a reduction in the assistance available to mortgaged home owners through Income Support. From October 1995 people taking out new mortgages no longer qualified for assistance with mortgage costs through Income Support for the first forty weeks of the claim. The entitlement of existing borrowers was reduced to assistance with half their mortgage interest from the ninth to the twenty-seventh week of any claim and the full amount thereafter. Borrowers are now expected to take out private insurance to cover themselves against the risk of unemployment or any other circumstances that would render them unable to maintain their mortgage repayments.

Looking back on the ten years of boom and slump in the British housing market, the first point to make concerns the extent to which the third such cycle in twenty years had a more damaging effect than its predecessors. The reasons for this have been the subject of much debate, but were to do with the height of the boom and the corresponding depth of the recession, which was made more painful because of the coincidence of high unemployment and low inflation. Whereas mortgaged home owners had experienced decades of real benefit from inflation, the combination of the deepest housing market recession in modern times and the lowest rate of inflation for thirty years meant that for the first time since before the Second World War home owners saw the value of their investment falling in cash terms. The rapid expansion of home ownership in the 1980s had been boosted by the increased availability of mortgage credit and the willingness of lenders to provide up to 100 per cent of the valuation; this had drawn into the market increasing numbers of low-income purchasers and they, and other heavily borrowed owners, were clearly most at risk of losing their homes when unemployment struck.

The second point to make here concerns the links between housing and the economy. In general terms the recent British experience illustrates the risks implicit in reliance on the markets for the achievement of policy objectives. There is also the more particular point that reliance on interest rates as the main tool of macroeconomic management meant that when economic policy dictated a hike in rates, the effect on the housing market was devastating; in effect the housing market was sacrificed in the attempt to dampen activity in the economy as a whole.

Finally in this section it is important to draw attention to the way that policy towards the housing market changed in the mid 1990s. As mentioned above, in the 1980s, when there was no shortage of demand in the housing market, the government resisted calls for the reform of mortgaged assistance to home owners, but in the depressed housing market of the mid 1990s the government made substantial cuts in support to home owners, including those in greatest need. As recently as 1992–93 the chancellor sought to take surplus supply out of the housing market by providing £570 million to permit housing associations to acquire unsold properties, but since that time there has been no sign of similar intervention to stimulate the market. The DOE white paper of 1995 was remarkably silent on the housing market, and there were no specific proposals to deal with problems such as negative equity, mortgage arrears and repossession. It seems that the Treasury preferred to see the housing market remain depressed than to unleash a new bout of unsustainable credit-based overconsumption. If a depressed housing market was the price that had to be paid for keeping down inflation, then they were prepared to pay it. Thus in the mid 1990s it was clear that housing policy was subordinated to economic policy to an even greater extent than in earlier years.

## Conclusion

In coming to a conclusion about eighteen years of Conservative housing policy the first point that must be acknowledged is that at least the Conservative governments knew what their priorities were: in housing perhaps more than any other part of the welfare state they stuck to the maxim of 'private good, public bad'. In their own terms, the Conservatives' housing policy was highly successful, raising the rate of home ownership in Britain from 55 per cent in 1979 to 67 per cent in 1995 and turning round the sixty-year growth of council housing. They also managed, eventually, to begin to withdraw mortgage interest tax relief, a task that for so long had appeared to be politically impossible. The housing policy debate was successfully moved onto Tory ground, so that there was no challenge to the right to buy, nor to the principle of local authority stock transfer, and no prospect of a return to large-scale house building by local authorities.

However, having been in office and committed to a particular set of priorities for so long, the Conservatives also exposed the contradictions and problems of their policies. For example a housing policy built around reliance on market mechanisms was bound to be vulnerable when general economic activity declined. This is partly a point about the way that markets tend to rise and fall (although not usually as wildly as the British housing market in the period 1986–92 – see Maclennan, 1994, p. 17), and partly about the need to recognise that actors and institutions driven by market forces cannot be expected to behave in ways that are consistent with the objectives of policy makers. The Conservatives lacked a policy for managing the housing market and this was very clearly revealed in the DOE white paper of 1995, which in 60 pages had nothing to offer on major problems such as negative equity and repossession.

The Conservatives' success in raising rents across all rented sectors exposed the tensions between housing and social security. Firstly, while the switch from bricks and mortar subsidy to personal means tested subsidies was coherent in housing terms, it had serious expenditure implications for the Department of Social Security, which, as the biggest spending department in Whitehall, always has the Treasury standing in attendance. Secondly, the deregulation of rents highlighted a longstanding feature of the housing benefit system. The British system is unusual (Kemp, 1994) in that it covers up to 100 per cent of housing costs, and in most cases, the calculation of entitlement is based on the actual rent paid. Deregulation and the move towards higher rents across the board have highlighted the way in which a market approach to rent setting required a limit to the state's liability to cover claimants' housing costs.

The tension between a market-based approach to rents and 100 per cent housing benefit produced a policy response: reducing benefit entitlement in some cases and increasing the pressure on tenants to bid down rents or look elsewhere. Some economists on the political right (Clark, 1994) argued that the logical direction was to move further towards breaking the link between housing benefit and actual rent, suggesting that claimants should be given a standard amount that reflected their household structure and local housing market conditions; they would then operate as consumers in a market, looking for the best accommodation available within their resources. The introduction of a reduction in housing benefit when the rent was deemed to be above average for an area can be seen as a move in this direction, but the real barrier to further progress is the low level of support provided to social security claimants.

On the conflict between housing policy and labour market policy, it is clear that high rents and low wages do not sit comfortably together. Part of the problem lies in the social security system and the way the Conservative government responded to the rising cost of housing benefit by making the rate of withdrawal of benefit steeper. It is this combination of high rents, low wages and steep housing benefit tapers that still makes the poverty trap particularly difficult to escape.

In the owner-occupied sector, too, the move to a flexible (that is less secure) labour market has worrying implications, because if people face employment futures in which they have less job security and if they have to plan for periods of unemployment throughout their working lives, then they are less likely to have the confidence to undertake the long-term commitment of mortgaged house purchase, and they are less likely to be seen as attractive customers by the lending institutions.

What, then, can be expected of the Labour government, given that it has a guaranteed five years in office? In the run-up to the election Labour was careful to make few commitments on housing, but there were three areas in which reasonably firm statements were made: the phased release of capital receipts from the sale of council houses, the removal of the compulsion on local authorities to put their housing management out to competitive tender, and the repeal of restrictions on the rights of homeless people introduced in the Housing Act 1996. In the context of the problems besetting the housing system these are very small-scale measures that, while welcome in themselves, will not go very far in dealing with the situation. If the £5 billion capital receipts said to be held by local authorities are released over the life of the parliament, the annual impact will do little more than restore the cuts in social housing investment expenditure made by Kenneth Clarke in his 1996 budget statement. It is unlikely that the released receipts will generate many new houses, for the money is more likely to be used to renovate existing council dwellings. Significant numbers of new houses would require increased public expenditure, and here Labour's room for manoeuvre has been severely restricted by the higher priority given to health and education, and by its pledge to stay within the overall spending plans set by the Conservative government for the first two years of the parliament. The escape route, canvassed by the Chartered Institute of Housing (Hawksworth and Wilcox, 1995), would be to abandon Britain's restrictive public expenditure conventions, which are out of line with other EU countries, and to allow social housing organisations to borrow for capital projects without counting against public expenditure totals. However, hitherto this has proved a step too far for Labour's Treasury team.

Apart from the issue of housing investment there is an urgent need for policy reform on rents and housing benefit. The Tories were forced to abandon their policy of annual real rent increases in social housing, but they left behind a system that is incoherent, hugely expensive and damaging to benefit recipients in terms of its poverty trap effects. Tackling the reform of housing benefit will be a major challenge to the Labour government, not least because of the way that the problems straddle the responsibilities and policies of different Whitehall departments.

Finally, the evidence points to the conclusion that housing strategies built around privatisation and marketisation have had their day. It is now clear that what is required is a new commitment to policies that will resolve the tensions inherent in the relationship between housing, social security and the labour market by recognising the benefits of intervention and the necessity of increased public expenditure if the serious problems of quality, quantity and affordability are to be tackled effectively. The growing tensions and difficulties that have been increasingly exposed in the last decade can not be resolved merely by adopting of different housing policies, because in large part they are due to factors that are not susceptible to narrow housing policy measures.

## Further Reading

The most valuable source of commentary and up-to-date statistical information on housing and housing policy in Britain is the annual *Housing Finance Review*, compiled by Steve Wilcox for the Joseph Rowntree Foundation. The new (fifth) edition of Peter Malpass and Alan Murie, *Housing*

*Policy and Practice* (London: Macmillan, 1998) includes a review of the eighteen years of Conservative government and an assessment of the prospects for housing under Labour. The collection of essays edited by Peter Williams, *Directions in Housing Policy* (London: Paul Chapman Publishing, 1997) contains valuable contributions from many leading housing scholars, as does the new edition of J. Goodwin, *Built to Last?* (London: Shelter, 1997). Books with a rather wider geographical frame of reference include Gavin McCrone and Mark Stephens, *Housing Policy in Britain and Europe* (London: UCL Press, 1995), and Mark Kleinman, *Housing and the State in Europe* (Aldershot: Edward Elgar, 1996).

# PART III

# CONTEMPORARY ISSUES IN BRITISH SOCIAL POLICY

## Introduction

The investigation of social policy in Britain, like the welfare state itself, is in a state of flux. In Part I, we saw how new challenges and changing circumstances have thrown up a wealth of new theoretical approaches to our welfare arrangements. In Part II, we saw how old issues now present themselves in a quite new light and how time-served assumptions no longer seem to apply even in the most conventional areas of social policy analysis. In Part III, we draw out a number of 'new' social policy issues (plus one very old one) in a rather more speculative fashion.

In Chapter 12 Gillian Pascall draws on what is now a very extensive base of knowledge and experience when investigating the distinctive ways in which the British welfare state is 'gendered'. She shows how women are at the very heart of social policy and charts the attempt to match their influence over the welfare state to their centrality within it. In Chapter 13 John Solomos discusses the complex ways in which 'race' has been incorporated/excluded in the British social policy regime. The discussion reveals a distinctive pattern of inclusion, exclusion and disadvantage.

John Barry (Chapter 14) develops the distinctive insights that have been brought to the welfare state from a green perspective. Issues of welfare, state and economy prove to be quite central to the politics of ecology and this approach yields a number of insights and policy recommendations that cut right across the more conventional political assumptions of left, right 'and' centre.

Poverty is a very ancient theme indeed, but as David Piachaud shows in Chapter 15, alongside some depressing continuities the incidence and salience of poverty has been transformed by societal change. Thus poverty, both old and new, constitutes both a continuing challenge to our institutions and an abiding source of shame to our divided if affluent society. Laura Cram (Chapter 17) traces the growing salience for UK actors of the European Union's 'social dimension', whilst Michael Cahill's innovative discussion on 'the great car culture' (Chapter 16) shows just how far we have still to go in rethinking what should count as social policy (and by extension, just what are the appropriate parameters of our concern with need, welfare and citizenship).

# CHAPTER 12

# Social Policy and Social Movements: Gender and Social Policy

GILLIAN PASCALL

Women are at the heart of welfare systems. They form the majority of paid employees in health, social care and education. More often than men they act as unpaid carers, as mothers and carers of frail elderly people and younger people with disabilities. As volunteers and neighbours providing care, women are more numerous than men. So in the public, private, formal, informal and voluntary sectors women are key – though not often powerful – providers of welfare.

Women also form the majority of those who need and use welfare systems. They are numerous among the poor, especially as lone mothers and elderly. Women as mothers need health care, secure income and housing for themselves and their children; as carers they need support from 'community care'; as elders they need health care, social support and secure pensions. As mothers, carers and elders they are less likely than men to earn enough to keep out of poverty.

While acknowledging the significance of social policy for women, feminist writers have often been highly critical of welfare systems in practice. Systems that appear equal are often deeply divided along gender lines. The policy hierarchy has men at the top, with women as a tiny – though now increasing – minority among prime ministers, cabinet members, MPs, top civil servants and quango members. Policy, then, has most often been made by men. Feminist analysts have contributed a powerful critique: men have constructed a social security system that privileges male contributors, a health system that empowers male-dominated medicine rather than female-dominated nursing or women patients, an education system delivering a gender-divided curriculum, housing policies that are predicated on men's incomes, and policies for 'community care' that devolve growing responsibilities onto unpaid women carers.

Feminists have also argued that the above areas comprise the central features of social welfare systems and, furthermore, that the nature of social provision in these areas cannot be properly understood without recognising their relationship to gender norms, assumptions and power relations. Feminist analyses of welfare states may be grouped into five key themes (Pascall, 1997):

- The provision of welfare, especially the extent and role of unpaid family work in welfare and male dominance of the formal institutions of welfare.
- The way welfare systems shape and are shaped by gender relations.
- Women's dependency on men and on welfare systems, and the extent to which women have access to autonomy through paid work and the ability to form autonomous households.
- Gender divisions in public and private life and the relation between 'public' and 'private'.
- Citizenship as a set of rights and obligations that is usually assumed to be universal, but in practice entrenches gender differences and the exclusion of women.

It has become increasingly difficult to write about women as a group. Ideologies of liberal feminism, socialist feminism and radical feminism have long led to divergent political programmes (Lovenduski and Randall, 1993). Writing about 'race' draws attention to differences between women; women from ethnic minorities have found white feminist analysis to be ethnocentric (Bhavnani and Coulson, 1986). Class also divides women. In everything from education and work opportunities to health and maternal experience, women's lives are shaped and divided by economic circumstances. Motherhood, paid work and career put women in different positions, which may lead to conflicting political demands and priorities. These divisions are real and must be acknowledged.

But feminism as a social and political movement also depends on women finding common purpose. The women's movement worldwide shares some concerns and objectives. In circumstances widely different from those in Britain, women tend to share unpaid family work, low pay and a small fraction of power in public and private life. Women's political action has always taken these as central concerns. The Women's Liberation Movement, which emerged in the 1970s, brought a surge of political activity, often described as a second wave, building on the suffragette feminism of the early twentieth century. Despite the decline of the Women's Liberation Movement, the women's movement has continued in various forms. For example women have continued to further feminist projects through positions in the state, social welfare services and academic arenas (Lovenduski and Randall, 1993).

# The Extent to Which Women's Needs are Not Met By the Welfare State

## Women's needs

Women's and men's basic needs are broadly the same: health and autonomy, and the income to resource these requirements (Doyal and Gough, 1991). But characteristically these needs are met in different ways and to different degrees – in the labour market, the family and welfare policy. Male power in all three institutions is reflected in women's lower earnings, lower share of household income, lesser entitlement to benefits and thus lesser satisfaction of needs. Men's power also challenges women's autonomy in personal life with inadequate levels of state protection against violence at home and sexual harassment at work.

Some different needs stem from traditional roles. Women are more likely to give time to parenthood and need the wherewithal to care for kin. Throughout the world women's health is compromised by reproduction; British women's need for health care includes the need for safe reproductive control (Doyal, 1995).

## Women and poverty

Women suffer poverty more than men for at least three reasons. Pay is clearly a key reason for women's generally lower incomes. Equal Pay Acts notwithstanding, women in full time paid employment earn 74 per cent of men's weekly earnings (median figures, *New Earnings Survey*, 1996, table A1.1). But many more women than men are in part-time work and take home less pay.

Marriage is a second factor. Men's greater earnings are not always redistributed to household members, while marriage and cohabitation break-down bring a high risk of poverty for lone parents. Caring, especially motherhood, is a third reason for low incomes. A growing tendency for women to hold on to paid work through the childbearing years is a significant current trend. But many women still tailor paid work to care for children and other kin. This extracts a heavy cost in lifetime earnings and pension contributions. It is certainly the case that women are more likely than men to have caring responsibilities for older kin that entail leaving jobs or reducing the number of hours of paid work. Of course, women themselves grow old, at which point the inadequacy of their pensions, caused by their having had to take time out of the labour market for child care and other reasons, brings poverty to growing numbers of female pensioners.

Finally, the welfare state offers only modest protection, especially to women. The postwar welfare state was built on the assumption that most men would be breadwinners, most women would be housewives and care for children and most marriages would last until death (Beveridge, 1942). National Insurance was intended to fill gaps in men's ability to provide for themselves and their families as a result of unemployment, sickness or death. Women would be dependent on men's earnings during marriage and on their husband's National Insurance contributions during widowhood. However most of the assumptions upon which National Insurance was built fit the state of affairs in the real world with decreasing accuracy. Men's incomes have become less secure, women are more likely to be in the labour market, marriage is more fragile. Women do still care for children, but the family wage system and the social security system built around it no longer meet their needs; social security has been refashioned to adjust to new realities but it is still made with the same cloth. Women's needs as carers are met, but at the meanest levels: thus lone parents are most likely to receive means-tested Income Support; mothers are entitled to Child Benefit for their children but nothing for themselves; carers may receive Invalid Care Allowance, which is lower than the contributory benefits to which men are more likely to be entitled. Consequently women make up a large majority of the recipients of Income Support, the residual, means-tested state benefit.

## Women's autonomy

Women's personal autonomy as citizens, wives, carers and mothers needs to be underpinned by welfare policies. The postwar welfare state appeared to establish universal citizenship, but it was soon clear that women's citizenship was to be second class (Lister, 1993). Beveridge recognised the work and the value of the work that married women contributed as housewives, but his design for a social security system gave them no independent personal status (Beveridge, 1942). They were to depend on men's incomes and on benefits paid to the household through men as breadwinners. Married women still have no rights to income as mothers; many depend on both their husbands and the state by receiving benefits through their partners. Increasingly, women have escaped total dependence on men's incomes by joining the labour market and keeping their stake in it for longer periods. But caring obligations, lower incomes and the nature of benefit rules give women less access to independent income and less of the autonomy this brings. Increasingly, women are supported by benefits outside marriage as lone parents. But this brings a fragile autonomy, as they are caught between caring obligations, low incomes and social disapproval.

Some women's lack of autonomy in relationships was brought to light by the refuge movement in the 1970s. Women's Aid began in 1971 to help women escape violent relationships. Refuges spread rapidly and brought evidence of the extent of domestic violence and the difficulty of escaping from violent partners (Binney *et al.*, 1981; Malos and Hague, 1993). Political action has brought legislation for safe housing and changes to police practice (Morley and Mullender, 1994), but refuges are still full to overcrowding and some legislation that helped women to find housing has been changed to deter lone parenthood (Pascall and Morley, 1996). Mothers of young children are particularly vulnerable to abuse from partners, being particularly likely to lack independent income or the means to find and pay for housing.

'Compulsory altruism' (Land and Rose, 1985) is a telling term used to describe the pressure people experience to do unpaid caring work. The personal autonomy of carers has been too little regarded (Finch and Groves, 1983). Many carers take on the responsibility gladly, often without question, and find reward in meeting the needs of a person they have loved and lived with. But there is a dark side: heavy personal costs in work, money and personal time. Community care policies are reducing alternatives, closing hospital beds and increasing the private, personal costs incurred by those in need of nursing and personal care. There may seem to be no choice about undertaking care, and caring may leave little time for anything else. Many carers – especially older carers and those looking after spouses – spend much more than a standard working week on heavy caring obligations.

The campaign for reproductive control, for women's 'Right to Choose', has been the most public campaign of the women's movement. Contraception, abortion, childbirth and the new reproductive technologies all pose issues about women's control over their bodies, with abortion campaigns the most politically prominent. Safe reproductive control has been central to the improvement of women's health in Western countries by enabling women to have fewer babies at safer intervals and safer ages. Such control is also central to other choices, for example about paid work and participation in public politics. However, neither the technology nor the choice are problem free. The relative hazards and benefits of contraceptive drugs and devices, overintervention in childbirth, in-vitro fertilisation and similar treatments for infertility have rarely been fully assessed and the recipients are rarely fully informed. Choice has not always been extended or placed unambiguously with women. Encounters with the male-dominated medical profession have made this area highly contested.

These four very different areas show the significance of welfare systems to women's autonomy. Without income as parents, housing, refuge from violence, nursing and social care, and reproductive control women have no autonomy. But as we shall see below, the form in which welfare has been provided has often compromised women's independence.

## Women's needs as carers

Does the welfare state meet women's distinctive needs as carers? Traditional ideas about the division of labour have been vigorously challenged, especially by the women's movement. Most women of working age are now in the labour market. Most men and women – especially younger ones – now believe that child care and household work should be shared. But in practice the traditional division of labour persists. Parenting is popular jargon, but mothering and fathering are very different activities. It is as mothers that women's needs are most distinct and pressing. Mothering reduces women's capacity to earn, but increases their need for income. Mothers cannot meet their obligation to care without income and housing.

The traditional solution to this problem was the family wage: earnings paid to men on behalf of women and children. But the 'family wage' has never been enough, especially for larger families, and its distribution and use have always been uncertain. For fifty years, some form of family allowance – now Child Benefit – has been paid to mothers in acknowledgement of their responsibility for children, and tacit acknowledgement that income paid direct to mothers was more likely to reach the children.

Mothers find Child Benefit important beyond its small amount because it is a reliable, regular income over which they have full control (Pahl, 1989). It meets some of the costs of children, but it does not cover the costs of mothers giving up paid work, adjusting hours or paying for substitute care. Furthermore its level was frozen by the Conservative government in the late 1980s, the Conservatives' policy being to use means-tested benefits such as Family Credit to concentrate money on poorer families.

Lone mothers have special difficulties providing for themselves and their children. Absent fathers have rarely contributed enough in maintenance to keep mothers and children out of poverty. Children's needs, low earnings, child-care costs and lack of nursery provision make paid work a difficult route to financial self-sufficiency, and only a small minority manage it. Most mothers have to depend on Income Support. The current policy is to push responsibility more towards fathers, through the Child Support Agency (CSA), and mothers, through paid employment. But the CSA has not yet wrested enough from fathers to make much impact on mothers, and the proportion of mothers on Income Support remains high. The Conservatives' policy was to see lone mothers primarily as mothers, with some attempt from the 1990s to encourage them to enter the labour market. The new Labour government's policy now appears considerably more stringent, making self-help through paid work a more decisive virtue and threatening benefit cuts for those lone mothers who refuse actively to seek work.

Some carers do now receive a benefit in their own right – Invalid Care Allowance. This was originally denied to married women, on the grounds that they would be at home anyway and could depend on their husbands for support. But now a majority of recipients are married women. As with Child Benefit there is evidence that recipients value Invalid Care Allowance as a very small independent income and as recognition of their caring contribution. But again this support for women as carers is very limited: the amount is small and dependent on the benefit entitlement of the person cared for.

Women's needs as carers are thus met in a very limited way by welfare policies. As mothers they and their children are assumed to be dependent on husbands for housing and income. When marriages break down mothers usually have to turn to Income Support. As carers of people with disabilities they may receive Invalid Care Allowance. But none of these situations entitles women to a fully independent income related to their caring responsibilities. The nearest we have come to this is Income Support for lone mothers, as long as the availability for work criterion has not been enforced.

## Women and 'universal' social services

Education and health care free at the point of use were two vital achievements of the postwar welfare state, and they continue to be of particular importance to women. The financing of health care through taxation brings health resources to women, whose participation in contributory, workplace or private schemes is less than that of men. The redistributive impact of these tax-funded services is favourable to women, whose unpaid work reduces income while often increasing need.

In the nineteenth century women were excluded from higher education and therefore from access to careers such as medicine. Into the 1980s girls trailed boys in school leaving qualifications, but now they are achieving better academic results than boys in most respects. Women's increasing access to university places – as mature or non-mature students, undergraduate or postgraduate – has been a phenomenon of the past two decades, and now the numbers or men and women at universities are approximately equal. Increased educational access and achievement are important factors in women finding better-paid work.

It is partly because the health and education services are so important to women that feminists have often criticised their structure and the nature of the services they provide. The NHS provides the clearest example of a gendered employment and power structure, with male and medical dominance. Schools too have a predominance of men in positions of power as heads; and in universities women account for only 7.5 per cent of the total number of professors. The impact of this on the services is a key issue. Women's encounters with men's medicine have often been unhelpful or experienced as hostile. In schools and universities the knowledge produced and conveyed has been criticised. The gender-divided curriculum has been effectively challenged with respect to younger children, but the higher reaches of sixth form and university studies are critically divided, with male domination of most courses leading to higher-paid work.

Health and education services have been sharply challenged by feminists as systems that carry men's power. But women's challenge to the traditional patterns of male dominance has been felt – perhaps most strongly – in education, where boys' poorer performance is becoming a matter for concern. In particular the many women who work in these institutions fight to make them fairer and more sensitive to women as workers, patients and students. The importance of these services to women is clear.

## The Nature of Proposals for Changes in Social Policy Coming from the Women's Movement

The demands of the Women's Liberation Movement in the 1970s were for equal pay, equal education and opportunity, child care, free contraception and abortion on demand, financial and legal independence for women, a woman's right to choose her own sexuality, freedom from intimidation by threat or use of violence or sexual coercion. For a brief period consensus about these aims was reached at national meetings. Subsequently they have been a reference point for a diversity of women's groups, women's studies courses and women researchers. Views often conflict, but there is still a recognisable feminist agenda.

As stated above, equal pay and equal opportunities were two of the founding demands of the movement. Improving women's labour market position would reduce poverty, increase the choices available to women with regard to having children or caring for others, and improve their opportunities, especially for participation in public life. The Equal Pay Act of 1970 was the first legislation to reflect the movement's second wave. It appeared to bring equal pay to men and women at work and did serve to reduce differentials, although the sharply divided labour market, with vertical and horizontal segregation, makes comparisons between men and women difficult. Nonetheless the legal system has failed to support women's claims: it is more than twenty years since this legislation came into effect but women's earnings as full-time workers are still only 74 per cent of men's.

Equal pay and opportunities have been pursued through the Equal Opportunities Commission, the labour movement, local authorities, public employers such as health authorities and universities, and some private employers such as banks. Legislation has been widened, especially by the application of European policy to the British situation, often stimulated by the Equal Opportunities Commission. Equal pay for equal value, and more equal conditions for part-timers have been won through this route. Campaigns have modified men's dominance of work environments and their operation in men's interests; and they have significantly altered the politics of paid work, with equality policies commanding widespread support. Campaigns continue for equal opportunity practices in appointments, promotions, care responsibilities and sexual harassment.

To enhance women's autonomy, reduce their dependence on men and reduce poverty, women need a transformation of the labour market: fairer pay, better access to better-paid work, flexibility for men and women to care for children and others, and parental leave. Women have used improved labour market access to keep themselves and their families out of poverty, increasingly holding on to paid jobs even when they have very young children.

But not all women are in the labour market – most lone parents, mothers of very young children, carers of the frail elderly and the elderly themselves depend on policies that provide income for those not in work. This has been the most gendered aspect of the welfare state, and the least successful for women. Independent income for women as carers is a long way from achievement. Prewar campaigns for family allowances were about women's economic position – many had no right to an independent income – as well as about children's poverty. Modern groups are more likely to seek some form of income for those responsible for the young and the old. Enhancing the Invalid Care Allowance would be the most modest route to this end, while a citizens' income would provide a more radical solution.

The way the welfare state has perpetuated women's dependence on men's incomes is a key critique. One of the women's movement's first demands was financial and legal independence for women. Disaggregation Now! campaigned for the separation of husbands' and wives' incomes for taxation and benefit purposes, which would also reduce the welfare state's part in making women dependent on men. Disaggregated taxation has happened and it does benefit better-off women. However, means-tested benefits are still based on couples' income and typically limit poorer women's ability to work when their husbands/partners are unemployed.

Women's action has targeted violence in the home, on the streets, in the media and at work. Women's groups argue that male power is expressed through marital violence, rape, pornography and sexual harassment at work. Women's Aid has been a national organisation since 1975, and refuges established through Women's Aid have created a new direction in social policy, with open access and cooperative self-support taking the place of bureaucratic gate-keeping and professional judgment. This has offered a deliberate challenge to welfare state traditions, an 'alternative political practice' (Lovenduski and Randall, 1993, pp. 307–8). Refuge provision has increased dramatically, but there are still inadequate facilities to meet the demand. Women's Aid seeks to offer (1) refuge to women suffering from domestic violence so that they can rebuild their lives in a supportive environment; (2) police protection for women in their homes and in refuges; and (3) access to longer-term housing for the victims of violent relationships. These are pressing needs that have to be met if women are not to be forced back into violent and dangerous situations.

Rape crisis groups and campaigning organisations such as the London Rape Crisis Group and Women Against Rape have similarly provided support, research and campaigns against the treatment of women in police stations and rape trials. They have stimulated widespread debate about the meaning, significance and impact of sexual violence against women. They have succeeded in changing the public perception of these crimes, establishing marital rape as a crime and improving police practices in some areas. Court procedures remain a trial for complainants, and perpetrators have a good chance of acquittal, so radical change in legal practices is called for.

Free contraception and abortion on demand were two of the original demands of the women's movement. Right to Choose advocates have confronted the Right to Life movement in many public debates about abortion. The National Abortion Campaign has been very effective in mobilising women to defend women's rights to abortion – the abortion law has changed little in thirty years. A wider politics of women's health has stemmed from similar concerns about reproductive rights and control. Women's health groups have formed on every subject – contraception, childbirth, fertility, cancer. Most seek better information about technological developments, putting women more in control; some are about self-help; many but not all are explicitly feminist. Women health workers – through groups such as the Radical Midwives Association and Women in Medicine – have used their position in the NHS to fight for a wider role for women midwives as carers in childbirth and woman-centred maternity care.

Choice about caring relationships is another key issue, represented in the women's movement agenda by demands for childcare, and later including care for others. Flexibility of work and benefits would enable women and men to combine paid and caring work. Support structures and alternative institutional and community provision for people with extra needs would make choices more real. Child care campaigns have been started by women in the labour market and in campaigns for women at work. The National Child Care Campaign, launched in 1980, aimed 'to build a mass national child care campaign around the demand for comprehensive, flexible, free democratically controlled child care facilities funded by the state' (Lovenduski and Randall 1993, p. 289). Later the Workplace Nurseries Campaign and the Working Mothers' Association also focused on child care. These organisations developed in a very hostile environment, where Conservative resistance to public spending was added to more traditional fears about eroding the proper role of women. By the end of the Conservative era, an ever-increasing number of women were combining motherhood with paid work, without state support. New Labour has changed the climate to make child care a central issue.

The claims of the Women's Liberation Movement in the 1970s – for equal pay, equal education and opportunity, child care, free contraception and abortion on demand, financial and legal independence for women, a woman's right to choose her own sexuality, freedom from intimidation by the threat or use of violence or sexual coercion – have continued to resonate through women's political action in the subsequent period. They have been disputed and developed, and some campaigns – especially for free contraception and equal educational opportunities – have been won in good measure. These are a recognisable agenda in the 1990s, and much more established in political debate than in the 1970s.

## Is the Women's Movement a New Social Movement?

So the women's movement is a significant agent in the development of the social policy agenda. But what *is* the women's movement and is it a new social movement? Defining the women's movement is complex. No single entity, organisation or membership has persisted over time, but rather there has been a shifting complex of organisations and individuals. Women's organisations have usually resisted traditional organisational structure, abjuring hierarchy and leadership, and relying on informality and social networks.

Neither can the women's movement be defined within the traditional terms of public politics. The claim of the Women's Liberation Movement that the personal is political represented an extension of the subject matter of politics. Feminists have argued that sexuality, relationships, families and workplaces are as political as parliament.

Political activity goes beyond public campaigns on self-help, cultural and educational activities and lifestyles. At one extreme suffragettes used direct action and civil disobedience by, among other things, chaining themselves to railings and going on hunger strike in prison. Mainstream public campaigns, engaging with parliamentary politics – especially defending abortion law reform – were key activities of second-wave feminists. Increasingly in the 1980s and 1990s women have acquired occupational positions from which they may pursue a feminist agenda, for example nursing, midwifery, teaching, higher education, social work and politics. But women have also sought to achieve goals outside public politics. Self-help has played a key role in establishing women's health groups, rape crisis centres and refuges from domestic violence. And the politics of personal relationships, sexuality, marriage and parenting are now part of everyday life.

Perhaps the most contentious word in the term 'new social movements' is 'new'. Dale Spender, in *There's Always Been a Women's Movement this Century* (1983), argues that the roots of the women's movement go much deeper than the 1960s. Some trace the movement further back than the current century, citing parallel activities in connection with sexuality, prostitution, child sexual abuse, marriage, education, employment and health in the 1850s.

## The Women's Movement and Public Politics

To what extent have ideas from the women's movement become embodied in public politics? Representation is critical and was the main aim of the suffragettes. The first woman MP took her seat in 1919, but through to the 1987 election there were never more than 30 women MPs out of around 630 members. The 1997 election marked a significant step in women's representation: there is now a critical mass of women – 120 women MPs – and this is likely to change the culture of government and policy will be subjected to scrutiny for its impact on women as well as men. But while the parliamentary change seems radical and irreversible, men still dominate: not quite one in five MPs are women. Women have become more numerous as cabinet members and government ministers, but Margaret Thatcher's tenure of the highest post seems likely to remain an exception in the immediate future.

Does representation mean that women MPs and ministers will represent women's interests? If so, will they articulate women's interests as groups in the women's movement have identified them? Women MPs would not claim to represent only women; neither could they reflect the diversity of opinions among women's groups. But the women's movement has entered the thinking of significant Labour politicians and academics. Their publications reflect women's movement ideas, for example Harman's *The Century Gap* (1993), Hewitt's critique of gendered working practices in *About Time* (1993), and Jowell's *Strategy for Women* (1996), written for the Labour Party.

The 1997 Labour government has developed government structures for women's policy, with a minister for women, a cabinet subcommittee for women and a women's unit within the Civil Service. These will coordinate the work of departments of state and monitor the impact of policy proposals on women. They have been criticised for their modesty, and especially for the appointment of a minister for women who already has a job as social security secretary. However, they represent a small increase in systems to focus government thinking about women.

The primacy given in Labour Party strategy to flexibility of work, parental leave and child care seems to be a clear result of the increase in women party activists and the influence of the women's movement. If applied with sensitivity, these policies could make it easier for parents – especially lone parents – to combine paid work with family commitments. The policies have wide support from women, including lone mothers, although the issue of benefit cuts for those who do not wish to undertake *paid* work, preferring the unpaid work of child care, remains a contested area. There is a real difficulty here. Responsibility and duty have become key words of New Labour as its leaders distance themselves from 'Old' Labour's language of rights. So far these new principles have been defined in traditionally masculine terms as the duty to undertake paid work. Consequent policies aim to enable women to contribute to social and economic life on the same terms as men, to support themselves and their children.

Care work, in this view, is thus identified as an obstacle to the duty of paid employment, care work as an obligation in its own right being placed well down the agenda. There is virtually no recognition of the difficulties that women face when providing good care for children and others in need while working in a discriminatory labour market. The idea that we cannot afford services that support care work – such as nursing care and Child Benefit – has become entrenched. If this is carried forward in Labour policy, as currently seems to be happening, then a Labour government could inflict significant damage on women, children, frail people in need of nursing care and their carers.

## Conclusion

To what extent have the women's movement and feminist writing changed the agenda of social policy as an academic subject? George and Wilding's key text of the 1970s and 1980s, *Ideology and Social Welfare* (1976), conceived significant ideologies along a left–right spectrum. This put market relations centre stage and sidelined work and relationships that took place outside the market in which women were primarily involved. The same authors' 1990s book, *Welfare and Ideology* (George and Wilding, 1994), sees feminism and greenism as distinct strands. Wilding argues that the questions raised by feminist analysis 'supply Social Policy with a new armoury of critical questions and a new agenda' (Wilding, 1992, p. 112). Other new texts take feminist thinking as part of the essential agenda of social policy in the 1990s. So feminist writers have asked new questions, affected our understanding of the welfare state in a quite fundamental way, and found their way into the mainstream of social policy literature.

More broadly, the women's movement has had a major impact on social policy in practice. Public politics and the political parties have been fairly resistant to women's participation in the formal political realm, particularly at national levels, with tiny percentages of women MPs until the current parliament. But the changing expectations of half the electorate are changing the content of public politics and the expectations of its leaders. Equal opportunities for women are widely accepted as a social goal – in education, industry, the civil service – though they may be far from attainment. The improved educational achievements of girls and young women and access to institutions of higher education are major gains of the past two decades. Provision and ideas about protecting women against men's violence have been adopted from the women's movement, with some public funding for refuges and institutional changes in police procedures. In Britain and elsewhere, women's use of the welfare services is greater than men's. Women's part in state institutions as nurses, teachers and social workers, as well as their need for services, gives them the opportunity and reason to change and defend the welfare state. Feminists have gained widespread acceptance for ideas that seemed revolutionary in the 1960s and 1970s and whose practice would be revolutionary now.

## Further Reading

Material and ideas in the above chapter are expanded in G. Pascall, *Social Policy: A New Feminist Analysis* (London: Routledge, 1997). Two collections of essays, by Christine Hallett for the Social Policy Association, *Women and Social Policy: An Introduction* (Hemel Hempstead: Harvester Wheatsheaf, 1996), and Mavis Maclean and Dulcie Groves' *Women's Issues in Social Policy* (London: Routledge, 1991) cover similar ground as does C. Ungerson and M. Kember, *Women and Social Policy* (London: Macmillan, 1997). Caroline Glendinning and Jane Millar's *Women and Poverty in Britain in the 1990s* (Hemel Hempstead: Harvester Wheatsheaf, 1992) and Lesley Doyal's *What Makes Women Sick* (London: Macmillan, 1995) are rather more specialised. Jane Lewis, in *Women and Social Policies in Europe: Work, Family and the State* (Aldershot: Edward Elgar, 1993), and Diane Sainsbury, in *Gender, Equality and Welfare States* (Cambridge: Cambridge University Press, 1996), offer a wider European context.

# CHAPTER 13

# Social Policy and Social Movements: 'Race', Racism and Social Policies

JOHN SOLOMOS

During the Conservative Party Conference in October 1997 Lord Tebbit chose to focus on a critique of what he saw as the dangers of multiculturalism for British society. Warning that multiculturalism was a 'divisive force' for society as a whole Tebbit warned that 'Unless we share standards, moral values, language and our national heritage, we will constitute neither a society nor a nation but just a population living under the same jurisdiction' (*Daily Telegraph*, 8 October 1997). In the aftermath of this speech there was intense debate in the popular media and within political institutions about the question of multiculturalism as a whole as well as specific policy dilemmas that face multicultural societies at the present time. It should be noted of course that both the Conservative Party and the Labour Party spoke out strongly against the populist tone of Tebbit's intervention, and the support he received from within mainstream politics was fairly limited (*Daily Telegraph*, 6 October 1997; *The Independent*, 12 October 1997). Indeed a number of senior political figures spoke out strongly in favour of at least one version of multiculturalism.

The limits of this acceptance of multiculturalism became clear, however, later on in the month when groups of Roma from Slovakia and the Czech Republic arrived at Dover and sought asylum on the basis that they were being persecuted in their countries of origin. Their arrival led to almost immediate expressions of concern in the tabloid press that Britain could become a 'soft touch' for would be refugees and economic migrants (*Sun*, 21 October 1997; Torode, 1997). The response of the new Labour government was to attempt to reassure the public that it would seek to maintain a tough stance on asylum and ensure that the new arrivals were sent back as soon as possible. Responding to the claim that the Roma were not genuine refugees, but simply 'Giro Czechs' intent on abusing the British welfare system, Mike O'Brien, the new immigration minister argued that: 'We want genuine refugees to get support, but people who are just coming to abuse the system, they're going to get a very firm response indeed' (quoted in the *Daily Mail*, 21 October 1997).

This is not the place to enter into the specific details and implications of these two events, but I have mentioned them at the beginning of this chapter in order to highlight a feature of policy debate about race and immigration that has shaped public debate in Britain ever since the 1960s: namely the contradictory balance between policies that accept the need for measures to tackle discrimination and ensure the integration of minorities with strong controls on the number of migrants and refugees who are allowed to enter in the first place. In one way or another this is a feature of public policy debate about race relations that has remained relatively constant over the past four decades, and I shall attempt to show in the course of this chapter that it provides the key to an understanding of how social policies connected with questions of race and immigration have developed.

In talking about race and social policy it is important to remember that we are engaging with an inherently politicised arena. Indeed we can only begin to understand the nature of policies in this field if we see them as the outcome of a range of concerns about the role of racial and ethnic minorities in societies such as our own. The interventions of politicians such as Lord Tebbit are but one facet of a much wider set of debates that have helped to shape how successive governments have responded to and racialised key aspects of policies about immigration, local politics, policing, housing, the inner cities, health and welfare over the past half century (Solomos, 1993).

This chapter offers a broad, interpretative look at the interplay between race and social policy. Taking as its starting point the history of social policies in this field, it will focus on recent trends and developments by exploring changing agendas and perspectives as well as analysing specific initiatives and proposals for changes that have emerged from within sections of minority communities. Following on from this it will focus on the ways in which current or emerging social policies in this field have been shaped and the controversies to which they have given rise. A key concern throughout the chapter will be to question some of the underlying assumptions that have dominated thinking in this field and to suggest some ways in which new critical perspectives can challenge them and lay the basis for new initiatives.

Before proceeding into the substance of this chapter it is worth noting that although the focus of the chapter is on race and racism we do not use these notions in an unproblematic manner. Indeed it is abundantly clear that in contemporary discourse ideas about *race, racism* and *ethnicity* have become the subject of intense debate and controversy (Solomos and Back, 1996). It is paradoxically the case that there is still confusion about what is meant by concepts such as race and racism, as evidenced by the range of terminological debates that have tended to dominate much discussion in recent years. It is perhaps partly the result of this focus on terminology that much of the academic debate in this field has remained somewhat abstract and unsatis-factory, and not directly helpful when addressing the everyday policy issues that are the focus of this chapter. But since it is not possible to engage directly with these theoretical disputes here, it is important to emphasise that we see race as a means of representing difference such that contingent attributes such as skin colour are transformed into essential bases for identities. But this is not to deny that race remains, at the level of everyday experience and social representation, a potent political and social category around which indivi-duals and groups organise their identity and construct a politics. As such, race is socially constructed; and blackness and whiteness are not categories of essence but defined by historical and political struggles over their meaning (for a more detailed account see Solomos and Back, 1996).

## Background and Context

The development of public policy responses to racial inequality in Britain dates back to the 1960s. Early debates were shaped by the dual concern about how best to deal with (1) the question of the arrival of sizeable numbers of migrants from the ex-colonies, particularly the West Indies and India and Pakistan, and (2) the social and economic issues that arose from the creation of racial minorities in many of the major urban conurbations in England. By the mid 1960s all the main political parties had converged around a policy agenda that accepted the need for tough immigration controls as a way of regulating the pattern of migration from the former colonies. The end result of this consensus can be seen in the long history of legislation, beginning with the 1962 Commonwealth Immigrants Act, which at first regulated immigration and then sought to stop it.

On the second issue, however, there was far less consensus between the main political parties about the need for legislation to promote the integration of those migrants and their descendants who had already arrived before the imposition of immigration controls. Both the Conservative and the Labour Party were formally committed to the idea of developing measures to tackle racial discrimination and promote at least a limited version of multicultur-alism. In practice, however, the legislation passed over the past four decades to deal with this issue was enacted during periods when the Labour Party was in power. Indeed, as is evident from Lord Tebbit's recent intervention, one strand of Conservative opinion has remained strongly opposed not only to the idea of 'multiculturalism' but to the legislation that has been passed since the 1960s.

It is not surprising, therefore, that ever since the 1960s there has been intense debate at both national and local levels about the form and substance of policy initiatives to tackle racial discrimination and inequalities that have been shaped by the effects of historical patterns of racism and domination. From this period onwards race relations policies in Britain can be said, in one way or another, to have been premised on the notion that the aims of public policy were threefold: (1) to encourage the gradual integration of racial and ethnic minorities by dealing with issues such as discrimination, education, social adjustment and welfare; (2) to promote better race relations by stopping new immigration while educating the population as a whole about the position of migrant communities; and (3) to allow minorities an equal opportunity to participate fully in all aspects of British society.

It is in this context that the question of what to do to about the social position of migrant communities once they had settled in British society emerged as a major dilemma for successive governments. Even in the early stages of migration there was an awareness that in the longer term the question of racial discrimination and inequality was likely to become a volatile political issue. During the 1970s and 1980s political attention began to shift from immigration controls to the future of racial and ethnic minorities in British society. Two issues caused particular concern:

- The negative response of sizeable sections of the majority white British population to the arrival of black migrants in considerable numbers.
- The frustration of black and ethnic minority communities who felt themselves excluded from equal participation in British society as a result of discrimination in the labour and housing markets, along with the related process of social and political exclusion.

Both these issues were perceived as potential sources of conflict that the government had to manage and control through interventions both nationally and locally. The core idea that underlay these interventions was the notion that it was important to develop policies to promote the integration of minorities in British society and allow the majority to feel comfortable with the development of a multicultural society.

The first attempts to deal with the potential for racial conflict and to tackle racial discrimination took two basic forms. The first involved the setting up of agencies, both nationally and locally, to deal with the problems faced by black migrants and to help the white communities understand the migrants. The second stage of the policy response, signalled by the passage of the 1965, 1968 and 1976 Race Relations Acts, was premised on the notion that the state should attempt to ban discrimination on the basis of race, colour or ethnic origin through legal sanctions and public regulatory agencies charged with the task of promoting greater equality of opportunity. Since 1977 the

Commission for Racial Equality (CRE), which was set up by the 1976 Race Relations Act as a quasi-governmental body, has encapsulated both elements of this strategy. The CRE is charged with the task of implementing legislation against discrimination as well as with the promotion of 'better race relations' in British society through initiatives aimed at both the public and the private sector (Hall, 1991).

It is also important to remember that, quite apart from race relations legislation and the work of bodies such as the CRE, there have been a variety of policy responses at both national and local government levels. The period since the 1980s, particularly in the aftermath of the urban unrest of 1981 and 1985, has seen a major transformation in the role of local authorities in the field of race and ethnicity (Ball and Solomos, 1990). A trend emerged for local authorities to develop policies aimed at promoting equality of opportunity in employment and ensuring that the services they provided took account of the multicultural nature of many urban communities. These measures were based on the manifest premise that local authorities had an important role to play in providing equal access to employment, education, housing and social services.

Part of the reason for the emergence of local authorities as key agents in the racialisation of social policy can be traced to the impact of the riots and unrest that took place throughout the 1980s. The combination of serious urban unrest and massive social and economic change helped to push racial inequality and the role of public policy in tackling it firmly onto the political agenda. Another aspect of this shift of attention from the national to the local during this period was the unwillingness of both the Thatcher and the Major administrations during the period from 1979 to 1997 to introduce new national initiatives in this field. As a result of the absence of new initiatives during this period the local environment became a key concern in public debates about race relations, particularly in relation to such issues as education, social services and housing.

The increasing role of local initiatives in this field was also related to another development, namely the emergence of a specific form of 'black politics' in places such as London, Birmingham and other major urban localities. This relatively new political environment saw sizeable numbers of political representatives from minority communities break into the local political system, and this was often combined with calls for minorities to use their influence in particular localities to transform not only the local but also the national political agenda. Developments in local authorities such as Birmingham, Tower Hamlets, Haringey and others since the 1980s have highlighted how the level of political incorporation of minorities into political institutions can have a direct impact on policy agendas and outcomes. While it is perhaps too early to make a full analysis of the longer-term impact of this political mobilisation it is clear that, at least in some areas, minority politicians have played an important role in attempting to transform policy agendas and influence the distribution of resources to specific race-related initiatives. Whatever the ambiguities of minority political participation, it is evident that in some localities it has been an integral element of the changing policy agendas that began to emerge in the 1980s.

## Policy Agendas and Issues

As a result of the developments outlined above, successive governments since the 1970s have based their policies on (1) their commitment to the objective of developing policies premised on the public commitment to tackling various aspects of direct and indirect racial discrimination, and (2) antidiscrimination legislation that aims to promote greater equality of opportunity and remedy other social disadvantages suffered by black minority communities in British society. These policies have been held together by the notion that the main objective of public policies in this field is to secure free competition between individuals and eliminate barriers created by racial discrimination. It is clear that, over the years, antidiscrimination initiatives and social mobility from within minority communities have had a major impact on the social make-up of minority communities (Modood *et al.*, 1997). But a wide range of research has pointed to the persistence of racial inequalities and the limitations of legislation as a tool for ensuring the social integration of minorities. The existence of antidiscrimination legislation by itself is not enough to deal with inequalities and processes of discrimination in areas such as employment, housing, health and social services. A variety of research projects carried out since the 1976 Race Relations Act came into force show that it has not prevented discrimination by employers. While successive governments have pointed to Britain's extensive legislation governing racial discrimination in the employment relationship as a sign of a commitment to rooting out discrimination, it is important to note that only a relatively small number of cases have been brought and that very few have been successful.

At the heart of these criticisms of the role of public policy in dealing with racial inequalities lies a pessimistic and negative evaluation of the role of state interventions that aim to use antidiscrimination initiatives as a means of ensuring greater equity and justice. As a number of writers have pointed out over the years, the very notion of using antidiscrimination legislation to promote equal opportunity is inherently contradictory and gives rise to a wide range of problems, both in terms of developing measures against discrimination and in understanding the changing nature of racial inequalities and policy agendas in British society.

Ironically, however, despite evidence that antidiscrimination policies have had at best a limited impact on the extent of racialised inequalities, there has been renewed interest in analysing the role of race in a wide range of social policy arenas. This is partly because the centrality of social policy to any rounded analysis of race and ethnicity has become even clearer as the dynamics of moving beyond immigration to the question of social inclusion and exclusion have become a key concern. On a whole range of issues, such as education, health, housing, policing and social services, the question of race has come to the fore in the context of both race-specific and wider social debates. These debates have focused on a variety of different but connected social concerns: for example the emergence of an underclass, rising rates of crime and violence, single parenthood, and the decay of the inner cities. Questions about race and ethnicity have played an important and highly problematic role in the formulation of these social issues and their associated policy agendas. But it is also clear that within contemporary policy discourses there is by no means agreement on what role national or local institutions have in shaping policies about race and ethnicity, or indeed on what kinds of policy responses are appropriate in this field (Law, 1996).

There are a number of complex configurations involved in the related social policy responses, not least because the salience of race in all these debates is predominantly expressed via coded or deracialised language. An analysis that seeks to unpack the complex relationship between race and social policy would not only need to provide a focus on the ways in which race dimensions have been marginalised within policy formations generally, but would also need to address the ways in which race dimensions have been problematically included within social policy formations.

The example of developments in the field of race and health is a case in point. Although for a number of years the health of minority communities was not an important feature of public policy, and indeed it can be said to have been marginalised, in more recent times there has been an explosion of both research and policy interventions in relation to this issue. There has been an on-going debate about how best to develop ethnic sensitivity and antiracist perspectives in the provision of public health, initiatives to deal with specific issues, health promotion, the employment of black and minority staff in the health service, and the promotion of equality of opportunity in the provision of health services. All of these initiatives in one way or another relate to the issue of what can be done to tackle the root causes of racial inequalities in health and the role of health policies in the development of antiracist perspectives (Smaje, 1995; Ahmad, 1993).

Similar points can be made about the changing nature of social policies on minority families and children. This is an area that has come to play an important role in the development of policies in this field, particularly within the context of local authorities and agencies involved in the care of children. The transracial placement of black and mixed-race children has been a particularly important area of controversy, both within minority communities and in the care professions. It is a question that has consistently attracted the attention of the popular media, particularly in the aftermath of the adoption of a 'same race' policy by most of the agencies concerned with this issue (Gaber and Aldridge, 1994). It is also an issue that has produced sharp criticisms from both the left and the right about the way in which a supposedly antiracist practice, namely 'same race' adoption, has been justified using very fixed notions of racial and cultural difference.

Perhaps the most important concern, certainly in many localities, for minority communities themselves has been the problem of racist violence. This is not surprising, given the extent of racist violence in the everyday social fabric of British society. A recent report from Human Rights Watch has highlighted the importance of this phenomenon in British society by pointing to the fact that between 1989 and 1996 the number of incidents trebled to 12199 (*Observer*, 11 May 1997). It is also an issue that has received much attention in both the local and the national media in recent years. Some of the most publicised cases, including the notorious attacks on Stephen Lawrence and Quddus Ali, have shown the deadly consequences that such violence can have on the everyday lives of minorities.

In terms of the wider policy arena, however, perhaps the most important issue to come to the fore of public debate in recent years has been the 'underclass', although it is clear that the usage of the concept in Britain is by no means as deeply racialised as it is in the United States. Some of this interest can be seen as the result of attempts to introduce the arguments of Charles Murray and other American neoconservatives into the British situation, largely inspired by right-wing think tanks such the Institute of Economic Affairs and the Centre for Policy Studies (Murray, 1990, 1994; Lister, 1996). But there has also been a much broader debate about the underclass within both academic and popular discourses. This has been stimulated partly by fears that the situation in Britain's 'inner cities' may be moving closer to the one that is prevalent in the United States. It is also the outcome of a concern that processes of racial exclusion are helping to create a situation where some sections of black communities feel socially and culturally excluded from the mainstream of British society. In particular attention has focused on the likely impact of unemployment and social exclusion on specific groups within minority communities, such as young men of West Indian or Bangladeshi origin. In some localities at least a concern with the 'underclass' has become a deracialised way of talking about such groups and the dilemmas they pose not only for welfare institutions but also for the police and other agencies.

It is of some interest to note, however, that this move towards more detailed accounts of social differentiation within minority communities has not resulted in more detailed accounts of the role of black and minority women. What little research has been done has pointed to the fact that gender is an important factor in shaping forms of racial inequality, and some of the most innovative research in this field has focused specifically on the position of black and minority women in relation to employment, education, welfare provision and related social policy issues. There is a clear need, however, for more empirically but theoretically informed research on the interplay between race and gender in structuring contemporary racial relations.

In contrast to the situation in other European societies the question of citizenship in relation to race and ethnicity has yet to become a key issue. Policy debates in Britain, unlike other European societies, have often not looked seriously at the issue of political and citizenship rights of migrants and their descendants. This is partly because it is widely assumed that such issues are not as relevant in this country. But it is also clear that ethnic minorities in Britain and elsewhere are questioning whether they are fully included in and represented through political institutions. This is partly because there is a growing awareness of the gap between formal citizenship and the *de facto* restriction of the economic and social rights of minorities as a result of discrimination, economic restructuring and the decline of the welfare state (see the Introduction to this volume and Chapter 3).

## The Continuing Relevance of Immigration

In the 1960s part of the justification for introducing tough controls on immigration was the argument that such controls would help to depoliticise immigration as an issue. It is evident, however, as we move towards the end of this century that the question of immigration is likely to remain an integral component of public debates about race and social policy. To return briefly to the example of the political response to the arrival of groups of Roma from the Czech Republic and Slovakia that we highlighted at the beginning of this chapter, one of the features of this debate was the way a combination of anti-immigrant rhetoric and popular stereotypes of migrants and refugees as welfare scroungers shaped the political response to this event. Sections of the tabloid press took the lead in using lurid headlines such as 'Invasion of the

Giro Czechs' and 'The Flood of Gipsies' to illustrate stories about the impact of the arrival of Czech and Slovak refugees on social services. Such stories illustrate how easily the images of 'migrants' and 'refugees' can converge with those of 'welfare scroungers' and other negative stereotypes (*Sun*, 21 October 1997; *Daily Mail*, 21 October 1997). But they also highlight the volatile and continuing influence of immigration as an issue in terms of social policy.

What needs to be emphasised, however, is that such images have not been limited to the Roma. They have been a key feature of policy debates and changes throughout the 1990s. In the period leading up to the 1993 Asylum and Immigration Appeals Act and the 1996 Asylum and Immigration Act, for example, there was widespread public debate about the issue of 'bogus' refugees, who were depicted as 'illegal' immigrants exploiting Britain's 'lax' asylum laws to take advantage of Britain's welfare benefits. As one tabloid paper (*Daily Mail*, 13 March 1995) commented in the period leading up to the 1996 Act: 'The easiest way to clamber on board the Great British Gravy Train is to enter the country on a visitor's visa or slip in illegally. Then if you're caught, just claim political asylum.' A Conservative MP put the argument against letting asylum seekers remain even more bluntly when he argued that:

> Our duties to our citizens include the duty to protect our welfare and benefit budgets and our housing system at a time of economic stringency . . . Those who should not be here but who have got round the system by false applications are of no benefit to our own people (Edward Garnier, *Hansard*, 2 November 1992, col. 61).

The 1993 Act was instrumental in curtailing access to housing and other social rights for asylum seekers. It was widely condemned by refugee and human rights organisations. But interestingly enough the political momentum in favour of even tougher controls continued and the end result of this pressure was the Asylum and Immigration Act 1996. This Act restricted access to child benefit, housing and other social security benefits, as well as extending the scope of the 'fast track' asylum appeals procedure with the introduction of 'White Lists'. The new housing provision means that only those who apply for asylum within three days of entry, and are without temporary accommodation, will be entitled to housing. This restriction also applies to Child Benefit and social security claimants. Lest the impression be given that the concerns expressed by the proponents of the new Act were driven solely by self-interest, these 'bogus' claimants were further accused of behaving immorally by making it difficult for genuine asylum-seekers, by 'clogging up the system' and prolonging the processing period.

The justifications forwarded for the need for new legislation were the increasing number of 'would-be migrants' who were exploiting Britain's asylum provisions, and the potential for a 'mass influx' from Eastern Europe. In fact the primary factors underlying the debate at the beginning of the 1990s were not dissimilar to those at the end of the Second World War – but now it was the end rather than the beginning of the Cold War (hence the perceived increase in the number of people coming from Eastern Europe, while the numbers coming from Africa and Asia remained constant); the crisis rather than the creation of the welfare state; unemployment rather than a labour shortage; and whereas after the war Britain's identity as the centre of the Empire was crumbling, it was now Europe which seemed to pose a threat to British identity and sovereignty, especially as a result of the drive to open internal borders.

## What Kind of Future?

It is clear that although the place of race may not be immediately apparent in many of the current debates that shape social policies in Britain, there are some arenas in which the question of race is at least an important theme. These issues include the underclass, rising rates of crime and violence, single parenthood, education, inner-city decay, disaffected youth and immigration. In all of these arenas policy changes in recent years can be seen as bringing questions about race and ethnicity more prominently into social policy.

When looking to the future a number of questions remain to be addressed. First, what kind of policies can be developed to tackle racial discrimination more effectively? Second, what can be done to develop a political agenda in relation to immigration that is not based on knee-jerk pressure to exclude migrants and refugees? Third, what kind of positive social policy agenda can be developed to deal with the position of both established communities and new migrants in the 1990s and beyond? There are no easy answers to these questions and the experience of the past two decades indicates that any set of policies will by no means achieve unanimous support in society as a whole. But perhaps a starting point for future policy agendas is the recognition that there is a need for a coordinated public policy to deal with various social, political and cultural aspects of the position of ethnic minorities in British society. In the past, policy initiatives have been at best *ad hoc* and piecemeal. This is partly because, although public policy has been committed for some time to the pursuit of equal opportunity and multiculturalism, there is no clear political and social consensus in British society about what this means, either ideologically or in practice. There is little agreement, for example, on the types of public policies that need to be developed to deal with discrimination in such areas as education, social policy and employment. Additionally, as recent debates about antiracism seem to indicate, there is also a denial that racial inequality is an integral feature of British society or that racism is an important issue.

In the period leading up to the Labour victory in May 1997 there was some hope that a new policy agenda could be developed in this field. The end of the long period of Conservative rule from 1979 to 1997 and the election of a Labour government gave rise to public debate about what kind of changes were likely to emerge (*Guardian*, 18 May 1997 and 2 July 1997). There was even talk of setting up a Human Rights Commission to combine the current work of the Commission for Racial Equality and the Equal Opportunities Commission. The argument in favour of such a move was that a multi-purpose agency would have more resources at its disposal and would also be more likely to attract public support. In practice, however, the period since May 1997 has seen a rather limited response and a marked reticence to confront head-on the question of reforming immigration and race relations policies. Part of the reason for this seems to be a fear that action in these areas could help to politicise questions about race.

Whatever the merits of such arguments it seems clear that there is still much confusion about the direction of policy reforms in this area. Because of the *ad hoc* nature of policy development it is difficult to talk of a national strategy to deal with the changing social and political agendas we face today. Rather we are likely to continue to see a patchwork of policies that are shaped by concerns about how best to manage what is commonly seen as a thorny political problem. But it is clear that racial and ethnic issues are and will remain a key concern for social policy and political institutions as we move towards the next century.

## Further Reading

There is an impressive array of literature on the development of immigration and race relations policies in Britain. There is also a growing body of comparative studies and theoretical texts. Interestingly enough the literature on the interface between race and social policies remains somewhat limited, and it is only in recent years that a number of writers have begun to address this obvious gap. An extensive list of recent research on a wide range of issue can be found in J. Butt and K. Mirza, *Social Care and Black Communities: A Review of Recent Research Studies* (London: HMSO, 1996). The most influential overview of race and social policy is Ian Law's *Racism, Ethnicity and Social Policy* (London: Prentice-Hall/Harvester Wheatsheaf, 1996). A broader but somewhat dated account can be found in Fiona Williams' *Social Policy: An Introduction* (Oxford: Polity, 1988). On wider dimensions of equal opportunity and social policies see B. Bagilhole, *Equal Opportunities and Social Policy* (London: Longman, 1997). For some contemporary accounts of race and aspects of care see W. I. U. Ahmad and K. Atkin (eds), *'Race' and Community Care* (Milton Keynes: Open University Press, 1996). For a detailed account of the social and economic position of minorities in Britain can be found in T. Modood *et al.*, *Ethnic Minorities in Britain: Diversity and Disadvantage* (London: Policy Studies Institute, 1997). A conceptual analysis of recent debates and controversies about race and social relations can be found in J. Solomos and L. Back, *Racism and Society* (London: Macmillan, 1996).

# CHAPTER 14

# Social Policy and Social Movements: Ecology and Social Policy

JOHN BARRY

While there have been some contributions from the green movement concerning social policy, it is fair to say that much of this is limited to the manifestoes of green parties. Green social theory, in general, has had little to say on social policy. Part of the reason for this is that many of the changes greens would like to see across a whole range of social policy areas – from housing to education to welfare provision – are typically argued to follow, almost 'naturally', from the (sometimes radical) changes they suggest to the contemporary organisation of industrialised societies as a whole. This is largely due to the extremely 'holistic' approach that is a distinctive feature of the green movement's thinking. One immediate result of this holistic approach is that ecological considerations cut across many traditional policy areas, and therefore require a newer, more integrated approach to policy making than has traditionally been the case.

The ecological perspective not only proposes some alternatives to contemporary social policy provision in terms of being motivated by a different set of political and social objectives. It also challenges dominant accounts of social policy instruments which by and large see the issue in terms of state-centred versus market-based instruments.

There are basically two ways of viewing the relationship between ecology and social policy. On the one hand one can focus on the 'ecological crisis' in general and the 'limits to growth' thesis in particular, and their implications for British social policy. On the other hand one can look at the contribution the green movement has to make to debates about social policy. Both of these will be explored in this chapter. In the first half, the ecological critique in terms of the 'limits to growth' is discussed, before moving on in the next section to some of the challenges the ecological critique has proposed for social policy. Three challenges are explored: the green emphasis on post-materialism and self-provisioning (communal self-reliance); its view of the relationship between inequality, social justice and economic growth; and its perspective on appropriate policy instruments in terms of state, market and community.

The second half of the chapter focuses on green social policy theory, illuminating the latter by focusing on two green social policy areas: green arguments for a basic income scheme and its connection to the place and role of work within green social policy strategy, and green health policy proposals. Following the conclusion, there is a brief assessment of the recent Labour government from a green social policy position.

## The Ecological Crisis and Limits to Growth

The implications of limits to growth for social policy are complex, contested and conjectural, given the sometimes fierce debates over the extent, character and severity of the 'ecological crisis' for human societies. An example of this contested character of many ecological problems relates to the uncertainty and conflict within the scientific community concerning 'global warming'. However, it is undisputed that a growing range of ecological problems face modern society ranging from global problems such as biodiversity loss and global warming, to more local problems such as urban pollution and the loss of rural hinterlands as a result of economic pressures for 'development'. Here I wish to focus on what is perhaps the most salient aspect of the ecological crisis in terms of social policy: the 'limits to growth' argument. The limits to growth argument (which has been a core aspect of the green critique of modern society for over thirty years), holds that an economy and society premised and organised on the basis of ever increasing economic growth is impossible ('unsustainable') within the finite ecological parameters of human societies. There are two aspects of limits to growth that need to be outlined.

The first are resource limits. This refers to the finite nature of the physical inputs needed by modern societies, such as fossil fuels for energy, fertiliser and plastics, and other ecological goods and services such as clean water and soil for food production. These inputs are finite. The second are pollution limits, that is, the finite capacity of ecological systems to absorb human-based pollution outputs and other side effects of contemporary economic systems. In short, the limits to growth argument simply states that the human economy (and society) is dependent upon 'nature's economy' (ecological systems). Given that the latter is a finite and closed system (apart from solar energy from the sun), it is impossible for the human subsystem (human economy and society) to exceed the finite boundaries of the larger ecological system of which it is a part. The upshot of this critique is that the experience of exponential economic growth (that is, year-on-year increases in economic 'throughput', as measured by GNP or GDP) is atypical and not a norm that can be expected to continue indefinitely. Thus the ecological critique has major implications for the economy of welfare in modern industrial societies, irrespective of whether welfare provision is primarily state-centred, market-centred or a mixed economy of welfare. The point is that welfare states are dependent upon economic growth to provide the financial resources with which to deliver the particular pattern of goods and services that characterise its social policy aims. The implications of the ecological critique can be then expressed as follows: what happens to social policy if economic growth is no longer assumed?

The implications of limits to growth for social policy are potentially radical. The contemporary welfare state has always been dependent upon a growing economy, for producing the tax base from which to fund social welfare provision, a view common to both left- and right-wing positions on the welfare state. Large-scale social welfare provision is called into question by the limits to growth position, and thus threatens the whole welfare state system. At the very least, the impact of a non-growing economy would be to force the state to shrink its social welfare budget in line with the decline in national income. On this reading, the ecological critique implies results that are suspiciously like the standard new right argument for the 'rolling back of the state' and slashing welfare budgets in the name of improving free market economic conditions and destroying the so-called welfare dependency culture. However this would be to misrepresent the ecological critique. The aims of new right critics of social policy are to (1) decrease the tax burden and (2) to introduce free market provision into the vacuum left by the shrinking of government, with the aim of (3) creating the conditions for more economic growth and an 'enterprise culture'. The ecological critique, on the other hand, is premised on (1) the unsustainable nature of continued economic growth (that is, its ecological impossibility) and/or (2) its political undesirability and (3) commitment to a third path for welfare provision that is removed from the state and the market.

The consequences of what many early ecological commentators called the 'steady-state economy' for social policy are far-reaching. One of the central tenets of the steady-state economy is that the economy is geared towards optimising as opposed to maximising production and consumption, a central part of which requires shifting the focus of social policy from welfare provision to being concerned with individual and collective well-being and quality of life. This transformation of social policy involves replacing welfare indicators, for example quantitative measures such as the standard of living, with qualitative indicators of well-being, a central aspect of which are non-material needs.

Taking the ecological context of social policy into account would mean that ecological considerations would have to be integrated as a core (rather than an optional) factor in social policy planning and strategy. Take housing as an example. The implication of limits to growth would be that social policy would focus on ways of reusing the existing housing stock rather than building more houses. In Britain, according to Irvine and Ponton (1988, p. 87), 'housing has hardly begun to be understood as part of the a socio-ecological system. The approach to house-building is short-life and resource-intensive, geared to growth-orientated economics.' The 'ecological cost' of housing policy would also mean that housing policy would stress the importance of domestic energy and water conservation, that is viewing the latter as scarce rather than as unlimited resources that can be ignored in housing policy planning. The adoption of an integrated, ecological approach would also imply that housing policy would be placed within the context of ecologically pertinent aspects of public policy such as transport policy and urban planning. Thus the separation of public from social policy is called into question by the green critique.

Radical green solutions to the problem of resource scarcity usually stress the importance of self-provisioning. For example Trainer (1991, p. 86) claims that 'our high per capita resource-use rates are due in large part to the fact that households and neighbourhoods produce for themselves so few of the goods and services they consume'. Thus there is not only a strong emphasis on decentralisation within green approaches to social policy, but decentralisation is also a constitutive aspect of the (re)creation of a more community-based social policy strategy, a key part of which rests on self-provisioning, understood to mean meeting and determining local needs locally, as far as possible. The more radical wing of the ecology movement wishes to replace both market and state completely with communal social relations, and thus perhaps in the process get rid of the need for 'social policy' as conventionally understood. Contemporary communitarians criticise the notion of 'social justice' and policies aimed to achieve it, on the ground that justice is a remedial virtue, useful for remedying flaws in social life: flaws that are the result of a decline in community. Likewise some greens view 'social policy' as a 'remedial' public activity, since it fills the gap that arises in advanced, industrialised societies in which the abstract association of the 'nation' has replaced the convivial patterns of social relations that are associated with that elusive entity 'community'. From this radical green view, the recreation of 'community' would obviate the need for extensive social policy measures. In short, as discussed below, the radical green argument rejects 'social policy' as conventionally understood in a search for improved social relations that would do away with or greatly reduce the need and/or desirability of present patterns of state-provided or state-managed social welfare.

However there are more 'realistic' green proposals – ones that accept the present institutional contours of the modern welfare state – and these have much to offer contemporary debates about social policy. This realistic green contribution is best termed a 'green social democratic' approach to social welfare, since the main aim is to 'green' the welfare state as opposed to create a completely 'green society'. That is, realistic greens seek the transformation rather than the transcendence of the welfare state, a central part of which is the 'greening' of social policy, which by definition presupposes the existence of state institutions (Barry, 1994, 1995). This realist green position will form the focus of the subsequent discussion.

## Challenges of the Ecological Critique for Social Policy

Whereas the main thrust of the limits to growth position is to question the possibility of continued economic growth (and those forms of social policy that are directly or indirectly dependent upon that growth), within the ecological movement this critique is supplemented (and indeed sometimes substituted) by the claim that economic growth is also unnecessary and in fact positively undesirable. That is, a green social policy is one that is not presaged on continuing economic growth and increasing financial resources for welfare provision. In this sense green social policy indicates, at least in its final aim, a 'post-fiscal' approach to welfare provision.

The general thrust of the ecological critique of contemporary industrialised societies challenges central assumptions of social policy within those societies. Primary among these is a questioning of the aim of social policy as providing citizens with the financial resources to enjoy some minimum level of material consumption of goods and services. The general trend of an ecologically aware social policy is for a shift from providing a particular bundle of goods and services that gives a particular standard of living, to focusing on how social policy can enhance the quality of life of citizens.

### Post-materialism and self-provisioning

Those greens who argue against the 'materialistic' lifestyles of contemporary liberal democracies (a critical perspective that is not coextensive with the green position) argue that such lifestyles (which social policy supports both directly and indirectly) are 'spiritually unfulfilling' as well as ecologically unsustainable (Dobson, 1995). A radical green version is given by Trainer in his book *Abandon Affluence!*, a title that speaks for itself. According to Trainer (1991, p. 85) a sustainable society would be one in which 'people would save, re-cycle, repair, wear out old clothes and look after things. They would be continually concerned to eliminate unnecessary use, to find more efficient ways, and to cut down on resource throughput.' From this critical perspective, social policy should focus either on providing and stressing the 'post-material' dimensions of well-being, or better still, on encouraging and supporting people to provide for their own needs.

Others such as Ferris (1993, p. 153) point out that 'it is not plausible, or in our view ethically acceptable, to expect poor communities to succeed in becoming more self-reliant without redistributive grants and subsidies from the state'. One way of addressing this justified concern is based on the prospects for a future 'greening of the state', where the state would support local, communal self-reliance. However, as discussed below, the green approach stresses that subsidies should be channelled through community-based institutions whenever possible, and only secondly through conventional state and private sector social policy instruments. This 'green social democracy' position sees the state transforming itself from a 'direct provider' to an 'enabler', that is, helping citizens to help themselves. This position is most characteristic of the view of the welfare state found in European green party programmes.

The green argument is that welfare capitalism has failed to fulfil non-marketed social/basic needs such as 'breathable air, living space, light, silence, drinking water, prevention of illness, preservation or reproduction of natural resources, good public transport, meaningful work and opportunities to use disposable time meaningfully' (Gorz, 1987, p. 6). The point about these needs is not only that they are essential to human individual and collective life, but also that they are not (as a rule) produced within human society but typically need to be protected from the effects of economic overdevelopment in order for them to be available. They are also largely located outside the exchange system of the formal, monetised economy. Hence to incorporate them into an understanding of social policy requires incorporating social policy into a wider understanding of the relationship between economic policy and its environmental impacts. In other words the 'greening' of social policy requires one to address the structural organisation of production and consumption within the formal, monetised economy, rather than simply being confined to the broad area of 'social consumption'. It also requires an expansion of the economy (and work) to include the informal social economy, as discussed later.

## Inequality, social justice and economic growth

In societies such as the welfare states of the West, state legitimacy is in part dependent upon a commitment to reduce inequality via redistributive measures. However, coexisting with this is the standard defence of economic inequality, which claims that it is necessary for creating the conditions for economic growth. In other words an unequal distribution of the benefits of socially produced wealth is a necessary condition of a growing, successful economy (less is said about the unequal distribution of the costs and risks of economic performance). Wealth and income inequalities are argued to be economic incentives that are absolutely essential if the best individuals are to be retained in the national job market and contribute to overall economic productivity and growth. The basic argument is that while some people gain more than others, everybody gains. This green critique of economic growth can also be regarded as an argument against the social inequalities that are a structural component of contemporary social and economic policies. The increase in inequality in Britain over the last twenty years can be interpreted as evidence of this relationship between economic growth and socioeconomic inequality. The green argument for a steady-state economy, or an economy in which maximising output or profits is not the dominant imperative, can also be seen as an argument for decreasing social and economic inequality. With an economy not geared towards maximising production, income and formally paid employment, the justification of an unequal distribution of socially produced wealth cannot be that it is required for procuring greater wealth production. In short, with the shift to a less growth-orientated society, the normative basis for social cooperation needs to be renegotiated, as does social policy.

The implications of this argument are dramatic for social policy, given that one of the central justifications for social policy is to reduce socioeconomic inequality via the redistribution of income, goods and services generated from a growing economy. The green argument is that if one wishes to reduce inequality, then accepting limits to growth may be a more realistic way of achieving it, since a less inegalitarian distribution of social wealth is more likely to be demanded in a non-growing economy. However, such talk of a principled rejection or downplaying of the traditional commitment to economic growth would obviously lead to strong resistance from both labour and capital interests, since it spells nothing less than the radical transformation of industrial society.

One interpretation of the green critique of orthodox economic growth is that economic *security* rather than economic *affluence* is important for a more equal social order within modern democracies. The green view is that it is the *distribution* of wealth within society, not the *absolute level* of wealth, that is important in a democratic political system. Similarly, the lessons for social policy are that what is important is the distribution of work (not just waged employment in the formal economy), free time and other 'public good' dimensions of a decent quality of life, such as quiet, pleasant and clean working and living environments and personal security. Whereas traditionally social policy has been concerned with the distribution of consumption, green social policy is centrally concerned with the distribution of productive opportunities (in the form of self-provisioning).

A less radical green position on economic growth is taken by Jacobs (1996), who makes an important distinction between economic growth that is understood as increases in personal disposable income (which is the dominant view) and economic growth that implies greater public, as opposed to private, spending and investment. The point is that public consumption of the fruits of economic growth does seem to imply less overall consumption (and potential ecological damage) than is the case with private consumption. An example of this is a shift to collective forms of provisioning, ranging from large-scale services such as public rather than private transport, to more micro-level shared services such as a clothes washing service rather than the use of individual washing machines and dryers. To offset the inevitable reaction that this shift towards collective consumption is unnecessarily draconian, there is also an argument for the continuation of individual consumption patterns premised on technological improvements in the 'ecological efficiency' of production. Thus one could imagine a green social policy in which the aim is to provide goods and services that are either produced and distributed in an ecologically sustainable manner and/or produced and consumed by a variety of units ranging from the individual to the household to collectives of individuals.

## The state, market and community

Absolutely central to understanding the green approach to social policy is the role and view of the state. Doherty's (1992, p. 102) statement that 'the greens have responded to new conditions and issues with a distinctively modern strategy based on accepting the limits of the state in guaranteeing social and political change' can be extended to include green thinking on social policy. While some of the more anarchistic greens' suspicion of the welfare state stems from their belief that 'while some of its origins were philanthropic . . . others reflected the government's desire for a healthy and educated supply of people for the production process and the armed forces' (Irvine and Ponton, 1988, p. 81), most greens would accept (at least in the short to medium term) the continuation of the welfare state system. With regard to the latter, the greens suggest an alternative to the management of society by the state (through social policy), a central part of which requires the decentralisation (and democratisation) of the state and its agencies. An example of this is the British Green Party's social welfare policy (1997, SW 204), which states that:

> We believe that a sustainable society would remove many of the causes of present day social problems. A return to smaller, more caring communities would reduce the need for both volunteers and social workers. The current role of welfare agencies would change and diminish; they would no longer carry the main responsibility for those in need.

Jacobs' (1996, p. 96) suggestion that 'publicly-raised funds should be directed into local, voluntary and community-based enterprises and organisations, with the twin aims of raising long-term employment and meeting social needs' is a recent expression of the broad ecological approach to social policy. Whereas traditional left and right social policy debate is largely confined to finding the appropriate mix of state and market mechanisms, the ecological approach to social policy is grounded in the 'social economy' or what is sometimes called the 'third sector', with the public or state and the private or market sectors being the other two. Part of this new 'mixed moral economy of welfare' finds expression in the increasing 'partnership approach' to local social provision. For greens the advantage of partnerships between the state and the voluntary and private sectors locally is that this will strengthen the local and informal economies (Kemball-Cooke *et al.*, 1991, p. 93) and foster genuine community economic development (Shragge, 1993).

The importance of this has to do with the green aim of rebuilding local communities. Thus the green preference for centring social policy on the social economy is not simply that the latter could provide services and activities that neither the state nor the market sector are able to provide, although this is of course important. It is also the preferred focus because delivering of social policy through the third sector would greatly facilitate the reinvigoration of communities. As Jacobs (1996, p. 100) puts it, 'community-based organisations tangibly raise levels of hope and self-confidence and a sense of social participation. By enabling people to work together for one another, they give expression to feelings of altruism and mutuality, and thereby help to regenerate a sense of community.' The recovery of community as a central plank in the overarching aims and methods of green social policy does not (as some critics of community have suggested) mean a return to closed, intolerant communities. Rather the green's appeal to community ought to be viewed as calling for the nation to be seen as a network (or community) of communities, coordinated by central state agencies but with local government and the third sector having increased autonomy and competence in the design and implementation of social policies. 'Meeting local needs locally' is thus a central objective of green social policy.

## Green Social Policies

While much of the preceding discussion has focused on the implications of the ecological critique for social policy at the 'meta' or general level, and on different policy instruments (market, state, community), there is also a discernible green position on particular areas of social policy. While much of the thinking on specific policies has stemmed from the need of green parties to produce clear policy prospects for election manifestoes, green approaches to social policy predate the rise of green political parties and are not related exclusively to electoral concerns. The latter, as one would expect, is particularly the case with the more radical green social policy proposals. For reasons of space, just two salient policy areas are discussed below. These are (1) the basic citizens' income scheme and the concept of work, and (2) green approaches to health policy.

### The basic citizens' income scheme and work

The provision of a basic citizens' income has been a central policy proposal within the green movement for at least the last twenty years. One of the main aims of this proposal is to free individuals from the need to engage in waged employment in the market or state sectors: a corollary of rejecting annual increases in economic growth as an overarching goal of public policy is that the era of 'full employment' (in the conventional sense) would end (Keane and Owens, 1986). Social policy objectives must also be premised on widening the concept of 'work' to include all those activities that sustain and enrich people's lives, and not simply be focused on cash transactions in the formal economy (Porritt and Winner, 1988, p. 155). As Jacobs (1996, p. 87) puts it, 'we must deal with both sides of the coin – not just the absence of work, but with work itself.' It is within this context that the basic income scheme is central to green thinking.

There are many facets to the basic income scheme, but we will only focus on a few of them. The first thing to note is that the basic income scheme is part of the greens' desire to shift taxation from labour to non-renewable resources and socially and environmentally damaging goods and services. The basic income scheme would be a central part of a radical overhaul of the tax and benefits system of modern economies, simplifying it by introducing a universal basic income to all citizens, regardless of whether or not they work in the formal economy. The British Green Party (1997, SW 402) also advocates the citizens' income scheme as a way of abolishing the stigma of means testing.

The second issue concerns one of the aims of the basic income policy. Basic income would distinguish 'employment', meaning waged work within the formal economy, from 'work', meaning unwaged activity within the informal economy. One of the advantages of the basic income scheme is that it would give public recognition (in the form of income) to the unpaid work of the household, such as caring for children, the sick and the old, food preparation, and other forms of domestic labour. Thus the basic income proposal fits with feminist arguments about the unpaid, gendered and unvalued nature of informal economic activity (Mellor, 1992). Another advantage of the scheme, according to the British Green Party (1997, SW 300), is that as a long term objective, 'the implementation of a Citizens' Income scheme combined with an informal economy would free members of a community to help each other and to organise the provision of many services currently supplied by the welfare state'.

One goal of the basic income would be to encourage individuals to discover the 'internal' goods of work, as opposed to valuing work purely in terms of the income it allows one to command. Typically the green argument is that the basic income would allow and encourage individuals – by themselves, in households and other collective organisations – to provide for themselves the things they need. Thus the state's role would be to provide individuals and communities with the wherewithal to help them meet their own needs (Gorz, 1983). In the long term, central state support would diminish over time as self-reliant, local economies became strong enough to provide the necessary economic resources to meet local needs locally. This argument for self-provisioning has already been identified above as a central aspect of the green position. In terms of the sphere of work, basic income would alter the pattern of production (and consumption) such that what Robertson (1985) has called 'ownwork' (located in the informal economy) would become an increasingly important component of individual well-being. That is, ownwork is not just about producing goods and services in the household or in other non-market, non-state ways, but would also lead to work being seen as intrinsically and instrumentally valuable for personal well-being.

Against the view that providing people with some minimum consumption level (via welfare transfers and benefits or policies aimed at full waged employment) ought to be the overriding goal of social policy, the radical green view (and one which it shares with older socialist values) is that providing people with rewarding productive work ought to be the aim of government policy. The British Green Party's social welfare proposal (1997, SWS 101) is premised on the separation of 'the twin conventional priorities of full employment and rising living standards'. Basic income would thus guarantee some minimum consumption level while also being part of a wider transformation of social policy in which self-provisioning would be central.

Thus while recognising that the diminution and eventual elimination of poverty ought to be a key social goal, the view of the 'good life' as one that is primarily associated with the consumption of goods (whether provided by the state or the market) is not consistent with green values. This does not mean that the greens completely opposed to material consumption, far from it. However the greens propose an alternative pattern of social policy provision in which 'well-being' – with emphasis on the opportunity of productive work for all and other essential components of a quality life, such as free time with one's family and friends – and not simply 'welfare' – with its bias towards economic considerations such as income maintenance and state-sponsored personal consumption – becomes the focus of social policy.

## Health

In keeping with its decentralist, local orientation, green health policy is guided by 'appropriate scale', that is, services should be located and delivered at the lowest level possible. As Irvine and Ponton (1988, p. 100) put it, 'wherever possible, medical help and advice would be dealt with at community level'. At the same time, green health policy also acknowledges that individuals have a responsibility to take care of their own health – the 'appropriate level' here being the individual, this being particularly the case when emphasis is placed on preventative medicine.

As well as espousing procedures such as midwife-assisted home births and the use of preventative rather than palliative medicine, green health policy proposals have as a common theme the need to restructure the relationship between citizens/clients and health professionals. The green emphasis on alternative/complementary medicine is motivated as much by a desire to 'empower' citizens to take care of their own health, as by the intrinsic health and other benefits of such forms of medicine. Discussing Gorz's thinking on health issues, Kenny and Little (1995, p. 283) state that the green vision he advocates implies that 'doctors should become "enablers" within the community, aiming to make individuals as self-reliant as possible in matters of health. Ultimately, the attainment of a healthy society will require the abolition of wages for work.' This last point, the link between health improvement and changes in the economic organisation of production, is thus another argument one can use for the basic income scheme and 'self-provisioning', as discussed above. Here as in so many other areas, the ecological argument is that one cannot talk of improving health care without also talking about the transformation of the economy, and thus of conditions outside the particular policy area under consideration.

For example, by expanding the concept of the 'environment' to include the urban, built environment (which is the everyday environment for the vast majority of citizens in advanced industrialised nations), one can establish the link between degraded urban areas, overcrowding, poor housing and so on, and ill-health, including mental illness. Modern medicine and health policy is flawed, according to the green movement, in its failure to recognise that the bulk of illness in modern societies is not accidental but predominately caused by socioeconomic and environmental conditions. That is, illness is an avoidable consequence of the way society is organised, and not just of personal, unpredictable events. An example of this is the link between asthma in children living in urban areas and pollution, largely, according to recent research, emissions from road traffic. The basic ecological position is that as long as what Margaret Thatcher called the 'great British car economy' is seen as central to the overall economic competitiveness or performance of Britain, then what is gained in economic growth will be paid for in part by the health of the younger generation. According to Jacobs (1996, p. 78), '1.3 million children in Britain – that is, one in seven – suffer from asthma, now shown to be aggravated, and possibly caused, by traffic pollution'. Thus changes in transport policy to lessen road traffic by encouraging public transport or taxing company cars, for example, can greatly contribute to decreasing the incidence of a range of respiratory-related illnesses. Because for greens, health (like most areas of social policy) cannot be separated from wider socio-economic and environmental conditions, such alterations in transport policy can be see as exercises in preventative medicine. Other examples of this type of preventative health care include alterations in urban planning so as to minimise the need for people to travel to basic amenities such as shops, schools, health care centres, entertainment and decrease the need for motorised transport and the infrastructure to support it. Thus green health policy is one that seeks to help improve the health of the human population by improving the 'ecological health' of the environment in which they live.

## Conclusion

The potentially radical insight of the green analysis is that the problems faced by the welfare state in general and social policy in particular will not be solved simply by appealing for more resources (which of course implies the continuation of economic growth). An ecologically sustainable social policy must, by definition, be premised on an ecologically sustainable economy, and this implies far-reaching structural (as well as technological) changes in the way the economy and state is organised. The green critique suggests that social policy needs to be detached from economic growth as much as possible. Recent trends have demonstrated that while national income has been rising, as has personal income for some, this has not been accompanied by a corresponding increase in levels of well-being and welfare that go beyond mere income (Oswald, 1995). A central part of the green approach to social policy is the need for alternative indicators and measures, ones not exclusively focusing on income or other measures derived from orthodox economics. Thus a key challenge for future social policy is to switch the focus from the 'mixed economy of welfare' to finding ways – through 'the mixed moral economy of well-being' – to provide citizens with public goods such as clean, safe and aesthetically pleasing local, urban and national environments, as well as productive work, free time and other components of a decent *quality of life* as opposed to the more conventional *standard of living* (Jacobs, 1995).

The strength of the ecological critique is its radical vision of an alternative way of organising our collective social life through specific social policies. Indeed one could predict that green social policy proposals will contribute increasingly to debate on social policy in the transition to a more sustainable society. It is thus both as an imaginative school of thought, seeking a 'third way' between state and market, and as the source of practical but radical policy proposals, that the ecological perspective can contribute to the future direction of British social policy.

Finally, a brief comment on the new Labour government. While nothing on the scale or nature of the green social policy proposals can be said to describe the policies of the new Blair administration, there are some signs that it is at least not immediately hostile to aspects of the ecological standpoint. There is some indication that the Blair administration is keen to see the status of the state change from a 'provider' to an 'enabler', as seen in Chancellor Gordon Brown's 'Welfare to Work' policy for example, and talk of decentralising the welfare system. At the same time the foreign secretary, Robin Cook, during the recent Earth Summit Plus 5 conference in New York, argued that 'more has to be less' in terms of the need for changes in lifestyles that the shift to a more sustainable society will require (*Guardian*, 27 June 1997). While this conceded a central aspect of the ecological critique of contemporary welfare economies, it was emphatically not accompanied by a consideration of the imaginative suggestions of the greens concerning, *inter alia*, alternative indicators and a shift of social policy away from welfare towards 'well-being', emphasising self-provisioning, divorcing well-being from economic growth and abandoning the pursuit of full employment, decentralising (and democratising) state agencies, and supporting community-based forms of self-provisioning, so that local needs may be met locally. At the moment there is little sign that the 'greening' of social policy is about to commence under the new Labour government, but some green social policy ideas stand a better chance of blossoming under it than under any previous British government, particularly because much of the green agenda is a 'post-fiscal' one, which ought to allay Treasury concerns about additional tax burdens.

## Further Reading

For a general overview of green politics see A. Dobson, *Green Political Thought: An Introduction*, 2nd edn (London: Routledge, 1995), which provides a good introduction to green ideas and the ecological critique. More detailed information on various green positions in a variety of social policy areas can be found in Green Party manifestoes, such as the British Green Party's 1997 election manifesto. Also useful are S. Irvine and A. Ponton, *A Green Manifesto: Policies for a Green Future* (London: Optima, 1988), and D. Kembell-Cook *et al.*, *The Green Budget: An Emergency Programme for the United Kingdom* (London: Greenprint, 1991).

Central figures in green social policy debates include Ivan Illich, *Deschooling Society* (Harmondsworth: Penguin, 1971), *Medical Nemesis: The expropriation of health* (New York: Pantheon, 1976) and *Disabling Professions* (London: Marion Boyers, 1977); Andre Gorz (1983, 1987); and James Robertson, *The Sane Alternative: A Choice of Futures*, 2nd edn (published by the author) and Robertson (1985). For commentaries on Gorz and Robertson's contributions to social policy, see Kenny and Little (1995) and Cahill (1995), respectively. For some discussion of the green contribution to social policy debates, see Cahill (1994) and P. Alcock, *Social Policy in Britain: Themes and Issues* (London: Macmillan, 1996). On the green argument for alternative indicators of well-being see V. Anderson, *Alternative Economic Indicators* (London: Routledge, 1991); and P. Ekins, *The Living Economy: A New Economics in the Making* (London: Routledge, 1990). J. Ferris, 'Ecological versus Social Rationality: Can there be green social policies?' (in Dobson and Lucardie, *The Politics of Nature: Explorations in Green Political Theory* (London: Routledge),1993) offers a good (if incomplete) overview of green thinking on social policy. M. Jacobs, *The Politics of the Real World* (London: Earthscan, 1996), is excellent and readable, and contains much of the most recent thinking on social and economic policy from the broadly 'realistic' end of the green political spectrum.

# CHAPTER 15

# Changing Dimensions of Poverty

DAVID PIACHAUD

This chapter is concerned with contemporary approaches to poverty and the challenges poverty poses for social policy. It looks at the nature of poverty in contemporary Britain and the different attitudes towards poverty adopted by different political perspectives. The chapter also explores why we should be concerned about (rising) poverty in Britain, concentrating on the effects of inadequate resources and the potential consequences of increasing child poverty. Finally, some consideration is given to possible social policy responses. Can poverty be alleviated purely by redistributing resources through social security payments or are other factors equally important? Does poverty relate to lack of time rather than simply money, and if so, what can governments do to remedy the problem? Again, it is important to understand how a lack of material resources can affect individual behaviour, especially consumption patterns and a perception of 'needs' that might be detrimental to good health. It may be that social policy makers need to think not only about income-related issues but also about different forms of intervention designed to change 'poor lifestyles' and tackle the causes of poverty.

## Poverty and Social Policy: Changing Conditions, Changing Assumptions

Social policy has been directed at many different goals – concerning health, education, the environment and the legitimation of the state, for example. One of the most central and constant goals in Britain during the twentieth century has been to relieve poverty. The Beveridge Report (1942) set out to eliminate the 'evil giant of want' by means of the social security system. Now many see that system as having failed. As shown in Table 15.1, social security spending increased by more than 50 per cent in real terms between 1979 and 1993/4, but over the same period the number in poverty (defined as those receiving less than half the average national income) more than doubled. This has led many to question and rethink the role of social policy in relation to poverty.

Table 15.1   **Social security and poverty**

|                                              | *1979/80*        | *1993/94*        |
| -------------------------------------------- | ---------------- | ---------------- |
| Social security expenditure (1994/5 prices)  | £48.3 bn         | £79.5 bn         |
| Number in poverty                            | 5.0 m (9%)       | 13.7 m (24%)     |

*Note*: In this and other tables, 'poverty' is defined as below half the average equivalised income (after housing costs).
*Sources*: DSS, 1993a, 1995, 1996a.

Concern about poverty has increased as society has become more unequal. Over the past twenty years the gap between rich and poor has increased dramatically. The share of income taken by the top fifth of earners before taxes and benefits rose from 43 per cent to 50 per cent between 1977 and 1995/6; after taxes and benefits their share rose from 36 per cent to 40 per cent of all income. In contrast the share of income going to the bottom fifth fell over this period. At present the disposable incomes of the top fifth are on average five times greater than those of the bottom fifth (Office of National Statistics, 1997). Poverty and inequality have clearly increased in Britain.

Before considering the current debate on policies aimed at alleviating poverty it is worthwhile considering how poverty has been defined and how social policy has addressed poverty. Poverty has been defined for research and policy purposes as arising when income is less than needs. Income determines command over resources and the range of choices and opportunities enjoyed; it is conveniently but not always accurately measured as net disposable income. Needs may be defined as absolute, with a fixed standard that does not change over time; this approach has been advocated by some on the political right. Most, following Townsend (1979), argue that needs must be seen as relative to the prevailing living standards and that as standards rise generally, so too must the poverty standard; for example a century ago nobody had a television whereas now in Britain the lack of a television (other than through choice) is an indication of poverty. Relative poverty is conveniently measured as income below half the national average, adjusted for household size.

Under the Beveridge plan, poverty was to be overcome by means of a social security system that would provide benefits during periods when earnings were interrupted due to sickness or unemployment, and that ensured an income in old age through the state pension. Social policy in this sphere was focused largely on income redistribution between periods in and out of work and over the life cycle. The Beveridge approach was based on two-parent families and the assumption that there would be full employment; growing prosperity would trickle down to benefit everyone or, to change metaphors in mid-stream, the rising tide would lift all boats.

Today many of the assumptions of Beveridge's world have collapsed. Unemployment, which never reached half a million in the 25 years after the war, rose to more than three million in the early 1980s and is now around two million. There has been a rapid rise in lone-parent families, most of whom depend on means-tested social security. While there are many more women in paid employment and contributing to social security, later labour-market entry and earlier retirement pose an economic and political challenge to the social security system. All these developments call the current policies on poverty into question.

In the next section alternative, often conflicting, views on the role of social policy in relation to poverty are reviewed. Then the basis for concern about poverty is discussed and some implications for policy are considered.

## The Diversity of Approaches to Poverty

The approach to social policy that has dominated most of the past two decades in Britain has been to limit the role of the state and pursue greater selectivity, most obviously by means-tested social security benefits. This is most clear in relation to unemployed people, for whom there have been a succession of cutbacks in national insurance benefits and increasing reliance on means-tested benefits. Advocates of this approach have argued that, with the limited funds available, it makes no sense to 'waste' benefits on those who do not need them – although for political reasons this argument has not been applied so enthusiastically to pensioners. Critics of means-tested benefits have emphasised low take-up rates, high administrative costs and the possible stigmatisation of recipients. Means testing inevitably involves withdrawing benefits from those with slightly higher incomes. This can lead to a poverty trap, creating a disincentive to work, to save, and in some cases for families to stay together. Instead of reducing dependence on state it could be that means-tested benefits increase welfare dependence.

The most extreme critics of social policy see it as part of the problem, not part of the solution. Murray (1984), for example, argues that any response to a social problem, however well-intentioned, only makes it worse. The suggestion is that you have to be cruel to be kind and therefore cutbacks in social security provision are needed to force people to take greater responsibility for themselves. This line of argument has been highly influential in the United States and has led to drastic reductions in welfare support for lone parents. The consequences of this in terms of poverty remain to be seen.

Some in Britain, as well as in the United States, see poverty as increasingly associated with an 'underclass'. Murray (in Lister, 1996) sees an underclass characterised by young unemployed men, unmarried mothers and increasing crime. The term underclass is, however, used in many different ways and with many different explanations. Some say it is due to mass unemployment, some that it is due to the inadequacy of social services, some that it is due to a culture of poverty; others argue that any differences in attitudes are the products of experiences, not the cause of different experiences. Each interpretation has different social policy implications. The clarity of the discussion would be much enhanced if the term 'underclass' were never used – and this would also reduce the stigmatisation, intentional or otherwise, that goes with the term.

Turning from approaches broadly associated with the political right, what have been the approaches on the left? The most straightforward approach to tackling poverty, particularly in the heyday of the Keynesian welfare states, was to redistribute income from the better-off to the poor. The extent of poverty is shown in Table 15.2 which shows the cost of closing the poverty gap and the tax consequences if this were done by redistribution. Technically it is a quite feasible policy to reduce poverty in this way. Yet at present the political likelihood of more redistribution is very low; for example the first Labour budget made no move to end the relative decline in the value of social security benefits, the chancellor ruling out the kind of increases in direct taxation that would be necessary to maintain or increase them in real terms.

Others have advocated a more comprehensive contributory social security system based on the predominant European model. The systems in continental Europe are mostly organised on an individual basis rather than on the family basis used in British social security and, compared with the British system, they are very expensive because they aim at 'income maintenance' rather than minimum income provision.

Many on the left have advocated a minimum wage as a means of tackling poverty, but it is not clear that its introduction would have as much effect on poverty as its supporters suggest. The minimum wage is certainly the subject

**Table 15.2  Poverty gap, 1993/4**

| | |
|---|---|
| Proportion in poverty | 24% |
| Mean poverty gap | 7% of equivalised income |
| Aggregate poverty gap | 1.7% of personal disposable income |
| Cost of bridging poverty gap | £5.3 billion |
| Cost equivalent to rise in standard rate of income tax | 3 p in the pound |

*Sources*: DSS, 1993a, 1995, 1996a.

of heated political argument. As the 1997 general election campaign made clear, the Conservatives opposed it on the grounds that it would destroy jobs and as a result add to poverty, while Labour supported it because the party believed it would enhance social protection and reduce poverty. However, while a minimum wage would serve to reduce the exploitation of workers, particularly women, its impact on poverty is likely to be quite limited. This is because, as Table 15.3 shows, most of the poor are not in paid employment at all. The main gains of a minimum wage are likely to be for women many of whom are in dual-earner families in the middle income range.

As many of the chapters in this book make clear, the most important shift in policy emphasis in recent years, affecting Labour, Liberal Democrats and Conservatives, has been towards supply-side policies to improve education and training. The objective is to enhance opportunity rather than to try to equalise outcomes. Rhetorically at least, the emphasis is on 'investment in people', particularly young people, whose skills are going to be required if Britain is to remain competitive in the rapidly evolving global market place (see Commission on Social Justice, 1994; Joseph Rowntree Foundation, 1995).

One important component of this shift has been the development of active labour market policies. The Job Seekers' Allowance, introduced by the Conservatives in 1996, required claimants to enter into a 'jobseeker's agreement' on the type of job sought and the steps to be taken to seek work. Labour's New Deal programme has four options to offer young people aged under 25 who have been unemployed for six months or more: a private sector job, with the employer receiving a £60 per week rebate for six months; work for a voluntary sector employer; a job with the Environmental Task Force; or a full-time training course. In contrast to the old Keynesian model of welfare, there is not a fifth option – doing nothing – so that in this respect the proposals may be seen as a form of US 'work-fare'.

The alternatives set out above by no means exhaust the range of potential solutions to poverty and it is worth mentioning three rather different proposals, all of which claim to be able to reduce its worst effects. First there is the idea, which has advocates on both left and right, of a basic or citizens' income (see McKay in this volume). Although an extremely expensive means

**Table 15.3  Numbers in poverty, 1993/4**

| Number in household: | |
| --- | --- |
| With one or more in paid employment | 1.7 million |
| With self-employed, unemployed, disabled or aged 60+ | 12.0 million |

*Sources*: DSS, 1993a, 1995, 1996a.

of tackling poverty (and one that consequently does not commend itself to politicians), the idea is important because it emphasises that many of the demarcations upon which social policy has been based – for example between the employed, unemployed and retired – are breaking down.

A second set of influences arises from the feminist movement and advocates of greater gender equality. In order to equalise employment opportunities the emphasis has been on extending child care; but it is not clear that this policy alone would have a significant impact on poverty. A paradoxical feature of the contemporary labour market is that there has been a large increase in two-earner families, which has served to reduce the extent of income poverty in such families, but also a corresponding increase in no-earner families, which has heightened the incidence of poverty in this group. While the lack of child-care facilities is certainly one factor in the lack of earnings, it is by no means the only explanation. As discussed in relation the minimum wage, the reduction of sex inequalities is an end in itself rather than a particularly effective means of reducing poverty, for which other policies will be needed.

A final approach that warrants mention is a child-oriented approach such as that put forward by Young and Halsey (1995). Concerned about the educational standard of many children, the number in care and on child protection registers, and about crime levels, they have called for a massive redistribution not only of income, but also of *time* and *concern* in favour of children. They argue for child-centred policies in many areas, including a 'parent wage' for mothers or fathers who stay at home to look after dependent children. The implementation of such a policy could have the rather 'conservative' effect of reversing the entry of women into the labour force, thus reducing family incomes and increasing income poverty. Nevertheless by starting out from a concern for the needs of children this approach does highlight the importance of reconsidering why poverty is a matter of central concern for social policy. It is this question that the next section addresses more generally.

## The Reasons for Concern About Poverty

Poverty is not an isolated phenomenon unrelated to other social issues. Rather it is both the consequence of broader social inequalities and a contributor to other social problems. Women, for example, are more likely than men to be poor. They receive lower rates of pay, more women than men are part-time workers with little social protection or pension rights, and women do the bulk of unpaid home and child-care work. All these factors contribute to their greater income and time provery, which is one component of gender inequality.

'Race' is another dimension of poverty. Those from minority ethnic groups are more likely to be unemployed or on low rates of pay in poor working conditions, and their treatment by the welfare state institutions is significantly worse. These factors contribute to poverty and reflect direct and indirect discrimination in society.

Poverty also contributes to poor education for children. For example, although there are individual exceptions, in general pupils in the most disadvantaged areas achieve lower educational standards than those in the most advantaged areas. How far educational performance can be improved by raising the standard of teaching and attainment in schools and how far it depends on reducing child poverty is now a matter of debate. What is clear is that poverty and education are inextricably linked.

Similarly there are large differences in health and mortality that are linked to income and social class. For example unemployment not only leads to poverty, often it also leads to ill-health and premature death. Children's development in terms of weight and height is worse in deprived areas. So poverty contributes to health problems, and in turn health problems contribute to poverty.

Thus concern about poverty must be part of a wider concern about gender and race inequality, and about the nature of education and health provision. It cannot be separated from the broad concerns of social policy, which are plainly to do with the individual and social consequences of at least two factors: inadequate resources for living generally and, more specifically, concern about children's opportunities and life chances.

## Inadequate resources

It is not the case that all resources and choices are directly determined by income. Education and health care are largely distributed through social allocation systems. A poor social environment – crime, insecurity, litter, noise – is not directly determined by income level, nor is the quality of community life. Yet all these are affected by income level.

There must be particular concern when resources are not adequate to cope with emergencies. The extent of vulnerability to uncertain life events is far greater for the poor. Equally there must be concern over poor health and low life expectancy, both of which are linked to poverty. But it is not enough to think solely in terms of income poverty. The ability to cope with emergencies may depend on savings and assets as much as on income. Health and life

**Table 15.4   Access to consumer durables**

|                                                      | Bottom 20% of income distribution (%) | Total population (%) |
| ---------------------------------------------------- | :-----------------------------------: | :------------------: |
| Proportion of individuals in a household with access to: |                                   |                      |
| Fridge or fridge-freezer                             | 99                                    | 99                   |
| Washing machine                                      | 87                                    | 93                   |
| Telephone                                            | 73                                    | 91                   |
| Central heating                                      | 76                                    | 85                   |
| Video recorder                                       | 71                                    | 82                   |
| Car or van                                           | 41                                    | 70                   |

*Source*: DSS (1996a), table 8.7.

expectancy, for example, depend on lifestyle decisions such as smoking and drinking as well as income.

In material terms many of the poor are not without assets, as shown in Table 15.4. But many of poor are far worse off than figures suggest in terms of expenditure on necessities – food, clothing, heating – because of very high expenditure on non-necessities such as tobacco, alcohol and useless foods. Half of those out of work spend less than 10 per cent of their household income on cigarettes; but one quarter spend over 20 per cent on smoking leaving far less for other expenditure (Marsh and McKay, 1994).

Food, clothing, heat and housing are basic requirements for existence in Britain. Many other needs are socially defined. Many perceived needs are the product of an insatiable generation of 'needs', promoted by the advertising industry, for example virtually all expenditure on cosmetics meets no real *need* but many, both male and female, perceive cosmetics as essential. Young and Halsey (1995, p. 14) refer favourably to Karl Marx's idea of the 'fetishism of commodities', commenting that, 'insofar as the modern economy makes people lust after things, it is subtracting value and energy from personal relationships and adding value and energy to objects.'

## Impact on children

Nearly one third of children in Britain are poor, three times the proportion in 1979. Children are substantially more likely to be in poor households than adults, as shown in Table 15.5. Thus the effect of poverty on children is a matter of special importance.

**Table 15.5   Children in poverty**

|  | *1979* | *1993/94* |
| --- | --- | --- |
| Number of children (million) | 1.4 | 4.2 |
| % of all children | 10 | 32 |
| Number of adults (million) | 3.6 | 9.5 |
| % of all adults | 9 | 22 |

*Sources*: DSS, 1993a, 1995, 1996a.

The opportunities and life chances of many children are diminished by:

● Poor diet and housing affecting health and education
● Poor parenting
● Poor education
● Poor socialisation

Once again, the question may be asked: to what extent is more income the answer? It is certainly *part* of the answer, and reversing the growth in relative poverty that has taken place since 1979 would redress many of its worst effects. However, if the government is correct in its view that self-respect comes from earning a living and not receiving 'hand-outs', then jobs are needed as well as income. Furthermore, as intimated above, more income is not necessarily the answer if it simply leads to extra drinking, smoking, junk food and obesity; nor will it help if, in the long run, if it is earned at the price of poorer parenting. Finally, more income can not directly resolve problems such as the loss of role models in the family, the breakdown of social control and even community collapse.

## The Implications for Policy

What, then can governments do to mitigate the incidence and effects of poverty? The traditional social policy response to poverty, as discussed earlier, has been to concentrate on meeting needs through social security. This approach is still crucial since most of the poor remain outside the labour market.

The emphasis of the new Labour government, to use President Clinton's words, is to give 'hand-ups not hand-outs'. But improved skills do not provide jobs unless the economy is run to ensure full employment. The welfare-to-work policy may be undermined if general employment is not expanding. Many on the political right favour neither hand-outs nor hand-ups but

**Table 15.6  Social policy and poverty**

| Macro policies affecting poverty | Economic and social policy<br>Policy on unemployment<br>Policy on retirement<br>Family policy<br>Social security policy |
|---|---|
| Micro features of income generation, e.g. hours and conditions of work | Policy on distribution of work by age, between men and women, between parents and non-parents |
| Micro features of consumption of resources, e.g. variations in expenditure | Policy on diet, smoking and drinking through regulation, promotion and counselling |
| Macro features of command over resources, e.g. public services, amenities and standards | Policy on education, health care, housing, physical environment and social environment |

instead want to hand back responsibility to individuals and families, putting all the emphasis on personal values and behaviour. It is no doubt true that there are individuals who have saved, gone on wonderful holidays and provided superb parenting to highly successful offspring on an income on which most could not begin to cope. But so what? Can everyone be expected to live like these paragons? If individual values have changed there are reasons for this change, so what are the economic and social pressures that have caused this to happen?

The damaging consequences of poverty are the product of both societal (macro) factors and individual (micro) factors. Both need to be considered if poverty is to be effectively tackled. When addressing social policy and poverty there is a need to think much more broadly than in the past. We need to think not merely about redistribution but also about tackling the social and economic causes of lack of income. We need to think about the process of income generation and its consequences, particularly for children. We need to think about influencing those features of personal behaviour that exacerbate poverty and worsen health, education and children's life chances. Finally we need to think about resources in much more broad terms than merely those purchased out of money incomes. The range of relevant policies will be discussed in turn and are summarised in Table 15.6.

## Tackling lack of income

In the past, as discussed earlier, social policy tackled poverty largely by means of redistribution through the social security system. Now it seems clear that social policy is often merely picking up the pieces caused by unemployment and family breakdown – it is providing a parsimonious palliative and is not getting to grips with the real problems. Ironically, welfare provision, particularly where income maintenance is concerned, is increasingly blamed for the very problems it is seeking to alleviate.

Tackling the lack of income requires a much broader approach to economic and social policy than has been apparent so far. Eliminating poverty, or even restoring poverty to its level in 1979, is an enormous challenge that requires political priority if it is to succeed. Achieving it entirely by redistribution would not restore the self-respect of those un-employed who could support themselves if the work opportunities were there – and in any case it is not politically conceivable. However, a concerted plan to tackle income poverty is feasible *if* the political will is there. Prime Minister Blair has said that if the Labour government fails to raise the incomes of the poorest it will have failed.

## Money and time

Income is clearly crucial in determining poverty. Yet concern with money income alone ignores what is involved in generating that income. To say that someone on £100 per week is poor but another on £120 is not poor is senseless if the former chooses to work only 10 hours and the latter has to work 100 hours per week. Many years ago Becker (1964) argued that the source of utility is not goods but the activity in which the goods serve as inputs: foods and kitchen equipment provide utility insofar as they produce meals. Yet what is also necessary to produce meals is the *time* to prepare and cook the food – and wash up ready for the next meal.

The differences in money income between men and women conceal the great differences in time spent working. For most women it remains the case that working time is predominantly unpaid. Of course the time spent in paid work can have adverse effects – on health for example, or parenting. Many children could not be said to suffer from money poverty but they receive little parental time and therefore, like many parents, can be said to suffer from time poverty.

## Personal behaviour

The spending of income has long been considered a private preserve in which the individual can be relied upon to maximise his or her welfare. Yet decisions about smoking and drinking are substantially influenced by the billions spent promoting these activities. They have serious consequences not only for the individual's own health and happiness but also for their children's life chances. Many who are not necessarily poor in income terms are reduced to poverty because of the amount they spend on tobacco, alcohol, gambling or drugs.

It is important to note that many smoke *because* they are poor; they are not primarily poor because they smoke. According to Marsh and McKay (1994, pp. 81–2):

> Unlike most people, the lowest income families really do have strong reasons for wanting to smoke. They alone in our society are under the greatest pressure, experience the greatest inequality of choice and opportunity in their lives. Some of them, especially the lone parents, feel they exist solely to service their children's daily needs. They have to do so at a level so basic it removes them entirely from the 'real' world of people who have comfortable homes, cars and holidays . . . smoking is their only luxury. They defend it, aggressively sometimes. In a world of many luxuries for others, one luxury for oneself becomes a necessity.

In relation to smoking, Marsh and McKay advocated not only higher benefits but also that the state should do everything it can to stop the promotion of smoking because success in this area would help reduce poverty as well as improve health. What they did not advocate was patronising calls for self-help and for people to try harder; they were concerned to tackle the social causes of individual behaviour. They called for government to take action of a novel kind: in effect to reorient social policy to influence the perception of 'needs'. It is possible that their demands have not fallen on entirely deaf ears: we have already seen (somewhat ill-fated) attempts by New Labour to ban tobacco advertising in sport, and this may be a step in the right direction. There is certainly a strong argument for the government to go further in an interventionist direction with regard to those forms of spending that exacerbate poverty – replacing the advertising of drink by alcohol education; replacing the phony claims of many food advertisments by clear and comprehensible nutritional guidance and product information; regulating gambling to protect the vulnerable addict; and tackling drug addiction in every possible way.

In relation to children, the state, if it is concerned with life chances, must take responsibility for promoting good, stable parenting. To be sure, bad parenting is certainly not confined to the poor – indeed a case can be made that it is the rich who treat their children the worst – but children in poor households are less likely to have the compensation – insofar as compensation is possible – of good education, space to escape to and play in, and good holidays.

## Public services, amenities and standards of the poor

Poverty in terms of money income is associated with poor health services, poor schools, a poor physical environment and an unsafe social environment. These features of the lives of many, though not all, who are poor in turn contribute to their own and their children's poverty. Yet none of these features can be improved by increasing individual money incomes. Indeed, the most common strategy adopted to obtain better-quality public services is to move geographically to a more prosperous and advantaged area – a remedy available to few of the poor.

If the damaging effects of poverty are to be alleviated then these public aspects must be improved. Indeed improving some of the public aspects of people's lives – such as environmental safety – may prove far more significant than the increase in private expenditure that would result from an increased money income. Indeed, if private spending is followed by the theft of the goods purchased – which is most common in poorer areas – increased income will not even result in material improvement.

This conclusion has consequences for all aspects of social policy, particularly perhaps for the role of the state, which has been allowed to diminish too far in recent years. The poor have the right to public services that are at least as good, perhaps better, than those available to the more prosperous. Yet currently the poor are generally treated worse. This is not to accept, as some suggest, that greater reliance on markets would be better for the poor; greater dependence on ability to pay would in general result in worse treatment for the poor. What this discussion suggests is that all social policies should be formulated and implemented with clear and conscious regard to their impact on poverty in general and on children and their life chances in particular.

An effective assault on poverty remains a challenge that our affluent society has yet to meet. Such an assault must involve tackling the causes of poverty – whether economic, social or individual – and it must recognise the need for redistribution towards those who, were it not for state welfare provision, would otherwise be in poverty. There is nothing inevitable about poverty. With the political will and sound social policy it can be overcome.

## Further Reading

Approaches to defining and measuring poverty are elegantly and succinctly discussed by Jo Roll, *Understanding Poverty* (London: Family Policy Studies Institute, 1992). British evidence on the extent and causes of poverty are lucidly reviewed in C. Oppenheim and L. Harker, *Poverty: the Facts*, 3rd edn (London: CPAG, 1996). The latest official estimates of poverty are set out by the Department of Social Security in *Households Below Average Income* (London: HMSO, 1997). An economic approach to poverty is A. B. Atkinson's *Economics of Inequality*, 2nd edn (Oxford:

Clarendon Press, 1983). Social explanations are discussed in Robert Holman's *Poverty: explanations of social deprivation* (London: Martin Robertson, 1978). Recent developments and controversies are discussed in Alan and Carol Walker (eds), *Britain Divided: the growth of social exclusion in the 1980s and 1990s* (London: Child Poverty Action Group, 1997).

CHAPTER 16

# Consumerism and the Future of Social Policy

MICHAEL CAHILL

The car and the consumer society that sustains it has produced new patterns of inequality and exclusion that social policy has to acknowledge. In a society built around mobility, the social exclusion that results from a transport system that prioritises the car demands investigation. This chapter takes the car as a key example of a technology that is heavily identified with consumer society and explores what it tells us about the relationship between consumerism and social policy.

Social inequalities abound in late-twentieth-century Britain; if anything they are more widespread and potent because of the wealth and attachment to consumer goods of the majority of the population. As J. K. Galbraith argued in relation to the United States: 'the government now rules with the support of the contented majority' (Galbraith, 1993). This two thirds majority is much less open to appeals for redistribution of wealth in favour of the poor. We live in a 'culture of contentment', where many believe that one of the primary purposes of life is to acquire consumer goods. Inequalities are made more obvious by the ever present media, which promotes the consumption of goods through advertising. The social problems of the next century will come in large part from the choices now being made by the contented majority. The way of life of that majority is built around certain assumptions that, if not unlearnt, will produce major problems; indeed they are already producing problems for themselves and for other people.

Consumerism as an ideology has become the key idea of the age, both New Labour and the Conservative Party are advocates of markets and consumers. Apart from a number of religious critiques of materialism and consumerism, the only real opposition comes from green thought and environmental activism. There can be no more potent symbol of the consumer society than the car. It personifies freedom, mobility and choice. The new Labour government's first document on transport policy declared in the foreword: 'The car remains an integral part of modern society. It has brought freedom, flexibility and mobility' (Dept of Transport, Environment and the Regions,

1997, p. 2). This is undeniable, although the immediate qualification has to be made that it has only been true for some people, some of the time, and one should question whether mobility is a desirable objective anyway.

Consumerism has become extraordinarily powerful in postwar Britain. There is a glaring contradiction at the heart of thinking at the close of the twentieth century. The economic system of the West has gone 'global', seducing its rival systems in China and the former state socialist societies in Russia and Eastern Europe. There are only a handful of states left in the world today who would describe themselves as socialist. The GATT agreements have meant that all countries are now part of a global market. Yet while the world's governments have become enamoured of markets as the way forward, the environmental consequences of the search for more and more profit has never been more apparent. It was in the 1990s that the world's experts on climatic change agreed that global warming was taking place. The car is recognised as a major contributor to global environmental problems, but car manufacturers are looking with considerable excitement at the vast new markets opening up in China, India (where car ownership is now growing at a rate of 25 per cent each year) and other parts of the world that have hitherto been too poor (or too sensible) to base their transport system on the private car. The desire for more and more consumer goods has taken on gigantic proportions not only in the West but now also in the developing world. The statistics on the size of the consumer market in the People's Republic of China make frightening reading (Smith, 1997).

Why are these issues of concern for social policy? Social policy has to be concerned not just with the income received by the poor but with the *opportunities* they have to spend this money and, more generally, with their quality of life. If poor people have to shop at expensive corner shops then this is important precisely because it means that their purchasing power is reduced (Piachaud and Webb, 1996). The relative importance of inequalities changes over time. The lack of a car in a society where public transport is cheap, efficient and extensive and public facilities are grouped closely together is not nearly as great as being carless in a society where the majority of the population have cars, public transport is poor or non-existent and public facilities are only accessible by car. Equally it can be argued that social policy ought to be about the protection of public services because those on low incomes gain more from them in terms of quality of life than the prosperous middle class. Public libraries, parks, recreation grounds and leisure centres all fall into this category. At a deeper level one can argue that the question of consumption is important because it may suggest that there has been a weakening of collective values and, as we shall see, the decline of collective values can have very direct consequences for the most vulnerable members of

society. Certainly the persistent stress on autonomy and personal independence leads us to wonder whether public provision will continue to be
sustained in the way that it has been. The emergence of low taxation regimes
in Western Europe suggests that there may be cause for doubt.

## The Importance of Consumption

In Britain we have moved from a society based around production, for
employment and jobs, to a society where many jobs are in the consumption
sector and in services. The needs and wants of consumers are endlessly
scrutinised, moulded and catered for. There is a gender dimension to this
shift as well, for the increase in women's employment has been largely in the
service and consumption sectors. The traditional division where paid
employment outside the home is synonymous with males and female
employment within the home – the housewife – is identified with women has
all but disappeared. There has been a move towards more dual-earner
families and an increasing number of households where the woman is the
main breadwinner. Given this new spending power associated with women it
is unsurprising that they are being targeted by manufacturers in a major way
(Lury, 1996, pp. 132–5). Minority groups such as the gay community have
also become recognised as big spenders in the sphere of leisure and services
(Chaney, 1996, p. 128). Consumerism has the power to embrace all in its
activities. This has been seen in the media, where commercial television has
been a major player for many years, but the influence of the advertisers has
now spread much more directly to the content of newspapers. The
proliferation of style and lifestyle supplements in the broadsheet press is
remarkable. They are sustained by a daily diet of advertising aimed at
segmented markets within the newspaper readership.

The good life in a consumer society denotes the possession of status goods
that differentiate us from other consumers. The totality of one's choices as a
consumer is one's lifestyle: the way that one uses goods and places (ibid.,
p. 5). Diverse life styles are now possible, which in their turn are advertised by
way of consumer goods. Groups advertise their differences by means of
consumer goods. Certain industries are key to this process: fashion, leisure,
retailing and motor manufacture among them. Consumerism has been able
to coopt ideas and movements to its way of viewing the world. For example
the feminist writer Naomi Wolf, in her book *Fire with Fire* (1994), argues that
women's spending power and new economic status should be used to acquire
social and political power. The 'green consumer' movement at the end of the
1980s was another example: one could shop but with a green conscience
(Elkington and Hales, 1988). Consumerism can be a form of young people's

self-expression, but of course only if they have the money. The attachment to hedonism that is marked in the 18–30 year olds is obviously predicated on the income to enjoy life in this way. This is not to argue that in the case of young people, or any other life-stage group, consumerism does not exist alongside other values, such as a commitment to quality of life or 'environmental values' (Wilkinson and Mulgan, 1995).

The consumer goods that we own provide us with an identity – they reflect our choice and signal to others 'who we are'. The practice of that self-expression has become for many of us the activity of shopping. In order to undertake this key activity it is essential to have money. The status of being a recognised consumer depends on having the money with which to carry off this act. Money has become much more important in Britain over the last two decades, with so much becoming commodified. Many children's leisure activities are now paid-for commercial activities. Sports such as badminton, squash and swimming have all been repackaged and now take place in private sector leisure centres with membership deals that keep out the poor and low-paid. Football, which came out of working-class self-association towards the end of the last century, is now firmly part of the entertainment industry. In reality many football clubs are football companies. Shopping is now a major leisure activity in Britain, and certain kinds of shopping have changed from chore to pleasure. Importantly, it is that ubiquitous piece of technology – the car – that gives us access to out-of-town superstores and leisure centres, and the myriad activities of the consumer lifestyle.

The dominance of consumer society means that a large number of people associate their lives of consumption with pleasure and freedom. They gain their identity from this world – identity has become a key word in the lexicon of consumer culture, denoting one's take on the world, one's orientation, one's selection of self. Giddens sees the many freedoms offered by this 'choosing self' as a basic constituent of a democratic society (Giddens, 1994), while Zygmunt Bauman (1994) writes of the 'seduced': the contented majority who are happily integrated into consumer society.

Either way there is a sense of a fragmented privatised society where it becomes increasingly difficult to sustain moral relationships – relationships based on a long-term commitment to others and to ideals – for the culture tells us that is best for us as individuals to 'stay loose'. Clearly if the sense of self is built upon the use of commodities and the purchase of goods in order to create or, more likely, to conform to an identity, then it is replacing structures and a culture that used to perform this work. At its most general, this is the enormity of the challenge that faces those who want to move to a more sustainable transport system – for there is great psychological invest-ment in the car. Consumer goods express one's social standing and cars are the perfect example: advertisers and manufacturers endow them with sexuality, style and power. The car has been described as 'the most psychologically expressive object that has so far been devised' (Marsh and Collett, quoted in Goodwin, 1995, p. 105).

## Consumerism

Since the advent of Thatcherism and its proven electoral success, much political rethinking has been concerned with an attempt to understand how society has changed – acknowledging, for example, the reduced role of class in voting behaviour and other areas of social life. It has also been concerned with a search for new integrative concepts that will enable people to form some sense of their common interests. New Labour's stress on 'community' – some of Tony Blair's speeches plainly echoing the communitarianism of the American sociologist, Amitai Etzioni (Driver and Martell, 1997) – is one instance of this search, while the rediscovery of 'citizenship' by many writers on the left is another. Conceptions of the social citizen, European citizen and global citizen have all been explored as possible alternatives to a consumer-led vision of the future (Van Steenbergen, 1994; Bulmer and Rees, 1996). These formulations – community, communitarianism, citizenship – have to contend with the extensive privatisation of life that modern technology permits and modern marketing promotes. Advertising, be it in print or on television, targets its audience as *individual* consumers.

Consumerism promotes itself as the way to achieve happiness, but the economic system of production and consumption that underpins this notion of happiness is bought at a high cost. The total amount of goods and services produced, the gross domestic product, is a measure of wealth but critics of capitalism have argued since the nineteenth century that this is inadequate. As John Ruskin was wont to say, 'there is no wealth but life'. The term 'quality of life' has become popular of late and can be defined in many ways (Offner, 1996), but if it is about more than the simple accumulation of goods by individual consumers then we can argue it is also about the social goods we share in common, whether we want to or not: the tap water we use, the air we breathe, the climate, the level of security, the environment in general. We could also extend this to say that 'quality of life' encompasses education and health, for these goods are a universal, non-private service for most people in this country. In addition the Index of Sustainable Economic Welfare includes many environmental costs in its calculation of well-being. These include the cost of car accidents, water pollution, air pollution, noise pollution, loss of habitat and loss of farmlands. According to this index, the real well-being of people in Britain has declined since 1980.

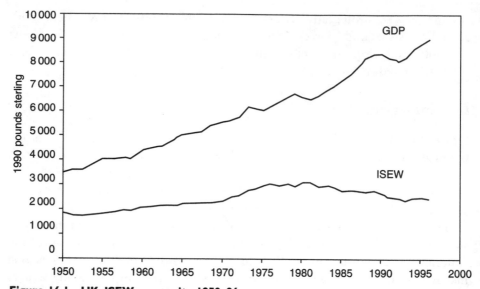

**Figure 16.1   UK–ISEW per capita 1950–96**
*Source*: New Economics Foundation/Friends of the Earth, *More isn't always better*, 1997.

So the promises held out by consumer goods cannot always be delivered. Once again the car is an obvious example: advertisers show us open roads and stunning vistas traversed by just one car. The familiar reality is congested roads, traffic jams and, increasingly, road rage.

## The Car

As the argument here suggests, the car has become the consumer good *par excellence* – the status symbol, the wheels, personal transport in a privatised world. It offers freedom – indeed it is claimed that it is the personification of freedom and mobility (Mulgan, 1997). Never before has a piece of technology been so fêted and become so much a part of the personhood of so many people. Cars have become *the* symbol of our age: the reverential tones in which cars are advertised in some commercials and the powers with which they are endowed imply that, although secularisation has become a powerful force, the desire to worship is still strong – it's just that it has been transferred to a machine. Some Christians would condemn this as idolatry, although in January 1996 the Anglican Cathedral in Coventry organised a service for the motor trade to commemorate 100 years of the car – an 1890s Daimler was driven down the aisle (Wolmar, 1996)! Helga Dittmar (1992) speculates that technologies have become extensions of ourselves. We can see the truth of this view when we remember that some people are unable to function if their car is unavailable. This phenomenon of car dependence has become widespread: a recent survey commissioned by the RAC revealed that 69 per cent of car-owning households agreed with the statement that 'A car is essential to our lifestyle and we would not want to be without one (Goodwin *et al.*, 1991, p. 38). Transport policy has been about facilitating mobility for motorists over the last four decades more, and about accommodating cities and towns to the demands of this technology. The new challenge is to reverse this process for the sake of the environment.

The social policy consequences of a car-based, car-dependent society have been documented in relation to health (Jones, 1995), community care (Jones, 1996), accidents (Erskine, 1996), children's mobility (Hillman *et al.*, 1990) and older people (Eurolink 1994). There is an extensive body of literature on the costs of road transport (Maddison *et al.*, 1996). It has been clear for some time now that the car-driving majority will have to reduce their use of the car significantly if Britain is to reach its target for carbon emissions reduction. There is also a need to achieve widespread changes in transport behaviour, with many more people walking and cycling. However the fear that a government might be regarded as 'anticar' and hence lose votes runs deep with government politicians, a fact amply demonstrated by the transport policies of the last Conservative government.

## The Conservatives and the Car

There were essentially two phases in the last Conservative government's 1979–97 transport policy. The first phase, which lasted from 1979 until the early 1990s, saw the primacy of the car in transport policy. The car was regarded as the highest form of transport yet invented and Margaret Thatcher spoke of a 'car-owning democracy'. In a way the car was the perfect privatised vehicle for the privatised family who had bought their own house without government encouragement. Marsh and Collett (1986, p. 11), in a book on the psychology of the car, observed that 'the use of the car as an extension of the home . . . remains a central feature of this automobile culture. Cars live in the home, in that most special of rooms we call the garage. When we take to the roads, a part of the home goes with us – a personal territory, an environment of security.' Roads were built to accommodate the car and it was believed at that time that new roads would strengthen the prosperity of an area (Department of Transport, 1989).

The 1990s saw a reversal, a U-turn, in these policies. This was amid growing pressure from those opposed to the new wave of road building occasioned by the government's transport policy, prompted by the Royal Commission on the Environment's 1994 report on transport, which warned that traffic pollution represented a serious public health danger and claimed that the particulates – microscopic airborne particles – from fuel were responsible for an excess mortality rate of 10 000 a year in Britain. Pointing out that the transport sector is a major source of the greenhouse gas carbon dioxide, the Commission said that the government's plans to reduce emissions were too limited to tackle the full extent of the problem. Among many recommendations a central argument was that the benign transport modes of walking or cycling should be greatly encouraged by government. From 1994 onwards the Conservative government was much more sympathetic to the environmental transport policy case. Two results of this new attitude were the publication of a cycling strategy and the development of a walking strategy (Department of Transport, 1996a, 1996b).

## Current Problems

For several years local authorities and central government have been trying to persuade motorists to get out of their cars and either use public transport or use their legs by walking or cycling. This is line with government thinking on sustainable development since the Earth Summit in Rio de Janeiro. A sustainable transport policy would prioritise walking and cycling, but on the whole these low-budget attempts to change the travel behaviour of the British population have been unsuccessful. For example the average number of journeys walked per person per year fell by 12 per cent between 1985 and 1995 (Department of Transport, 1996b), while cycling accounts for less than 2 per cent of trips in Britain (Department of Transport 1996a). This is not surprising given the paltry sums that have been allocated to the public education initiatives. The motor car lobby is much better funded: indeed 20 per cent of the advertising industry's spending is generated by motoring and car advertisements (Goodwin, 1995, p. 108). The implications of a sustainable policy are considerable for the average driver in the West, requiring a reduction in total mileage and use of the car and, in order to achieve this, much higher fuel taxes. Of course the difficulties in the way of such a policy will be severe for it will require a government that not only can convince the population of the need to accept limits on consumption, but is also prepared to pursue an environmentally friendly transport policy against the perceived interests of national and international firms. Local Agenda 21 is a illustration of how great the task is. Local authorities have been pursuing the implications of sustainability across a range of policy areas. Agenda 21 illustrates the possibility of raising environmental and global awareness even with scarce resources (Selman, 1996).

Public service advertising seems to have been useful in changing attitudes towards drinking and driving, but little or nothing has been spent on recognising the rights and needs of the most vulnerable road users: pedestrians. Although the fall in road deaths in Britain to around 3500 a year is to be welcomed, it seems to have been achieved by encouraging a climate of fear in which fewer vulnerable users are killed because there are fewer of them on the streets. The deaths and serious injuries inflicted by motorists each day on each other and on pedestrians and cyclists are well documented. For too long road deaths have been accepted as a normal part of our transport system.

Two areas that are not routinely recognised as a social welfare problem seem to bear out the communitarian case that there has been a loss of social order and shared values (see Etzioni, 1993, 1997). The first is pavement parking. This often forces vulnerable pedestrians into the road in order to continue their journey, thus exposing them to the danger of passing traffic. Visually impaired people and others with mobility difficulties are particularly at risk from this form of antisocial behaviour. Arguably the pressures on parking space have become so intense in certain areas that pedestrians, many of whom also happen to be motorists, tolerate this behaviour. Equally, although they see that it is inconvenient, they do not think about the consequences for those with impaired mobility such as many older, frail people. The National Consumer Council found in their 1995 national survey of pedestrians that 27 per cent of respondents thought pavement parking was a problem, which was a slight increase on the 1986 figure of 24 per cent (National Consumer Council, 1996, pp. 18–19). Pavement parking means that those with mobility problems quickly learn that the local environment is hazardous, and sometimes they just do not bother to travel. This is what the planners call 'trip inhibition'.

Pavement parking, then, makes a small but very real contribution towards making the pedestrian environment both less safe and less hospitable. It also provides a dilemma for law enforcement. In an age of increasing traffic congestion, when motorists are faced with the question 'do I park on the pavement or do I not?', they are going to be facing the 'shall I park illegally?' dilemma more often (it is an offence to drive onto the footpath under the 1835 Highway Act). One of the problems with this area of the law is that the police do not enforce it because their main objective is to keep traffic moving, and a car parked partly on the pavement may not be obstructing the road and slowing the traffic. But lack of enforcement of the law can mean that it is increasingly flouted – as we have seen with speed limits (Hillman and Plowden, 1996) – and this can be socially corrosive.

It is at this point that the force of communitarian thinking of the kind espoused by Etzioni comes into play. Etzioni argues that there is a moral voice within each of us that needs to be cultivated and is based upon shared moral values. Presumably for all but the most individualistic and anti-authoritarian, the enforcement of speed limits falls into this category. This is not the case with pavement parking. The sad tale of pavement parking is a good example of the current lack of moral voice in the community, for it is likely that enforcement of the traffic regulations by the police would now be met by strong public disapproval. Part of the problem for traffic wardens and others who face the unenviable task of enforcing traffic regulations is the hostility they meet in the course of their job. Road rage is not only a phenomenon experienced by other motorists but can be vented against road users of all kinds. However it is in this area of 'middle-ground' morality – the middle ground between individual decision making and the claims of the wider society – that communitarianism, by reminding individuals of their social duties, has a contribution to make.

Another example is the new and dangerous practice of cycling on pavements, not on those parts of pavements that are specially designated cycleways for shared use but on the footpath where all users should walk. This seriously threatens the mobility rights of older people who are frail or vulnerable in other ways. Once more the phenomenon can be understood, given that the enormous rise in the number of motor vehicles on our roads is displacing other road users, first the most vulnerable, the pedestrians, and then the cyclists. Those cyclists who have not been frightened off the roads altogether have found pavements a relatively safe route and free from the clear dangers posed by traffic. In the absence of cycle routes in the 1980s, many cyclists turned pavements into cycle routes. The popularity of mountain bikes, especially the many variants for children, meant that many parents invested hundreds of pounds in these bikes, but it was unsafe for their children to ride on the roads. The pavement beckoned as a safe route. There was only one problem: the legitimate users – indeed the only legal users – were pedestrians. So began a new form of death – death by collision with a bicycle, which has despatched a number of people, mainly older frail people, to an untimely end.

## Changing Values?

The above examples of pavement parking and cycling suggest that there has been a change in social attitudes, perhaps occasioned in some part by the mobility decisions of the majority of the population. The contented majority make infrequent use of pavements as thoroughfares, except for the shortest journeys. Any vigilance they have about transport tends not to be about pavements but roads. An alternative approach would contend that communities ought to agree on some rules about pavement use and then urge every individual to try to uphold and sustain these. This could mean that children who cycle on the pavements will be reprimanded, but it must also mean that the community can easily obtain a 20 m.p.h. zone in the immediate neighbourhood.

Few would deny that the car is a technology that has got out of hand and needs to be curbed, but it will be a brave government that begins this process. While in opposition in 1995 the Labour Party ditched a transport policy document because it was felt to be too anticar (Wolmar, 1995). Yet as the 1990s draw to a close and evidence accumulates on climate change, species extinction, global warming, world hunger and growing financial inequality, both women and men in the Western world must confront the wider consequences of their individual endeavours. The radicals and feminists of the 1960s and 1970s insisted that the personal was political – now an ecological green perspective has picked up this theme once more, arguing that the actions of individuals matter. In transport policy the task is to persuade millions of people to use their cars less in their daily lives. Not to give them up altogether, although if more people were to do this it would be a boon, but to use them *less*. If the destructive impact that our way of life is having on the planet is to be curbed, then travel decisions have to be altered in innumerable ways.

Communitarian thinking of the kind advocated by Etzioni encourages us to think of communal ways of resolving problems and agreeing on solutions. There are some grounds for optimism. The sentiments expressed in opinion polls are nowadays considerably pro-public transport and environmentally friendly. For instance the 1997 edition of *Social Trends* records that, in response to the statement 'many more streets in cities and towns should be reserved for pedestrians only' 68 per cent of respondents agreed. Likewise 64 per cent felt that cyclists and pedestrians should be given more priority in towns and cities, even if this made things more difficult for other road users.

The move away from viewing cars as a symbolic expression of our personality to seeing them primarily as a form of personal transport will probably also need to be part of a health promotion strategy. This would focus on the sedentary lifestyles of the British population. Fifteen per cent of men and 17 per cent of women are obese while 43 per cent of men and 30 per cent of women are overweight (*Guardian*, 2 May 1997). Moreover there is anxiety about children's fitness: 'the current level and pattern of children's activity is a cause for grave concern' (Armstrong in Hillman, 1993, p. 41).

## Consuming Less

At the heart of the contemporary obsession with consumption is the car –
much of the social organisation of consumerism is built around it. For
example, out-of-town shopping centres, out-of-town leisure centres and many
other aspects of modern life are built around (a usually unconscious)
acceptance of car dependence. Such dependence is a social problem that, as
we have seen, has health, environmental and social welfare consequences
(Freund and Martin, 1993). Furthermore the social inequalities that flow
from this are many and various. Future social policies designed to keep faith
with sustainability will need to promote accessibility rather than mobility.

'People who have cars are able to develop a lifestyle totally different from
those who do not have access to a car. It is a lifestyle characterised by low
density living, a high activity rate, greater freedom from routine tasks, and the
capacity to respond spontaneously to social and leisure opportunities as they
arise' (Weaver in Goodwin, 1995, p. 109). This lifestyle has been the key
factor behind the dispersal of people from urban areas to the suburbs and
then from the suburbs to the countryside. In the countryside the possession of
a car means that access to work locations at some remove is possible, so
journeys to work have become longer. At the same time there is an increasing
trend to relocate urban employment in greenfield or semirural locations,
which presents considerable difficulties for those employees without a car.
However we need not be unduly pessimistic. The increasing trend towards
home working and teleworking will remove the need for many of the
commuter journeys that now take place. In land-use planning Britain is
witnessing the small beginnings of car-free housing estates along the lines of
those that have existed in Germany for some years (*Independent*, 15 February
1997).

If we take green arguments seriously, then it is the area of consumption
that there needs to be a change in the behaviour of the majority of people in
Britain. Quite simply the British eat too much, drive too much and do not
exercise enough. The limits that are needed derive from the need to conserve
energy and reduce carbon emissions. Behavioural change is key to this for
there needs to be a radical shift in how other transport modes are perceived.
Clearly there are many journeys that cannot be feasibly undertaken by the
sustainable modes of cycling and walking. Yet if cycling and walking were
taken up by large numbers of people then we would see an improvement in
the nation's fitness level and health status.

Alongside these developments and the formulation of a healthy transport
strategy at both local and central government level, fiscal measures will be
required. There is considerable scope for raising petrol duties along the lines

suggested by the Royal Commission on Environmental Pollution in its 1994 report, with an annual increase in the real price of fuel so that the price doubles between 1994 and 2004. Road pricing would further encourage motorists to be more careful in their use of the road and would offer a further source of revenue for improved public transport as an alternative to motoring.

The story of the car in the late twentieth century is replete with lessons for future social policy makers. It demonstrates the dangers of allowing one technology to dictate not only transport policy but also the shape of cities, towns and social arrangements. It highlights the fact that consumer goods have social consequences because of the way in which men and women use them, and this can generate new inequalities. One could also suggest that it makes clear that the concept of citizenship is going to be far more valuable in the new century than the language of consumerism.


## Further Reading

Yiannis Gabriel and Tim Lang, *The Unmanageable Consumer* (London: Sage, 1996) is an invaluable discussion of the many concepts of the consumer in the Western world. Peter Freund and George Martin's *The Ecology of the Automobile* (Montreal: Black Rose Books, 1993) is a provocative American book that illustrates how cars attained their hegemony in the world's transport system: one chapter is specifically devoted to social inequalities and the car. John Whitelegg, *Critical Mass Transport, Environment and Society in the Twenty-first Century* (London: Pluto Press, 1997) situates the British transport problem in a gobal context of consumerism and unsustainable lifestyles. The Royal Commission on Environmental Pollution's *Twentieth Report: Transport and the Environment – Developments Since 1994*, Cmnd 3752 (London: HMSO, 1997) makes a case for radical change in the British transport system.

CHAPTER 17

# UK Social Policy in the European Union Context

LAURA CRAM

One of the most significant developments to affect British social policy was the accession of Britain to the European Economic Community (now the European Union, EU) in 1973. Although EU legislation is extremely limited in scope, as a member state Britain is legally bound to implement certain pieces of social law that have been created and agreed upon at the European level. The EU has often been described as a system of 'multi-level governance' (Marks, 1992), or as a 'multitiered system' (Leibfried and Pierson, 1995) within which decisions taken by the 15 member states at the EU level have a fundamental effect on both policies and politics at the national level in each of those states.

The emphasis in recent years on the spectre of EU social intervention by UK opponents of the European social dimension has encouraged a distorted picture of the extent to which EU social legislation is binding. In practice this is very limited. There has never been consensus on what the role of the EU ought to be in the field of social policy. A coherent European social model can hardly be said to have emerged. Rather the social policy of the EU has developed in something of a 'stop-go' manner. Dogged with controversy since its inception, it is perhaps hardly surprising that relatively few pieces of EU social legislation have reached the statute book and many of those that have been ratified are dramatically watered down versions of the original proposals. However, while the scope of binding EU social policy may have been exaggerated in recent years, especially during the 1997 general election campaign, this does not mean that EU social policy has had no impact on British social policy. The *direct* impact of EU legislation, although limited to a few policy areas, is nevertheless important, while the *indirect* effects of EU activities in the social field may in the long term prove to be even more significant for UK citizens and for the future shape of UK social policy.

# What is EU Social Policy?

One of the most startling features of EU social policy, from a UK perspective, is the rather peculiar definition of social policy that has emerged at the EU level. Many of the areas of policy that are traditionally considered to constitute social policy in most member states, especially redistributive issues such as social security, are dealt with by the EU only tangentially. It is only since the Maastricht Treaty came into force in 1993 that there has been any formal mention of, for example, public health and education as areas of competence at the EU level and still the power of the EU to act in these areas is very limited and strictly circumscribed by the principle of subsidiarity. This principle implies that the EU institutions should act in any policy area only where member states cannot themselves carry out these tasks satisfactorily (Nielsen and Szyszczak, 1993, p. 30). As a result EU social policy has largely come to consist of the development of rule-making or regulatory policies that set minimum standards to be achieved by member states, for example regarding health and safety measures in the workplace, but which do not require a redistribution of wealth; of non-binding declarations or recommendations of the member states, often referred to as 'soft law' (see Wellens and Borchardt, 1989), which may be politically significant but which do not impose any legal obligations on national governments to implement their provisions; and, most recently, of legislation based on agreements, for example on parental leave and part-time work, achieved through the process of 'social dialogue' between representatives of European employers and European trade unions. Binding legislation (that is, legislation that member states are legally obliged to implement in their own countries) in the social field is still restricted to a very small number of policy areas.

Most of the binding EU legislation in the social field is devoted to the establishment of an institutional framework at the EU level: establishing decision rules (such as those governing the operation of the European Social Fund), setting up advisory and standing committees, or creating permanent organisations such as the European Foundation for the Improvement of Living and Working Conditions. The very limited number of provisions that directly affect the well-being of European citizens include a relatively small number of regulatory policies in the areas of Health and Safety, the equal treatment of men and women, the protection of workers, and social security for migrant workers. To these may be added a number of small-scale EU social programmes involving direct EU expenditure such as the Helios Programme for people with disablties (see Cram, 1993, pp. 138–40; 1997, ch. 4). A broader range of social issues such as public housing, the elderly, education and public health are, meanwhile, the subjects of an array of non-binding soft law provisions. In this context it is easy to understand how European social policy could be dismissed as 'Heavy on Symbolism . . . and Light on Substance' (Tsoukalis, 1993, p. xiii).

Traditionally the development of EU social policy has been viewed as an adjunct to the achievement of the EU's economic goals and as each successive treaty has been drawn up the question of how much power to concede to the EU in the social field has proved controversial. Since the creation of the European Economic Community (EEC) with the signature of the Treaty of Rome in 1957, a stream of treaty preambles, summit declarations and, more recently, conclusions of the European Council have highlighted the significance that the various heads of state and government attribute to the social dimension. There has, however, long existed a tension between the declarations of the member states and the reluctance of the same member states to turn their rhetoric into reality via the introduction of binding EU legislation in the social field. In order to understand why the particular pattern of EU social policy that is evident today has emerged and how it impacts upon the UK, it is necessary to understand the history of EU social policy development (even prior to the UK's accession in 1973) and the different roles played by some of the key actors involved in decision-making at the EU level.

## The Development of EU Social Policy

### Key actors

*The European Commission* is the executive body of the EU. It is charged with the role of 'guardian of the treaties' and is responsible for providing the dynamic for further integration. The Commission has the right to initiate policy and legislation and is responsible for ensuring that legislation is implemented by member states.

*The Council of Ministers* is composed of member-state ministers who are brought together to deliberate and decide upon legislation that falls within their department's competence. Hence social policy issues are debated by the Council for Social Affairs. This is the main decision-making body within the EU although it may increasingly legislate on the basis of codecision with the European Parliament.

*The European Council* developed from the summit meetings of the heads of state and government of the EU. This institution developed on an extra-treaty basis and was only formally recognised with the introduction of the Single European Act (SEA) in 1986. It is the only EU forum in which the EU heads of state and government have a formal role to play.

The influence of the *European Parliament* (EP) has increased since it became directly elected in 1979 rather than appointed by the member states. The EP must issue an Opinion before legislation can be passed in the Council of Ministers. The Single European Act also provided for an enlarged and more formalised role for the EP through the introduction of the 'cooperation procedure', while the Maastricht Treaty allowed the EP to legislate in certain policy areas on the basis of 'codecision' with the Council of Ministers.

*The European Court of Justice* (ECJ) is responsible for interpreting and enforcing EU law, both that which is stated in the treaties and all secondary legislation that follows from this. There are fifteen judges, one from each member state.

*The Economic and Social Committee* (ESC) is divided into three groups, representing trade unions, employers and consumer interest groups. The ESC has to be consulted by the Council or the Commission in cases laid down in the treaty or on any subject where this is deemed appropriate. The ESC may also draw up opinions on its own initiative. However it has remained a consultative body and its influence on EU decision making has been relatively small.

*Social Partners* is the title used to refer to the official representative of the European employers organisations and of the European trade unions who are invited to participate in the process of social dialogue at the EU level.

## Key events

### *After the Treaty of Rome – Establishing a Role for EU Social Policy*

The goals expressed in the preamble to the Treaty of Rome (1957) exhibit broad aims concerning the nature of the new socioeconomic order in the making. However the actual social provisions in the treaty, which empower the EU institutions to enact policies in this area – Articles 117–128, Part 3, Title III – are vague and often ambiguous. Only Article 119, concerning the application of the principle of equal pay for equal work and inserted at the inistence of French employers who were concerned that the other member states would gain a competitive advantage through cheaper labour costs, was clearly specified (see Brewster and Teague, 1989, p. 55). The importance of this became clear in the late 1970s, when almost no social legislation was passed by the Council of Ministers other than that on equal treatment for men and women, for which a clearly specified legal imperative existed. In general the provisions in the Treaty of Rome are modest, supporting only minimal intervention in order to promote the free movement of workers between the member states. Under the provisions of the Treaty of Rome, social policy legislation can be passed only as a result of a unanimous decision by the Council of Ministers. In such a controversial area, involving major issues of taxation and expenditure, it is hardly surprising that the member states found it difficult to achieve the degree of consensus required on any but the most innocuous of policy proposals.

The European Commission has, however, always taken a dynamic approach to the interpretion of the social provisions of the EU treaties (Collins, 1975, p. 188). Although this has not always proved successful, it can be argued that Commission's activities have at the very least helped to shape the emergence of EU social policy at the margins. Furthermore it might be argued that the seeds sown by the Commission in the 1960s and 1970s, when little binding legislation was passed by the Council of Ministers, may have begun to bear fruit in the 1990s. In the 1960s and 1970s the Commission was beginning to learn how to capitalise on the rhetorical commitment of member states to the social dimension; was promoting the development of social dialogue between European employers and trade unions; encouraging the incorporation of a broad range of citizen groups into the policy-making process; and, last but not least, had begun to make use of research and small-scale action programmes, for example the poverty programme, to prepare the ground for future action should the opportunity arise.

From the outset the Commission attempted to define its relationship with the member states to allow itself maximum flexibility in the social field. The Treaty of Rome was interpreted by the Commission as a declaration of the member states' ambitions in the social field and the Commission consistently sought to hold the member states to ransom over their treaty commitments. The ambiguities in the treaty's references to social policy were interpreted by the Commission as providing increased scope for Commission action. Thus the Commission stated that the 'comparative lack of precision in the Treaty forces the Commission to interpret certain of the articles . . . it is not the Commission's intention that the interpretation shall be restrictive; it cannot conceive that the Community has not got a social purpose' (European Commission, 1959, p. 107).

From early on the Commission also sought to to draw in non-governmental actors to support its work on the harmonisation of social systems. Trade unions, employers' associations and member governments participated in *ad hoc* committees. Working parties composed of representatives from both sides of industry examined the problems of collective bargaining, protection at work for women and young workers and the length of the working week. Throughout this period the Commission showed scant regard for the opinions of the member states. For member states, meanwhile, 'such moves by the Commission suggested that governments might be bypassed and action encouraged which was unwelcome to them' (Collins, 1975, p. 191). Ultimately the member states signalled their discontent by refusing to cooperate with the Commission. No meetings of the Council of Ministers for social affairs were held between October 1964 and December 1966 (ibid., p. 195; Holloway, 1981, p. 54).

On 19 December 1966 the deadlock situation was finally resolved on the basis of what became known as the Veldkamp Memorandum. The subsequent agreement, struck in the Council of Ministers, strictly curtailed the role of the Commission in social affairs and represented a clear triumph for the Council of Ministers over the Commission (Collins, 1975, p. 196; Holloway, 1981, p. 55). As a result the Commission's approach to social policy in the late 1960s and early 1970s was inevitably more restrained. The Commission, reluctant to clash with the Council again, adopted a notably more circumspect approach to social affairs, concentrating far more on technical matters and provisions stipulated in the treaty.

Meanwhile the Commission learned to capitalise upon the rhetoric of the member states. It quickly learned to couch its proposals for new social policies in the language of economic and monetary union favoured by the heads of member states at the Hague summit in 1969 and the Paris summit in 1972. In Paris, for example, the member states had declared their intention to 'strengthen the Community by forming an economic and monetary union, as a token of stability and growth, as the indispensable basis of their social progress and as a remedy for regional disparities'. The Commission was asked to draw up an action programme to help achieve these ends by 1 January 1974.

In response to this request from the Council, the Commission continued to assert its independence in the social field. In practice, however, it took a pragmatic approach to the elaboration of the Social Action Programme (SAP), which 'consisted of measures for which it was felt, rightly or wrongly, that there was a broad political consensus among the nine member governments' (Shanks, 1977, p. 13). Until 1975 the SAP seemed to run according to plan, but even in 1974 and 1975, when progress was still being made, there was a growing tendency for the member states to water down any policies that involved the expenditure of EU resources. By 1976 progress on the SAP had 'slowed to a trickle' (ibid., p. 16). Each of the Commission's 36 proposals had to be argued separately in the Council in pursuit of a unanimous agreement, and by the mid 1970s the political will to pursue an active EU social policy seemed to have waned. In contrast with the situation a decade earlier, however, in 1976 it was declining economic circumstances that had the effect of making national governments more protectionist rather than the overzealous activities of the Commission. Moreover this time the Commission's activity in the social field did not grind to a halt.

Despite the obvious lack of support from the Council of Ministers after 1975, the Commission continued to pursue a wide range of activities in the social field. It was able to continue its catalytic research activities (during this period the Poverty Programme and the Action Programme for Health and Safety were established and entered into their second phases) and to promote the institutional development of EU social policy. A number of EU organisations and committees in the social field were established during this period (for example the Standing Committee on Employment, the European Foundation for the Improvement of Living and Working Conditions, and committees dealing with the social problems of agricultural workers, inland navigation, equal opportunities for men and women, railways and road transport). Finally, the Commission made a sustained effort to implement the remaining provisions of the Treaty of Rome. In 1973 the first EU legislation on equal opportunities was adopted and throughout the late 1970s and early 1980s the work of the Commission in promoting the harmonisation of Equal Opportunities legislation continued. The Court of Justice also took the opportunity during this period to underline clearly the social goals of the Community: 'these are not limited to economic activity, but must at the same time ensure, through common action, social progress and pursue the continuous improvement of living and working conditions of the European peoples, as is stressed in the preamble to the Treaty' (ECJ, 8 April 1976, Case 43/75, Defrenne II).

However by the late 1970s the evident lack of enthusiam for development of the social dimension on the part of most member states, combined with the almost certain veto of any social policy proposals by the newly elected Thatcher administration in Britain, made rapid legislative advances in the social field appear a distant prospect. Although the Commission, supported by judgements of the Court of Justice and numerous declarations from the European Parliament, sought to prepare the ground for future action, without a change in the political opportunity structure little advance in the social dimension appeared likely.

### From L'Espace Sociale to the Single European Act – Relaunching the Social Dimension

The event that was to facilitate far-reaching changes in the political opportunity structure for the development of EU social legislation was the completion of the internal (or single) market in 1992. In the mid 1980s the Commission sought to justify its actions in the social field in terms of facilitating the realisation of the internal market and ameliorating any negative consequences that it might generate. By the mid 1980s the Commission's strategy was two pronged. Aiming to circumvent the institutional obstacles, not least the British veto, which had been hampering the development of the European social dimension, the Commission sought first to revitalise the social dialogue: proposing that legislation might be based upon agreements emerging from discussions between employers and trade unions at the EU level. Second, the Commission encouraged proposals from member states that there should be alterations to the treaty provisions governing the development of EU social policy, not least that there should be a shift away from strict unanimity and towards qualified majority voting (QMV) on social policy measures.

The Commission was well prepared to make good use of the opportunity for action when a renewed declaration of support for EU intervention in the social field came from member states in the Council of Social Affairs Ministers in 1984. The Commission rapidly submitted a new medium-term social action programme, which was approved by the Fontainebleau European Council in June 1984 and provided the Commission with a basis upon which to build its plans for the social dimension. Carefully couched in language that emphasised the importance of social policy for the completion of the internal market, the currently popular rationale for EU intervention, the action programme sought to revitalise the social dialogue between employers and trade unions. Jacques Delors, then president of the European Commission, argued that negotiation between management and labour (the 'social partners') should constitute one of the cornerstones of the revitalised 'social area', or 'L'Espace Sociale', in the EU.

On Delors' initiative, what became known as the 'Val Duchesse Dialogue', between the social partners was launched in 1985. Intended as an important step towards revitalising the social dimension in the EU and drawing an important constituency of actors into the EU social policy process, the Val Duchesse talks proved disappointing in practice. Hesitation on the part of employers to participate in any dialogue that sought to reach a binding agreement scuppered the Commission's ambitious intentions. The 'Joint Opinions', finally issued, were vague and loosely worded and committed neither party to any specific action. Employers agreed to sign the final texts only on condition that the Commission would not make use of the joint opinions as the basis for any legislation (Brewster and Teague, 1989, pp. 96–7). However 'Delors knew that the exercise would initially be more about confidence building than about immediate results' (Ross, 1995, p. 377). Indeed subsequent developments in the Single European Act, the Maastricht Treaty and the Amsterdam Treaty bear testimony to the way in which the role of the social partners has developed and become institutionalised in the EU social policy process. As so often, the initial faltering steps initiated by the Commission have proved to have a lasting impact on the development of EU social policy.

Meanwhile the negotiations over the Single European Act (1986/7) and the future direction the EU was to take, provided the Commission with the opportunity to launch a renewed offensive on the social dimension. While the British government in particular strongly opposed Commission intervention in social affairs, some concession in this area was the price that had to be paid for the economic benefits expected from the internal market. Broad statements of commitment to social progress, although perhaps less ambitious than those in the Treaty of Rome, figured once again in the preamble to the Single European Act. In contrast the social provisions of the revised treaty remained vague. The actual advances in the social provisions were rather confusing. Article 118A, for example, allowed for qualified majority voting on matters of health and safety for workers, while Article 100A stated that matters concerning the 'rights and interests of workers' must be subject to unanimous voting. However Article 118b did enshrine the concept of the social dialogue within an EU treaty, and the stated commitment to economic and social cohesion in the EU provided an important starting point for action on the part of the Commission. Meanwhile Margaret Thatcher, then the prime minister of Britain, mistakenly insisted that the procedural changes in the SEA did not effectively change the right of individual countries to veto proposals that were considered contrary to their national interest (Brewster and Teague, 1989, p. 39). She was shortly to realise just how wrong she had been.

### The Social Charter to the Maastricht Treaty – a Step Too Far for Britain

The SEA provided the basis for the Delors initiative, which sought to give substance to the social dimension of the internal market (Venturini, 1988, p. 27). The Commission's revived attempts at a dynamic interpretation of its role in the social dimension were soon, however, to bring it into a head-on confrontation with the British government, and Margaret Thatcher was to learn how the Commission could use its administrative role to counteract the aims of the British administration. Ultimately this was to result in Britain's refusal to sign the Community Charter of Fundamental Social Rights for Workers, popularly known as the 'Social Charter', and later in the British decision to opt out of certain aspects of the Maastricht Treaty (1991/3).

Conscious that to be seen as continually blocking the Commission's social policy initiatives was bad politics, and anxious to influence the direction of EU social policy, in 1986 the British government, with the support of Ireland

and Italy, had presented its own 'Action Programme for Employment Growth'. The basis of this proposal was a non-interventionist EU policy, based largely on improved training, providing help to the self-employed and entrepreneurs and encouraging labour market flexibility. It was passed by the Council of Ministers with little difficulty. Minor amendments were made to the text to incorporate the 'social dialogue' principle and the programme was ratified unanimously. In theory this was a major achievement for the Conservative government, since proposals that are not supported by the Commission are rarely adopted by the Council (Brewster and Teague, 1989, pp. 98-9). However the six-monthly progress reports required of the Commission indicate the Commission's efforts to countervail the programme's objectives of decentralisation and deregulation. The Commission divided the action programme into separate initiatives and classified them under existing EU programmes and initiatives. The radical British programme thus appeared as little more than an adjustment to existing policy aims. The Commission was clearly using its position 'as helmsman of policy development to frustrate the key objectives of Britain government by identifying proposals in the Action Programme which correspond broadly with previous EU initiatives' (ibid., p. 99).

Meanwhile the SEA was rapidly followed up by a high-profile onslaught by the Commission on the social dimension. In particular the Commission made maximum use of those provisions which facilitated qualified majority voting in the Council of Ministers and allowed the British veto to be circumvented. The British government was so disturbed by the use made by the Commission of its new-found powers in the social area that it chose not to sign up even to the non-binding Community Charter of Fundamental Social Rights for Workers in 1989. The Social Charter itself was merely a 'solemn declaration' with no binding effect and was heavily laced with references to the principle of subsidiarity. The Commission had, however, rapidly drawn up an action programme with a detailed list of proposals for legislation based on the Social Charter. The British government feared that the social proposals emanating from the Commission's action programme would be linked to Article 100a of the Single European Act, which allowed for qualified majority voting in the Council (Rhodes, 1991, p. 262). Any proposals passed on the basis of qualified majority voting in the Council of Ministers would also have been legally binding in Britain, even though it had not signed the Social Charter. The British position was supported by employers, who also feared the consequences of the generalised use of qualified majority voting (Tyszkiewicz, 1989, p. 23). These reservations proved justified when the then Commissioner for social affairs, Vasso Papandreou, announced that the Commission would use Article 118a (allowing for qualified majority voting) as a basis for the implementation of the action programme wherever possible.

By 1991 the high-profile relaunch of the social dimension, and the Commission's manipulation of the SEA provisions, may have contributed to the British Conservative government's decision to opt out of the rather limited provisions of the Maastricht social agreement. The question of EU social policy had a very high profile in UK domestic politics during this period, and for the then Prime Minister John Major it became imperative to demonstrate that his government would not be pushed around by its European partners or by the European Commission. This was a crisis situation for the development of EU social policy, a situation that would prove impossible to resolve until there was a change of administration in Britain on 1 May 1997. Contrary to popular belief, however, Britain never opted out of all aspects of EU social policy. Indeed John Major signed up to certain provisions of the Maastricht Treaty that actually strengthened the European social dimension.

The Maastricht Treaty brought about two sets of changes with significant consequences for the legal basis of EU action in the area of social policy. First, changes were made to the main body of the EU Treaty that could affect the social policy activities of all the member states (including the UK). When the Maastricht Treaty entered into force in November 1993, what was previously Title III on Social Policy became Title VIII of Part Three of the Treaty ('Community Policies'), entitled Social Policy, Education, Vocational Training and Youth. The revised provisions in the main body of the Maastricht Treaty strengthened and extended the powers of the EU institutions in the areas of public health, education and vocational training. The British government was party to these aspects of the treaty throughout, even though it chose to opt out from the Social Agreement. Second, a Social Protocol (Protocol 14) was signed by all of the member states (again including the UK) entitling the EU member states, with the exception of the UK, to press ahead with social policy in the areas identified by, and using the instruments specified in, the attached Agreement on Social Policy. The Social Agreement was, the protocol stated, to facilitate the activities of those member states who had expressed a wish 'to continue along the path laid down in the 1989 Social Charter'. The UK was not entitled to participate in the deliberations on or the adoption of proposals made on the basis of Protocol 14 and the Social Agreement. In turn, legislation adopted on this basis was not applicable to the UK nor was the UK to incur any financial costs as a consequence of such legislation.

Perhaps the most significant aspect of the social agreement was the institutionalisation of the role of social dialogue in Articles 3 and 4. As a result of these provisions, agreements for legislation were reached by the social partners on the issues of parental leave and part-time work. At last it appeared that the early work of the Commission in encouraging this dialogue was beginning to have an impact. The Commission, meanwhile, always keen for the UK to opt back into the entirety of the social dimension, this time was not so quick to maximise its use of the provisions contained in the separate Social Agreement.

Since the change in government on 1 May 1997 the legal basis of EU social policy has become increasingly more complex. Although Prime Minister Tony Blair has agreed to opt back into all of the social provisions of the treaty, this cannot be achieved immediately. Until the Amsterdam Treaty, signed by all 15 member states on 2 October 1997, is ratified by all of the member states (a process that could take up to two years) the UK will not be legally bound by any legislation or agreements achieved on the basis of the Maastricht Social Agreement alone. A special procedure has been agreed between the 15 member states to the effect that all measures passed as legislation so far on the basis of the Social Agreement (for example on European works councils and parental leave), and any further legislation that is passed before the Amsterdam Treaty is ratified, shall be retabled in the Council of Ministers and must be agreed upon unanimously by all the member states.

## Amsterdam and Beyond

During the Amsterdam summit of the heads of the 15 EU member states (16/17 June 1997) it was agreed that the provisions of the social agreement could be incorporated into the revised version of the Maastricht Treaty. Once it has been ratified the Amsterdam Treaty, signed on 2 October 1997, will become the new legal basis for the development of EU policies. The Amsterdam Treaty has met with a mixed response from the Commission and social activists alike.

Title VIII of the Maastricht Treaty on 'Social Policy, Education, Vocational Training and Youth' has been adapted in the Amsterdam Treaty to incorporate the existing provisions of the Social Agreement. This development has been broadly welcomed. However a number of organisations, not least the European Trade Union Congress, have stated that as this progress is not matched with more extensive qualified majority voting, it 'therefore does not suggest significant headway being made in European social policy in the future' (*Agence Europe*, 20 June 1997, p. 5). A new Title VIa, covering employment, has been included in the Amsterdam Treaty and confirms the commitment of the member states to 'work toward developing a coordinated strategy for employment and particularly for promoting a skilled, trained and adaptable workforce and labour markets responsive to economic change'. In addition the new Article 6a has added a non-discrimination clause to the treaty. This allows the EU to 'take necessary measures to combat any kind of discrimination based on sex, race or ethnic origin, religion or belief, disability, age or sexual orientation'. However, although this provision has been welcomed, both the European Anti Poverty Network and the European Commission have argued that the requirement for unanimous voting on measures in this area will seriously impede its utility (*Agence Europe*, 23 June 1997, p. 15 and 26 July 1997, p. 15). As with each of the treaties discussed above, much will depend on what is made of the Amsterdam Treaty provisions, how they are interpreted and how they are implemented. Only with time will the full implications of the Amsterdam Treaty with regard to the development of British social policy become clear.


# EU Social Policy and its Impact on the UK

The Conservative administration's hostile attitude towards the development of EU social policy during the premiership of Margaret Thatcher (1979–90), followed by the Conservative government's 'opt-out' of some of the social aspects of the Maastricht Treaty during John Major's premiership (1990–97), have made this issue very salient in British domestic politics in recent years. Britain (and particularly the Conservative Party) has developed a reputation for strong opposition to the development of social legislation at the European level. This was not always the case. Indeed Conservative Prime Minister Edward Heath was, along with Chancellor Willie Brandt of Germany and President Georges Pompidou of France, one of the early supporters of the development of a social dimension to the European Union, which he felt would help to place a 'human face' on the mainly economic goals of the common market (Taylor, 1983, p. 206; Shanks, 1977, p. 8). Likewise, fellow member states have often used Britain's recalcitrance as a useful screen to hide their own reluctance to act on social policy matters (Lange, 1992, p. 246). Nevertheless the UK's reputation as an 'awkward partner' (George, 1990) is difficult to shake off. Despite the declaration by Tony Blair's Labour government – almost immediately after it was returned to office on 1 May 1997 (*Agence Europe*, 5–6 May 1997, p. 4) – that it intended to opt back into the social provisions of the Maastricht Treaty as soon as possible, some member states remain sceptical about the UK's intentions. Even after agreement on the Amsterdam Treaty, the other member states and the Commission await evidence of full UK cooperation in the social field, which can only come with time.

The salience of the question of EU social policy in the last two British general elections bears testimony to its importance to domestic politics. It has also had a very real impact on UK social policy in at least three respects. First, certain pieces of EU social legislation confer specific rights or obligations upon UK citizens that national courts are bound to recognise and uphold (for example provisions for the protection of pregnant workers and equal treatment of men and women at work). This is known as the principle of *direct effect* and is clearly of major importance for UK citizens. Although not specifically stated in the EU treaties, it is now generally accepted that when there is conflict between provisions of EU law and the domestic law of one of the member states, EU law is supreme over national law. This principle of *supremacy* means that even if there are only a few pieces of EU social legislation, they may prove to be highly significant for UK citizens. Moreover, even if the UK government fails to introduce relevant national legislation to formalise the rights and obligations conferred on UK citizens by EU legislation, it may find that the European Court of Justice will rule that the provisions of EU legislation are *directly applicable* and hence apply within the UK even without the usual enabling legislation (see Nugent, 1994, pp. 218–19). Thus the limited scope of EU social legislaton is no excuse for ignoring its impact. EU social law has very real and direct implications for UK citizens, albeit within a limited sphere.

Second, as Britains have become more aware of how the EU functions and what powers it has in the social field, new channels of influence and access to the decision process have opened up to UK citizens. As decisions on social policy within the 'multitiered system' of the EU are no longer possible to control solely at the national level, interest groups, new social movements and public sector organisations have increasingly sought to shift the focus of their activities to include action at the EU level. These activities include the traditional work of lobbying decision makers (see Mazey and Richardson, 1993), but groups have also learned to seek more formal contact at the EU level by, for example, participating in advisory groups and committees established by the EU institutions. Moreover, some of the better organised and resourced actors, for example the Trade Union Congress (TUC) and the Equal Opportunities Commission (EOC), have learned to make use of the European Court of Justice to ensure that the rights conferred by European social law are in fact fully upheld in the UK.

Finally, a more intangible effect of the development of the European social dimension may be its long-term impact on the pattern of UK social policy development. As UK actors who have traditionally operated at the national level are increasingly working in collaboration with their counterparts from the other member states at the European level, whether in Euro-groups or in less formal conferences and consultations, it appears that some of the ideas and values traditionally associated with more continental traditions of social policy may be filtering through to the UK. For example the recent demands by the TUC for the development of a 'social partnership' and 'social dialogue' with UK employers might be viewed in this light (*Financial Times*, 22 May 1997, p. 8).

## Conclusion

EU social legislation may be limited in scope but it is extremely important for the development of UK social policy. As has become clear, seeds sown by the Commission in the 1960s, for example concerning the concept of 'social dialogue', are beginning to bear fruit in the 1990s within the borders of the UK.

Although the UK has recently altered its stance on EU social policy and has chosen to participate with its European counterparts in all of the social aspects of the Amsterdam Treaty, a huge increase in the volume of EU social legislation should not be expected. The controversy that has dogged the development of the EU social dimension is unlikely to disappear overnight and the Amsterdam Treaty does not reflect a rapid rise in mutual trust and consensus on the issue of EU social policy. In particular the refusal to extend qualified majority voting on social issues highlights the residual unwilling-ness of member states to give up power over this sensitive policy area. From the UK perspective, the Blair administration has insisted on a two-year period, dating from the signature of the Amsterdam Treaty, before the measures agreed by the other member states on the basis of the Maastricht social agreement are legally required to be implemented in the UK. Mean-while, Blair's pre-election emphasis on the need for a flexible, deregulated labour market in the UK should caution against any assumption of a dramatic change in the UK negotiating position on EU social issues.

However, although many found the Amsterdam Treaty disappointing in parts, particularly with regard to the largely exhortatory provisions in its non-discrimination clause, it should be remembered that it marked the first step towards the issues of race, disability, age and sexual orientation being included in an EU Treaty. The inclusion of these issues and the likely encouragment of marginalised groups to participate at the EU level may have a significant impact in the long term. In particular the example of how alternative channels of access for UK groups at the EU level have been utilised by women's groups and trade unions and the institutionalisation of the roles played by these actors (for example through the social dialogue, advisory committees, inter-groups) in the EU policy process may prove salient for other marginalised groups in the future.

# Further Reading

Those wishing to learn more about how the European Union functions and how its policies impact upon its member states should read N. Nugent's *The Government and Policies of the European Union* (London: Macmillan, 1994). Those wishing for more detailed information on official developments in EU social policy should visit their local European Documentation Centre, where they can consult the original texts. European watchers should also consult the daily bulletin *Agence Europe*. More specifically, on EU social law and how it has developed, Nielsen and Szyszczak, *The Social Dimension of the European Community* (Copenhagen: Handelshojskolens Forlag, 1993) is a very useful text. For details of how EU social law is implemented in Britain, see N. Burrows and J. Mair, *European Social Law* (Chichester: John Wiley and Sons, 1996). For an overview of the development of EU social policy and a discussion of the degree of convergence in national welfare regimes in Europe, see L. Hantrais, *Social Policy in the European Union* (London: Macmillan, 1996). For a discussion of how and why the EU social policy process has developed in the form that it is evident today and how this affects the current output of EU social policy, see L. Cram, *Social Policy in the European Union* (London: Macmillan, forthcoming).

# Conclusion

NICK ELLISON AND CHRIS PIERSON

In this brief conclusion we draw on the wealth of theoretical and empirical evidence of developments in British social policy to answer just two questions. First, in what almost everyone recognises to be quite new circumstances for the British welfare state, just how much has social policy in Britain really changed? Is the newly emergent 'competition' or 'work-fare' state set to overwhelm whatever remains of the Keynesian welfare state apparatus? Are we really witnessing a transition from 'collectivist' to 'individualised' forms of social welfare? Or, second, is it possible that the excitement of discovering the new has led us to underestimate elements of continuity with the past? Perhaps it is possible that *new* forms of 'community' or 'citizenship' will check the seemingly irreversible tide towards privatised and atomised forms of welfare.

## Change . . .

There can be little doubt that the British welfare state has changed profoundly in the past twenty-five years. The assumptions that informed thinking about the roles and purposes of welfare in the 1940s and 1950s have been fundamentally challenged. All of the chapters in Part I deal with the fragmentation of the social democratic, collectivist ethos that characterised the postwar welfare state. Pierson (Chapter 1) charts the rise of a range of challenges to the social democratic orthodoxy, beginning in the 1970s with the criticisms of neo-Marxists and neoliberals, but then developing through the perspectives of feminist and antiracist writers. It may be that these perspectives are part of a more general acknowledgement that the old, institutionally homogeneous welfare state may no longer be sustainable in the face of the range of demographic, economic and political pressures, imagined or not, that are attributed to 'globalisation'.

Pierson's chapter sets the tone for much of what follows. Accounts of normative change in Part I examine the abandonment of traditional assumptions about the welfare state in relation to the evolving ideological positions of the major political parties (Ellison, Chapter 2), the current understanding of citizenship and need (Lister and Hewitt, Chapter 3 and 4), and finally with regard to the context of a possible welfare future in the shape of an 'associative' welfare state (Hirst, Chapter 5). If the ideological positions of the political parties show clear signs of convergence around a new social policy consensus that privileges duty and opportunity above rights and social protection, this new consensus displays a robustly positive approach to questions of individualism and pluralism. Although free market 'individualism', so beloved by the new right, continues to be treated with scepticism in many quarters, the older, universalist-collectivist understandings of 'citizenship' and 'need' have nevertheless been recast in terms of the new interest in pluralism and 'difference' emerging from the new social movements. While the developing critiques by feminists (Pascall, Chapter 12), anti-racists (Solomos, Chapter 13) and greens (Barry and Cahill, Chapter 14 and 16) have proved highly significant in terms of their ability to repoliticise and reprioritise the social policy agenda, reducing the influence of new right perspectives in the process, the strength of these different interests is itself proof of the extraordinary intellectual diversification and fragmentation of social policy over the past two decades.

This fragmentation has both contributed to and been exacerbated by the sustained assault by successive Conservative governments on the traditional institutional configuration of the Keynesian welfare state – against the background of endemically high unemployment. Each of the chapters in Part II discusses the impact of this assault on the major areas of British social policy. At the root of change lies the ethos of the 'new public management', that curious hybrid that decentralises delivery mechanisms while increasing central control over strategy and policy (Hoggett, 1996). Where welfare is concerned, the chapters in Part II clearly show how areas of provision originally organised and delivered by the state have now been either privatised, as in the case of housing, or subjected to the new discipline of the internal market, as in many areas of health, education and the personal social services. While the state continues to control public sector financing and key policy decisions, these initiatives have contributed to a significant erosion of the traditional distinction between the 'public' and the 'private' sector. Although such a development is not necessarily a 'bad thing', a number of contributors raise the question of whether welfare state services have become resource-led as opposed to needs-led (Nettleton, Chapter 8, Langan, Chapter 10), explicitly recognising a major departure from the needs-oriented, collectivist perspective of the Keynesian welfare state.

It may be argued that the organisation of delivery mechanisms should take second place to the efficient provision of social goods and services that allow needs to be met on an equitable basis. The problem is that many of the contributors to Part II, and to this book as a whole, doubt that equity – let alone equality – can be guaranteed under the new managerialism. They discuss a range of factors, different in each policy area, that conspire against the fair distribution of social goods and services, the most important of which is surely the jettisoning of the goal of full employment (Whiteside, Chapter 6) and the associated tightening of the income maintenance system (McKay, Chapter 7). Arguably, at least, the result of a decade or more of social policy reform is an increasingly divided society where access to high-quality social goods such as housing and education is dependent on an ability to command certain 'resources' – notably full-time employment – which furnishes opportunities for better educational facilities in cleaner, relatively crime-free environments. Meanwhile those with greater needs, particularly the unemployed and welfare-dependent older people, will either be forced to take whatever opportunities happen to be on offer or, in the case of the retired, remain dependent on meagre state pensions.

Finally, when considering the issue of fragmentation and change in British social policy, it is vital to take account of the impact of the European Union. Although the emergence of an integrated 'European welfare state' is highly unlikely, the EU's increasing influence in domestic social arrangements is a certainty. Through the operations of the European Court of Justice, for example, the EU is likely to affect – indeed has already affected – the rights and duties of British citizens (Cram, Chapter 17). In this way Europe poses a clear challenge to the hitherto accepted idea that national governments exercise total control over domestic social policy. It may be, as Cram hints, that those groups who become dissatisfied with the existing levels of domestic social provision, or with the manner in which they are treated by British welfare institutions, may begin to look towards Europe as a potential source of redress. Whether or not Britain remains an 'awkward partner', British citizens can expect to be affected by European social legislation and can also expect to use their European 'citizenship' as one means of exercising influence over domestic social and political issues.

## . . . and Continuity?

Change has undoubtedly been the dominant theme in British social policy since the late 1970s, as the chapters in this book generally acknowledge. It is important, however, not to become so preoccupied with this dimension that elements of continuity with the Keynesian welfare state are entirely ignored or forgotten. For one thing the state itself plainly remains a key actor in the strategic conduct of welfare policy. Battered by globalising forces and, in the eyes of some commentators (Strange, 1996), certainly reduced, the state has nevertheless continued to exercise a high degree (some would say an extraordinarily high degree) of control over the direction and development of domestic social policy. Although observers such as Paul Pierson (1994) have commented on the resilience of Keynesian welfare institutions in the face of Conservative reforms, the paradox appears to be that whether or not these reforms have been successfully implemented – and the verdict here is inevitably mixed – the state has retained its powers of surveillance and control, as well as its formidable organisational capacity. Quite crucially, and despite two decades of trying, social expenditure has not been reduced. The annual social security budget alone is now in excess of £100 billion.

Outside the central state itself, what are the main elements of continuity with postwar welfare collectivism? Most obviously, health, education, the income maintenance system and the personal social services continue to be controlled, if not delivered, by the state or state agencies. Only housing has been largely – though by no means wholly – removed as a key area of social provision (Malpass, Chapter 11). Aspects of Keynesian ambitions remain entrenched in these key sectors. The short introduction to Part II notes that free health care at the point of delivery, comprehensive schooling and contribution-based social security benefits remain enshrined as central elements of British social policy that continue to inform ideas of social justice. The overwhelming majority of the population continue to depend on the state sector for education and health services. The universality (and equality?) of these services is being increasingly compromised, however, as user-charging in health, decentralised organisational and financial autonomy in education and increased means testing in income maintenance take effect.

Where welfare theory is concerned, it is relatively easy to comment on clear-cut changes – the effective subordination of Marxist critiques and the increasing disillusionment with new right solutions have given way to the developing interest in new pluralist ideas associated with the 'new social movements'. But continuities also exist here. 'Citizenship' is once again on the political agenda: the discussions on how it may best be understood and applied reveal concerns not only about the nature of equity and social justice, but also about how the universalist assumptions implicit in the idea can be made to chime with new demands for recognition and 'social inclusion' from groups who, quite properly, also wish to retain a clear sense of their own identity. Echoes of past ideological struggles between individualists and collectivists, pluralists and centralisers can also be heard, even as these old lines of division cease to provide adequate tools for understanding, let alone resolving, the complexities involved in efforts to reconstitute our conception of the role and nature of social policy.

# The Future of British Social Policy

What do the studies in this book suggest about the future of the British welfare state? Two possibilities are of particular interest. There is, first, the possibility of a continued move towards a 'competition' or 'work-fare' state, a tendency that is already inscribed in some of the institutional arrangements of British social policy. At the same time we need to take seriously a second radical alternative to the challenge posed by the 'break-up' of the Keynesian welfare state — that is the call for new forms of social provision that are 'neither state nor market'. These two approaches will be discussed in turn.

## The work-fare state – a possible future

One possibility is that governments will move still further in the direction of 'contracting out' services and 'devolving' responsibility to individuals and their families. We should expect that governments will seek to transfer the costs of welfare provision (perhaps most consequentially in terms of old age pensions) onto individual citizens. In twenty years time we shall all be paying more for access to health, education and pensions (the biggest three areas of government social expenditure). Current reforms point up two overwhelming concerns on the part of policy makers. In those areas of welfare activity that relate directly to the economy (unemployment compensation, education and training, the transition from education to work) there will be a growing emphasis on *competitiveness* – defined in terms of national economic performance *and* the individual's capacity to 'perform' by accepting the new conditions of 'flexibility' and seizing the opportunities on offer. Elsewhere (that is, in benefits and services not directly related to the 'flexible' labour market) the persistent concern will be *controlling costs*. The new right's agenda – slashing state social expenditure and allowing everyone to buy private services – looks increasingly fantastic. We shall all have to buy more private provision (if we can afford it), but the state's commitment to welfare provision will continue to be enormous. Such a vision does not appear to hold out much comfort to the most vulnerable members of society and those – frequently women – who either choose or have to look after them. It could of course be said that those most in need will continue to be supported by state welfare services. Good intentions to the contrary, the difficulty is that, in a 'work-fare' environment, it is not clear how well governments will be able to meet their social commitments in the face of continuing downward pressure on direct taxation and persistent demands for cost-effectiveness. On this reading, extensive means testing and/or potentially high levels of 'coercion' as governments demand a specific performance for the receipt of social goods and services mark out a bleak welfare future.

## Beyond state and market: A new collectivism?

Need the future be as gloomy as this prognosis suggests? A number of contributors to this volume suggest that a 'work-fare state' is not the only possible response to the collapse of traditional state welfare forms. Such critics argue for alternative forms of collective or communal provision, possibly guaranteed, but not usually delivered, by the state. Prominent amongst these (and raised in Chapters 5, 7 and 14) is the call for provision of a citizens' income as the bedrock of communal social provision. All three chapters argue that what is clearly a collective good could be used to provide individuals with the resources to enable them to enjoy a sufficiently good quality of life without having to rely upon means-tested goods and services. They variously insist that a citizens' income is justified on the basis of citizenship, addresses traditional objections to the 'social control' element in state provision and is consonant with new forms of economic organisation (including the end of full employment). In Hirst's view (Chapter 5), a basic income could be used to underpin a more communal or 'associative' approach to welfare, freeing individuals to make 'voluntary' contributions in the form of unpaid work or local service provision. Those writing from an ecological perspective welcome the possibilities that a citizens' income would present for local communities to establish forms of 'self-provisioning', which could free individual members from dependence on central state resources and controls.

# Beyond the Welfare State?

Institutionally, it would appear that the advocates of a work-fare future have the upper hand. The only major British party to have pledged to a citizens' income – the Liberal Democrats – has now withdrawn that commitment, and whilst the advocates of a basic income have some very powerful prudential arguments on their side, it is hard to envisage the tax consequences of its introduction being 'saleable' in the current fiscal climate. But the future is not to be fought out exclusively between these two tendencies. In an age where the state does less, it may still choose to regulate more. The ability to avoid the most inequitable and residual outcomes of a changing welfare agenda may now depend (even more than in the golden days of the Keynesian ascendancy) upon the skill and dexterity of those politicians and policy-makers who want to temper efficiency with equity. The challenge for them is formidable.

# Bibliography

Abbott, D., P. Broadfoot, P. Croll, M. Osborn and A. Pollard (1994) 'Some Sink, Some Float: National Curriculum Assessment and Accountability', *British Educational Research Journal*, vol. 20, no. 2, pp. 155–174.

ADC/AMA (1995) *Housing Finance Survey 1995–96* (London: Association of District Councils/Association of Metropolitan Authorities).

Ahmad, W. I. U. (1993) *'Race' and Health in Contemporary Britain* (Milton Keynes: Open University Press).

Ainley, P. and A. Green (1996) 'Missing the Targets: the new state of post-16 education and training', *Forum*, vol. 38, no. 1, pp. 22–23.

Alcock, P. (1987) *Poverty and State Support* (London: Longman).

Allsop, J. (1995) *Health Policy and the NHS Towards 2000* (London: Longman).

Amin, A. (ed.) (1994) *Post-Fordism: a Reader* (Oxford: Blackwell).

Anderson, V. (1991) *Alternative Economic Indicators* (London: Routledge).

Ascher, K. (1987) *The Politics of Privatisation: Contracting Out Public Services* (London: Macmillan).

Atkinson, A. B. (1989) *Poverty and Social Security* (Hemel Hempstead: Harvester Wheatsheaf).

Atkinson, A. B. (1995) 'The Welfare State and Economic Performance', *National Tax Journal*, vol. 48, pp. 171–98.

Atkinson, A. B. (1996) 'The Case for a Participation Income', *Political Quarterly*, vol. 67, no. 1, pp. 67–70.

Audit Commission (1986) *Making a Reality of Community Care* (London: HMSO).

Audit Commission (1992) *The Community Revolution: The Personal Social Services and Community Care* (London: HMSO).

Audit Commission (1994) *Seen But Not Heard: coordinating community child health and social services for children in need* (London: HMSO).

Audit Commission (1995) *Briefing on GP fundholding* London: HMSO).

Baldock, J. (1989) 'United Kingdom – a perpetual crisis of marginality', in B. Munday (ed.), *The Crisis in Welfare: an International Perspective on Social Services and Social Work* (Hemel Hempstead: Harvester Wheatsheaf).

Ball, S. (1990) *Politics and Policy Making in Education: Explorations in Policy Sociology* (London: Routledge).

Ball, S. J., M. Maguire and S. Macrae (1997) 'The Post-16 Education Market: Ethics, Interests and Survival', paper presented at the 6th Quasi-Markets Conference, University of Portsmouth, 10–11 April.

Ball, W. and J. Solomos (eds) (1990) *Race and Local Politics* (London: Macmillan).

Bamford, T. (1990) *The Future of Social Work* (London: Macmillan).

Barnes, M. (1996) *Care, Communities and Citizens* (London: Longman).

Barr, N. (1993) *The Economics of the Welfare State*, 2nd edn (London: Weidenfeld and Nicolson).

Barr, N. and F. Coulter (1990) 'Social Security: solution or problem', in J. Hills (ed.), *The State of Welfare: The Welfare State in Britain Since 1974* (Oxford: Clarendon Paperbacks).

Barry, J. (1994) 'Beyond the Shallow and the Deep: Green Politics, Philosophy and Praxis', *Environmental Politics*, vol. 3, no. 3, pp. 369–94.

Barry, J. (1995) 'Towards a Theory of the Green State', in S. Elworthy *et al.*, (eds) *Perspectives on the Environment 2: Interdisciplinary Research on Politics, Planning, Society and the Environment* (Aldershot: Avebury).

Barry, J. and J. Proops (1996) 'Local Employment Trading Systems: Connecting Citizenship and Sustainability?', End of Award Report, Economic and Social Research Council Research Project (Ref: L 320253192).

Bauman, Z. (1994) *Alone Again: ethics after certainty* (London: Demos).

Bebbington, A. and A. Kelly (1995) 'Expenditure Planning in the Personal Social Services: Unit Costs in the 1980s', *Journal of Social Policy*, vol. 24, no. 3, pp. 385–411.

Becker, G. (1964) *Human Capital* (New York: Columbia University Press).

Benhabib, S. (1992) *Situating the Self: gender, community and postmodernism in contemporary ethics* (Cambridge: Polity).

Benton, T. (1993) *Natural Relations: ecology, animal rights and social justice* (London: Verso).

Benzeval, M., K. Judge and M. Whitehead (1995) *Tackling Inequalities in Health* (London: King's Fund).

Beveridge, W. H. (1942) *Social Insurance and Allied Services*, Cmnd 6404 (London: HMSO).

Beveridge, W. H. (1948) *Voluntary Action* (London: Allen and Unwin).

Bhavnani, K. and M. Coulson (1986) 'Transforming socialist feminism: the challenge of racism', *Feminist Review*, vol. 23, pp. 81–92.

Binney, V., G. Harkell and J. Nixon (1981) *Leaving Violent Men: A study of refuges and housing for battered women (WAF/DE Research Team)* (Manchester: Women's Aid Federation).

Blackburn, R. (1997) 'Reflections on Blair's Velvet Revolution', *New Left Review*, vol. 223 (May/June), pp. 3–16.

Blair, T. (1994) *Socialism* (London: Fabian Society).

Blair, T. (1995) 'End the give and take away society', *Guardian*, 23 March 1995.

Blair, T. (1996) *New Britain: My vision of a young country* (London: 4th Estate).

Blair, T. (1997) 'Seven Pillars of a Decent Society', lecture, Southampton, April.

Bookchin, M. (1986) *The Modern Crisis* (Philadelphia: New Society Publishers).

Bowe, R., S. J. Ball and A. Gold (1992) *Reforming Education and Changing Schools: case studies in policy sociology* (London: Routledge).

Bradshaw, J. (1971) 'The concept of social need', *New Society*, 30 March 1971.

Bramley, G. (1994) 'An Affordability Crisis in British Housing: Dimensions, Causes and Policy Responses', *Housing Studies*, vol. 9, no. 1 (January), pp. 103–24.

Brewster, C. and P. Teague (1989) *European Community Social Policy: its impact on the UK* (London: Institute of Personnel Management).

Bridges, D. and C. Husbands (eds) (1996) *Consorting and Collaborating in the Education Marketplace* (Hove: Falmer).

Britton, A. J. C. (1991) *Macroeconomic Policy in Britain, 1974–87* (Cambridge: Cambridge University Press).

Brown, G. (1997) 'Why Labour is Still Loyal to the Poor', *Guardian*, 2 August 1997.

Brown, M. and S. Payne (1994) *Introduction to Social Administration in Britain*, 7th edn (London: Routledge).

Bulmer, M. and A. M. Rees (1996) *Citizenship Today: the contemporary relevance of T. H. Marshall* (London: UCL Press).

Butcher, T. (1995) *Delivering Welfare: the Governance of the Social Services in the 1990s* (Buckingham: Open University Press).

Butler, J. (1990) *Gender Trouble: feminism and the subversion of identity* (London: Routledge).

Butler-Sloss, E. (1988) *Report of the Inquiry into Child Abuse in Cleveland 1987* (London: HMSO).

Cahill, M. (1994) *The New Social Policy* (Oxford: Blackwell).

Cahill, M. (1995) 'Robertson', in V. George and R. Page (eds), *Modern Thinkers on Welfare* (London: Prentice-Hall).

Cannan, C. (1994/95) 'Enterprise Culture, Professional Socialisation and Social Work Education in Britain', *Critical Social Policy*, vol. 42, pp. 5–19.

Carr, W. and A. Hartnett (1996) 'Civic education, democracy and the English political tradition', in J. Demaine and H. Entwistle, *Beyond Communitarianism: Citizenship, Politics and Education* (London: Macmillan).

Casey, B. and S. Creigh (1989) ' "Marginal" groups in the Labour Force Survey', *Scottish Journal of Political Economy*, vol. 36, no. 3, pp. 282–99.

Central Statistical Office (1995) *Social Trends 25* (London: HMSO).

Central Statistical Office (1997) *Social Trends 27* (London: HMSO).

Cerny, P. (1990) *The Changing Architecture of Politics: Structure, Agency and the State* (London: Sage).

Chaney, D. (1996) *Lifestyles* (London: Routledge).

Clark, G. (1994) *Housing Benefit: Incentives for Reform* (London: Social Market Foundation).

Clarke, J. and J. Newman (1992) *The Right to Manage: a second managerial revolution* (Milton Keynes: Open University).

CML (1991) *Housing Finance* (London: Council of Mortgage Lenders, November).

Cohen, S. (1995) 'The mighty state of immigration controls', in J. Baldock and M. May (eds), *Social Policy Review 7* (Canterbury: Social Policy Association).

Coles, B. (1995) *Youth and Social Policy: Youth citizenship and young careers* (London: UCL Press).

Collins, D. (1975) *The European Communities: the social policy of the first phase* (London: Martin Robertson).

Comité des Sages (1996), *For a Europe of Civic and Social Rights* (Brussels: European Commission).

Commission on Social Justice (the Borrie Commission) (1994) *Social Justice: Strategies for National Renewal* (London: Vintage).

Coote, A. and D. Hunter (1996) *New Agenda for Health* (London: IPPR).

Cram, L. (1993) 'Calling the Tune Without Paying the Piper? Social Policy Regulation: The Role of the Commission in European Union Social Policy', *Policy and Politics*, vol. 21, pp. 135–46.

Cram, L. (1997) *Policy-making in the European Union: Conceptual Lenses and the Integration Process* (London: Routledge).

Crook, A. and P. Kemp (1996) 'The Revival of Private Rented Housing in Britain', *Housing Studies*, vol. 11, no. 1, pp. 51–68.

Cross, M. (1993) 'Generating the "new poverty": a European comparison', in R. Simpson and R. Walker (eds), *Europe: for richer or poorer* (London: CPAG).

Dahrendorf Commission (1995) *Report on Wealth Creation and Social Cohesion in a Free Society* (London: The Commission on Wealth Creation and Social Cohesion).

Daly, H. (ed.) (1973) *Toward a Steady-State Economy* (San Francisco: W.H. Freeman).

Deacon, A. (1995) 'Spending more to achieve less? Social security since 1945', in D. Gladstone (eds), *British Social Welfare Past, Present and Future* (London: UCL Press).

Deacon, B. (1995) 'The globalisation of social policy and the socialisation of global politics', in J. Baldock and M. May (eds), *Social Policy Review 7* (Canterbury: Social Policy Association).

Deakin, N. (1994) *The Politics of Welfare: Continuities and Change* (Hemel Hempstead: Harvester Wheatsheaf).

Dean, H. (1991) *Social Security and Social Control* (London: Routledge).

Dearing, R. (1994) *The National Curriculum and its Assessment: A new framework for schools* (London: SCAA).

Deem, R., K. Brehony and S. Heath (1995) *Active Citizenship and the Governing of Schools* (Buckingham: Open University Press).

Denham, A. (1996) *Think-Tanks of the New Right* (Aldershot: Dartmouth).

Department for Education and Employment (1996) *Self-government for Schools* (London: HMSO).

Department of the Environment (1995) *Our Future Homes: Opportunity, Choice, Responsibility*, Cm 2901 (London: HMSO).

Department of Health (1989) *Working for Patients*, Cm 555 (London: HMSO).

Department of Health (1991a) *The Patient's Charter* (London: HMSO).

Department of Health (1991b) *Child Abuse: A Study of Inquiry Reports 1980–1989* (London: HMSO).

Department of Health (1991c) *Patterns and Outcomes in Child Placement* (London: HMSO).

Department of Health (1992) *The Health of the Nation: a strategy for health in England*, Cmnd 1986 (London: HMSO).

Department of Health (1995a) *Variations in Health: What can the Department of Health and the NHS Do?* (London: HMSO).

Department of Health (1995b) *Child Protection: Messages from Research* (London: HMSO).

Department of Health (1996a) *Opportunity and Choice: primary care – the future* (London: HMSO).

Department of Health (1996b) *The Government's Expenditure Plans 1996–97 to 1998–99*, Cmnd 3212 (London: HMSO).

Department of Health (1997) '8th Wave Fundholding Deferred', http:/www.coi.gov. uk/coi/depts/GDH/coi8907c.ok, 20th May.

Department of Health and Social Security (1993) *NHS Management Inquiry (Griffith's Report)* (London: HMSO).

Department of Social Security (1993a) *The Growth of Social Security* (London: HMSO).

Department of Social Security (1993b) *Containing the Cost of Social Security – The International Context* (London: HMSO).

Department of Social Security (1994) *Social Security Department Report 1994*, Cmnd 2513 (London: HMSO).

Department of Social Security (1995) *Social Security Department Report* (London: HMSO).

Department of Social Security (1996) *Households Below Average Income: 1979–1993/4 (HBAI)* (London: HMSO).

Department of Social Security (1996) *Social Security Statistics* (London: HMSO).

Department of Social Security (1997) *Social Security Departmental Report The Government's Expenditure Plans 1997–8 to 1999–2000*, Cmnd 3613 (London: HMSO).

Department of Social Security (1998) *A New Contract for Welfare* (London: HMSO).

Department of Transport (1989) *Roads for Prosperity* Cm 693 (London: HMSO).

Department of Transport (1996a) *The National Cycling Strategy* (London: HMSO).

Department of Transport (1996b) *Developing a Strategy for Walking* (London: HMSO).

Department of Transport, Environment and the Regions (1997) *Developing an Integrated Transport Policy* (London: HMSO).

Dilnot, A. and M. Kell (1989), 'Male Unemployment and Women's Work', in A. Dilnot and I. Walker (eds), *The Economics of Social Security* (Oxford: Oxford University Press).

Dilnot, A. and S. Webb (1989) 'The 1988 Social Security Reforms', in A. Dilnot and I. Walker (eds), *The Economics of Social Security* (Oxford: Oxford University Press).

Dittmar, H. (1992) *The Social Psychology of Material Possessions* (Hemel Hempstead: Harvester Wheatsheaf).

Dixon, J., A. Harrison and B. New (1997) 'Is the NHS Underfunded?', *British Medical Journal*, vol. 314, pp. 58–61.

Dobson, A. (ed.) (1991) *The Green Reader* (London: Andre Deutsch).

Dobson, A. (1995) *Green Political Thought: An Introduction*, 2nd edn (London: Routledge).

Dobson, A. and P. Lucardie (eds) (1993) *The Politics of Nature: Explorations in Green Political Theory* (London: Routledge).

Doherty, B. (1992) 'The Fundi-Realo Controversy: An analysis of four European Green parties', *Environmental Politics*, vol. 1. no. 1, pp. 95–120.

Dorling, D. and J. Cornford (1995) 'Who Has Negative Equity? How House Price Falls in Britain Have Hit Different Groups of Home Buyers', *Housing Studies*, vol. 10, no. 2, pp. 151–78.

Doyal, L. (1995) *What Makes Women Sick: Gender and the political economy of health* (London: Macmillan).

Doyal, L. and I. Gough (1991) *A Theory of Human Need* (London: Macmillan).

Driver, S. and L. Martell (1997) 'New Labour's communitarianism', *Critical Social Policy*, vol. 53, no. 17, pp. 27–46.

Dunnell, K. (1995) 'Are We Healthier?', *Population Trends*, vol. 82, pp. 12–18.

Eardley, T., J. Bradshaw, J. Ditch, I. Gough and P. Whiteford (1996) *Social Assistance in OECD Countries: Synthesis Report*, (Research Report No. 46), Department of Social Security (London: HMSO).

Echols, F. H. and J. D. Willms (1995) 'Reasons for School Choice in Scotland', *Journal of Education Policy*, vol. 10, no. 2, pp. 143–56.

Edwards T., J. Fitz and G. Whitty (1989) *The State and Private Education: an evaluation of the assisted places scheme* (Lewes: Falmer).

Elkington, J. and J. Hales (1988) *The Green Consumer Guide* (London: Victor Gollancz).

Ellison, N. (1994) *Egalitarian Thought and Labour Politics: Retreating Visions* (London: Routledge).

Ellison, N. (1997) 'From Welfare State to "Post-Welfare" Society? Labour's Social Policy in Historical and Comparative Perspective', in B. Brivati and T. Bale (eds), *New Labour in Power: precedents and prospects* (London: Routledge).

Elworthy, S., K. Anderson, I. Coates, P. Stephens and M. Stroh (eds) (1995) *Perspectives on the Environment 2: Interdisciplinary Research on Politics, Planning, Society and the Environment* (Aldershot: Avebury).

Employment Department Group/DSS (1994) *Jobseeker's Allowance*, White Paper, Cmnd 2687 (London: HMSO).

Enthoven, A. (1985) *Reflections on the Management of the NHS* (London: Nuffield Provincial Hospitals Trust).

Erskine, A. (1996) 'The Burden of Risk: who dies because of cars?', *Social Policy and Administration*, vol. 30, no. 2, pp. 143–57.

Esping-Andersen, G. (1990) *The Three Worlds of Welfare Capitalism* (Oxford: Polity Press).

Etzioni, A. (1993) *The Spirit of Community* (New York: Simon and Schuster).

Etzioni, A. (1997) *The New Golden Rule: community and morality in a democratic society* (London: Profile Books).

Eurolink Age (1994) *Mobility and Transport: meeting the needs of older people with disabilities* (London: Eurolink Age).

European Commission (1959) *Second General Report of the European Commission* (Brussels: European Commission).

Evans, M. (1996) 'Fairer or Fowler? The effects of the 1986 Social Security Act on family incomes', in J. Hills (ed.), *New Inequalities: The changing distribution of income and wealth in the United Kingdom* (Cambridge: Cambridge University Press).

Farnham, D. and C. Lupton (1994) 'Employment relations and training policy', in S. Savage, R. Atkinson and L. Robins (eds), *Public Policy in Britain* (London: Macmillan).

Ferris, J. (1993) 'Ecological versus Social Rationality: Can there be green social policies?', in A. Dobson and P. Lucardie (eds), *The Politics of Nature: Explorations in Green Political Theory* (London: Routledge).

Field, F. (1995) *Making Welfare Work: Reconstructing Welfare for the Millenium* (London: Institute of Community Studies).

Field, F. (1996a) *How to Pay for the Future: building a stakeholders' welfare* (London: Institute of Community Studies).

Field, F. (1996b) *Stakeholder Welfare*, Choice in Welfare Series no. 32 (London: Institute of Economic Affairs).

Finch, J. and D. Groves (1983) *A Labour of Love: Women, Work and Caring* (London: Routledge & Kegan Paul).

Firestone, S. (1971) *The Dialectic of Sex: the case for feminist revolution* (London: Jonathan Cape).

Flynn, N. (1997) *Public Sector Management*, 3rd edn (Hemel Hempstead: Harvester Wheatsheaf).

Forder, J., M. Knapp and G. Wistow (1996) 'Competition in the Mixed Economy of Care', *Journal of Social Policy*, vol. 25, no. 2, pp. 201–21.

Forrest, R., P. Leather, D. Gordon and C. Pantazis (1995) 'The Future of Home Ownership', *Housing Finance*, August, pp. 9–15

Franklin, B. and N. Parton (eds) (1991) *Social Work, the Media and Public Relations* (London: Routledge).

Freund, P. and G. Martin (1993) *The Ecology of the Automobile* (Montreal: Black Rose Books).

Gaber, I. and J. Aldridge (eds) (1994) *In the Best Interests of the Child: Culture, Identity and Transracial Adoption* (London: Free Association Books).

Gabriel, Y. and T. Lang (1995) *The Unmanageable Consumer: contemporary consumption and its fragmentations* (London: Sage).

Galbraith, J. K. (1993) *The Culture of Contentment* (Harmondsworth: Penguin).

Gamble, A. (1992) 'The Labour Party and Economic Management', in M. Smith and J. Spear (eds), *The Changing Labour Party* (London: Routledge).

Gamble, A. (1994) *The Free Economy and the Strong State*, 2nd edn (London: Macmillan).

Garfinkel, I. and R. Haveman (1977) *Earnings Capacity, Poverty and Inequality* (New York: Academic Press).

George, S. (1990) *An Awkward Partner: Britain in the European Community* (Oxford: Oxford University Press).

George, V. and P. Wilding (1976) *Ideology and Social Welfare* (London: Routledge and Kegan Paul).

George, V. and P. Wilding (1994) *Welfare and Ideology* (Hemel Hempstead: Harvester Wheatsheaf).

Geras, N. (1983) *Marx and Human Nature: a refutation of a legend* (London: Verso).

Gewirtz, S., S. J. Ball and R. Bowe (1995) *Markets, Choice and Equity in Education* (Buckingham: Open University Press).

Giddens, A. (1994) *Beyond Left and Right* (Oxford: Polity Press).

Glennerster, H. (1994) 'Health and Social Policy', in D. Kavanagh and A. Seldon (eds), *The Major Effect* (London: Macmillan).

Goodwin, P. (1995) *Car Dependence: a report for the RAC Foundation for Motoring and the Environment* (London: RAC).

Goodwin, P., S. Hallett, F. Kenny and G. Stokes (1991) *Transport: The New Realism* (Transport Studies Unit: University of Oxford).

Gordon, D. M. (1996) *Fat and Mean – the corporate squeeze of working Americans and the myth of managerial 'downsizing'* (New York: Martin Kesseler Brooks/The Free Press).

Gorz, A. (1983) *Ecology as Politics* (London: Pluto).

Gorz, A. (1987) 'Reshaping the Welfare State', *Praxis International*, vol. 6, no. 1, pp. 5–16.

Gough, I. (1979) *The Political Economy of the Welfare State* (London: Macmillan).

Gough, I. (1983) 'The Crisis of the British Welfare State', *International Journal of Health Services*, vol. 13, no. 3, pp. 459–77.

Grace, G. (1995) *School Leadership: Beyond Education Management: An essay in policy scholarship* (London: Falmer).

Gray, A. and B. Jenkins (1993) 'Markets, Managers and the Public service: the changing of a culture', in P. Taylor-Gooby and R. Lawson (eds), *Managers: New Issues in the Delivery of Welfare* (Buckingham: Open University Press).

Gray, J. (1992) *The Moral Foundations of Market Institutions* (London: Institute of Economic Affairs).

Gray, J. (1997) *Endgames: questions in late modern political thought* (Cambridge: Polity).

Green Party (1997) http://www.gn.apc.org/greenparty/policy/.

Griffiths, R. (1991) *Seven Years of Progress – General Management in the NHS*, Management Lectures no. 3, mimeo (London: The Audit Commission, 12th June).

Hakim, C. (1982) 'The social consequences of high unemployment' *Journal of Social Policy*, vol. 11, no. 4, pp. 433–67.

Hall, S. (1991) 'Old Identities and New Ethnicities', in A. D. King (ed.), *Culture, Globalisation and the World System* (London: Macmillan).

Halpin, D., S. Power and J. Fitz (1997) 'Opting into the Past? Grant-Maintained Schools and the Reinvention of Tradition', in R. Glatter, P. A. Woods and C. Bagley (eds), *Choice and Diversity in Schooling: Perspectives and Prospects* (London: Routledge).

Ham, C. (1992) *Health Policy in Britain: the politics and organisation of the NHS* (London: Macmillan).

Ham, C. (1997) 'Foreign Policies', *Health Service Journal*, vol. 107, pp. 24–7.

Harding, T. (1992) 'Questions on the Social Services Agenda', in T. Harding (ed.), *Who Owns Welfare? Questions on the Social Services Agenda*, Social Services Policy Forum Paper no. 2 (London: NISW).

Harman, H. (1993) *The Century Gap: 20th Century Man/21st Century Woman – how both sexes can bridge the century gap* (London: Vermilion).

Harrison, S., D. Hunter and C. Pollitt (1990) *The Dynamics of British Health Policy* (London: Unwin Hyman).

Hattersley, R. (1997a) 'Why I'm No Longer Loyal to Labour', *Guardian*, 25 July 1997.

Hattersely, R. (1997b) 'The Poor Need Cash and Need it Now', *Guardian*, 14 August 1997.

Hawksworth, J. and S. Wilcox (1995) *Challenging the Conventions* (Coventry: Chartered Institute of Housing).

Hayek, F. A. (1960) *The Constitution of Liberty* (London: Routledge & Kegan Paul).

Hayek, F. A. (1982) *The Constitution of Liberty* (London: Routledge & Kegan Paul).

Heelas, P. and Morris, P. (eds) (1992) *The Values of the Enterprise Culture: the moral debate* (London: Routledge).

Heffernan, R. and M. Marqusee (1992) *Defeat from the Jaws of Victory: Inside Kinnock's Labour Party* (London: Verso).

Hennessey, P. (1992) *Never Again: Britain, 1945–51* (London: Jonathan Cape).

Henwood, M. (1992) 'Demographic and Family Change', in T. Harding (ed.), *Who Owns Welfare? Questions on the social services agenda*, Social Services Policy Forum Paper no. 2 (London: NISW).

Hewitt, M. (1993) 'Social movements and social need', *Critical Social Policy*, vol. 37, pp. 52–74; also in D. Taylor (ed.), *Critical Social Policy: a reader* (London: Sage, 1996).

Hewitt, P. (1993) *About Time: The Revolution in Work and Family Life* (London: Rivers Oram Press).

Hill, M. (1990), *Social Security Policy in Britain* (Aldershot: Edward Elgar).

Hill, M. (1993) *The Welfare State in Britain: A political history since 1945* (Aldershot: Edward Elgar).

Hill, M. (1996) *Social Policy A Comparative Analysis* (London: Harvester Wheatsheaf).

Hillman, M. (ed.) (1993) *Children, Transport and the Quality of Life* (London: Policy Studies Institute).

Hillman, M., J. Adams and J. Whitelegg (1990) *One False Move . . . a study of children's independent mobility* (London: Policy Studies Institute).

Hillman, M. and S. Plowden (1996) *Speed Control and Transport Policy* (London: Policy Studies Institute).

Hills, J. (1997) *The Future of Welfare: a guide to the debate* (York: Joseph Rowntree Foundation).

Hirst, P. (1994) *Associative Democracy* (Oxford: Polity Press).

Hirst, P. (1997a) 'The Global Economy – myths and realities', *International Affairs*, vol. 73, no. 3, pp. 409–25.

Hirst, P. (1997b) *From Statism to Pluralism* (London: UCL Press).

Hirst P. and G. Thompson (1996) *Globalisation in Question: the international economy and the possibilities of governance* (Oxford: Polity Press).

Hodkinson, P., A. C. Sparkes and H. Hodkinson (1996) *Triumphs and Tears: Young People, Markets and the Transition from School to Work* (London: David Fulton).

Hoggett, P. (1996) 'New Modes of Control in the Public Service', *Public Administration*, vol. 74, pp. 9–32.

Holliday, I. (1995) *The NHS Transformed: a guide to the health care reforms* (Manchester: Baseline Books).

Holloway, J. (1981) *Social Policy Harmonisation in the European Community* (Farnborough: Gower).

Holman, B. (1993) *A New Deal for Social Welfare* (Oxford: Lion).

Holmans, A. (1991) 'The 1977 National Policy Review in Retrospect', *Housing Studies*, vol. 6, no. 3, pp. 206–19.

Hood, C. (1991) 'Public Management for all Seasons', *Public Administration*, vol. 69 (Spring), pp. 3–19.

Hooper, C. (1996) 'Men's Violence and relationship breakdown: can violence be dealt with as an exception to the rule?', in C. Hallett (ed.), *Women and Social Policy. An Introduction* (London: Harvester Wheatsheaf).

House of Commons Health Committee (1995) *Priority Setting in the NHS: purchasing*, vol. 1, annex 1 (London: HMSO).

Hudson, R. and A. M. Williams (1995) *Divided Britain*, 2nd edn (London: Belhaven).

Hunter, D. (1991) 'Managing Medicine: a response to crisis', *Social Science and Medicine*, vol. 32, pp. 441–8.

Hutton, W. (1996) *The State We're In* (London: Vintage).

Hutton, W. (1997) *The State to Come* (London: Vintage).

Irvine, S. and A. Ponton (1988) *Not 1986, A Green Manifesto: Policies for a Green Future* (London: Optima).

Jacobs, M. (1995), 'Environmental Change and the Concept of "Standard of Living", ESRC, Global Environmental Change Programme (Phase III) Research Fellowship.

Jacobs, M. (1996) *The Politics of the Real World* (London: Earthscan).

Jessop, B., H. Kastendiek, K. Nielson and O. K. Pederson (1991) *The Politics of Flexibility: Restructuring State and Industry in Britain, Germany and Scandinavia* (Aldershot: Edward Elgar).

Jessop, B. (1994) 'The Transition to post-Fordism and the Schumpeterian workfare state', in R. Burrows and B. Loader (eds), *Towards a Post-Fordist Welfare State?* (London: Routledge).

Jones, A. (1992) 'Civil rights, citizenship and the welfare agenda for the 1990s', in T. Harding (ed.), *Who Owns Welfare? Questions on the Social Services Agenda*, Social Services Policy Forum Paper no. 2 (London: NISW).

Jones, H. and K. Kandiah (1996) *The Myth of Consensus: New Views on British History, 1945–64* (London: Macmillan).

Jones, L. (1995) *Transport and Health: the next move* (London: Association for Public Health).

Jones, L. (1996) 'Putting Transport on the Social Policy Agenda', in M. May, E. Brunsdon and G. Craig (eds), *Social Policy Review 8* (London: Social Policy Association).

Jones, M. (1996) 'Full Steam Ahead to a Workfare State?', *Policy and Politics*, vol. 24, no. 2, pp. 137–57.

Jordan, B. (1987) *Rethinking Welfare* (Oxford: Blackwell).

Joseph Rowntree Foundation (1995) *Inquiry into Income and Wealth* (York: Joseph Rowntree Foundation).

Jowell, T. (1991) 'Challenges and Opportunities', conference speeches delivered by Virginia Bottomley and Tessa Jowell, distributed with *Caring for People*, 4.

Jowell, T. (1996) *Strategy for Women* (London: The Labour Party).

Katzenstein, P. J. (1985) *Small States in World Markets* (Ithica, NY: Cornell University Press).

Keane, J. and J. Owens (1986) *After Full Employment* (London: Hutchinson).

Kelly, A. (1991) 'The New Managerialism in the Social Services', in P. Carter, T. Jeffs and M. Smith (eds), *Social Work and Social Welfare Yearbook 3* (Milton Keynes: Open University Press).

Kelly, D., G. Kelly and A. Gamble (eds) (1997) *Stakeholder Capitalism* (London: Macmillan).

Kembell-Cook, D., M. Baker and C. Mattingly (eds) (1991) *The Green Budget: An Emergency Programme for the United Kingdom* (London: Greenprint).

Kemp, P. (1994) 'Housing Allowances and the Fiscal Crisis of the Welfare State', *Housing Studies*, vol. 9, no. 4, pp. 531–42.

Kenny, M. and A. Little (1995) 'Gorz', in V. George and R. Page (eds), *Modern Thinkers on Welfare* (London: Prentice-Hall).

King, D. (1987) *The New Right* (London: Macmillan).

King, D. (1993) 'The Conservatives and Training Policy, 1979–92', *Political Studies*, vol. XLI, no. 2, pp. 214–35.

King, D. (1995) *Actively Seeking Work? The Politics of Unemployment and Welfare Policy in the United States and Great Britain* (Chicago: University of Chicago Press).

King, D. (1997) 'Employers, Training Policy and the Tenacity of Voluntarism in Britain', *Twentieth Century British History*, vol. 8, no. 3, pp. 383–441.

Klein, R. (1995) *The New Politics of the NHS*, 3rd edn (London: Longman).

Klein, R., P. Day and S. Redmayne (1996) *Managing Scarcity: priority setting and rationing in the NHS* (Buckingam: Open University Press).

Krugman, P. (1994) 'Does Third World Growth Hurt First World Prosperity?', *Harvard Business Review*, July–August: 113–21.

Labour Party (1989) *Meet the Challenge, Make the Change* (London: Labour Party).

Labour Party (1990) *Looking to the Future* (London: Labour Party).

Labour Party (1995) *Renewing the NHS: Labour's agenda for a healthier Britain* (London: The Labour Party).

Labour Party (1997) *New Labour Because Britain Deserves Better* (London: Labour Party).

Land, H. and H. Rose (1985) 'Compulsory altruism for some or an altruistic society for all?', in P. Bean, J. Ferris and D. Whynes (eds) *In Defence of Welfare* (London: Tavistock).

Langan, M. (1993a) 'The Rise and Fall of Social Work', in J. Clarke (ed.), *A Crisis in Care: Challenges to Social Work* (London: Sage/Open University).

Langan, M. (1993b) 'New Directions in Social Work', in J. Clarke (ed.), *A Crisis in Care: Challenges to Social Work* (London: Sage/Open University).

Langan, M. and J. Clarke (1994) 'Managing in a Mixed Economy of Care', in J. Clarke, A. Cochrane and E. McLaughlin (eds), *Managing Social Policy* (London: Sage).

Lange, P. (1992) 'The Politics of the Social Dimension', in A. Sbraggia (ed.), *Euro-Politics: Institutions and Policy-Making in the 'New' European Union* (Washington: Brookings).

Lash, S. and J. Urry (1987) *Disorganised Capitalism* (Oxford: Polity Press).

Law, I. (1996) *Ethnicity and Social Policy* (London: Prentice-Hall/Harvester Wheatsheaf).

Layard, R., S. Nickell and R. Jackman (1991) *Unemployment: Macro-economic performance and the labour market* (Oxford: Oxford University Press).

F. Lazco, A. Dale, S. Anter and G. N. Gilbert (1988) 'Early retirement in a period of high unemployment', *Journal of Social Policy*, vol. 17, no. 3, pp. 313–33.

Leibfried, S. P. and P. Pierson (1995) 'Multitiered Institutions and the Making of Social Policy', in S. Leibfried and P. Pierson (eds) *European Social Policy: between fragmentation and integration* (Washington: Brookings Institution).

Lenaghan, J. (1997) 'Central Government Should Have a Greater Role in Rationing Decisions', *British Medical Journal*, vol. 314, pp. 967–70.

Leontieff, W. and F. Duchin (1986) *The Future Impact of Automation on Workers* (New York: OUP).

Lewis, J. (1992) 'Gender and the Development of Welfare Regimes', *Journal of European Social Policy*, vol. 2, no. 3, pp. 159–73.

Lewis, J., P. Bernstock and V. Bovell (1995) 'The community care changes: unresolved tensions in policy issues and implementation', *Journal of Social Policy*, vol. 24, no. 1, pp. 73–94.

Lewis, J., P. Bernstock, V. Bovell and F. Wookey (1997) 'Implementing care management: issues in relation to the new community care', *British Journal of Social Work*, vol. 27 (February) pp. 5–24.

Liberal Democratic Party (1997) *Make the Difference: The Liberal Democrat Manifesto* (London: The Liberal Democratic Party).

Lilley, P. (1993) *Benefits and Costs: Securing the Future of Social Security*, MAIS Lecture delivered on 23 June 1993.

Lister, R. (1989) 'The Politics of Social Security: An Assessment of the Fowler Review', in A. Dilnot and I. Walker (eds), *The Economics of Social Security* (Oxford: Oxford University Press).

Lister, R. (1993) 'Tracing the contours of women's citizenship', *Policy and Politics*, vol. 21, no. 1, pp. 3–16.

Lister, R. (1994) 'She Has Other Duties: Women, citizenship and social security', in S. Baldwin and J. Falkingham (eds), *Social Security and Social Change: New Challenges to the Beveridge Model* (Hemel Hempstead: Harvester Wheatsheaf).

Lister, R. (1996) 'In Search of the "Underclass" ', in R. Lister (ed.), *Charles Murray and the Underclass*, IEA Choice in Welfare Series no. 33 (London: Institute of Economic Affairs).

Lister, R. (ed.) (1996) *Charles Murray and the Underclass*, IEA Choice in Wlefare Series no. 33 (London: Institute of Economic Affairs).

Lovenduski, J. and V. Randall (1993) *Contemporary Feminist Politics: Women and Power in Britain* (Oxford: Oxford University Press).

Lowe, R. (1993) *The Welfare State Since 1945* (London: Macmillan).

Lury, C. (1996) *Consumer Culture* (Oxford: Polity Press).

Mace, J. (1995) 'Funding Matters: a case study of two universities' response to recent funding changes', *Journal of Education Policy*, vol. 10, no. 1, pp. 57–76.

Maclennan, D. (1994) *A Competitive UK Economy: the challenges for housing policy* (York: Joseph Rowntree Foundation).

Maclure, S. (1988) *Education Reformed* (Sevenoaks: Hodder and Stoughton).

Maddison, D., D. Pearce, O. Johansson, E. Calthrop, T. Litman and E. Verhoef (1996) *The True Costs of Road Transport* (London: Earthscan).

Malos, E. and G. Hague (1993) *Domestic Violence and Housing: Local Authorities' responses to Women Escaping Violent Homes*, Bristol Papers in Applied Social Studies, no. 19 (Bristol: Women's Aid Federation England/School of Applied Social Studies).

Malpass, P. (1990) 'Housing Policy and the Thatcher Revolution', in P. Carter, T. Jeffs and M. Smith (eds), *Year Book of Social Work and Social Welfare* (Milton Keynes: Open University Press).

Malpass, P. (1993) 'Housing Policy and the Housing System Since 1979', in P. Malpass and R. Means (eds), *Implementing Housing Policy* (Milton Keynes: Open University Press).

Malpass, P., M. Warburton, G. Bramley and G. Smart (1993) *Housing Policy in Action* (Bristol: School for Advanced Urban Studies, University of Bristol).

Mandelson, P. (1997) 'A Lifeline for Youth', *Guardian*, 15 August 1997.

Marks, G. (1992) 'Structural Policy in the European Community', in A. Sbragia (ed.), *Euro-Politics: Institutions and Policy-Making in the 'New' European Union* (Washington: The Brookings Institution).

Marquand, D. (1991) 'Civic republicans and liberal individualists: the case of Britain', *Archive Européenne de Sociologie*, vol. XXXII, pp. 329–44.

Marsh, A. and S. McKay (1994) *Poor Smokers* (London: Policy Studies Institute).

Marsh, P. and P. Collett (1986) *Driving Passion: the psychology of the car* (London: Jonathan Cape).

Marshall, T. H. (1950) *Citizenship and Social Class* (Cambridge: Cambridge University Press).

Marshall, T. H. (1963) 'Citizenship and Social Class', in T. H. Marshall, *Sociology at the Crossroads and Other Essays* (London: Heinemann).

Marx, K. (1975) *Early Writings* (edited by L. Colletti) (Harmondsworth: Penguin).

Marx, K. and F. Engels (1976) 'The German Ideology', in *Collected Works, Volume 5*, translated by C. Dutt, W. Lough and C. P. Magill (London: Lawrence and Wishart).

Mays, N. (1997) 'The Future of Locality Commissioning', *British Medical Journal*, vol. 31, no. 4, pp. 1212–13.

Mazey, S. and J. Richardson (1993) *Lobbying in the European Community* (Oxford: Oxford University Press).

McCormick, J. and C. Oppenheim (1996) 'Options for Change', *New Statesman and Society*, 26 January 1996.

McLaughlin, E. (1994) 'Flexibility or Polarisation?', in M. White (ed.), *Unemployment, Public Policy and Changing Labour Markets* (London: PSI).

Mead, L. (1986) *Beyond Entitlement: the Social Obligations of Citizenship* (New York: The Free Press).

Meekosha, H. and L. Dowse (1997) 'Enabling citizenship: gender, disability and citizenship', *Feminist Review* vol. 57, forthcoming.

Mellor, M. (1992) *Breaking the Boundaries: Towards a feminist, green socialism* (London: Virago).

Millar, J. (1994) 'Lone Parents and Social Security Policy in the UK', in S. Baldwin and J. Falkingham (eds), *Social Security and Social Change: New Challenges to the Beveridge Model* (Hemel Hempstead: Harvester Wheatsheaf).

Minford, P. (1991) 'The Role of the Social Services: A View from the New Right', in M. Loney, R. Bocock, J. Clarke, A. Cochrane, P. Graham and M. Wilson (eds), *The State or the Market: Politics and Welfare in Contemporary Britain*, 2nd edn (London: Sage).

Mitchell, D. (1991) *Income Transfers in Ten Welfare States* (Aldershot: Avebury).

Modood, T. *et al.* (1997) *Ethnic Minorities in Britain: Diversity and Change* (London: Policy Studies Institute).

Mohan, J. and K. Woods (1985) 'Restructuring Health Care: the social geography of public and private health care under the British Conservative government', *International Journal of Health Services*, vol. 15, no. 2, pp. 197–217.

Monkton, C. (1993) 'Universal Benefit', *Citizens Income Bulletin*, vol. 16, pp. 3–6.

Morley, R. and A. Mullender (1994) *Preventing Domestic Violence to Women*. Police Research Group Crime Prevention Series Paper 48 (London: Home Office Police Department).

Mouffe, C. (1993) *The Return of the Political* (London: Verso).

Mulgan, G. (1997) *Connexity: how we live in a connected world* (London: Chatto and Windus).

Murray, C. (1984) *Losing Ground* (New York: Basic Books).

Murray, C. (1990) *The Emerging British Underclass*, IEA Choice in Welfare Series No. 20 (London: Institute of Economic Affairs).

Murray, C. (1994) *Underclass: The Crisis Deepens*, IEA Choice in Welfare Series No. 20 (London: Institute of Economic Affairs).

National Consumer Council (1995) *Problems for Pedestrians* (London: National Consumer Council).

Nationwide (1996) *Housing Finance Review*, January.

Nazroo, J. (1997) *The Health of Britain's Ethnic Minorities* (London: Policy Studies Institute).

Nettleton, S. and G. Harding (1994) 'Protesting Patients: a study of complaints made to a Family Health Service Authority', *Sociology of Health and Illness*, vol. 16, no. 1, pp. 38–61.

New Economics Foundation/Friends of the Earth (1997) *More Isn't Always Better* (London: New Economics Foundation).

NFHA (1995) *CORE Lettings Bulletin No. 21* (London: National Federation of Housing Associations).

NHSME (1992) *Local Voices: the views of local people in purchasing for health*, EL (92), p. 1.

Nielsen, R. and E. Szyszczak (1993) *The Social Dimension of the European Community* (Copenhagen: Handelshojskolens Forlag).

Nugent, N. (1994) *The Government and Politics of the European Union* (London: Macmillan).

O'Connor, J. (1996) *From Women in the Welfare State to Gendering Welfare State Regimes*, Special Issue, *Current Sociology*, vol. 44, no. 2, p. 124.

OECD (1977) *Towards Full Employment and Price Stability* (Paris: OECD).

Offner, A. (ed.) (1996) *In Pursuit of the Quality of Life* (Oxford: Oxford University Press).

Ohmae, K. (1990) *The Borderless World* (London: Collins).

Oldfield, A. (1990) *Citizenship and Community. Civic Republicanism and the Modern World* (London: Routledge).

Oldman, C. (1991) *Paying for Care: Personal Sources of Funding Care*, York: Joseph Rowntree Foundation.

Oliver, M. (1992) 'A Case of Disabling Welfare', in T. Harding (ed.), *Who Owns Welfare? Questions on the Social Services Agenda*, Social Services Policy Forum Paper no. 2 (London: NISW).

Oliver, M. (1996) *Understanding Disability: From Theory to Practice* (London: Macmillan).

Oppenheim, C. and L. Harker (1996) *Poverty the Facts*, 3rd edn (London: CPAG).

Organisation of Economic Cooperation and Development (OECD) (1989) *Economics in Transition* (Paris: OECD).

Oswald, A. (1995) 'Happiness and Economic Performance', mimeo (London: Centre for Economic Performance, London School of Economics).

Pahl, J. (1989) *Money and Marriage* (Basingstoke: Macmillan).

Pahl, R. (1990) 'Prophets, ethnographers and social glue: civil society and social order', mimeo: ESRC/CNRS Workshop on Citizenship, Social Order and Civilising Processes, Cumberland Lodge, September.

Parker, H. (1989) *Instead of the Dole: An enquiry into the integration of the tax and benefit system* (London: Routledge).

Parker, H and H. Sutherland (1994) 'Basic Income 1994: redistributive effects of transitional BIs', *Citizens' Income Bulletin*, vol. 18 (July), pp. 3–8.

Parton, N. (1991) *Governing the Family: Child Care, Child Protection and the State* (London: Macmillan).

Parton, N. (1996) *Child Protection and Family Support: Tensions, Contradictions and Possibilities* (London: Routledge).

Pascall, G. (1997) *Social Policy: A New Feminist Analysis* (London: Routledge).

Pascall, G. and R. Morley (1996) 'Women and homelessness: proposals from the Department of the Environment – 1 Lone Mothers', *Journal of Social Welfare and Family Law*, vol. 18, no. 2, pp. 189–202.

Pateman, C. (1988) 'The Patriarchal Welfare State', in A. Gutman, (ed.), *Democracy and the Welfare State* (Princeton, NJ: Princeton University Press).

Pateman, C. (1989) *The Disorder of Women* (Oxford: Polity Press).

Pedersen, S. (1993) *Family, Dependence, and the Origins of the Welfare State* (Cambridge: Cambridge University Press).

Penna, S. and M. O'Brien (1996) 'Postmodernism and Social Policy', *Journal of Social Policy*, vol. 25, no. 1, pp. 39–62.

Perraton, J., D. Goldblatt, D. Held and A. McGrew (1997) 'The Globalisation of Economic Activity', *New Political Economy*, 2, no. 2, pp. 257–78.

Piachaud, D. (1980) 'Social Security', in N. Bosanquet and P. Townsend (eds), *Labour and Equality: A Fabian Study of Labour in Power, 1974–79* (London: Heinemann).

Piachaud, D. and J. Webb (1996) *The Price of Food: missing out on mass consumption*, (London: STICERD, London School of Economics).

Pierson, C. (1991) *Beyond the Welfare State?* (Oxford: Polity).

Pierson, P. (1994) *Dismantling the Welfare State?* (Cambridge: Cambridge University Press).

Pinch, S. (1997) *Worlds of Welfare: Understanding the Changing Geographies of Welfare Provision* (London: Routledge).

Piven, F. F. and R. Cloward (1993) *Regulating the Poor: The Functions of Public Welfare*, 2nd edn (New York: Vintage Books).

Plant, R. and N. Barry (1990) *Citizenship and Rights in Thatcher's Britain: Two Views* (London: Institute of Economic Affairs).

Polanyi, M. (1944) *The Great Transformation: The Political and Economic Origins of Our Time* (Boston: Beacon Press).

Pollard, A., P. Broadfoot, P. Croll, M. Osborn and D. Abbott (1994) *Changing English Primary Schools? The Impact of the Education Reform Act at Key Stage One* (London: Cassell).

Pollert, A. (1991) *Farewell to Flexibility* (Oxford: Oxford University Press).

Porritt, J. and D. Winner (1988) *The Coming of the Greens* (London: Fontana).

Powell, E. and I. Macleod (1952) *The Social Services – needs and means* (London: Bow Group).

Power, S. (1992) 'Researching the impact of education policy: difficulties and discontinuities', *Journal of Education Policy*, vol. 7, no. 5, pp. 493–500.

Rainwater, L., M. Rein and J. E. Schwartz (1986) *Income Packaging in the Welfare State: A comparative study of family income* (Oxford: Clarendon Press).

Ransom, S. (1995) 'Theorising Education Policy', *Journal of Education Policy*, vol. 10, no. 4, pp. 427–8.

Ress, P. (1997) 'Health Care Systems for the 21st Century', *British Medical Journal*, vol. 31, no. 4, pp. 1407–09.

Rhodes, M. (1991) 'The Social Dimension of the Single European Market: National Versus Transnational Regulation', *European Journal of Political Research*, vol. 17, pp. 245–80.

Rifkin, J. (1995) *The End of Work* (New York: Torcher/Putnam).

Riley, D. (1992) 'Citizenship and the welfare state', in J. Allen, P. Braham and P. Lewis (eds), *Political and Economic Forms of Modernity* (Cambridge: Polity).

Robertson, J. (1985) *Future Work: Jobs, Self-Employment and Leisure after the Industrial Age* (Aldershot: Gower).

Robinson, R. (1996) 'The Impact of the NHS Reforms 1991–1995: a review of research evidence', *Journal of Public Health Medicine*, vol. 18, no. 3, pp. 337–42.

Roche, M. (1992) *Rethinking Citizenship* (Oxford: Polity).

Rodrik, D. (1997) *Has Globalisation Gone Too Far?* (Washington, DC: Institute for International Economics).

Rose, N. (1992) 'Governing the enterprising self', in P. Heelas and P. Morris (eds), *The Values of the Enterprise Culture* (London: Routledge).

Ross, G. (1995) 'The Delors Era and Social Policy', in S. Leibfried and P. Pierson (eds), *European Social Policy: between fragmentation and integration* (Washington: Brookings Institution).

Rowntree, S. B. (n.d.) *Poverty: a study of town life* (London: Nelson).

Royal Commission on Environmental Pollution (1994) *Eighteenth Report: Transport and the Environment*, Cmnd 2674 (London: HMSO).

Rubery, J. and F. Wilkinson (eds) (1994) *Employer Strategy and Labour Markets* (Oxford: Oxford University Press).

Rustin, M. (1994) 'Flexibility in Higher Education', in R. Burrows and B. Loader (eds), *Towards a Post-Fordist Welfare State?* (London: Routledge).

Sabel, C. (1995) 'Bootstrapping Reform: rebuilding firms, the welfare state and unions', *Politics and Society*, vol. 23, no. 1, pp. 5–48.

Sainsbury, D. (1994) *Gendering Welfare States* (London: Sage).

Scott, J. (1994) *Poverty and Wealth: Citizenship, Deprivation and Privilege* (Harlow: Longman).

Scottish Labour Party (1997) Keynote Speeches, Scottish Labour Party Annual Conference, Gordon Brown, 8 March, Eden Court, Inverness.

Seale, C. (1993) 'The Consumer Voice', in B. Davey and J. Popay (eds), *Dilemmas in Health Care* (Milton Keynes: Open University Press).

Seddon, T. (1994) 'Assessing the institutional context of decentralised school management: schools of the future in Victoria', *Discourse*, vol. 15, no. 1, pp. 1–15.

Seldon, A. (1981) *Wither the Welfare State?* (London: Institute of Economic Affairs).

Selman, P. (1996) *Local Sustainability* (London: Paul Chapman).

Shanks, M. (1977) *European Social Policy Today and Tomorrow* (Oxford: Pergamon Press).

Shaw, E. (1994) *The Labour Party Since 1979: crisis and transformation* (London: Routledge).

Shragge, E. (ed.) (1993) *Community Economic Development: In search of empowerment* (Montreal: Black Rose Books).

Simkins, I. (1995) 'The Equity Consequences of Education Reform in England and Wales', *Educational Management and Administration*, vol. 23, no. 4, pp. 221–32.

Sinclair, J., R. Seifert and M. Ironside (1995) 'Market-driven reforms in education: Performance, quality and industrial relations in schools', in I. Kirkpatrick and M. M. Lucio (eds), *The Politics of Quality in the Public Sector* (London: Routledge).

Skidelsky, R. (1996) 'Welfare Without the State', *Prospect*, January, pp. 38–43.

Slater, P. (1997) *Consumer Culture and Modernity* (Oxford: Polity).

Slemrod, J. (1995) 'What do Cross-country Studies Tell Us About Government Involvement, Prosperity and Economic Growth?', *Brookings Papers on Economic Activity*, 2: 373–431.

Smaje, C. (1995) *Health, Race and Ethnicity: Making Sense of the Evidence* (London: King's Fund).

Smith, M. and J. Spear (1992) *The Changing Labour Party* (London: Routledge).

Smith, R. (1997) 'Creative Destruction: Capitalist Development and China's Environment', *New Left Review*, vol. 222 (March/April), pp. 3–41.

Social Services Inspectorate (SSI), (1996) *Progress through Change: The Fifth Annual Report of the Chief Inspector 1995/96* (London: HMSO).

Solomos, J. (1993) *Race and Racism in Britain*, 2nd edn (London: Macmillan).

Solomos, J. and L. Back (1996) *Racism and Society* (London: Macmillan).

Solow, R. (1990) *The Labour Market as a Social Institution* (Oxford: Blackwell).

Soper, K. (1981) *On Human Needs* (Hemel Hempstead: Harvester Wheatsheaf).

Spender, D. (1983) *There's always been a women's movement this century* (London: Pandora).

Spicker, P. (1993) *Poverty and Social Security: Concepts and Principles* (London: Routledge).

Spicker, P. (1996) 'Understanding Particularism', in D. Taylor (ed.), *Critical Social Policy* (London: Sage).

Springborg, P. (1981) *The Problem of Human Needs and the Critique of Civilisation* (London: Allen and Unwin).

Standing, G. (1992) 'The Need for a New Social Consensus', in P. Van Parijs (ed.), *Arguing for Basic Income: Ethical Foundations for a Radical Reform* (London and New York: Verso).

Strange, S. (1996) *The Retreat of the State* (Cambridge: Cambridge University Press).

Strong, P. and J. Robinson (1990) *The NHS: under new management* (Milton Keynes: Open University Press).

Stephenson, O. and P. Parsloe (1993) *Community Care and Empowerment* (York: Joseph Rowntree Foundation).

Taylor, C. (1992) *Multiculturalism and 'the Politics of Recognition'* (Princeton, NJ: Princeton University Press).

Taylor, P. (1983) *The Limits of European Integration* (London: Croom Helm).

Taylor-Gooby, P. (1997) 'In defence of second-best theory: state, class and capital in social policy', *Journal of Social Policy*, vol. 26, no. 2, pp. 171–92.

Terrill, R. (1974) *R. H. Tawney and His Times* (London: Deutsch).

Thompson, S. and P. Hoggett (1996) 'Universalism, selectivism and particularism: towards a postmodern social policy', *Critical Social Policy*, vol. 16, no. 1, pp. 21–43.

Timmins, N. (1996) *The Five Giants: A biography of the welfare state* (London: HarperCollins).

Tomlinson, B. (1992) *Report of the Inquiry in London's Health Service, Medical Education and Research (The Tomlinson Report)* (London: HMSO).

Tonge, J. (1997) 'Britain', in H. Compston (ed.), *The New Politics of Unemployment* (London: Routledge).

Tooley, J. (1996) *Education without the State* (London: Institute of Economic Affairs).

Torode, J. (1997) 'Must Britain be Europe's Soft Touch?', *Daily Mail*, 21 October 1997.

Townsend, P. (1979) *Poverty in the UK* (London: Allen Lane).

Townsend, P. (1996) *A Poor Future* (London: Lemos and Crane).

Trainer, T. (1991) *Abandon Affluence!*, in A. Dobson and P. Lucardie, *The Politics of Nature: Explorations in Green Political Theory* (London: Routledge).

Tsoukalis, L. (1993) *The New European Economy* (Oxford: Oxford University Press).

Tudor-Hart, J. (1971) 'The Inverse Care Law', *The Lancet*, 27 February, pp. 405–12.

Tyszkiewicz, Z. (1989) 'Employers View of the Community Charter of Basic Social Rights for Workers', *Social Europe*, vol. 1, p. 90.

Van Parijs, P. (1992) *Arguing for Basic Income: Ethical Foundations for a Radical Reform* (London and New York: Verso).

Van Parijs, P. (1995) *Real Freedom for All* (Oxford: Oxford University Press).

Van Steenbergen, B. (ed.) (1994) *The Condition of Citizenship* (London: Sage).

Van Zanten, A. (1996) 'Market Trends and the French School System: overt policy, hidden strategies, actual changes', *Oxford Studies in Comparative Education*, vol. 6, no. 1, pp. 63–76.

Venturini, P. (1988) *1992: The European Social Dimension* (Brussels: Commission of the EC).

Vincent, A. and R. Plant (1984) *Philosophy, Politics and Citizenship: the life and thought of the British idealists* (Oxford: Blackwell).

Walford, G. (1996a) 'School Choice and the Quasi-market', *Oxford Studies in Comparative Education*, vol. 6, no. 1, pp. 7–15.

Walford, G. (1996b) 'School Choice and the Quasi-market in England and Wales', *Oxford Studies in Comparative Education*, vol. 6, no. 1, pp. 49–62.

Walker, A. (1993) 'Community Care Policy: from consensus to conflict', in B. Bornat, C. Pereira, D. Pilgrim and F. Williams (eds), *Community Care: a Reader* (London: Macmillan).

Walker, C. (1993) *Managing Poverty: The Limit of Social Assistance* (London: Routledge).

Waslander, S. and M. Thrupp (1995) 'Choice, competition and segregation: an empirical analysis of a New Zealand Secondary school market, 1990–1993', *Journal of Education Policy*, vol. 10, no. 1, pp. 1–26.

Webb, S. and B. Webb (1911) *The Prevention of Destitution* (London: Longman Green).

Webster, C. (1991) *Aneurin Bevan on the National Health Service* (Oxford: Wellcome Unit for the History of Medicine).

Weiss, M. and B. Steinert (1996) 'Germany: competitive inequality in educational quasi-markets', *Oxford Studies in Comparative Education*, vol. 6, no. 1, pp. 77–94.

Wellens, K. C. and G. M. Borchard (1989) 'Soft Law in European Community Law', *European Law Review*, vol. 14, pp. 267–321.

West, A. and P. Sammons (1996) 'Children with and without "Additional Educational Needs at Key Stage 1" in Six Inner City schools – teaching and learning processes and policy implications', *British Educational Research Journal*, vol. 22, no. 1, pp. 113–28.

White, M. and J. Lakey (1992) *The Restart Effect* (London: PSI).

Whiteside, N. (1988) 'Unemployment and health: an historical perspective', *Journal of Social Policy*, vol. 17, no. 2, pp. 177–94.

Whitty, G. (1989) 'The new right and the national curriculum: state control or market forces', *Journal of Education Policy*, vol. 4, no. 4, pp. 329–42.

Whitty, G., T. Edwards and S. Gewirtz (1993) *Specialisation and Choice in Urban Education: The City Technology College Experiment* (London: Routledge).

Wilcox, S. (1994) *Housing Finance Review 1994–95* (York: Joseph Rowntree Foundation).

Wilcox. S. (1995) *Housing Finance Review 1995–96* (York: Joseph Rowntree Foundation).

Wilcox, S. (1997) *Housing Finance Review 1997–98* (York: Joseph Rowntree Foundation).

Wilding, P. (1992). 'Social Policy in the 1980's', *Social Policy and Administration*, vol. 26, no. 2, pp. 107–16.

Wilkinson, H. and G. Mulgan (1995) *Freedom's Children: work, relationships and politics for 18–34 year olds in Britain today* (London: Demos).

Wilkinson, R. (1996) *Unhealthy Societies* (London: Routledge).

Williams, F. (1992) 'Somewhere over the rainbow: universality and diversity in social policy', in N. Manning and R. Page (eds), *Social Policy Review 4* (Canterbury: Social Policy Association).

Wistow, G., M. Knapp, B. Hardy and C. Allen (1992) 'From providing to enabling: local authorities and the mixed economy of care', *Public Administration*, vol. 70 (Spring), pp. 25–45.

Wolf, N. (1994) *Fire with Fire: the new female power and how it will change the twenty-first century* (London: Chatto and Windus).

Wolmar, C. (1995) 'Labour in U-turn over new transport policy', *The Independent*, 26 October 1995.

Wolmar, C. (1996) 'Spirit of Godiva rides again as cathedral celebrates cars', *The Independent*, 18 January 1996.

World Health Organisation (WHO) (1985) *Targets for Health for All* (Copenhagen: WHO).

Yeatman, A. (1993) 'Voice and representation in the politics of difference', in S. Gunew and A. Yeatman (eds), *Feminism and the Politics of Difference* (Sydney: Allen and Unwin).

Young, M. and A. Halsey (1995) *Family and Community Socialism* (London: Institute for Public Policy Research).

Yuval-Davis, N. (1991) 'The citizenship debate: women, ethnic processes and the state', *Feminist Review*, vol. 39, pp. 58–68.

# Index

*Note*: page numbers in **bold** type refer to illustrative figures or tables.